Teaching
READING
to Children

SECOND EDITION

Teaching
READING
to Children

LAWRENCE E. HAFNER
Florida State University
Tallahassee

HAYDEN B. JOLLY
Learning Services Center
Clarksville, Tennessee

Macmillan Publishing Co., Inc.
NEW YORK

Collier Macmillan Publishers
LONDON

Macmillan Publishing Co., Inc.
866 Third Avenue, New York, New York 10022

Collier Macmillan Canada, Inc.

Library of Congress Cataloging in Publication Data

Hafner, Lawrence E.
  Teaching reading to children.

  Previous ed. published in 1972 as: Patterns of
teaching reading in the elementary school.
  Includes bibliographies and index.
  1. Reading (Elementary) I. Jolly, Hayden B.
II. Title.
LB1573.H116 1982   372.4'1   81-1793
ISBN 0-02-348780-1   AACR2

Printing: 1 2 3 4 5 6 7 8   Year: 2 3 4 5 6 7 8 9

To Mary and Charlotte

Preface

This book is a comprehensive discussion of how to help children learn to read and to continue improving reading skills throughout the elementary grades. Reading instruction should be guided by excellent theory and principles. Therefore, we base our strategies and techniques on such principles. The result is an abundant array of practical procedures that work.

Our feedback on their value comes from (1) our own experience as regular classroom teachers in grades one through six, (2) our pre-service students whom we direct and supervise as they diagnose and teach pupils, (3) in-service teachers whom we teach in course work and/or workshops, and (4) teachers and reading specialists throughout the country with whom we are in contact. The instructional procedures work very well and we are proud to recommend them.

Learning should be guided; therefore, we have provided a set of objectives at the beginning of each chapter and a summary, study questions, learning activities, and recommended readings at the end of each chapter. Working the study questions allows a student to grasp the material in the detail that gives power. Reading the summary provides the broad framework necessary to "see the forests." Then doing the learning activities brings the reader several further steps toward mastery. We have shunned simplistic self-checks in favor of the more comprehensive procedures outlined above. We invite you to delve into the book and judge for yourself.

L. E. H.

H. B. J.

Contents

SECTION IV

Evaluating Capacity and Achievement and
Applying Results to Teaching Children
Reading

SECTION V

Organizing for Better Reading Instruction

Reading Foundations

CHAPTER 1
Foundations of Reading

OBJECTIVES

As a result of thoroughly processing the material in this chapter the reader should be able to state/explain the following:

1. *Some misconceptions of reading and the implications of these misconceptions for the teaching of reading.*
2. *The importance of the concept of constructing meaning.*
3. *The working definition of the reading process used in this text.*
4. *Implications of usable definitions of the reading process.*
5. *The meaning of decoding printed words.*
6. *The development of meanings.*
7. *The difference between literal comprehension and interpretation.*
8. *The process of inference.*
9. *The definition, importance, and process of critical reading.*
10. *The highlight of the total reading act and its implication for the teaching of reading.*
11. *Several valid principles for teaching students to read well.*

MISCONCEPTIONS OF READING

It is essential that teachers know what reading is, for their idea of the reading process determines how they teach reading. There are teachers and parents who do not understand the key ideas in the reading process. Some people teach as if reading were only calling words accurately. Others think it is the ability to get a rough idea of the meaning of a passage. Still others consider their pupils competent readers if they understand the material well enough to answer simple questions of fact. Although this last conception of reading is closer to the truth than the conception of reading as word calling, all these ideas fall short of what

3

reading entails because they fail to include the function of probing for implied meanings.

The apparently harmless view that reading is "getting" meaning *from* the printed page leads to faulty educational practices. Mr. Doe, a fourth-grade teacher, thinks reading is primarily a matter of getting meaning, and he cannot understand why his pupils do so poorly on reading achievement tests. Perhaps it would help his understanding if he were asked to derive the meaning from this sentence: "His mètier was the fabrication of habergeons."

What do the readers do if they do not "get meaning"? They build or construct meaning. There are facts that lie behind symbols, and the readers must be able to reconstruct them if they are to comprehend the page. To do so they must bring to the page building blocks of meaning and an ability to reason. Then they will be able to manipulate ideas so as to understand the intended meanings.

A USABLE DEFINITION OF READING

The definitions of reading by psychologists and reading specialists note that the reader has to convert printed language to some kind of overt or covert speech and also understand the message intended by the array of symbols.

The working definition of reading that will be used in this text places great emphasis on reading as a language analysis process that by definition involves thinking for the purpose of developing meaning. Reading is a process of looking at written language symbols, converting them into overt or covert speech symbols, and then manipulating them so that both the direct (overt) and implied (covert) ideas intended by the author may be understood.

Reading, then, is a thinking process stimulated by language decoded from printed symbols. In this thinking process, conceptualizations of the author conveyed by the language are related to one another in a way that makes the author's intended message understandable.

If you can decode the written sentence ⟨Wǒ sȳihwan kàn Jūng-gwo shū⟩ but you do not understand it, you are not really reading. By our definition, if words convey no meaning, reading is not taking place. An important implication of this view of reading is that knowledgeable parents and teachers will insist on a continuing program of concept-language development in the schools and at home.

FOUR ASPECTS OF THE READING PROCESS

What do people do when they read? Our answer is based, in part, on a reading structure developed by William S. Gray in several of his writings. Mature readers engage in the following activities when they read thoughtfully:

They decode printed words.
They comprehend meanings.
They react to the meanings they have developed.
They use some of the meanings.

Decoding Printed Words

Decoding, or converting, print to overt or covert speech is a necessary first step in reading. This process of identifying printed words may be taught using the procedures recommended in this text. But to independently decode a word, students must learn the characteristic associations between combinations of *graphemes* (letters) and the *phonemes* (sounds) represented by them. In beginning reading, for example, they will learn to associate *ch* with the sound in *ch*erry, *oa* with the sound in *oa*k and b*oa*t. Learning these and other associations and how to use context in conjunction with the associations makes it possible to independently convert printed symbols to speech symbols.

Comprehending Meanings

Another important process requires the reader to comprehend the meanings of words, phrases, and sentences. At first, the meanings must be readily identifiable. As readers explore books they will encounter words whose meanings they do not know. Teachers will continually need to help readers develop those meanings by relating vocabulary to their experiences.

In reading, meanings are developed in context, in a sentence setting. The sentence appears to be the basic reading unit, but the reader usually must bring to the page one or more meanings of a word, for much of our language is communicated in sentences made up of words combined in particular patterns or structures. Therefore, the reader needs contexts comprised largely of familiar meanings and structures.

Readers have a twofold job in understanding the author. They must try to determine the *literal* meanings intended by the author and also the *implied* meanings. (Remember, the writer *implies*; the reader *infers*.) That is, understanding involves both literal comprehension, or the understanding of the basic, directly stated ideas of the author, and interpretation, or the understanding of the implied or indirectly stated meanings.

Literal comprehension and interpretation can be illustrated by examples of questions used to teach these abilities. The first set of questions, based on a sixth-reader selection titled "Ready for the Flood," requires literal comprehension of the material.

1. Who was Miesje?
2. What did Mr. Wielemaker and Jacob do with the animals?
3. What did Mother carry upstairs?

The following questions require interpretation, or inferential reading, because the answers are implied rather than directly stated. The reader must reason his way to conclusions.

1. In what country did this story take place?
2. Why was it important for Mother to be calm? To look calm?
3. Who was Jacob?
4. Why did the loft suddenly seem much smaller?

Ready for the Flood[1]

As Kees entered the kitchen, he saw all sorts of strange and unusual things going on. Mother was dressing Sjaantje; Trui was bustling about, her face as pale as a sheet; and Father and Jacob were putting on their gum boots. But the strangest thing of all was that Miesje, the cat, was rushing about on the table, and nobody chased her off.

"You've got to help," Father said to Kees. "The water might get as far as here. Mother will tell you what she wants you to do. Sjaantje will have to help, too. Now get on—all hands on deck."

"Mr. Wielemaker and I will take the animals out of the sheds," Jacob told them. "We'll take them onto the Blue Dike. They ought to be safe there, for the time being anyway, because it's farther inland."

Kees had stopped thinking about Grandfather; only the present seemed to matter now. There was a lot of work to be done, hard work. For a brief moment he was worried at the thought of the poor animals having to leave their warm sheds to be driven into the dark night in this raging storm and icy rain.

Trui had recovered a little from her fright. "What shall we do first?" she asked.

"Mr. Wielemaker thought we should get everything ready in the loft first," Mother told her.

Kees noticed that Mother was trying hard to look calm, but that her voice was trembling.

"First we two will have to fetch Jacob's bedding from the hayloft. Kees and Sjaantje will help us bring up the bedding from our bed. If the ground floor should get flooded, we'll at least be all together upstairs," she said.

Kees got the pillows from his parents' bed and took them upstairs. Sjaantje followed with a couple of sheets, and Mother brought up the mattress.

They put everything on the floor of the main loft, next to the children's and Trui's little attic rooms, Jacob usually slept in an attic off the hayloft, above the cow shed. "I like to sleep near my friends," he always said.

Soon all the bedding was upstairs. "The men will sleep here," Mrs. Wielemaker said to Trui. "We shall sleep in your room. Let's make up their beds now."

The loft suddenly seemed much smaller and quite different. "It looks rather cosy with all these beds," Kees said. He and Sjaantje went on lending Mother a hand. All sorts of things had to be taken upstairs—a paraffin stove, matches, candles, provisions. The place looked just like a shop. Trui had brought up two whole hams, a side of bacon, and several sausages from the larder.

---

[1] "Ready for the Flood" opens Chapter Three of *The Tide in the Attic* by Aleid Van Rhijn (New York: Abelard-Schuman, Criterion Books, 1962; and London: Methuen, 1962). Reprinted by permission of Abelard-Schuman Limited and Methuen & Co. Ltd. (It also appears in *Wide Horizons, Book 6*, by Helen M. Robinson et al. [Chicago: Scott, Foresman, 1965]).

"If need be, we can hold out for quite a while," she said.

All this time Kees could hear the loud peal of the bells above the roar of the storm.

To infer the author's implied meanings the reader needs to use the clearly stated information to deduce them. Such a process takes place in reading to answer question 1, "In what country did this story take place?" The solution: Dikes are found in the Netherlands. Trui and Sjaantje are Dutch (Netherlands) names. This story takes place where there are (1) dikes and (2) people called Trui and Sjaantje; therefore, this story must take place in the Netherlands. In answering the question "Who was Jacob?" the reader has to be able to see relationships. Solution: Jacob calls the head of the house "Mr. Wielemaker," so Jacob is not a member of the family. He works for the Wielemakers and he sleeps at the Wielemakers' home, but not with the family. The reader sees this as being a pattern of living characteristic of the domestic servant or hired hand. Experience and reasoning ability are clearly involved in this solution. Or the readers may need to induce a meaning, that is, they may have to read particular facts and come up with a general statement that ties the facts together. They do this when they correctly answer a question such as "What kind of person is Mother?" (Try answering the question yourself, in order to understand the point about inducing meaning.)

When readers infer,[2] they bring meaning in the form of additional information and/or the reasoning they do. Reading love letters is a familiar illustration of inferential reading, of reading between the lines. People probably do their best and their worst inferential reading at these times. They do the best because they are trying to wrest every bit of implied meaning from the letters and the worst when they make inferences not warranted by the information given or past experience with the individual who has written the letters.

It is easy to see how three very important factors in reading are word knowledge, reasoning, and seeing relationships among ideas. Readers must understand the meanings of the words, the component parts of the message; they must be able to reason to determine the meanings of unfamiliar words and to determine the author's implied meanings; and they must be able to see relationships among ideas to develop meanings.

Reacting to Meanings

A third aspect of the reading process is reacting to meanings. Persons who react critically to the printed page virtually "talk back" to the author. They react because they seek truth; the critical reaction is a creative process for determining the truth and relevance of a statement. Readers compare related statements within the story or text to see if they are consistent, and they compare such statements with the statements and findings of other authorities who write on the same topic.

---

[2] *Fer* is a Latin root meaning "bring" or "bear."

Huelsman (1951) tells us that in this relentless pursuit of truth called critical reaction we consider thoughtfully, in the light of facts that are known and valid standards of judgment, (1) the significance of what is read, (2) its general worth, and (3) its accuracy or quality.

The necessity of teaching students to read critically is obvious so long as we find statements such as the following in science texts: "The earth was formed by gases which broke off from the sun and then cooled." This cannot be stated as a fact. At best, it may be stated as a hypothesis that someone is trying to prove, but it is not a known fact.

When readers move into the popular media, into less objective fields than science is purported to be, they find ample opportunity to read with a gimlet eye, to read critically. A typical news report about battle D in war X between countries Y and Z might appear as follows:

> The enemy was driven back 500 yards along a front five miles long. Heavy losses were inflicted upon the enemy while our casualties were extremely light. Our planes also bombarded an enemy airfield, destroying fifty planes on the ground.

The facts of the matter are these:

1. The enemy was driven back 150 yards at several points along a two-mile front.
2. Fifty enemy were killed.
3. Forty-five of our troops were killed.
4. We hit an auxiliary field and knocked out five fighters, two helicopters, and one jeep.

Applying Meanings

Finally, readers apply the meanings. As they interpret and react, they make conscious and subconscious decisions about integrating ideas into their beings, accepting and making them part of themselves, to use as a basis for thoughtful action. It is this integrating of ideas and applying of new insights that constitute the fourth phase of the mature reading act. This application stage needs to be the goal for which the reader strives. As we instruct our students *in* reading, we aim for personal and social growth *through* reading; we strive for intelligent behavior change.

Not everything a person reads is immediately useful; some of it is stored for future refinement and use. The more persons know as a result of reading, the greater the backlog of experiences they can draw upon for various purposes. Through reading, people mature and become more interesting and useful individuals. Also, some of the material that students consider enjoyable, stories about people like themselves, can help to develop appreciation for the problems and predicaments of others and how others handled these problems.

As we interpret and react, then, we combine new ideas with old ones and develop still newer and better ideas. The ideas permeate the flexible, insightful reader, and under appropriate conditions can overflow into useful, intelligent action that is the product of the total reading act.

SOME PRINCIPLES OF TEACHING READING

Some principles of teaching reading that are rooted in what is known about reading are the following:

1. *Teach students to demand meaning from the printed page.* If students know that they are going to be held accountable for the meaning of printed text, they will more likely process the text in a manner that forces them to give evidence of understanding. Purposes that stimulate meaningful processing include the following:

   a. Read the (segment) and tell me in your own words . . . .
   b. Read the (segment) and tell me what you see in your mind.
   c. Draw a picture of something that you read about.
   d. Read and find the answers to these questions.
   e. Identify the important idea in this (segment).
   f. Read this (segment) and tell why the author wrote it.
   g. Compare one author's ideas about topic A with another author's ideas on the same topic.

2. *Emphasize the use of several techniques for teaching students to identify words.* Too many students do not have an opportunity to make the number of responses needed daily in order to associate a given printed word or phrase with the spoken form. Also, the teacher might fail to use a variety of good techniques for teaching the associations.

One should not place too much emphasis upon requiring certain pupils to "sound out" words. For any number of reasons such an emphasis will slow readers down so much that they are not reading fluently enough to gather meaning or to use partial pronunciation in connection with context so as to identify words.

Chapter three contains word identification techniques that can be used to teach a student how a word is constructed without involving phonics. (If the student happens to know some of the elements, fine, but don't add this phonics burden onto the student.) These techniques are especially useful for students who are weak or not far advanced in phonics.

3. *Teach students several techniques for identifying words independently.* Frank Smith (1979) notes that we pay too much attention in reading to the graphic cues (printed stimulus array) in trying to decode. More attention should be given, especially after a basic stock of nucleus [at sight] words have been learned, to the overall meaning—the context. If we do this, we will do more *sampling* of graphic cues, predict what is coming in the text, and then verify our predictions. In this way there will be a continual interplay between the graphic array sampling and verification through context. With respect to independent word identification skills, teachers can do the following:

   a. Teach certain grapheme-phoneme associations such as

   $t \rightarrow /t/$ $ai \rightarrow /\bar{a}/$ $ph \rightarrow /f/$ and the like.

These associations can be taught *inductively*,[3] using known nucleus words that contain the element. The technique is taught in chapter three.

b. Teach students to use context to eliminate certain meaning possibilities, thereby mapping out a more likely area of meaning.

c. Teach the use of meaning cues in tandem with graphic cues. If a student on his/her instructional level is reading fluently and for meaning, then the student can combine context with a minimum knowledge of grapheme-phoneme associations to identify a word not yet in his/her store of nucleus words; for example, all of the words except *mower* are known words in the following sentence:

Charlie was cutting the grass with the *mower*.

Under the conditions given and with the minimum knowledge mentioned including ⟨m⟩ → /m/, the student will have no problem.

d. As students progress, teach them to use *glossaries* and *dictionaries* as aids to pronunciation and meaning.

4. *Make absolutely sure that a student is being taught reading at his/her instructional reading level.*[4] This is extremely important. More problems are created in the schools by requiring students to read material that does not match their instructional reading level than by almost any other practice. This practice overwhelms and discourages students and is probably one of the precursors of juvenile delinquency. Furthermore, reading materials in the content areas must also be at the student's instructional reading level.

5. *Provide many reading materials at the student's independent reading level*[5] *so that fluency can be developed.* Just as piano students need to develop fluency and a sense of confidence by spending part of their time playing pieces they have already learned or are at a level lower than that at which they are being instructed, so must reading students develop fluency and confidence by rereading selections and by reading other interesting material at a level lower than their instructional level. They need a variety of interesting materials at their independent reading level.

6. *Develop and maintain a strong program of general vocabulary development as well as content area vocabulary development.* Characteristically, students at all educational levels have rather mediocre vocabularies. How could it be otherwise, given the unstimulating conditions that exist in many schools and homes?

It is important that adults have a strong vocabulary *consciousness* so that their children and students will develop an appreciation of words. If students do not hear their parents and teachers express nuances of meaning through carefully selected words and phrases, then everything positive will be labeled

[3] They can also be taught (1) *deductively*: give the rule and then examples, and (2) through the use of *games*.

[4] Level at which one comprehends at least 75% of the material and can read aloud without making more than 1 error every 20 words.

[5] Level at which one comprehends at least 90% of the material and makes only 1 or 2 word recognition errors per 100 words.

"cool," "great," or "nice" and everything negative, "square," "dumb," or "yukky."

Because vocabulary and general information are necessary for success in reading, parents, teachers, and students should plan and carry out vocabulary development programs and constantly strive to help students increase their store of general information.

If students see that parents and teachers are greatly concerned about vocabulary, as evidenced by their diction,[6] they are more likely to become interested in improving their own vocabularies. Vocabulary development, however, is a lifelong process.

A related problem is aliteracy, or the lack of the reading habit. Programs such as the minimum standards programs (in various states) ignore aliteracy and "fail to anticipate the vicious cycle of adults who do not choose to read, in turn creating children who do not read and who do not choose to read."[7]

7. *Since reading is a communication process, one must provide many occasions for reading and utilize various kinds of reading material, especially material from the home and materials developed by students and teachers.*

Let us provide a few examples of such materials/activities:

class newspaper	typewritten letters from friends
experience stories	and relatives
reading and writing commercials	graded stories
poetry	songs
magazines	catalogues
student-written stories	menus

8. *Obtain and use testing materials that are valid and reliable.* Some materials that are valid as measures of certain skills should not be used because the skills should not be measured, at least not as often as they are being measured. If they must be measured, an inordinate amount of attention should not be given to the results in comparison with the results of important tests.

Let us explain why, for example, too much emphasis should not be placed on phonics testing and the results of phonics tests:

   a. Phonics elements are abstract and difficult to learn. It is harder to learn a phonic element than it is to learn several words. Research by Mills (1956) points to the great difficulty that low-intelligence children have in learning to read by a phonics-oriented approach. Bright children often do well on phonics approaches, but low-ability children do not.
   b. Overemphasis on phonics in the beginning stages may well lead to a lack of attention to comprehension, a phenomenon often observed in the schools.
   c. Fragmented learning becomes the end goal. Rather than seeing phonics

---

[6] Diction means *choice* of words, not merely enunciation.
[7] Larry Mickulecky. "A Changing View of Literacy." *Reporting on Reading.* 5 (3) (April 1979), p. 5.

as one (and not the most important) means of decoding, it becomes the end itself. *Meaning* is the goal.

   d. Too much emphasis is placed on the graphic symbol with concomitant neglect of context. It is difficult for most students to sound out entire words. However, a strong emphasis on context (as pointed out earlier) plus partial phonics cues is easier and more significant decoding.

   9. *Obtain and utilize reading materials that will meet the needs of students.*
Many of the existing materials meet the needs of students. How they are introduced, taught, paced, and monitored determines whether they are successful or unsuccessful.

   10. *Utilize teaching procedures that help students learn to think better and to achieve better.*

SUMMARY

Teachers' ideas of the nature of the reading process and of the goals of reading determine how they teach reading. Those who think that reading is restricted to either pronouncing words accurately or "getting" meaning tend to overemphasize oral reading and to neglect the development of concepts, their labels, and the probe for meaning.

Reading is a thinking process stimulated by language symbols decoded from printed symbols. Obviously, it is also a perceptual process, but the key thinking process involved is reasoning.

The complete reading process involves four basic facets. First, people decode print to speech. The classroom teacher will help students become independent decoders by teaching them various skills, such as the ability to associate certain graphemes with certain phonemes and to use context to understand meaning.

Also, readers comprehend the meanings of words, phrases, and sentences. Meanings in listening and in reading are developed in context, often in sentence and paragraph settings. Not only must students become adept in literal comprehension—or understanding the directly stated facts—but they must also learn to interpret the implied or indirectly stated meanings, to infer or bring in meaning in the form of additional information and reasoning processes so as to develop the many relationships among the ideas.

Readers who react critically to the printed page talk back to the author because they seek the truth. They must reflect, in the light of known facts and valid standards of judgment, on the significance of what is read, its general worth, and its accuracy or quality.

Finally, people strive to apply those meanings that are worthy of application and in need of it. Not everything we read is immediately useful, but, as a result of reading, a person can build a backlog of experiences upon which to draw for various intellectual and social purposes.

The goals, then, are to teach students to read purposefully, to seek accurate knowledge, and to act wisely on the basis of valid, relevant knowledge.

LEARNING ACTIVITIES

1. List 15 reading tasks of varying levels of complexity. The tasks should be described well enough so that a person has an idea of what is involved in each task, for example, reading a recipe for making a lemon pie, reading an editorial in a metropolitan newspaper, and reading an article in *Reader's Digest*. Write each task on a separate index card. At different times ask several people to arrange them in the order of complexity. Tabulate the results; for example, compute the average ranking for each reading task. Also, try to determine if there is anything in the backgrounds of the people that would account for differences as well as similarities in the way they rank the tasks.

2. Construct a new alphabet. Write a brief story or other reading selection using your alphabet. Teach someone to read your selection. (You may draw pictures—stick figures will do—to accompany your story.) What did you learn?

3. Select a paragraph or two of reading material and write two literal comprehension and three interpretation questions. Make sure the interpretation questions require the reader to infer the answers. Explain the dynamics of thinking involved in answering each interpretation question.

4. Visit a classroom and look for examples of teachers using valid principles of teaching reading. Note them. (If you see incorrect practices, make a mental note and write them down later.)

5. Make a reading selection more difficult by substituting harder (less frequently used) words and by making more complex sentences. Then select two people of approximately equal reading ability. Ask one person to read the original selection and the other person to read the difficult version: ask them to (1) read the selections aloud and (2) explain what they read. What did you learn?

6. Analyze current letters to the editor and/or editorials and identify examples of misinformation and/or poor reasoning.

STUDY QUESTIONS

1. What are some misconceptions about the reading process? How might these misconceptions affect the teaching of reading?

2. What is verbalism?

3. Why is it important to think of reading as (re)constructing meanings?

4. Explain our definition of reading as you understand it.

5. What are some implications of the acceptable definitions of reading given in the text?

6. What is meant by "decoding printed words"?

7. What skills does a reader use to independently convert printed symbols to speech symbols?

8. Differentiate the terms *imply* and *infer.*

9. What happens if we present the reader with unfamiliar contexts?

10. What is the twofold job readers have in understanding authors?

11. Differentiate *literal comprehension* and *interpretation,* or inferential reading.

12. What did you learn from studying the Netherlands selection and the related questions and discussion?

13. When do you do your best inferring? worst inferring?

14. What, not counting perception, are the key factors in reading?

15. Explain what you know about critical reading.

16. Why should we consider application of ideas gained through reading to be important?

17. Which four principles for teaching reading seem most important to you? Explain.

RECOMMENDED READING

AUKERMAN, ROBERT C. and LOUISE R. AUKERMAN. *How Do I Teach Reading?* New York: John Wiley & Sons, 1981. Chap. 1.

CUNNINGHAM, PATRICIA M. "A Compare/Contrast Theory of Mediated Word Identification." *Reading Teacher,* 32(7) (April 1979), 774–778.

EBERWEIN, LOWELL. "Does Pronouncing Unknown Words Really Help?" *Academic Therapy,* 11(1) (Fall 1975), 23–29.

FARR, ROGER and NANCY ROSER. *Teaching a Child to Read.* New York: Harcourt Brace Jovanovich, Inc., 1979. Chap. 1.

LAMB, POSE and RICHARD ARNOLD (Eds.). *Reading: Foundations and Instructional Strategies.* Second Edition. Belmont, CA: Wadsworth Publishing, Inc., 1980. Chaps. 1–4.

PEARSON, P. DAVID. "A Psycholinguistic Model of Reading." *Language Arts,* 53(3) (March 1976), 309–314.

RANSOM, GRAYCE A. *Preparing to Teach Reading.* Boston: Little, Brown and Company, 1978. Chap. 1.

YAP, KIM ONN. "Relationships Between Amount of Reading Activity and Reading Achievement." *Reading World,* 17 (October 1977), 23–29.

REFERENCES

HUELSMAN, C. B., Jr. "Promoting Growth in Ability to Interpret When Reading Critically in Grades Seven to Ten." In *Promoting Growth Toward Maturity in Interpreting What Is Read,* Supplementary Educational Monographs, No. 74. Chicago: University of Chicago Press, 1951, 149–153.

MICKULECKY, LARRY. "A Changing View of Literacy." *Reporting on Reading,* 5(3) (April 1979), 5.

MILLS, ROBERT E. "An Evaluation of Techniques for Teaching Word Recognition." *Elementary School Journal,* 56 (1956), 221–225.

SMITH, FRANK. *Reading Without Nonsense.* New York: Teachers College Press, Columbia University, 1979.

CHAPTER 2
Strategies for Preparing the Child to Read

OBJECTIVES

As a result of thoroughly processing the material in this chapter the reader should be able to state/explain the following:

1. *The meaning of reading readiness and the key abilities needed for reading.*
2. *The relative importance of some basic factors.*
3. *The selection of tests to assess readiness for reading.*
4. *The types of behaviors that militate against success in reading.*
5. *The nature of perceptual skills in reading acquisition and how these skills can be improved.*
6. *The role of personality and sociocultural-economic factors in reading acquisition.*
7. *The importance of cognitive development (intelligence and language) in reading acquisition.*
8. *The means of assessing and developing cognitive abilities.*
9. *The educational factors that operate in reading acquisition and the results of preschool stimulation of disadvantaged children.*
10. *The nature of experimental and dynamic readiness instruction.*

WHAT IS READING READINESS?

Readiness is a state of general maturity manifested in the ability and willingness to perform certain cognitive, perceptual, and educational tasks needed for learning to read without too much difficulty. If it is too difficult, the child is not ready.

Importance of Subabilities

An Analogy from Sports. Sometimes a teacher finds it difficult to explain to a parent the importance of a child's having the subabilities needed for

15

reading. But the use of an analogy from the field of sports might help parents, especially fathers, understand the readiness concept.

Let us consider what a lad must be able to do, what subabilities he must have, if he is going to propel himself over a bar that is, say, 16 feet above the ground. To succeed in pole vaulting at that height he must have strength, speed, coordination, kinesthetic sense, the desire to be successful, and the ability to understand and follow instructions.

What is the meaning of this pole vaulting analogy? To the extent that one does not have these subskills and qualities, his pole vaulting performance will suffer. Also, among pole vaulters who attain the same height there are differences in arm strength, running speed, and the like. But by different combinations of ability strengths they are able to achieve the same results. However, if one is noticeably weaker in several of these abilities than others, he will probably not perform as well.

Similarly, there are subabilities necessary to reading that can be employed in varying combinations to learn to read. Everything we do requires sets of subabilities.

THE KEY ABILITIES NEEDED FOR READING

Vocabulary, Reasoning, Attending, and Decoding

Vocabulary and reasoning are key components in the reading process, and there is a need to decode words and to attend to the task of learning to read in order to succeed at it. The various subabilities related to reading can be organized into (1) intelligence-language-cognitive abilities, (2) perceptual abilities, and (3) educational abilities. These abilities are interrelated so that educational abilities, for example, also involve mental or perceptual ability.

Intelligence-Language-Cognitive. The intelligence-language-cognitive abilities relate to word knowledge, number knowledge, manipulating ideas, seeing relationships expressed in language, expressing oneself in language, and taking several dimensions of a concept into consideration to rightly understand it. Piaget found that decentration and conservation abilities begin to mature around the age of seven. Piaget's work is discussed toward the end of this chapter.

Perceptual. The perceptual abilities are *auditory discrimination* (ability to hear likenesses and differences in similar speech sounds), *auditory memory* (ability to hear and reproduce given sequences of words or digits), *auditory segmentation* (ability to segment a spoken word into its constituent parts), *visual discrimination* (ability to see likenesses and differences among letters of the alphabet and among words), *visual-sequential memory* (ability to see an array of visual figures and to reproduce them in the same sequence), *near-point vision* (ability to maintain focus on material at a distance of approximately 18 inches), *visual-motor skills* (ability to perform such tasks as doing jigsaw puzzles, copying patterns, and writing), and *auditory-visual association* (ability to associate an auditory symbol with a visual symbol).

Educational. The previously discussed abilities as well as personality and sociocultural-economic factors interact with school influences to produce what are called educational abilities. These include such motivational-attentional and book orientation facets as understanding the idea of reading,[1] wanting to read, being able to concentrate and attend to reading instruction, following teacher directions, handling a book and equipment, reading from left to right, keeping one's place on the page, and so forth.

Relative Importance of Some Basic Factors

The importance of the contributions that basic factors make to reading achievement varies, depending upon whether one is talking about reading at the reading acquisition level (usually in first or second grade) or a more advanced level. Let us at this point make some general comments regarding the roles of intelligence abilities and perceptual abilities. These ideas will be modified by detailed analyses in subsequent sections.

At the reading acquisition level, reading apparently[2] is largely a *perceptual* task. The reading tasks do not require much intellectual power as measured by most intelligence tests. These tasks require much ability in visual and auditory discrimination and the ability to make auditory-visual associations. Therefore, the correlation between intelligence and reading at the first-grade level is only 0.35; but for visual discrimination and reading, for example, the correlation is 0.60, a marked relationship (Bond and Wagner, 1966). Intelligence accounts for only 12 per cent of the variation in reading scores, whereas visual discrimination accounts for 36 per cent of the variation in such scores.

In the intermediate grades, however, more students achieve well in phonics, but reading is now more of an intellectual or thinking task. Therefore, the correlation between reading and intelligence at the fifth-grade level is 0.60; at this level intelligence accounts for 36 per cent of the variation in reading scores (Bond and Wagner, 1966). These findings were corroborated by Bruininks and Lucker (1970). At these levels visual discrimination makes little contribution to the variance in reading scores.

Validity of Readiness Concept

From our files we recount the case of a four-year-old girl who could read second-grade material with understanding. She also scored average for seven-year-olds on a reading readiness test. At age five years, four months, she earned

[1] Vernon (1957) states that the child's cognitive clarity about the nature and purpose of the reading process is an aid in learning to read. If pupils are confused about the relation of speech to reading, they will experience difficulty in learning to read.

[2] We say "apparently" because there is some well-founded speculation that certain visual and auditory abilities are undergirded by, or may well be facets of, intelligence.

an IQ of 157 on the *California Test of Mental Maturity* (CTMM) and an IQ of 157 on the *Stanford-Binet Individual Test of Intelligence* (L-M) while scoring at the fourth-grade level on a standardized reading test. It might be well to note, too, that this child was particularly advanced in auditory and visual discrimination skills and could write words on her little chalkboard beginning at age three. There was no trouble in learning to write lowercase letters shortly thereafter. The same requisite skills are used by early readers as by average second-grade children.

FORMAL ASSESSMENT OF READINESS FOR READING INSTRUCTION

Subtests/Factors in Selected Measurement Batteries

Teachers use readiness tests, intelligence tests, and tests of psycholinguistic abilities in addition to observation to determine children's strengths and weaknesses in readiness factors. The following discussion should familiarize the reader with a variety of instruments and inventories used in readiness diagnosis. Reading methods instructors will also make available copies of appropriate tests.

Readiness Tests. Group readiness tests usually require the recognition of the correct response rather than a creative response; exceptions are the responses made in visual-motor subtests. Instead of discussing the mechanics of test construction and administration, the emphasis here will be on the factors measured by group readiness tests and what certain specific, commercial readiness tests measure.

auditory blending: ability to blend the individual sounds of words (that have been spoken by the examiner at the rate of one per second). Useful in blending the parts of words that have been "sounded out."

auditory discrimination: ability to perceive likenesses and differences in speech sounds. A necessary ability for learning phonics skills.

basic concepts
   quantity: knowledge of concepts such as much-little, many-few, big-little.
   space: knowledge of concepts such as near-far, here-there, up-down.
   time: knowledge of concepts such as now-then, slow-fast.

learning rate: percentage of words remembered of those taught to mastery criterion an hour previously (word identification). This information is especially valuable when other readiness data are equivocal (that is when the data don't clearly indicate probable success or failure).

letter recognition: ability to give the names of printed letters.

listening (also called auditory comprehension): the ability to understand a spoken message.

numbers: usually relates to the ability to count.

visual discrimination: ability to perceive differences among letters or among words.

visual-motor coordination: ability to coordinate hand and eye movements in tasks such as copying a figure, completing an incomplete figure, and tracing a maze.

vocabulary: ability to understand words; often tested by having the pupil select the picture that depicts the meaning of the word spoken by the examiner.

word recognition: ability to select the word (from among foils) spoken by the examiner.

Through careful observation, the alert teacher does a pretty good job of determining readiness for initial reading instruction. But most teachers' judgments can be aided by wise use of reading readiness tests such as the following:

Murphy-Durrell Diagnostic Reading Readiness Tests. Helen Murphy and Donald D. Durrell. New York: Harcourt Brace Jovanovich, 1964. Can be used in kindergarten and in grade 1. Three subtests: (1) phoneme perception, (2) visual discrimination, and (3) learning rate.

Metropolitan Readiness Tests (1976 edition). Joanne R. Nurss and Mary E. McGauvran. Level I. For use in kindergarten or in grade 1 (in the first few weeks) with groups judged to be at a relatively low level of skill development. Six subtests: (1) auditory memory, (2) rhyming, (3) letter recognition, (4) visual matching, (5) school language and listening, (6) quantitative language, and an optional test, copying.

Table 2-1. Readiness Factors and Tests that Measure Them

	Boehm Test of Basic Concepts	Metropolitan 1976 Level II	Murphy-Durrell
VISUAL (MOTOR)			
Visual discrimination (matching)		x	
Visual-motor coordination		x	
Letter recognition		x	x
BASIC CONCEPTS			
Space	x		
Time	x		
Quantity	x		
AUDITORY			
Auditory discrimination		x	x
Auditory blending**			
NUMBERS			
Quantitative concepts		x	
Quantitative operations		x	
Numbers			
VOCABULARY/COMPREHENSION			
(auditory mode)			
Comprehension*		x	
Vocabulary			
Understanding sentences†			
School language		x	
WORD RECOGNITION			
Word recognition**			
LEARNING RATE			
Learning rate			x

*Spache Diagnostic Reading Scales
†Durrell-Murphy Listening Test
**Gates-MacGinitie Readiness Skills Test

Level II. For use at the end of kindergarten or in the early weeks of grade 1. Six prereading subtests: (1) beginning consonants, (2) sound-letter correspondence, (3) visual matching, (4) finding patterns, (5) school language, (6) listening, and two optional quantitative subtests, quantitative concepts and quantitative operations, and an optional test, copying.

Boehm Test of Basic Concepts. Ann E. Boehm. New York: Psychological Corporation, 1971. Use in kindergarten and grade 1. Measures knowledge of 50 words representing three kinds of basic concepts: (1) quantity, (2) space, and (3) time.

Individual Readiness Test. Because it is difficult to be sure a child is doing the best he/she can when he/she responds on group tests, a teacher might well consider administering an individual readiness test to some of his/her pupils. Not only can rapport be established with the child but the teacher can obtain more insight into the dynamics of a child's thinking in these individual testing situations.

The Van Wagenen Readiness Scales by M. J. Van Wagenen, published by Psycho-Educational Laboratories, Minneapolis, are designed for use in kindergarten, grade 1, and grade 2. Subtests and examples of items follow:

1. "Listening Vocabulary" (can be given to groups of children): The child is presented with five pictures. Teacher says the name of one of the items; the child marks the corresponding picture.

2. "Range of Information": The child is asked questions on a variety of topics. Following are not actual test questions but are similar to them: "What animal has a very long neck and is covered with spots?" "In what games is a touchdown made?"

3. "Perception of Relations": "You wear a hat on your head and a glove on your _____."

4. "Opposites": "When I say warm, you say _____." "When I say east, you say _____."

5. "Memory span": The child is instructed to repeat a sentence that the examiner reads: "The house is white." "In spring the rains come and the flowers grow."

6. "Word Discrimination": The child is instructed to look at a row of five words and pick out the one word that is different from the others: "girl girl grill girl girl."

7. "Word Learning": The child is taught to associate the spoken form of five words with their printed forms. Then he/she is asked to pronounce these words as they are presented one at a time on cards.

Special or Unusual Features. (1) The profile chart for recording part scores. (2) Word-learning test. (3) The intelligence quotient can be obtained through use of appropriate conversion tables. (4) There are several means of estimating verbal comprehension ability. (5) The test measures verbal comprehension, perception, and word-learning abilities.

Informal Tests. A number of tests that can be devised by the teacher are described in Chapter 7. Sample tests are shown in Appendix A.

Prediction Studies Using Measurement Batteries

Some of the most accurate prediction of achievement has been done by using combinations of carefully selected tests. Several research studies exemplifying this approach follow:

Book (1974) developed an index for the early (kindergarten) identification of academically high-risk children to provide school personnel with information useful in developing academic programs.

Tests used were the following: the Metropolitan Readiness Test (MRT); the Bender-Gestalt Test (B-G), a visual-motor test; the Slosson Intelligence Test (SIT); and the Stanford-Binet Intelligence Test (S-B). In December 1972 the SIT was administered to all children thought to be of low or below average intelligence. In April 1973 the SIT and the other tests were administered. Six diagnostic categories based on present program criteria were established and each child assigned to one of them:

Category	S-B IQ	MRT Score	B-G Error Score	Placement
(1)	80 or less	47 or less	10 or more	EMR class
(2)	81–93	48 or less	10 or more	extended readiness
(3)	94 or higher	below 48	10 or more	extended readiness
(4)	94 or higher	below 48	9 or less	extended readiness and/ or tutorial program
(5)	94 or higher	49–57	9 or less	extended readiness
(6)	94 or higher	58 or higher	9 or less	enrichment program

A high correlation was found between the diagnostic category to which the child was assigned and end of grade 1 achievement; the same relationship existed for end of grade 2 achievement. At the end of second grade (N = 219), only one child failed to make as much progress as he/she would have been predicted to make, and 27 children did better than expected.

Kapelis (1975) studied the predictive validity of the Meeting Street School Screening Test (MSSST) and the Slingerland Prereading Screening Procedures (SPSP) and compared them with the validity of teachers' predictive judgments. End of grade 1 criterion measures were the word knowledge, word discrimination, and reading subtests of the Metropolitan Achievement Test.

Reading was best predicted by including the total SPSP and the MSSST language and SPSP auditory discrimination scores in the prediction equation. This combination produced a Multiple R of 0.77 and accounted for 58.9 per cent of the variation in reading scores.

Teachers' Ratings As Achievement Predictors

To test the assumption that affective responses obtained from instruments measuring teachers' perception of pupils' maturity and pupils' self-perceptions are correlated with scores on highly cognitive achievement tests, White and Simmons (1974) applied a statistical analysis to the scores obtained by beginning first-graders on the Metropolitan Readiness Test, the Behavioral Maturity Scale, and the I Feel-Me Feel test; the latter is a self-concept measure. Only the teachers' perception of academic maturity as measured by the Behavioral Maturity Scale was a significant predictor (r = 0.71) of readiness to do first-grade work (as measured by the Metropolitan Readiness Test).

Reading Readiness Inventories. In the first inventory which follows, most of the information can be obtained by the teacher through informal testing or observation. Hearing acuity, binocular vision, and mental age will be obtained through formal testing. The key items are marked with an asterisk and should be considered important in a minimum assessment.

Table 2-2. Hafner-Jolly Reading Readiness Inventory

Name _____ M.A. _____†

Birthdate _____ C.A. _____
         Month   Date   Year

	Rating		
	Good	*Average*	*Poor*
Hearing acuity			
Audiometer*	_____	_____	_____
Low whisper (15 inches)	_____	_____	_____
Comments _____			
Auditory discrimination			
Initial sounds	_____	_____	_____
Medial sounds	_____	_____	_____
Rhyming sounds*	_____	_____	_____
Comments _____			
Auditory blending	(+)		(0)
Two-phoneme words (e.g., s-o, i-t)	_____		_____
Three-phoneme words (e.g., t-a-b, r-ā-n)	_____		_____
Four-phoneme words (e.g., k-r-ə-m, p-r-i-z)	_____		_____
Five-phoneme words (e.g., ȯ-r-ə-n-j, p-ē-a-n-ō)	_____		_____
Comments _____			
Binocular vision (Keystone Telebinocular Test)			
Binocular acuity (nearpoint)*	_____	_____	_____
Binocular coordination*	_____	_____	_____
Comments _____			
Visual discrimination	(+)		(0)
Matches one letter (from choice of two letters) to model letter	_____		_____

Table 2-2. (Continued)

	Rating		
	Good	Average	Poor
Matches one letter (from choice of four letters) to model letter*	————		————
Selects words that contain two given letters at beginning of word (e.g., sm soup sail smile am smack)	————		————
Comments _____			
Social adjustment			
Pays attention to instruction	————	————	————
Respects rights of others*	————	————	————
Awaits turn for teacher's attention	————	————	————
Concentrates on learning tasks*	————	————	————
Comments _____			
Emotional adjustment			
Accepts teacher's authority*	————	————	————
Follows directions*	————	————	————
Comments _____			
Mental development			
Mental age*	————	————	————
Quality of questions asked	————	————	————
Memory (ability to retain information)	————	————	————
General alertness*	————	————	————
Wants to learn to read*	————	————	————
Comments _____			
Language development			
Recites exact plot of a story after hearing it once	————	————	————
Expresses ideas	————	————	————
Vocabulary usage*	————	————	————
Articulation	————	————	————
Sentence structure	————	————	————
Understands and uses basic concept words (e.g., in-out; near-far; high-low; above-below; small-big; here-there.)	————	————	————
Comments _____			
Letter and word reading			
Identifies lowercase letters*	————	————	————
Identifies capital letters	————	————	————
Simple oral spelling	————	————	————
After one hour remembers several words that had been learned to a mastery criterion*	————	————	————
Comments _____			

Table 2–2. (Continued)

	Rating		
	Good	Average	Poor
Visual-motor coordination			
Use of hands	————	————	————
Use of feet	————	————	————
Use of body	————	————	————
	(+)		(0)
Copies a circle (three-year-old task)	————		————
Copies a square (five-year-old task)	————		————
Copies letters (five- to six-year-old task)*	————		————
Copies a diamond (seven-year-old task)	————		————
Comments _____			
Health			
General condition of health*	————	————	————
Nutritional status	————	————	————
Summary remarks and recommendations: _____			

† or VCA (Verbal Comprehension Age), measured by the *Hafner-Smith Verbal Comprehension Test.* See Appendix A.

PERCEPTUAL SKILLS IN READING ACQUISITION

Visual Discrimination

The ability to tell likenesses and differences in visual forms, such as letters, is visual discrimination. A gross (easy) discrimination task, for example, is differentiating *box* and *tree*; a fine (hard) discrimination task is involved in differentiating *candy* and *dandy* or *cad* and *cab*.

Importance. Visual discrimination ability is important to reading acquisition. Balow (1963) found that girls are quite a bit better in reading than boys. The girls' superiority in visual discrimination was determined to be the basis for their superiority in reading. In a study by Bryan (1964), visual perception was found to be a better predictor of reading achievement in grade 1 than the Metropolitan Readiness Test or an intelligence test.

Measurement. There are several ways to measure visual discrimination achievement. Have pupils (1) note which of several letters is different from the other letters in an array, (2) note which of several letters is the same as a model or stimulus letter, or (3) note which word is the same as a model word.

Developing Visual Discrimination Ability. There are many ways to develop visual discrimination:

1. Talk about[3] characteristics of one letter compared to (and different from) another, especially as you write the second letter.

2. Have the student select the letter (of two letters) that is like the model letter and circle it:

	y			t			o	
(y)		o	x		t	o		c

3. Have the student select the letter (from an array of letters) that is like the model letter and circle it:[4]

(Easy)	g	m	g	h	o	x
	v	w	x	t	n	v
	o	c	j	e	o	y
(Hard)	m	n	a	h	m	u

Games

TITLE: Have You Got a Match?

TYPE OF READING ACTIVITY: Letter discrimination.

OBJECTIVE: Pupils will learn to discriminate letters by making fine differentiations in order to match like letters.

MATERIALS: Set of cards with pairs of letters printed on them.

PREPARATION: On plain 3 X 5 cards, print pairs of letters, some of which match. Put cards in a stack, face down. Children take turns drawing a card. Child looks at card and tells whether or not it matches. When he/she answers correctly, the child keeps the card. The one who has the most cards at the end of the game (all cards used) or end of the time period is declared the winner.

Examples of Cards:

e	o	a	x	r	y	j	k	k	n
c	m	a	l	r	v	b	t	k	h

---

[3] Teaching must be accompanied by discussion and examples; otherwise, it is merely testing and not teaching.

[4] Spache and Spache (1977) comment, "Distinctive feature training, as in matching given stimuli to a sample utilizing memory, has been shown to give better letter name learning results than similar training which does not require memory."

Visual-Auditory Association (Letter Recognition)

One aspect of visual perception takes the task beyond discrimination and requires the pupil to associate a name or a sound with each letter of the alphabet.

Importance. The ability to name the letters of the alphabet that have been presented in random array has a marked relation (r = 0.60) to success in beginning reading. However, it is now thought that ability to learn letter names is a function of intelligence and that it is the latter ability that helps children to learn the letter-name associations and the regular reading tasks. Being able to give *sounds* for letters transfers more readily as an aid to reading than does giving the names for the letters of the alphabet.

It could well be that what one does with letter-name or letter-sound knowledge is the important factor. Letter-name knowledge is useful to a person in thinking and talking about similarities and differences among printed words. Letter-sound facility would be more beneficial in attempts to "sound out" parts of words (not the whole word), although we are not advocating a synthetic phonics approach to reading acquisition.

Measurement. There are ways to measure visual-auditory association ability:
1. Name a printed letter: (f → /ef/) or
2. Give the characteristic sound (f → /f/) associated with it.

Learning the Alphabet. Children who have not associated the spoken alphabet names with key spoken words may have fun with the following activity:

Alphabet Rhyme. Children will enjoy learning the following rhyme and saying it. You can record it on tape for children to listen to on their own. Some children may enjoy chanting it as they skip rope or engage in some other rhythmic activity.

A is for angel, B is for ball.
C is for cuts
We get when we fall.

D is for doggy, and E is for eel.
F is for food
That we eat at each meal.

G is for gum and H is for hair.
I is for I
Don't want that gum there.

J is for juicy, K is for kite.
L is for lumps
From bumps in the night.

M is for Mama, N is for nose.
O is for open
But never for close.

P is for Papa, Q is for queen.
R is for robot
To know one is keen.

S is for Santa, T is for tree.
U is for uncle
Who's so nice to me.

V is for violet, W for wheel.
X is for X-ray
To see how you feel.

Y is for yogurt, Z is for zoo.
This has been fun
For me and for you.

                                        L. E. Hafner

Developing Letter-Sound or Letter-Name Associations. Prior to the reading of words you may want to teach the pupils to associate the correct sound with each of the following consonants and consonant digraphs: *b, c(k), d, f, g, h, j, k, l, m, n, p, q, r, s, t, v, w, y, z, ch, sh, th, wh.* The following exercises will help to develop the associations:

1. *(Writing) Letters of (Initial) Consonant Sounds.* When good auditory discrimination of initial sounds in spoken words has been developed, introduce the written form of letters. For each consonant there will be a picture whose name begins with that letter. Superimposed upon the picture will be the letter that represents the beginning sound. (This is an old trick that has been picked up by several basal series in recent years.) For example, when introducing the letter *b,* specifically sensitize the pupils to the sound *b* by having them give names of things that start with the sound they hear at the beginning of *bread* and *banana.* Then have them look at the top of the work page for the letter that says *b* (or that says the sound we hear at the beginning of *ball*).

Have the pupils trace over the *b* that is superimposed on the ball. Then write some *b*'s on the chalkboard and let several pupils trace over them. Each time, they say the sound of *b* as they write it. Then proceed to the other pictures. Say each word, listen for the beginning sound, and write the letter *b* quickly as they print it.

2. *Exercise for an Initial Presentation of Letter-Sound Association.*

> T: "Who can tell me a word that starts like ball?"
> P: ["Bear"]
> T: "Fine. We have here some pictures of things whose names begin like the word ball. [Show pictures of a bat, a bee, a bell, or any other suitable illustrations for words beginning with b.] How do these words begin?"
> P: _____.
> T: [Draw a ball on the chalkboard. Superimpose the letter b over the ball as you say] "The word ball begins with this letter." ["Bat, bee, and ball begin with the letter b."]
> T: [Print b, x, and t on the chalkboard and then say words beginning with various letters. Have several pupils at the chalkboard and let them take turns pointing to b when they say a word beginning with b.]

3. *Follow-up, Reinforcing Exercises. Exercise a:* Hand out a duplicated sheet of several pictures identified correctly. Let pupils trace over the outline of the *b* that is next to each picture. *Exercise b:*

> T: "Here is our special picture of the ball. The letter b is the one we write for the sound that begins the word ball." [Affix the picture to the chalkboard with Plasti-Tak. Then place in a column, one at a time, pictures of things whose names begin with b.]
> T: "How do all these names begin?"
> P: "With the same sound" or "with a b" or "like ball."
> T: "Yes, they begin with the sound the letter b stands for." [Have several b's printed on the chalkboard—one by each picture—that pupils can trace over.]

Exercise c: Place on the chalk ledge three pictures of things whose names begin with the letter *b* and one picture for the letter *m*. Place a piece of Plasti-Tak on the back of each picture.

> T: "I am going to put this letter (b) on the chalkboard. What word does it stand for on our special picture?"
>
> P: "Ball."
>
> T: "Ball, because we hear that sound at the beginning of ball."
>
> T: "All together now, tell me the name of each picture as I point to it. [Do it.] Who wants to find a picture whose name begins like the sound this letter stands for?"
>
> P: _____.
>
> T: [Show pupil how to affix picture next to the letter b.]
>
> T: [Continue with other pictures.]

4. *Exercises for Differentiating Members of a Group.* The following kinds of exercises can be used when introducing other letters. For example, the letters *b*, *m*, and *t* can be part of a group of letters that you teach at about the same time. These are in one group because they are not likely to be confused with one another. You would *not* teach *b*, *p*, and *d* in a group; nor would you teach *b*, *h*, and *g*. *Exercise a:*

> T: [Distribute pictures of things whose names begin with b, t, or m. Place in front of the group three boxes. Print a large legible b on one box, a t on the second, and an m on the third.]
>
> T: [Pointing to b] "Brian, do you have a picture whose name starts with the sound of this letter?"
>
> P: _____.
>
> T: [Continue with t and m, but do not use all the pictures. After a while change the activity. Let a pupil come forward with a picture, show it to the class, let the class pronounce the name. Then have the pupil place it in the correct box in such a way that the pupils can see the letter on the box as he places the picture into it.]

Exercise b: Prepare a mimeographed sheet with special pictures for the letters *b*, *t*, and *m* at the top. The sheet should also contain two columns of pictures whose names begin with *b*, *t*, or *m*. In the blank space to the right of each picture the pupils are to write in the appropriate beginning letter. [If the children are not adept at writing, they can be presented with a multiple-choice array of three letters for each picture. They are to circle the appropriate letter for each picture.]

5. *Oral Context plus Beginning Letters.* Context clues and beginning consonant letter clues help a child to identify a word. In the readiness stage oral context is used. In the following exercise the teacher reads all but the last word of a sentence. Pupils determine from the context which words would make sense at the end of the sentence. The next time, however, they must provide a word that begins with the printed letter that is presented at the end of the sentence.

> T: "I will say a sentence, but I will not say the last word in the sentence. You
> tell me the last word: "When the man went camping, he took along his __.'"
> P: ["Children," "wife," "fishing pole." and so on.]
> T: "All right. This time I will say the sentence again. Only this time the last word
> must begin with the letter that is behind my hand." [Say the sentence again and
> at the end uncover the printed t, which is on the card] "What is the word?"
> P: "_____" [Count as correct any word beginning with t that makes sense in the
> context.]

Other sentences could be (1) "Every car has a spare t__." (2) "It's fun to climb a t__." (3) "At the zoo we saw a b__." (4) "Put your money in the b__." (5) "Many people drink m__." (6) "Children like to go to the m__." (7) "One of the days of the week is M__."

6. *Differentiating Letters of the* m, t, b *Group (Context plus Letters).* To give practice in differentiating letters of the *m, t, b* group use sentences such as these:

1. Cereal comes in a __. (b)
2. Some nights we get light from the __. (m)
3. You shouldn't get __. (m)
4. Put the spoon on the __. (t)
5. I got stung by a __. (b)
6. Ouch! I stubbed my __. (t)

Each sentence can be recorded on the audio tape portion of a *Language Master* card. The appropriate letter can be printed on the card.

Further Activities for Developing Letter-Name or Letter-Sound Associations

ACTIVITY 1: Pay Attention.

Directions: Distribute one card to each child. On each card will be a letter of the alphabet—letters that have been studied up to that point. Say: "I am going to name a letter. If you have the letter on your card, hold it up and I will check it." [As a variation, let a pupil go from child to child and read their letters. Exchange letters and repeat the game and variation.]

ACTIVITY 2: Chalkboard Delight.

Directions: Write on the chalkboard in random order the letters you have been and are studying. Call on a child, then point to a letter and ask him/her to give its name. [A long pointer can be useful.]

ACTIVITY 3: Writing the Letter.

Directions: "I am going to say a word. Think of the sound at the beginning of the word. Write the letter that stands for the sound."

Example: "bird" "tree" "swing"

More Games for Teaching Visual-Auditory Association
(Letter Recognition)

TITLE: <u>Initial Consonant Wheel.</u>   NAME: <u>Connie Baker</u>
                                                         <u>Trigg County, Ky., 1975</u>

TYPE OF READING ACTIVITY: Letter recognition.

OBJECTIVE: The child will learn to recognize and pronounce the initial
                  consonant of each word.

MATERIALS: Poster board, pictures, glue, felt markers.

PREPARATION: Give each child a wheel made from the poster board containing
                  pictures plus a second wheel with the initial consonants fastened
                  to it. The child matches the initial consonant with the right
                  picture. For example, he/she would match "baby" with the
                  initial sound "b." Also, he/she must pronounce the name of
                  the picture and initial consonant.

READINESS-LETTER KNOWLEDGE

<u>Directions:</u> The child is to identify the letter upon which he tosses the bean bag.
Letters are taped to the tile floor. The child is given a bean bag and asked to remain

behind a given line. From there he throws the bean bag. He must be able to identify the letter where his toss lands.

A Useful Mediating Device. The following device, brought to our attention by Paul McKee and Frank Laubach, and others, can be used to teach letter-name associations and/or letter-sound associations. One side (picture with letter superimposed) is the teaching side. The other side (letter alone) is the testing side. In teaching these associations, you and the pupils must agree on the name of the picture. Examples of cards—teaching sides—follow:

Capital Letter Practice

RADIO AND TV STATIONS

Directions: Pin initials of local and area radio and TV call letters on the pupils. Pupils may ask,

"Who is WONS?"
"Who is WCTV?"
"Who is WTAL?" "Who is WGLF?" "Who is WTNT?" "Who is WANM?"

Matching Capital and Lowercase Letters

WORD WHEELS

Directions: "Word wheels may be made with capitals on the outside wheel, small letters on the inside in random order. Two children see how quickly they can go around the wheel matching the capital and the small letters. A third child checks to see that pairs of letters are correctly made" (Durrell, 1956).

Auditory Discrimination

The ability to tell likenesses and differences in sounds is called auditory discrimination; for example, differentiating the following: /m/ - /n/, /mĭs/ - /nĭs/, /mĭt/ - /mĭn/, /pit/ - /pat/.[6]

Importance. Elkonin (1979) notes the importance of auditory discrimination: "It is important that these (analytic) experiences with the sound aspect of language *precede* the learning of alphabetic characters as symbols for sounds." Auditory discrimination ability is useful for learning grapheme-phoneme associations that help in developing independent word identification skills. Therefore, one can view the attempt by some teachers to teach "phonics" to children who have poor auditory discrimination as a rather pathetic venture.[7]

Measurement. Auditory discrimination can be measured in a number of ways:

1. Say three words (two of which rhyme) and ask the student which word does *not* rhyme. Examples: how, now, box; can, sat, ran; bone, bowl, tone.

2. Say two words and ask if they are the *same* or *different*. Examples: I, too; wall, caught; box, pox; five, five; sing, sink; fan, van; them, them.

Development. Auditory discrimination is not fully developed in one-fourth of second-grade pupils, but it can be improved through training, according to Murphy (1943). She instructed first-grade children in auditory discrimination, and the result was steady and consistent gains in auditory discrimination and reading achievement.[8]

---

[6] To be auditory tasks, these words must be spoken, without visual representations.

[7] Although it seems reasonable to assert that auditory discrimination is important for success in phonics, Spache (1976) and Groff (1975) question its value in *initial* reading acquisition.

[8] All groups given training showed superior reading achievement, on the average, in several tests given in grade 1, except for one very low-ability group that did not exceed its matched control group. Spache and Spache (1977) point out that Murphy's auditory discrimination training appeared to be successful

Durrell and Murphy (1953) report the case of a ten-year-old boy with an IQ of 170 who, although his speech was excellent and his cognitive grasp of phonics was good, had a reading vocabulary of only 60 words. During testing at the Boston University Reading Clinic it was discovered that he was deficient in phoneme perception. When given training in auditory discrimination, the boy said, "I knew that there was a trick to it. The words have sounds in them and you just match the sound with the way the word looks. I suppose that's why they taught me phonics all these years." During the next three months the boy made eight years' progress in reading.

A variety of activities can be used to develop auditory discrimination. Examples follow:

1. *Nursery Rhymes.* After reading a familiar nursery rhyme to children, pick out a couplet, read it again to the children, and ask them which words sound alike:

> T: "Little Bo Peep
>   Has lost her sheep."
>   "Now, which words sound alike (or rhyme)?"
> P: "Peep and sheep."
> T: (If children do not respond as expected, you can reread the couplet, emphasizing the rhyming parts.)
> T: "Which words sound alike (or the same)?"
> P: "_____"
> T: "pEEP and shEEP sound alike. Peep and sheep rhyme. Another word that rhymes with peep and sheep is _____."
> P: "sleep, deep, creep . . . ."

Of course, you may need to study a number of these couplets over a period of several days and possibly weeks before some children "get it."

2. *Listening for Rhyming Similarities.*

> T: "I am going to say two words. You listen carefully and tell me which of the two words rhymes with way: Tom, may." (You may have to do it over and say, "Does Tom or may rhyme with way?")
> P: "May."
> T: "Can you think of other words that rhyme with way and may?"
> P: "Play, day, say, Kay, Faye . . . ."

Games to Develop Auditory Discrimination

"What's in the 'Fridge'?" (Let the children take turns in answering.) Ask, "What's in the refrigerator that begins with /ī/?" The child responds and then points to another child to give a different item beginning with /ī/. Next, give another letter sound such as /b/. Repeat the procedure. Other places to use are

---

because the reading program stressed a phonics approach. We point out that children who are weak in auditory discrimination would do better in reading acquisition if they were not taught by a phonics approach. According to Mills (1956), slow learners seem to have the most difficulty when taught by a phonics approach.

the supermarket, the bedroom, the pantry or cupboard, the drugstore [pharmacy], the farm, the zoo, and the like.

"I'm Going to Canada (or to the United States)." Get yourself and your group together in a circle and say to the person to your left, "I'm going to Canada and I'm going to see a 'home.'" That person says something like, "I'm going to Canada and I'm going to see a 'mountain.'" Continue in a clockwise direction. The idea is to say a word that begins with the same *sound* with which the previous player's word ended.

"I Am the King." This game requires some creativity. You start the game by saying, "I am the king. And I can sing." Whoever has a couplet raises his/her hand, and you acknowledge one. Possible offerings: "I am a plumber and I'm a hummer." "I am a wall and I'm pretty tall." "I am a car and I'm going far."

Auditory Segmentation

Auditory segmentation is (1) the ability to hear the separate sounds in spoken words, for example, *orange,* and be aware that you have made an /r/ sound or a /j/ sound, and (2) the ability to hear in sequence the separate sounds in spoken words.

Importance. Murphy and Durrell (1964) in discussing the importance of auditory segmentation state that "the key ability in beginning reading is that of identifying the separate sounds in spoken words. This the child must do before he can match the sounds in spoken words with their forms in print."

How then does one teach children to note sequences of sounds in words and to differentiate the separate sounds? Briefly, the procedure involves looking at a picture of a familiar object beneath which there are as many spaces on a diagram as there are sounds in the spoken word and placing a "counter" in a diagram space for each sound of the word as it is spoken. One sound is made at a time, in sequence, of course, and a counter is placed in the diagram space. See Figure 2-1 for an exercise on the word *man.*

One does not use letters in this procedure. The boxes, the counters, and then the sounding out are gradually eliminated. In the last stage, the child names the object in the picture and then tells the teacher how many *sounds* are in the word.

PERSONALITY FACTORS

Various personality factors seem either to facilitate or to impede learning to read. These factors operate differentially in various combinations to achieve these effects. Personality factors also interact with intellectual or cognitive factors, resulting in various cognitive styles of approaching and executing academic tasks.

Grimes and Allinsmith (1961) found that first-grade children who are both highly compulsive and highly anxious overachieve greatly when taught to

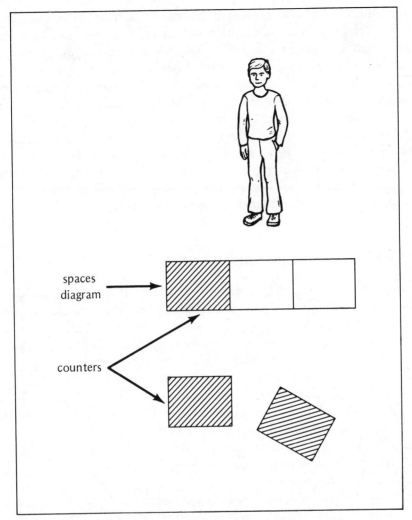

spaces
diagram →

counters

Figure 2–1. Material used to teach a pupil that words are formed from separate sounds. The counter for /m/ is in place. (After Elkonin, 1973).

read by a phonics method, which provides a structured setting of rules, systematic arrangement, and certainty in problem solving. Children who are highly anxious and low in compulsivity underachieve when taught by the whole-word method, which operates in a relatively unstructured setting.

Individuals who are low in ego strength—have a poor self-concept—have difficulty in attending to learning situations in sufficient quantity and adequate quality to learn or to apply what little they may have learned. Wattenberg and Clifford (1964) discovered that ego strength has a strong correlation with reading achievement. The pupil, then, must be able to concentrate if he is to achieve well in reading. Benger (1968) found a high correlation between a concentration rating and first-grade reading achievement.

Camp and Zimet (1974) studied the relationship of teacher rating scales to behavior observations and reading achievement of first-grade children. They found that "children who have a high rate of off-task behavior, including non-deviant teacher contacts, are likely to have lower mental ages, poorer achievement, and lower teacher ratings of positive behavior."

The key idea, however, is not whether a child manifests some particular personality trait but whether the trait works to impede or to facilitate the concentration necessary for learning to read.

Learning conditions can be arranged so that children can concentrate more adequately and therefore be able to capitalize on opportunities to learn (Grimes and Allinsmith, 1961; Skinner, 1968; and Palmer and Hafner, 1979). Arranging learning conditions implies attention to fitting methods and materials to the intellectual and personality characteristics of the learner.

SOCIOCULTURAL-ECONOMIC FACTORS

Observation alone points to great differences in the sociocultural-economic milieus of various families. Because adequate concepts, attitudes, and motivations for learning tend to flourish in well-to-do environments (although there are many exceptions), some children have decided developmental advantages, or at least the potential for advantages, over other children. Mickelsen and Galloway (1973) point out that the many subcultures in our country determine to some degree children's experiences and concepts, speech, attitudes, and values. Some children from these cultures do not key into the middle-class schools and their formalized methods of reading instruction. However, in the dominant middle-class culture many children have engaged in school-like activities for quite some time before entering school and know what to expect in school and how to cope with it.

A study by Riden (1957) showed that in poor residential areas the degree of culture in the home correlates positively with reading achievement. Therefore, even among poor families, the family with cultural advantages produces better readers than the family with fewer such advantages. Hill and Giammateo (1963) found that socioeconomic status affects school achievement, including reading, and that children from lower socioeconomic levels at that time did not overcome this cultural level by the end of grade 3.

At present varied groups of people are lumped together under a common index of poverty. However, there is a group of people who are abjectly poor; these people can be called paupers. Allen (1970) observed that the regular poor "seem to share values and behavioral attributes with the middle class above them rather than with the abjectly poor below them." The pauper is thought of as being apathetic and fatalistic.

Another important point is that people classified as being alike on the economic index of poverty are very unlike. They, for example, would not be alike in psychological traits because the poor include, among others, the child and the aged, the unemployed and the unemployable, the vagrant and the migrant, and the physically sick and the mentally sick. Also, the psychological meaning of being poor is different for blacks than it is for whites. Allen (1970) suggests, "For whites, poverty may be more frequently related to personal problems of disturbed personality, intellectual inferiority, or motivational deficits."

Deutsch (1967) constructed a deprivation index utilizing scores on several variables (parents' aspirations for children, crowdedness of the house, mother's presence at breakfast, absence of father). Research shows the deprivation index is independent of social class. Middle-class children can be deprived, too. However, when applied to a group of elementary school children from the slums, a significant correlation was found between scores on the deprivation index and scores on reading level. Children who are deprived, according to the index, did less well in reading than the children who are not deprived, evidently regardless of social class.

Not only do children from backgrounds of poverty do more poorly on standard tests and other indices of school achievement than do middle-class children but the difference increases as the children progress through the schools. There are critics who say that the tests are not culturally fair; however, these tests do predict academic achievement. Also, it is the culture of the middle class to which many people aspire.

Kohn and Cohen (1975) conducted a large-scale study in New York City. Emotional impairment in the first grade was found to be unrelated to social class and race. Underachievement (on the Metropolitan Readiness Test) was found to be a function of social class, race, and preschool emotional impairment. Children who were rated apathetic and withdrawn during the preschool period were significantly less advanced in reading readiness skills (MRT) than children who were rated alert and assertive.

Durkin (1963) studied children who had already been reading when they started first grade. Several cultural aspects were associated with this early reading. The following characteristics obtained among early readers as compared with normal readers: (1) The educational level of the mothers was higher. Because children spend much time with mothers prior to school entrance, this fact can be a decided advantage in terms of cultural stimulation. (2) These children came from smaller families. In smaller families one ordinarily can expect more time for interaction between parent and child, resulting in more and higher-level language interaction for the child. (3) They were read to by parents. Being read to results in stimulation of children's language development, a sense that parents are interested in them, and an idea of what reading is.

COGNITIVE ABILITIES IN READING ACQUISITION

As stated earlier, cognitive abilities are those processes that involve thinking, meaningful language use, and problem solving. In its earliest stages in infancy, thinking does not require language; thinking precedes verbal language.

Intellectual development is a long-term process that takes place as a person operates upon (interacts with) his/her environment. The cognitive schemata (structures) that are part of this development are used in the continuing drive for physiological and psychological *equilibrium.* This equilibrium or balance is attained as the result of two interrelated adaptive processes: *assimilation* and *accommodation.*

One categorizes and processes new information in terms of cognitive schemata—concepts, principles, and strategies—that exist at the time; that is assimilation. When people encounter something they cannot process using existing schemata, they adapt themselves to the situation by modifying schemata to fit reality. This means (1) modifying a concept, principle, or strategy, or (2) developing a new concept, principle, or strategy. This adapting is accommodation.

During the *sensorimotor stage* of development (Chronological Age or CA up to 1½ or 2 years), the child "learns to represent the world with (1) visual images, which serve as internal symbols, and (2) motor symbols, such as imitation, which serve as signs. Toward the end of this period, verbal symbols are also used to represent thought. During this stage, visual images, motor symbols, and verbal symbols are used to represent thought. For Piaget, thought precedes language, and only later does the process become somewhat reciprocal (Hafner, 1977).

In the first substage of the *preoperational stage* (CA 1½ or 2 to 4 years), the "child begins to use mental symbols, especially words, to represent absent things or events. And the child runs these events off in serial order" (Hafner, 1977).

The reasoning of the child in the second substage (CA 4 to 7 years) is (1) *egocentric*—cognitive operations and language are marked by present action and from the child's viewpoint, (2) *perceptually oriented*—words are defined by describing them or telling how they are used, and (3) *marked by irreversibility,* shown by the child's difficulty in classifying. Language is structured by logic and is a sophisticated tool used in understanding the environment. But language must have its symbol system grounded in concrete experience if it is to bring out understanding. Through the interplay of several forces—action modifications, language, and socialization—intelligence is transformed from practical intelligence to thought. Language enables people to describe their actions, bring about the past even though objects they have acted upon are not present, and to anticipate future actions to the point where words sometimes substitute for actions that are then not performed. Language also leads to thought on a broader plane of communication where thought is socialized. In this way language is the vehicle for concepts and ideas that belong not only to self but to everyone.

During the next developmental stage, the *concrete-operational stage,* the child is acquiring the ability to *classify,* to *order,* and to *reverse thinking action.* Briefly stated, reversibility means, for example, that the child can go back and forth in the vertical classification hierarchy (flower ↔ rose, for example) and also note that not only is 3 + 5 equal to 8 but so is 5 + 3. Another advance in classification over the previous stage where a child cannot conceive of a man as being both a father and a mailman, for example, is his/her ability in this stage to see that a man in fact can be both a mailman *and* a father.

Related to the process of reversibility is that of *inversion*: an operation performed can be cancelled in one's mind. For example, a person who sees water poured from a cup to a glass can in his mind imagine the water being poured from the glass back into the cup. Because of the ability to reverse, one acquires the principle of *invariance* or *conservation*. That is, one learns that although a substance undergoes a physical transformation such as shape, the amount is still the same.

The concrete-operational child also improves in the ability to put things such as sticks of various sizes into *serial order*. Hafner (1977) points out that when the seriation operation is firmly developed, the principle of transitivity is comprehensible: If T is larger than U and U is bigger than V, it is understood internally (through thinking alone) that T is bigger than V. "This is a type of logical thinking. Research shows that people do not have to wait until the formal operational stage of development to do certain kinds of valuable mental manipulations if the component concepts used in the manipulations are understood. Therefore, to say that a child cannot do any logical thinking before age 11 or 12 is not true."

Discussion of the formal operations stage is not pertinent to our discussion of readiness for reading, but before leaving this topic it would be well to discuss briefly the organization of the cognitive structures in Piaget's theory. Piaget (1952) has shown that each new cognitive structure is always more highly organized and differentiated than its predecessor. Regarding this point by Piaget, Layzer comments as follows:

> Each new structure is always more highly organized and more differentiated than its predecessor. At the same time it is more adequate to a specific environmental change. The intermediate stages in the development of a given structure are not rigidly predetermined (there are many different ways of learning to read or ski or play the piano), nor is the rate at which an individual passes through them, but in every case cognitive development follows two basic rules (Piaget, 1967): Every genesis emanates from a structure and culminates in another structure. Conversely, every structure has a genesis.

Importance of Cognitive Development: Intelligence and Language

It may well be that the reader can more readily assimilate information about the relationships between intelligence/language and success in reading acquisition than between Piagetian tasks and reading; therefore the latter, which may require more accommodation, will be discussed in the next section.

Intelligence. Bond and Dykstra (1967) noted a median correlation of 0.50 between intelligence and reading acquisition (end of grade 1), as measured by the *Pintner-Cunningham Primary Test of Mental Ability* and the paragraph meaning subtest of the *Stanford Reading Test*, respectively. Because measured intelligence in this instance accounts for only 25 per cent of the variation in reading scores ($V = r^2$: variance = correlation squared), it is not of itself a good predictor of success in reading at the grade 1 level. However, people with high IQs usually do well in reading acquisition and those with low IQs ordinarily do poorly in that task. It is difficult to predict the achievement of individuals in the middle range of intelligence.

Another facet of intelligence is *mental age*. Our experience with children in the first and second grades shows that reading acquisition is much easier, more fun, and generally more profitable when the child has the intellectual maturity represented by a mental age of six and a half rather than five. For the child's sake we must strongly consider a mental age of about six and a half before beginning reading instruction seriously. Mitigating factors are visual discrimination, a child's eagerness to learn, nearpoint vision, teacher capability, and quality of instructional materials. We are not so much hinting at beginning earlier when these factors are optimal as strongly suggesting a delay during which negative aspects are corrected or allowed to develop positively. There is scarcely anything worse than getting a child going on a downward spiral, and inept instruction of immature pupils is a sure way of bringing about such a negative state.

Language Abilities. Fry, Johnson, and Muehl (1970) compared the oral language of above-average readers in grade 2 with that of below-average readers. Twenty pictures were used as stimuli to the children's stories. The good readers were more fluent and had larger vocabularies. They were also more likely to create stories with meaning, whereas the poorer readers were more prone to enumerate picture content.

Measurement of Cognitive Abilities

Intelligence. Intelligence is measured by individual tests and group tests. The latter generally require reading whereas the former do not: one would not use a reading test to assess capacity to learn to read. Intelligence tests can be divided roughly into three kinds of tasks: verbal, performance, and nonverbal; the nonverbal usually involve arithmetic computation, perceptual tasks, and spatial tasks done in group tests and utilizing pencil and paper. Several kinds of intelligence tests, including the *Wechsler Individual Scale for Children,* are discussed in the section on evaluation.

The following factors on the WISC do differentiate good readers from poor readers, with the poor readers getting lower scores on these subtests: general information, arithmetic reasoning, auditory memory, and coding. Such tests are quite abstract, whereas tests on which poor readers do relatively well—picture arrangement, block design, object assembly, and the like—are more concrete. For a thorough discussion of the use of the WISC scores in reading diagnosis, see Searls(1975).

Relationship of Piagetian Tasks to Mental Ability, Readiness, and Reading

At the outset it must be pointed out that Piagetian tasks and intelligence test tasks are different. In a real sense, intelligence tasks are achievement tasks, whereas the development of reasoning in Piagetian tasks is almost entirely unrelated to school achievement among average and bright six- and seven-year old children (De Vries, 1974).

Also, Piagetian (cognitive) tasks are more highly related to reading readiness tasks than to reading achievement at the first-grade level. There is a higher relationship between cognitive tasks and reading in later grades. In the second grade, for example, a group of readers at grade level succeeded at Piagetian conservation tasks, whereas the children who were reading below grade level failed on these same tasks (Cox, 1976).

Finally, there is a wide variety of Piagetian tasks: (1) decentration, (2) conservation, and (3) dream.

Decentration. The decentration concept refers to the child's ability to decenter from his own point of view—to be less egocentric—and also to look at several aspects of a visual configuration so as to differentiate it from a similar appearing configuration.

Elkind, Larson, and Van Doorninck (1965) found that in grades 3 through 6 slow readers were significantly less adept at figural decentration than were average readers of comparable age, intelligence, and sex. The findings do not prove the role of decentration in reading but show that the more decentered a child's perception, the better its reading ability.

Conservation. Pulaski (1971) offers a simple definition of conservation: "Conservation is the ability to realize that certain attributes of an object are constant, even though it changes in appearance." There are three aspects of conservation that can be used as landmarks of cognitive development: conservation of quantity, acquired by the average child at the age of seven; conservation of weight, acquired at the age of nine; and conservation of volume, acquired at about age eleven.

Conservation and Reading. Conservation and decentration are both related to reading achievement. In fact, conservation and decentration are closely interrelated. The preoperational child (Cox, 1976) attends to "isolated parts of a complex stimulus whereas an older child will see the stimulus as an integrated whole with multiple parts." In order to determine the developmental sequence involved, Elkind, Kegler, and Go (1964) compared children between the ages of four and nine years. Nearly all of the four-year-olds saw specific parts of a visual display. The kindergarten and first-grade children saw only the wholes, and the children beyond grade 2 saw the wholes and the parts as an integrated whole; for example, they would say, "a scooter made out of candy" or "a man made out of fruit" in response to the arrays.

Cox (1976) points out that these studies suggest that the thinking of nonconservers is often dominated by perceptual centering, interfering with the form of the word that the child must perceive. In order to succeed in a conservation task, a child must differentiate between relevant and irrelevant stimuli (Gelman, 1969). Similarly, to succeed in reading, the child must differentiate distinctive features of letters to facilitate correct responses to symbols. When this has occurred, the child can learn the rules for putting together meaningful units (Cox, 1976).

Cox concludes that if one insists on teaching preoperational children (remember, there are still some such children in grades 2 and 3) to try to read, "special help should be given in abstracting rules and systems by the use of concrete materials such as wooden letters, phonics games, rhyming games, and print charts. If basic rules are not carefully taught, any type of transformation of material will be disastrous." The present text suggests a special kind of visual scrutiny exercise in which word parts are compared with the whole word, using movable magnetic letters. The use of magnetic or felt letters facilitates taking words apart and putting them together again so as to see the relationship of letters to larger parts and to wholes. A reading program by Smith, Rowell, and Hafner (1972) also facilitates the study of constituent parts of words.

Dreams. De Vries (1974) studied average and bright six- and seven-year-old children, using intelligence tasks, Piagetian tasks, and the reading section of the *Metropolitan Achievement Test*. She found that only mental age and the Piagetian "dream" task correlated reasonably well with reading tasks on the MAT.

The Piagetian perspective leads to the view that education's aim should be the long-range cognitive, emotional, social, and moral development of the individual. Academic achievement as an educational goal would then be proportionally reduced and placed in this larger developmental perspective.

Piaget's tests are not a substitute for tests of reading ability, for example, but their meaning becomes clearer when placed in the broader context of Piaget's theory of development.

DEVELOPING COGNITIVE ABILITIES

Some Activities Conducive to Intelligence-Language Development

The opportunities for children to interact with, manipulate, and learn the names of things encountered in exploration are myriad. Children must be allowed to interact with their environment and should have someone around to help them learn labels for the things and situations that they encounter. The mother who allows her three-year-old to climb on a chair to help bake and who lets the child measure, sift, mix, knead, roll, and pour; who talks with her child; and listens and responds about what they are doing contributes to language development.

What are some other activities engaged in by preschool children that provide opportunities for language development? (Remember, some mothers, for any number of reasons—good, bad, and indifferent—curtail or completely disallow activities of these kinds.) The following are examples of one three-year-old girl's activities, always accompanied by an active interchange of conversation:

1. Poured rice through a funnel into a kettle. (Child also noted that the funnel was like the hat worn by the Tin Man in the *Wizard of Oz* movie.)

2. Child dressed herself.

3. Child talked on the telephone (spoke to friends and relatives; called Santa Claus, after mother dialed; called the "time" man).

4. Looked through the picture albums and discussed the pictures, for example, the recent trip to Grandma's and the trip to Hawaii and Japan.

5. Watched Captain Kangaroo and was able to discuss with her mother, father, or older brother some of the things taking place in the program.

6. Played grocery store, set up with all kinds of groceries, toy cash register, money, checkout counter, and so on. (Her older sister was usually available to take part.)

7. Played fashion show (accompanied by appropriate fanfares, descriptions, programs, and appreciative audience; the latter was very important).

8. Played taking an airplane trip. (This is especially meaningful if the child has taken airplane trips.)

9. Made "moon animals" out of Glo Glob material and talked about these animals (done in conjunction with viewing astronauts' trip to the moon).

10. Played waitress. (This activity was especially interesting for her because the waitress is somewhat in control and the total activity involves much communication: reading menus, taking orders—scribbling and writing some letters of the alphabet—on a pad, talking with the "customers" about the order, inquiring about their needs, and so forth.)

In addition, the child very much loved being read to.

Some of these activities can be carried on in preschool and first-grade classrooms, particularly with children who have not had the advantage of engaging in such activities at home. Unfortunately, some children have not had the advantages others have had and it will be necessary to provide activities to aid the language development of the less fortunate.

Oral Context Exercise. Practice in reasoning is provided by saying a sentence and leaving off the last word, asking a child to provide it.

1. Many children ride to school on a school _____. [bus]
2. At Christmas time people like to sing _____. [songs, carols, hymns]
3. On Saturday afternoon Daddy likes to watch _____. [television, sports]
4. Whenever I cross a street, I am very _____. [careful]
5. When little children go to bed, someone might tell them a bedtime _____. [story, tale]

Dramatizing Stories. First-grade children like to dramatize familiar stories. They know the plot and dialogue of such favorites as "Goldilocks and the Three Bears," "The Three Little Pigs," and "Billy Goats Gruff." With the teacher's help they can develop the basic scenes, including simple stage settings. Teachers in private schools can draw on a number of familiar Bible stories to dramatize.

Playing Store. Children engage in language activity both when they plan how they want to set up their store or shop and when they operate it. Supermarket-type stores may not provide as much chance for customer-proprietor talk as the little shop where the clerk and customer still engage in conversation about the merchandise. Types of stores and shops that provide fine opportunities for language development are curio shops, jewelry stores, clothing shops, stationery stores, and hardware stores.

Classifying. In doing classification work children will profit from being helped to determine the defining attributes that certain things have in common. For example, in talking about desserts, they will be led to see that most desserts are sweet and that they are usually eaten last during a meal. To make children aware of attributes it is well to have as a preliminary activity a game in which children describe a number of things.

1. *Describing things.* A car: "It's got four wheels and a steering wheel and you ride around in it." A rabbit: "It's got long ears and it jumps around," or "It's little and furry and it's got long ears." After children are made cognizant of various attributes, you should have better responses to the problem of seeing what various things have in common. Another way of classifying things is on the basis of use.

2. *Sorting real objects that belong together.* Assemble such items as pliers, hammer, soap, toothpaste, saw, screwdriver, hand lotion, shampoo. Let children sort them into two groups on the basis of use. Develop correct verbal labels or class names (tools, cleaners or cleansers). Additional categories of real items that could be assembled in the classroom are writing tools, kitchen tools or utensils, clothing, costume jewelry, musical instruments, hair clips, flowers, pets.

3. *Finding pictures of things that belong to a certain class.* Children may know that certain things go together or fall within a certain category by simple association with a class name without having thought much about the attributes. Following are some classes of things for which children may find pictures to cut out: desserts, meats, animals, sports, flowers, furniture, houses, apartments, fireplaces, machines, workers, toys. When you have collected pictures of a certain class, bring out through observation and discussion what the members of a class have in common.

Problem-Solving Activities. The interest here is in situations that stimulate thinking and the use of language in developing possible solutions to problem situations. Problem situations such as the following may be posed:

1. How can first-graders earn money to buy something they want?
2. How do you get people to drive carefully?
3. How do you find a new game to play?
4. How do people build houses?

5. How do you make a jack-o'-lantern?
6. How do you play baseball?
7. How do you bake cookies?

The discussions may lead, in some instances, to experimentation to verify proposed solutions or to field trips, to find out how a house is built, for example, or to obtain more information and to verify claims and conjectures.

Show and Tell. Children love to talk about things they do and things they own. They have many experiences in common that give a common background, but they perceive experiences in individual ways. Children also have unique experiences.

Set aside a period early in the morning to allow pupils to tell about their experiences and to show objects and pictures related to these experiences. Katie's story of her trip to Hawaii consisted of a torrent of words, beautiful pictures, and colored slides and showing off her little grass skirt, lei, and overseas flight bag from the airline. Sandra was equally proud of her trip to the zoo in the nearby metropolis. She was somewhat shy at first, but warmed up to the task as she told about the funny noise the peacock made and how very big the Bengal tiger was.

Neither could one ever forget how proud Freddy was, standing in front of the class telling how he accompanied his father one Saturday in the big milk truck to pick up milk from the dairy farmers. The farmers asked his father if he was a good helper and his father said, "The best!" Freddy told the class how much fun it was to sit in the big cab and zoom along the highway, up and down the rolling hills on the way to the big city to deliver the milk to the dairy. Freddy, with the help of his teacher, showed the colored slides of himself sitting in the cab, of some of the cows in the fields, and of the huge dairy. No six-year-old boy was ever more proud or articulate than Freddy was that day during Show and Tell. And he really enjoyed answering his classmates' and his teacher's questions about the great trip with Dad.

Making and Exhibiting Collections. Six-year-olds collect everything, from beat-up-looking butterflies found in the backyard to exquisite dolls bought during travels in foreign countries. Every child can have a collection of some kind; an observing teacher can help some of the timid (or perhaps some of the disadvantaged) children get started. Some pointers in making and exhibiting collections follow:

1. Items in a collection should be properly labeled (oral and written).
2. Help children make the association of the label or name with the item.
3. When children are interested and where it is feasible, help them make further classifications of items in their collections.
4. Where necessary, help interpret to parents the values of collecting and the significance of their children's collections in particular.
5. Make available picture books related to the collections of the children.
6. Make available appropriate books for the gifted children who can already do some reading.

7. Encourage discussions of the collections.

8. Try to relate collections to other activities in the curriculum. (In fact, some collections may stem from unit work in content fields.)

Using Language Kits to Stimulate Discussions. Dunn and Mueller (1966) studied the efficacy of the initial teaching alphabet and the *Peabody Language Development Kit* with grade 1 disadvantaged children. The PLDK lessons "are intended to stimulate oral language and verbal intelligence, and therefore to enhance school progress." The experimental program, which lasted many months, resulted in significant enhancement of school achievement. Other applications have confirmed that PLDK alone, and in combination with the initial teaching alphabet enhance the overall oral language development and verbal intelligence of children. Written by Lloyd M. Dunn and James O. Smith and published by the American Guidance Service, Inc. of Minneapolis, the kits are available at several levels.

Level 1 of the PLDK is designed to be used with children who function at a mental age of four and a half to six and a half years of age. Therefore, it can be used with intellectually average kindergarten children and slower pupils in any grade 1 class. The kit stresses a general oral language development and verbal intelligence program involving associative, convergent, and divergent thinking.

Developing and Using a Home-Community Language Kit. The types of materials found in a commercial language kit can be developed by using local resources. The possibilities are limitless and are, to a great extent, a function of the imagination, perseverance, and enthusiasm of the teacher. Some of the materials that might be assembled are (1) photographs of places, people, and events in the community (you may want to have some of the pictures enlarged); albums with transparent pages for mounting photographs; (2) displays of community enterprises and places of interest provided by historical societies, the chamber of commerce, industries, and other local groups; (3) realia (real objects such as specimens of local wildflowers or natural resources, local manufactured products, and similar categories selected by pupils and teacher).

A home community language kit seems to have several advantages: (1) children can contribute ideas for things to discuss; (2) children can contribute pictures of people, things, and events in the community; (3) children are familiar with their home community; (4) children can be specifically encouraged to relate experiences they have had at home and at certain places in the community; (5) these experiences can be related in the context of a topic or a specific place or event in the community that is being studied; (6) children and teacher can identify with many of the situations and draw upon concrete experiences and imagery.

Puppets. A hand puppet may serve a child as an extension of his/her personality, as a friend, as a character with which he/she can have a conversation. A puppet, then, can be a helpful ally for the timid child as well as the bold one. Puppets can be made from socks, cloth, and sacks; faces can also be painted on one's hand so it can serve as a puppet. They can be used in free conversation or dramatization or in skits for which a script has been written.

Predicting the Outcome of a Story. The ability to predict the outcome of a story or to supply a suitable ending for a story segment is an important factor in success in reading. Any brief story may be used for the prediction exercise. You may want the children to be *convergent* in this kind of activity; ask a pupil to tell what he/she really thinks happens, how the story really ends.

When you tell part of a story that usually does not have an ending and ask the children to tell what could happen, you may encourage more *divergent* answers. Examples of story beginnings that you may use are these:

1. Cal Jones is in the first grade. He and his family are going to Tampa (or any nearby metropolis) Saturday to do some shopping in the department stores. Cal has saved three dollars. When Cal gets to the first department store . . .
2. Sandra Smith wanted to play with Jimmy Brown. She went over to Jimmy's house and knocked at the door. . . .
3. Once there was a boy named Jerry. One day Jerry was watching some children learn to skate. Jerry had never tried to skate. He said, "You kids aren't very good skaters. If I put on skates, I could skate without falling down." So the children helped Jerry put on a pair of skates. Then . . .

EDUCATIONAL FACTORS IN READING ACQUISITION

Throughout the chapter we have referred to educational factors. This section will report some work on the stimulation of disadvantaged children. Because of the great interest in early childhood intervention, let us discuss the work of Robert Aaron (1968), who studied preschoolers to determine the percentage of stimulated disadvantaged children (compared to advantaged children) who could attain certain language/reading behaviors. Aaron studied the observational data gathered by Gesell and associates (1940) on the reading and writing behaviors of high intelligence preschoolers—ages one to five years—who lived in a high socioeconomic environment.

> We have compiled the data with the idea of using them in at least two major ways. (1) As a yardstick by which to measure our project children in a longitudinal fashion. This should help us establish whether our stimulation program is accelerating the children past the reference behaviors at an increasingly earlier age. (2) As a device to help precisely define the behavioral differences among children in our population by race, sex, and socioeconomic status, tasks not undertaken by previous researchers. A diagnostic test was constructed, composed of a series of hurdles which the child had to attempt to pass. In the course of this interaction with such things as books, words, pictures, and paper and pencil, the child evidences his degree of sophistication in the areas of picture reading, letter and word reading, handling books, and book-related behaviors. Some behaviors were not easy to elicit without elaborate stage setting and were put in the schedule of behaviors that would be collected by applying systematic observation efforts to activities in the room where the behaviors were most likely to occur.
>
> The first major testing with the instrument was an effort to look at some of the

Research and Development Center population along two dimensions, socioeconomic level (high and low) and stimulated versus traditional kindergartens. We also wanted to see if the low-income child, with benefit of the stimulation, approximated Gesell's (1940) high-income child of 28 years ago.

Discussion of Results

A general analysis of the data leaves one clear conclusion. When compared with advantaged children from professional-level families, who are in a traditional kindergarten, the stimulated disadvantaged group shows a clear superiority in the following ways:

1. More perform effectively in auditory memory.

2. In book-related behaviors, there is among the disadvantaged subjects more ability in the mechanics of book handling and more knowledge of how to care for books. The experimental subjects know, in a significantly greater ratio, that the purpose in looking at a book is to "read."

3. Indices of reaction to print indicate that the experimental group is extremely word-conscious, and quite sophisticated toward reading.

4. The project children clearly surpassed the advantaged controls in capital letter knowledge, recognition of own first name, knowledge of sign words in and out of context, simple oral spelling, sight word knowledge, interest in small letters, visual discrimination of word form, and number who had begun to develop a sight vocabulary.

The writing behaviors test clearly shows the influence of the Research and Development Center's writing-spelling program. On the progressively more difficult task of copying geometric shape models, the stimulated children were clearly superior. In behaviors involving the production of letters and words, as a group, they were again well ahead of the control group.

Experimental Instruction

Tailored Enrichment Services. Sturgis, Iacono, and Kunce (1974) provided a full range of supplemental and tailored enrichment services to first-grade pupils. The pupils had been assessed individually and their unique needs were diagnosed. Some of the special programs were linguistic reading, basal reading, oral language development, perceptual motor activities, family counseling, multimedia math, and basic skills.

During the latter part of the year, the pupils were given subtests of the *Metropolitan Achievement Tests.* In order to determine if pupils responded differentially according to IQ, the pupils (both experimental and control) were divided into subgroups of high IQ (115 or more), average IQ (100 to 114), and low IQ (99 and less). Significant differences favoring the experimental group obtained only for the low-ability group, in which differences were significant in the following areas: word knowledge, word discrimination, reading, and arithmetic.

Whisler (1974) taught 75 visual memory/visual discrimination lessons to an experimental group of first-graders; that amounted to 15 minutes of instruction each day for 15 weeks. Both the experimental and the control groups received basal reader instruction. Post-testing revealed the experimental group to be significantly higher $(p < 0.01)$[9] than the control group in both word reading (Cooperative Primary Test) and visual discrimination. Most of the key stimulus words used in the experimental teaching were introduced in the reading series in use or were listed in the Dolch Basic Sight Vocabulary list. One doesn't know whether to attribute the gains to (1) the visual memory training, (2) the visual discrimination training, (3) the fact that key first-grade words were used, or (4) some combination of these three factors.

Sewell and Severson (1974) sought to examine the relationship between achievement and a number of variables shown to be associated with learning ability, including IQ, to determine their predictive effectiveness on the word reading and arithmetic subtests of the *Metropolitan Achievement Tests*. Sixty-two first-grade black children were individually tested on the *Wechsler Intelligence Scale for Children* (WISC) and tasks from three learning assessment strategies, only one of which—diagnostic teaching—was effective in predicting achievement.

In diagnostic teaching the child was shown five previously unknown words and was told what each word was. Then the cards were shuffled and he was tested; there were three trials. Also, the words were learned under three different conditions of reinforcement: (1) feedback of correctness of response, (2) social praise, and (3) tangible reinforcement—a piece of candy for every two correct responses made.

Results showed that IQ correlated moderately with achievement. In general, diagnostic teaching exceeded IQ in predictive effectiveness. IQ on the basis of WISC correlated 0.55 with word reading. Diagnostic teaching (social praise condition) correlated 0.63 with word reading and took much less time.

DYNAMIC READINESS INSTRUCTION

Mrs. Connie Sneed, kindergarten teacher in the Walter T. Moore School in Tallahassee, exemplifies the best in dynamic readiness instruction through a give-and-take among pupils and herself. The following activities, done toward the end of the kindergarten year, also would be appropriate in grade 1.

The first activity related to the ham and eggs Mrs. Sneed had prepared for her kindergarten class. Some comments about that eating experience were on a

---

[9] p means probability; p = 0.01 means that only 1 in 100 obtained differences was a matter of chance; the inference is that the differences are real.

special language experience bulletin board:

What I feel when I eat

I like the eggs
and the ham, and it
was good.
                     Leigh

At first I thought it didn't look
good. But when I tasted the ham
it was good, but the eggs—yuk!
                             John

It make me feel
good and I like it.
                     Steven

I felt good about it. And I like it.
                             Gretchen

It looked yuck, but I taste it
and it taste good.
                             John

Making Pancakes. Mrs. Sneed talked with the children as they prepared the batter for pancakes. After much planning, this activity provided opportunities in language, auditory discrimination, and visual discrimination. In the class were pupils with a wide range of backgrounds and abilities, but everyone participated.

T: "Pancakes starts with a _.
Ss: "/p/."
S[1]: "P̄ is for pancakes."
S[2]: "P is for pears."
S[3]: "P is for Peter Pan."
S[4]: "Peter and the Wolf."
T: "What is this?" (Holds up a large cookie sheet.)
Ss: "Sheet."
T: "What does it start with?"
Ss: "/sh/."
T: "Give me some other words that start with /sh/."
Ss: "ship" "sheep" "Shelley" "Shawn" "sugar."
T: "If we make only consonants, can we have an o͟?"
S: "No."
T: "Can I use /kā/ ⟨k⟩?"
S: "Yes."
T: "/wī/ ⟨y⟩."
S[1]: "yarn."
S[2]: "wild."
S[3]: "No, wild starts with a ⟨w⟩."
T: "Let's do vowels now."
S: "/a/ ⟨a⟩."
S: "apple."
T: "/yü/ ⟨ū⟩."
S: "Utopia."
T: "If we had all the alphabets,[10] how many would we have?"
S: "Twenty-six."

[10] A shorthand colloquial expression referring to the letters of the alphabet.

T: "Tell me how you made the syrup."

Ss: "Put two cups of brown sugar in a pan."

"You put some butter in it."

"And some water."

"And some syrup."

T: "Why syrup?"

S: "To make it taste like maple."

T: "Yes, because we didn't have any maple flavoring."

S^1: "Then we heated it. And it bubbled up. b-b-b-l."

T: "What did you do after you made it?"

S: "Put it in a jar."

T: "What did you do with the pan?"

S: "Washed it."

T: "How did you make your pancakes?"

Ss: "We used pancake flour."

"Milk."

"Eggs."

"Oil."

T: "What did you do with all that?"

S^1: "We mixed it."

T: "What did we do with it?"

S: "Put it on the griddle and cooked it."

T: "Here is how you get your pancakes. I will point to a pancake letter and you give me several words that start with the letter. (Each child in the class had a letter to identify and, therefore, a pancake to eat.)

SUMMARY

A person can learn to read if willing and able to perform certain necessary cognitive, perceptual, and educational tasks. There is no need to impose a strain on children by rushing them into initial reading instruction if a sensible delay coupled with continued readiness instruction will enable them to learn with enthusiasm at a later time. Children's egos are more important but unfortunately parents' ego needs or teachers' timetables (crystallized in part by outside pressure) often interfere with reason and, consequently, with the welfare of children.

In a sense, reading acquisition is largely a perceptual task. The perceptual factor declines in importance by the intermediate grades when perceptual tasks such as discriminating among printed words have been pretty well mastered. At that point, reading is more of an intellectual task of reasoning to develop relationships among ideas.

A child who learns to read with meaning will show the necessary readiness attributes—cognitive and perceptual—to support the acquisition of reading, whether the chronological age is four, six, or nine years.

Aspects of readiness can be assessed through use of readiness tests, intelligence tests, and observation of children's behaviors. In some studies measurement batteries have been used to predict success in initial reading acquisition. Behavioral maturity scales/indexes and readiness inventories can also be used to guide observation of children to determine readiness. It has also been established which kinds of behaviors militate against success in reading acquisition.

In teaching perceptual skills, one should differentiate between visual discrimination and visual-auditory association. Being able to give the common sounds associated with the letters of the alphabet transfers more readily as an aid in reading than does the ability to give the names of the letters. When letter-sound relationships are taught, concrete mediating devices should be used.

There are proponents and opponents for auditory discrimination as an important factor in beginning reading. It is safe to say, however, that it is important for success in phonics.

Children vary in their cognitive styles and in the personality traits and/or problems they may bring to the reading task. The important point is whether these factors work to impede or to facilitate the concentration necessary for learning to read.

Socioeconomic factors affect achievement. There is a need to become more knowledgeable about the different kinds of poverty that exist and the differential effects of race upon achievement. The various studies show that factors such as deprivation, low social class, language deprivation, emotional impairment, and failure experiences have a deleterious effect on general readiness and on reading achievement in particular. On the other hand, early readers compared to average readers have mothers who have higher education levels, come from smaller families, and were read to by parents.

This chapter delineated the basic concepts in Piaget's cognitive theory and discussed the high points of the developmental stages. Also explained were the importance of considering mental age in conjunction with visual, motivational, and instructional factors in deciding when a child is ready to learn well and the relationship of Piagetian tasks to mental ability, readiness, and reading, with special emphasis on the roles of decentration, conservation, and dream tasks. Conservation and decentration are related positively to reading achievement.

Many preschool and school activities conducive to intelligence-language development were detailed. These involve manipulation and social interaction including experiences and related language activities.

After discussing the positive effects on book-related behaviors of stimulation activities with disadvantaged preschoolers, the chapter offered several kinds of experimental instruction.

LEARNING ACTIVITIES

1. Observe three first-grade children of varying ability and fill out the "Hafner-Jolly Reading Readiness Inventory" for each child.

2. Assuming one of the children you observed is a nonreader, what kind of statement can you make about the child's readiness to read?

3. If one child is already reading, explain how his readiness report relates to the quality of his reading.

4. What kinds of instruction would you prescribe for the child you observed who is weak in reading readiness?

5. Make a set of alphabet cards that superimposes letters over figures. Teach the alphabet to a child.

6. Select a child who is weak in auditory segmentation (hearing separate sounds in spoken words) and auditory blending and begin teaching him/her to improve these skills using the Elkonin technique.

7. Visit several classrooms where readiness instruction is taking place. List strengths and weaknesses in the instruction.

STUDY QUESTIONS

1. After reading the chapter, explain what reading readiness means.
2. What are the key abilities needed for reading acquisition?
3. Why does the importance of intelligence increase as one goes through the grades?
4. Explain why early reading is not a fluke.
5. Explain the importance of such readiness factors as learning rate, auditory discrimination, and visual discrimination.
6. Why, in your estimation, are results on arithmetic reasoning and auditory memory subtests important in determining readiness for reading?
7. Do you think the prediction index developed by Book is worth the effort it took? Why, or why not?
8. What is the value of systematic observation by the teacher?
9. Why in your estimation is it important to have discrimination training before association instruction?
10. Which techniques would you use to best ensure the development of letter-name or letter-sound associations? Explain those you selected.
11. What is the importance of auditory discrimination to reading?
12. How would you develop auditory discrimination?
13. Which sociocultural-economic factors affect reading achievement?
14. Explain *assimilation* and *accommodation*.
15. What in the child's development at the *preoperational* stage impedes reading acquisition? Explain.
16. What changes in the *concrete operational* stage favor reading development? Explain.
17. What kinds of argument can you offer for generally not beginning reading instruction until a child attains a mental age of about six and a half years?
18. What are some ways of stimulating intelligence-language abilities?
19. Why does it seem important that we included the section on educational factors in reading acquisition?
20. What are the advantages of dynamic instruction over workbook instruction?

RECOMMENDED READING

ANASTASIOW, NICHOLAS. *Oral Language: Expression of Thought*. New York: International Reading Association, 1971.

AUKERMAN, ROBERT C. and LOUISE R. AUKERMAN. *How Do I Teach Reading?* New York: John Wiley & Sons, 1981. Chap. 2.

DURKIN, DELORES. *Teaching Them to Read.* Boston: Allyn & Bacon, Inc., 1974.

ELKIND, DAVID. *Children and Adolescents: Interpretive Essays on Jean Piaget.* 2nd ed. New York: Oxford University Press, 1974.

HITTLEMAN, D. R. *Developmental Reading: A Psycholinguistic Perspective.* Skokie, Ill.: Rand McNally & Company, 1978. Chap. 6.

JOHNSON, T. D. *Reading: Teaching and Learning.* New York: St. Martin's Press, 1973. Chap. 2.

OLLILA, LLOYD. "Reading: Preparing the Child." In P. Lamb and R. Arnold (Eds.). *Reading.* Belmont, CA.: Wadsworth Publishing Co., Inc., 1980. Chap. 9.

SPACHE, GEORGE D. and EVELYN SPACHE. *Reading in the Elementary School.* 4th ed. Boston: Allyn & Bacon, Inc., 1977. Chap. 7.

REFERENCES

AARON, ROBERT L. Publication 68–10. Athens, Ga.: Research and Development Center in Educational Stimulation, 1968.

ALLEN, V. L. "The Psychology of Poverty: Problems and Prospects." In V. L. Allen (Ed.). *Psychological Factors in Poverty.* Chicago: Markham, 1970, 367–381.

BALOW, IRVING. "Sex Differences in First Grade Reading." *Elementary English,* 40 (March 1963), 303–312.

BENGER, K. "The Relationships of Perception, Personality, Intelligence, and Grade One Reading Achievement." In H. K. Smith (Ed.). *Perception and Reading.* 12 (1968), 112–123.

BOND, GUY L. and EVA B. WAGNER. *Teaching the Child to Read.* 4th ed. New York: Macmillan Publishing Co., Inc., 1966.

BOND, GUY L. and ROBERT DYKSTRA. "The Cooperative Research Program in First-Grade Reading Instruction." *Reading Research Quarterly.* 2 (1967), 5–142.

BOOK, R. M. "Predicting Reading Failure: A Screening Battery for Kindergarten Children." *Journal of Learning Disabilities,* 7 (1974), 43–47.

BREKKE, B. W. "An Investigation of What Relationships Exist Between a Child's Performance of Selected Tasks of Conservation and Selected Factors of Reading Readiness." Unpublished doctoral dissertation, University of North Dakota, Grand Fork, 1971.

BRIGGS, BARBARA C. "An Investigation of the Effectiveness of a Programmed Graphemic-Option Approach to Teaching Reading to Disadvantaged Students." *Journal of Reading Behavior.* 5 (Winter 1972–1973), 35–46.

BRUININKS, ROBERT H. and W. G. LUCKER. "Change and Stability in Correlations Between Intelligence and Reading Test Scores Among Disadvantaged Children." *Journal of Reading Behavior,* 2(4) (Winter 1970), 295–305.

BRYAN, Q. R. "Relative Importance of Intelligence and Visual Perception in Predicting Reading Achievement." *California Journal of Educational Research,* 15 (January 1964), 44–48.

CAMP, B. W. and S. G. ZIMET. "The Relationship of Teacher Rating Scales to Behavior Observations and Reading Achievement of First-Grade Children." *Journal of Special Education,* 8 (Winter 1974), 353–359.

COX, M. B. "The Effect of Conservation Ability on Reading Competency." *Reading Teacher,* 30(3) (December 1976), 251–258.

DEUTSCH, MARTIN. *The Disadvantaged Child.* New York: Basic Books, 1967.

DEVRIES, R. "Relationships Among Piagetian, IQ, and Achievement Assessments." *Child Development,* 45 (September 1974), 746–756.

DURKIN, DELORES. "Children Who Read Before Grade One: A Second Study." *Elementary School Journal,* 64 (1963), 143–148.

DURRELL, DONALD D. and HELEN A. MURPHY. "The Auditory Discrimination Factor in Reading Readiness and Reading Disability." *Education, 73* (1953), 556–560.

DURRELL, DONALD D. *Improving Reading Instruction.* New York: Harcourt Brace Jovanovich, 1956, p. 77.

ELKIND, DAVID, R. P. KEGLER, and E. GO. "Studies in Perceptual Development II: Part-Whole Perception." *Child Development, 35* (1964), 81–90.

ELKIND, DAVID, M. LARSON, and W. VAN DOORNINCK. "Perceptual Decentration Learning and Performance in Slow and Average Readers." *Journal of Educational Psychology,* 56(1) 1965, 50–56.

ELKONIN, D. B. "USSR." In John Downing (Ed.). *Comparative Reading: Cross-National Studies of Behavior and Processes in Reading and Writing.* New York: Macmillan Publishing Co., Inc., 1973.

FOX, BARBARA C. "How Children Analyze Language: Implications for Beginning Reading Instruction." *Reading Improvement,* 13(4) (Winter 1976), 229–234.

FRY, M. A., C. S. JOHNSON, and S. MUEHL. "Oral Language Production in Relation to Reading Achievement Among Select Second-Graders" In D. J. Baker and P. Satz (Eds.). *Specific Reading Disability.* Rotterdam, Netherlands: Rotterdam University Press, 1970, 123–159.

GELMAN, R. "Conservation Acquisition: A Problem of Learning to Attend to Relevant Attributes." *Journal of Experimental Child Psychology,* 7 (1969), 167–187.

GESELL, ARNOLD and others. *The First Five Years of Life.* New York: Harper & Row, Publishers, 1940.

GRIMES, J. W. and W. ALLINSMITH. "Compulsivity, Anxiety, and School Achievement." *Merrill-Palmer Quarterly,* 7 (1961), 247–271.

GROFF, PATRICK. "Reading Ability and Auditory Discrimination: Are They Related?" *Reading Teacher,* 28(8) (May 1975), 742–747.

HAFNER, LAWRENCE E. *Developmental Reading in Middle and Secondary Schools: Foundations, Strategies, and Skills for Teaching.* New York: Macmillan Publishing Co., Inc., 1977.

HILL, EDWIN and M. GIAMMATEO. "Socio-economic Status and Its Relationship to School Achievement in the Elementary School." *Elementary English, 40 (1963),* 265–270.

INHELDER, BARBEL. *The Diagnosis of Reasoning in the Mentally Retarded.* New York: The John Day Co., Publishers, 1968.

KAPELIS, L. "Early Identification of Reading Failure: A Comparison of Two Screening Tests and Teacher Forecasts." *Journal of Learning Disabilities,* 8 (December 1975), 638–641.

KOHN, M. and J. COHEN. "Emotional Impairment and Achievement Deficit in Disadvantaged Children—Fact or Myth?" *Genetic Psychology Monographs,* 92 (August 1975), 57–78.

KOPPITZ, E. M. *The Bender Gestalt Test for Young Children.* New York: Grune & Stratton, Inc., 1964.

KRETSCHMER, J. C. "Toward a Piagetian Theory of Reading Comprehension." *Reading World,* 14 (March 1975), 180–187.

LAIRD, A. W. and J. P. CANGEMI. "When Are Children Ready to Learn to Read?" *Reading Improvement,* 12 (Spring 1975), 47–49.

MICKELSON, N. I. and C. G. GALLOWAY. "Verbal Concepts of Indian and Non-Indian School Beginners." *Journal of Educational Research,* 67 (1973), 55–56.

MILES, J., P. J. FOREMAN, and J. ANDERSON. "The Long and Short Term Predictive Efficiency of Two Tests of Reading Potential." *The Slow-Learning Child,* 20 (November 1973), 131–141.

MILLER, HARRY B. *Programmed Educational Techniques in Reading.* Monroe: Northeast Louisiana University, 1974.

MILLS, ROBERT A. "An Evaluation of Techniques of Teaching Word Recognition." *Elementary School Journal,* 56 (January 1956), 221–225.

MORPHETT, M. V. and C. WASHBURNE. "When Should Children Begin to Read?" *Elementary School Journal,* 31 (1931), 496–503.

MURPHY, HELEN A. "An Evaluation of the Effect of Specific Training in Auditory and Visual Discrimination on Beginning Reading." Unpublished doctoral dissertation, Boston University, 1943.

MURPHY, HELEN and D. DURRELL. "Manual of Directions," p. 1. *Murphy-Durrell Diagnostic Reading Readiness Tests.* New York: Harcourt Brace Jovanovich, Inc., 1964.

PALMER, BARBARA C. and LAWRENCE E. HAFNER. "Black Students Get an Edge in Reading." *Reading Horizons,* 19(4) (Summer 1979), 324–328.

PIAGET, JEAN. *The Origins of Intelligence in Children.* New York: International Universities Press, 1952.

——. *Six Psychological Studies.* New York: Random House, 1967.

PULASKI, M. A. S. *Understanding Piaget.* New York: Harper & Row, Publishers, 1971.

RIDEN, S. M. "The Effects of Environment on the Reading Ability of Eight-year-old Children." *British Journal of Educational Psychology,* 27 (1957), 225–226.

SEARLS, EVELYN F. *How to Use WISC Scores in Reading Diagnosis.* Newark, Del.: International Reading Association, 1975.

SENNA, C. (Ed.) *The Fallacy of I. Q.* New York: The Third Press, 1973.

SEWELL, T. and R. A. SEVERSON. "Learning Ability and Intelligence as Cognitive Predictors of Achievement in First-grade Black Children." *Journal of Educational Psychology,* 66 (December 1974), 948–955.

SKINNER, B. F. *The Technology of Teaching.* New York: Appleton-Century-Crofts, 1968.

SMITH, EDWIN H., C. GLENNON ROWELL, and LAWRENCE E. HAFNER. *The Sound Reading Program.* Waco, Texas: Education Achievement Corporation, 1972.

SPACHE, GEORGE D. *Investigating the Issues of Reading Disabilities.* Boston: Allyn & Bacon, Inc., 1976.

SPEER, O. B. and G. S. LAMB. "First Grade Reading Ability and Fluency in Naming Verbal Symbols." *Reading Teacher,* 29 (March 1976), 572–576.

STURGIS, D. K., C. U. IACONO, and J. T. KUNCE. "Parental Advantagement, IQ, and Differential Responsiveness to an Education Enrichment Program." *Psychology in the Schools,* 11(3) (July 1974).

TRIGG COUNTY, KENTUCKY. Federally funded Workshop. *Vocabulary Games.* 1975

VERNON, M. D. *Backwardness in Reading.* Cambridge: Cambridge University Press, 1957.

WATTENBERG, W. W. and C. CLIFFORD. "Relation of Self-Concepts to Beginning Achievement in Reading." *Child Development,* 5 (1964), 461–467.

WHISLER, N. G. "Visual-memory Training in First Grade: Effects on Visual Discrimination and Reading Ability." *Elementary School Journal,* 75 (October 1974), 51–54.

WHITE, WILLIAM F. and M. SIMMONS. "First Grade Readiness Predicted by Teachers' Perception of Students' Maturity and Students' Perception of Self." *Perceptual and Motor Skills.* 39 (August 1974), 395–399.

Developing Basic Reading Acquisition and Independent Word-Identification Skills

CHAPTER 3
Strategies for Teaching Initial Reading Acquisition

OBJECTIVES

As a result of thoroughly processing the material in this chapter the reader should be able to state/explain the following:

1. *The principles to apply in order to do the best job of teaching initial reading acquisition.*
2. *The formula for continuous progress in learning to read.*
3. *The characteristic emphases in basal reading methods.*
4. *Each step of a basal lesson plan and the purpose of these activities.*
5. *Activities for teaching word-identification techniques.*
6. *The "nail-down" word-identification strategies to use with any approach or materials for teaching initial reading acquisition.*
7. *How to teach function words through use of special illustrated phrases.*
8. *How to teach the language-experience approaches.*
9. *The characteristic emphases in the rational-meaning method and the structural linguistic method.*
10. *How a psycholinguistically oriented, programmed reading approach works.*

There are any number of methods by which children can learn to read. This chapter presents four methods: (1) basal, (2) language-experience, (3) synthetic language-experience, and (4) linguistic. Programmed methods and audio-visual methods of teaching reading are discussed in Chapter 10. A teacher who knows a method well can use that method to teach children to read but will not forget to use appropriate self-instruction materials and methods so that instruction can be geared to mastery and paced to the child's rate of learning.

Regardless of the methods used, the teacher will apply certain principles in order to do the best job:

1. Have the pupils make many responses during the day.

2. Pace the material so that the pupils make correct responses.

3. Before moving on, try to make sure pupils master each step in a sequence.

4. Make sure that a pupil is making a high percentage of correct responses, for then he/she learns better and improves self-concept.

5. Provide the background necessary for the achievement of the expected response.

6. When a pupil is to make an association between a letter and a sound, make sure he/she (a) hears the sound clearly, (b) sees the letter clearly, and (c) concentrates on the association.

7. When a pupil is to make an association between a printed word and its spoken form, make sure he/she (a) hears the word clearly, (b) sees the printed word clearly, and (c) concentrates on making the association.

8. Exaggerate the visual aspect that the pupil is to learn.

9. Make sure the pupil understands the meaning of the words and phrases for which you are trying to establish visual-auditory association.

10. As you are teaching the visual-auditory associations by the various "nail-down" methods, be sure also to place the words in written contexts for the pupil to read.

11. Encourage the pupil to use both graphic cues and meaning/syntactic cues in identifying words as he/she is reading text.

12. Practice for fluent reading of sentences and paragraphs, and also check on pupil's grasp of the meaning.

13. Utilize the pupils' strengths.

14. Try either (a) to overcome their relevant weaknesses or (b) to work around them, that is, build on their strengths.

15. Continue to build a pupil's conceptual background.

16. For continuous progress in learning to read emphasize this minimum formula: Continued progress in learning to read = correct pacing + practice of correct responses + mastery at each step + thoughtful fluent reading + continued language and concept development. Always demand and obtain meaning.

As will be made clear in Chapter 10, available self-instruction materials can make execution of these principles possible to the pupil working alone. The emphasis of this present chapter is on some common materials used in direct teaching by the teacher.

BASAL METHOD

Characteristic Emphases

Basic Idea. In most basal reading programs children are taught letter-name or letter-sound associations and then they are taught to identify words. These words are then used in sentence and story context in order to provide meaningful reading material that will be interesting to the children.

Then the pupils are taught component parts (phonic elements) such as *th*, *ea,* and how to apply this knowledge of word parts in order to identify words. The meaning of textual material is emphasized at all times so that contextual clues can be used along with phonics skills to identify words and to understand the textual material as a whole.

The textual material, in the form of stories, is used as a vehicle for teaching both reading skills and an appreciation for reading. After sequences of reading skills are developed by the authors, the skills are slotted into the lesson plans that are placed in the teachers' guidebook.

Elementary Word-Identification Skills. In many basal readers the letter-sound relationships are taught inductively, highlighting the common phonic element in a matrix of known sight words containing a given element. These letter-sound relationships are taught gradually over a period of one to three years. Yet it is possible to teach them beginning with the first few sight words if there is a phonic element common to two of them.

Another way to teach such a phonic element is to compare a known word with a new word containing the same element to bring out the key or phonic element common to them both. For example,

```
                          ┌──key part
previously learned word: ship
           new word: shall
```

Discussion of the identical part and how it looks and sounds alike in both words will help the pupils to learn the new element and, with further practice, to remember it and apply it in unlocking other words.

Organization for Teaching Reading Skills. Following is a detailed outline of a lesson plan format that is typical of the kind used in the basal approach.

Step One: Preparation for Reading

1. Developing background. In order to set the stage for reading a story, the teacher can engage in one or more of the following activities: (a) have pupils read a brief related story; (b) read to the pupils a related poem; (c) discuss experiences, pictures, and objects related to the topic of the story. (Most basal series provide suggested introductions.)
2. Presenting vocabulary. Help the pupils with both the perceptual and the conceptual aspects of new words in a story. For example, point up how a new word is similar in appearance to a known word. Discuss the words in sentence context. Present the new word in a written context. Use the sentence context plus a known phonic element (an initial letter sound) in the word to unlock its pronunciation.
3. Further preparatory work (independent). Pupils may do practice exercises— duplicated or in skills workbook—that are provided in the basal series materials or exercises devised by the teacher.
4. Dictionary practice. Help pupils to locate new words in the picture dictionary in the back of their reader. In the dictionary each word is used in a key sentence in order to further develop and clarify the meaning of the word.

Step Two: Reading the Story

1. Silent reading (independent). In order to let the pupils enjoy the story in its entirety without fragmenting it, have them read the whole story silently in response to a single motivating question. Check their comprehension by calling for the answer to the original question. Either restate the question as originally asked or in a paraphrased form. If you are properly pacing the materials to the pupils and teaching for mastery, they should be able to read silently with little or no trouble.

2. Guided oral reading. The pupils should read parts of the story in response to various kinds of questions. Here they will be required to (a) read to prove a point, (b) make deductions, (c) read between the lines, (d) understand story implications, (e) predict outcomes, (f) read to follow directions, (g) locate information, (h) dramatize a story and (i) interpret a character's emotions. It is during guided oral reading in particular that the comprehension skills are applied in response to teacher questioning and the pupils' own needs.

Step Three: Teaching Skills

1. Independent activities. Those children who need the work may do appropriate word-identification and comprehension exercises in duplicated exercise sheets or in the skills workbook.

2. Teacher-directed activities. The teacher may select (from among those suggested) activities designed to develop interest in reading. Some of the activities suggested are (a) preparing for a dramatization, (b) testing to check progress, (c) reviewing phonics skills, (d) playing phonics games, (e) working with pupils on their dictionaries, (f) making a chart about some classroom procedure such as the rules for good oral reading, (g) making up original stories from the pupils' reading words, and (h) constructing sentences from word cards. When these activities are done properly they help to reinforce the words and skills that are being taught. They provide the pupils with another opportunity to make correct responses and to be reinforced for making them.

3. Taking care of individual differences. Careful observation of a child's performance plus frequent testing will enable a teacher to determine which kinds of activities will help a child improve skills through specialized practice. Some of the activities from which a teacher can choose, in addition to those already suggested, are (a) children working in pairs, (b) kinesthetic practice (tracing over dotted outlines of words) with words while saying them, (c) building words in a pocket chart or on a magnetic board, (d) making a booklet of rhymes or experience stories, and (e) playing a phonics game.

4. Related activities. The reading lessons can be enriched through use of suggested activities such as the following, which can be related to the topic of the story: (a) making a booklet, (b) drawing a picture about a story scene a pupil likes best, (c) reading a related story, (d) singing a song, and (e) writing (copying) a story (dictated by the pupils) that has been written on the chalkboard by the teacher.

Note: Prior to the opening of school in the fall a teacher should check the list of suggested related stories in the teachers' guidebook and should make sure to have available as many of these books as possible.

Activities for Teaching Word-Sound Associations. Word-sound associations may be taught with the following activities: (1) associating the sound of a word with the printed form, (2) associating the picture of a word with the printed form, (3) reinforcing association through multimodal activities such as tracing over dotted outlines of the word while saying it, (4) labeling pictures that have been cut out of magazines and catalogues, (5) incorporating into exercises words learned from simple experience charts, (6) building words (a) with alphabet cards, (b) with magnetic alphabet, (c) by writing.

Role of Nucleus Words. Most basal series advocate the teaching of meaningful words presented in meaningful printed context. Basically two types of words are taught as nucleus words: first, those words with irregular letter-sound relationships (*of, there, here, is*) that would make the word hard to sound out; second, those words for which the pupils lack skills to determine the pronunciation. By de-emphasizing the sounding out of words—part by part—reading may be done more fluently, and therefore may be done to obtain ideas. However, this idea presupposes step-by-step mastery of the words. Each nucleus word must be "nailed down" by each pupil.

Basic Materials and Exercises. An alert teacher can incorporate many kinds of materials into a basal series method. Usually the basic materials and exercises include books, teachers' guides, workbooks, word cards, phrase cards, tape cassettes, dictionaries such as picture dictionaries or illustrated dictionaries in the back of readers, and self-help selections. The last are brief selections containing a reference picture, and caption sentences accompany many exercises; this setup allows the child to refer to these pictures and sentences when necessary while doing the rest of the exercise. Finally, basal series have available specific skills tests and reading achievement tests. Some series have criterion-referenced tests.

Sequence

The general sequence for teaching the beginning reading skills according to this approach can be outlined. Both the general sequence and the sequence of elements included under a given point will vary from series to series. The following sequence is similar to the sequence of beginning reading skills in a number of series:[1]

> Teaching letter-sound and/or letter-name associations.
> Teaching nucleus words: associating the printed form of a word with the spoken form, using nail-down strategies.

---

[1] A more complete and accurate idea of the sequence for a given reading series will be obtained by looking at the publishers' scope and sequence charts or in teachers' manuals.

Strengthening the association of the printed and the spoken form of a word through careful visual scrutiny of the form of the whole word and its parts.
Teaching rudimentary, independent word-identification skills.

a. Letter-sound associations.
   1) Consonant (letter)-sound (if not taught during readiness training).
   2) Initial consonant digraph-sound.
   3) Consonant blend-sound.
b. Processes.
   1) Inductive and deductive teaching of letter-sound associations.
   2) Comparison of known word with new word containing a like element.
   3) Substitution of initial letter sounds in known words to form new words.
c. Context aids
   1) Use of sentence meaning plus partial pronunciation to unlock words.
   2) Development of independence in word identification through use of self-help references.
d. Structural clues.
   1) Recognition of variants of known words.
   2) Recognition of contractions of known words.
   3) Looking through a whole word in order to identify it.

Teaching Procedures

How does one actually go about teaching reading skills in a basal reading series? Following are (1) a story, "The Big Lion," and (2) a sample lesson plan for a directed reading lesson based on the story:

The Big Lion

(P. 21) Dad said, "There is a big lion at the zoo."
   "A big, big lion?" said Susan.
   "Yes, a big, big lion." said Dad.
(P. 22) Jack said, "Dad, can we go to the zoo to see the lion?"
   "Yes. Do you want to go, Susan?"
   "No, I don't like lions. The lion can hurt me," said Susan.
(P. 23) "You are silly, Susan," said Jack. "Maybe it has no teeth."
   "Funny lion, no teeth," said little Larry. "I want to see funny lion—no teeth."
(P. 24) So they all got in the car. They went to the zoo.
   They went to the big lion's cage.
   "There he is," said Jack.
(P. 25) "He is big," said Susan. "Big lion," said Larry.
   "Look at the man. He gave the lion some meat," said Dad.
(P. 26) "Look at his big teeth," said Jack.
   "The man's big teeth?" said Susan.
   "No, silly. The lion's," said Jack.
   "You know something funny?" said Susan.
   "What?" said Jack.

"I bet he has a big toothbrush," said Susan.

"The man?"

"No, silly, the lion."

Step One: Preparation

1. Developing background. Any one of the following activities can be used to build background for reading the story: (a) showing slides of a trip to the zoo, (b) letting children tell what they have seen at a zoo, (c) reading a poem about a lion or about a zoo.
2. Presenting vocabulary (New words: lion, zoo). For zoo: Say, "I'd like to go to the zoo." Try to elicit, "I want to go, too," write that sentence on the chalkboard, and have it read. Underline the word too and have it pronounced. Say, "Which word rhymes with too, city or zoo?" Write zoo under too and point up the way in which they look alike and different. To present lion: Pass out a duplicated sheet that has a picture of a lion, with the word lion printed under it. Under the word lion is the same word (lion) in dotted outline form. Have the pupils say the word while looking at it; then the pupils say the word lion while tracing over the dotted outline form.
3. Further preparatory work (independent). Work the reinforcement exercise on page 15 of the reading workbook.
4. Dictionary practice. Have the pupils find zoo and lion in the picture dictionary at the back of the book.

Step Two: Reading the Story

1. Silent reading (independent). On the chalkboard write the number of the page on which the story begins (page 21). Ask the pupils to turn to it in their readers and read the title of the story. Say, "Read the story to yourself to see if both Jack and Susan go to the zoo."
2. Guided oral reading.
(P. 21) "What is the title of our story?"
   "What did Dad say about the big lion?"
(P. 22) "Who wants to see the lion, Jack or Susan?"
   "What did Jack say?"
   "What did Susan say?"
   "How do you think Susan felt?"
   "Read what Susan said the way you think she said it."
(P. 23) "How did Jack try to make Susan feel better?"
   "How would you say Jack's words if you wanted to make Susan feel better?"
(P. 24) "Did they go to the zoo?"
   "How do you know?"
(P. 25) "What did little Larry say about the lion?"
   "What did the man do for the lion?"
(P. 26) "Let's do the last page like a play." [Call for volunteers and select a person for each part. After they "perform," select another cast and let it perform.]

Step Three: Teaching Skills

1. Independent activities. (a) Let those pupils who can profit from it do the practice exercise on the duplicated exercise sheet. (b) Those who need it can do the follow-up pages in the skills workbook.

2. Teacher-directed activities. (a) Making up original stories: Help the pupils use the words they can read to make up stories in the pocket chart. The words they have learned can be placed where they can see them (chalk ledge, another pocket chart, and so on). If they suggest a word that has not been set out, write the word on a blank card or try to obtain it from the set of cards that comes with the series. (b) Working on the pupil dictionaries: Using the series dictionary, which contains all the words in the first-level readers, locate the two new words of this story, lion and zoo. Then have the pupils close the dictionary and see if they can locate the words. Refer to the alphabet to show that l is in the middle section. Ask the pupils if they should look in the middle part of the dictionary for the word. Ask them where z is in the alphabet. Ask them in which part of the dictionary they would look to find z—first, middle, or last.

   Have the sentences read and discuss them. Call for other sentences. If the pupils are making their own dictionaries, guide their entry of the word in their dictionaries. Suggest that they draw pictures to go with the words. Where appropriate pictures are available, they may be cut and pasted onto the correct pages.

3. Taking care of individual differences. (a) Kinesthetic practice: Select two or three words that pupils have been having difficulty with. Write them in dotted outline form. Have the pupils trace each word several times as they say it. Put each word in sentence context on newsprint and display it on an easel or on the bulletin board. (b) Experience reading chart: Able pupils will enjoy reading an experience reading chart based upon their visit to a zoo.

4. Related activities. (a) Copying an experience reading chart. The pupils who dictated the story about their visit to the zoo may enjoy writing the story (or segments of it) on large sheets of paper. (b) Stories to share: "Animals Use Their Tails," in Did You Ever? By Adda Mai Sharp (Austin, Texas: Steck, 1957). A Day at the Zoo. by Marion Conger (New York: Simon and Schuster, 1950).

STRATEGIES FOR TEACHING WORD IDENTIFICATION

Nail-down Strategies to Use with any Approach

In various reader systems children may learn some letter-sound associations before learning to read words. Therefore, the inchoate stages of learning to read may emphasize associating printed forms of letters with the spoken forms. The pupil does not learn how to sound out words part by part in these beginning stages but learns how to differentiate each word from other words. Also, teacher discussion of the plot and the story provides contexts that help the child recall the pronunciation of the word. Some activities to use in developing associations between the printed form of the word and the spoken form follow.

Association of the Printed Word with a Picture. Because we move in a left-to-right progression in reading and because in developing an association the printed form should precede the spoken or picture form, the printed word should be to the left of the picture.[2]

T: [Display the card containing the word and the picture.]

[Cover the picture with the hand or with a blank card. Focus attention on the printed form; this action is imperative or the association cannot be made. Then show the picture. Elicit the spoken word from the pupil(s). After a number of paired presentations of printed word and picture, the printed word ball should elicit the response "ball" from the pupil(s).]

Language Master. Anytime after you teach a child to look at a word from left to right you can use the *Language Master* device to identify the word and to provide repeated practice as an aid in learning to pronounce it. A *Language Master* card containing a printed word and a magnetic tape recording of the pronunciation of the word is placed in the machine. The child can see the printed form as he/she hears it spoken on the loudspeaker.

Sets of cards with a prerecorded tape firmly affixed to the bottom of each card are available. Blank cards and tapes may also be used by the teacher to write any words on them and to record the spoken forms, too. You may pick out a series of cards for the child or a small group of children to practice or you may let a child choose his/her own cards.

Also available are cards that contain common phrases used in reading. You may want to point to each word in the phrase at first in order to make sure the pupil is making the correct associations between printed words and spoken forms of the words.

Part-Whole Comparison. Instruction that emphasizes inspecting very carefully the component parts of words is useful in helping a child identify a word and remember it. Phonics is not entailed in this procedure—only careful visual scrutiny.

T: [Print word on the chalkboard or magnetic board.]

cool

"Here is the beginning of the word [pointing to c], here is the middle part of the word [pointing to the oo], and here is the ending part [point to l]."

T: "Now watch again as I write cool on the chalkboard. It begins like this [write c], then you write this [oo], and at the end you write this [l]."

---

[2] To avoid the negative connotations of a "look-say" approach, follow the teaching of a few words with the "part-whole comparison" strategy and/or the "knowing what a word is and what it isn't" strategy.

T: "Look carefully at the word cool. —Now close your eyes. Can you see the word cool? —If you can't, take a quick peek."

T: [If you are using the magnetic board, you can allow children to manipulate the letters, going from a slightly jumbled form of the word to the correct form. You may want to use a model at first. After a while you can check to see if they can rearrange the letters from memory.]

T: [Put another word, such as can, on the board. Go through the same procedure.]

T: [Leave the two words, cool and can, on the board and then write parts of each word on the board, one word at a time, and ask which word it is a part of. This procedure sets the stage for examining these components of the words: ool, an, coo, ca, co. The first two segments require a grosser discrimination to be made than do the last two—ca, co.]

Knowing What a Word Is and What It Isn't. Many times people get married knowing what their future spouse is but not what he/she is not. In like manner, pupils sometimes think they really know a word (or teacher thinks so) but find that when they must differentiate it from a similar word, they didn't really know the word because they did not know what it was not.

The use of exemplars and nonexemplars helps the pupil differentiate a word from words that have similar graphic cues. A pupil in learning the association between ⟨dog⟩ and /dóg/ should recognize exemplars of ⟨dog⟩—dog and *dog*—and nonexemplars—*fog* and *doll.*

Technique One. Directions: Write a word on the board, for example, dog and say, "This word is dog." Write other words on the board and each time ask if the word is dog. When a word is not dog, the pupils should tell why it is not dog. Finally, point to the words, and each time you point to dog have the children say /dóg/.

Model word: dog
Comparison words: doll dog fog for dog door bog fog dog

Target Word	Comparison Words	Sample Responses
dog	fog	"The first letter is f, but in dog it is d." "The first part is wrong."
dog	dog	"Yes, that's dog. Right! All the letters are the same."
dog	for	"The first letter is wrong and the last one is too."
dog	doll	"No. These words are different at the end. They just don't look the same."
dog	dog	"Dog. Same letters. They look just alike."

It is useful when comparing words to use felt letters and a flannel board or magnetic or plastic letters. At other times you may erase each comparison word as you complete the comparison and write the next word right under the target word.

Technique Two. Directions: The directions for this exercise are to be read by the teacher or an assistant. The words and pictures are duplicated. Several sets may be placed on one page. Pass out copies to the pupils involved. Then say, "Look at the word to the left of the picture of the forest. What is the word? (Pause.) Right— forest. Below the word and picture are several words. Put a check mark (√) by the words that are exactly the same as the word by the picture, the word <u>forest</u>. Say the word quietly as you check it. When the word is not <u>forest</u>, underline the part that is different. Let's do an example:"

forest	![forest scene]

fon<u>d</u>est	foot	fondest	foot
forest	forest	follow	for
for __	farthest	foot	forest
	forest	forest	fort

Tracing a Word While Saying It. One way of helping children develop the association between the printed and the spoken forms is to have them trace over the word as they say it. In addition to the forced visual inspection involved in this procedure, there is the kinesthetic reinforcement that it provides.

The word to be traced can be written on a chalkboard or on a piece of paper. It can either be written lightly or in dotted outline form; in either case it should be large enough so that the child can trace over it without taxing his/her visual-motor capacities. Once again you are helping the child with the *sequence* of the letters and the *component* parts of the word.

have   have

Illustrated Rhyme Phrases. An activity that requires of the teacher only whimsy and a minimum amount of talent in art is using illustrated rhyme phrases. These phrases can be used to teach both concrete words and abstract (function) words such as *in, on, a,* and so on. If taught as sight words, they serve as "readiness" work for phonics.

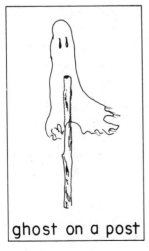

ghost on a post   fox in a box   cat at bat

Further Strategies for Identifying Words

The Programmed Work Sheet. To reinforce word-sound associations make a column of words on the left-hand side of the page and simple pictures representing the words on the right side. Pupils can cover the right-hand column. After pronouncing a word in the left-hand column, the pupil uncovers the picture and receives either a positive reinforcement or a correction. Examples:

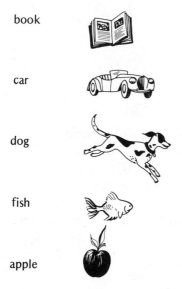

book

car

dog

fish

apple

(For variation, present the same words and pictures in a different order: *fish, car, dog, apple, book.*)

Illustrated Phrases for Teaching Function Words. Some of the important words that help the English language to function properly are *a, and, are, have, here, how, I, in, is, it, of, the, that, this, to, what, when,* and *where.* As children are learning these words one can teach them sentences that become increasingly less stilted than the sentences in many beginning materials and more like the natural language that they speak. In teaching these words one takes advantage, to some extent, of the letter-sound associations the pupils know, of meaningful context, and of opportunities to make responses provided by repeated, meaningful practice. These words must be mastered. The pattern for teaching them follows:

1. Present a large illustrated card that contains a phrase or sentence.[3]
2. Have the children memorize the phrase and be able to point to the word corresponding to the one they are saying.
3. Present on a duplicated sheet the picture and phrase that were on the card, along with other pictures and matching phrases previously taught.
4. Have the phrases read.

---

[3] On this large illustrated card or sheet the word that is being taught should *not* be dotted, but it may be underlined. This large card may be placed on the wall where children can easily see it.

5. Below the pictures have dotted outlines of the word in question so that the children may trace over as they say it:

Word   Illustrated Phrase

a

a boy

and

chair and table

are

Are you sleeping?

have

The children have toys.

here

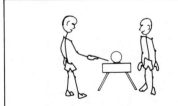

Look here

Word	Illustrated Phrase

how

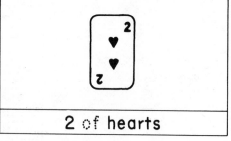

Tell me how

is

Jack is happy.

it

Jill is it.

of

2 of hearts

the

See the boy and the dog.

Word	Illustrated Phrase

that

Look at that flower.

this

Take this apple.

to

Take me to your leader.

what

What a big cone.

when

Say when.

ANALYTIC LANGUAGE-EXPERIENCE METHOD

Characteristic Emphases

Basic Idea. In the language-experience approach to beginning reading, the pupils read stories about their own experiences that the teacher has written on the chalkboard or on chart paper. How is this done? (1) The teacher engages the pupils in a discussion about some experience they have had. (2) The pupils offer sentences about the experience. (3) The teacher writes (prints) the sentences on the chalkboard. (4) Under the guidance of the teacher the stories are committed to memory.[4] (5) The pupils learn to associate the spoken sentences with printed sentences, then the spoken phrases with printed phrases, and finally the spoken words with the printed words. This procedure, as can be seen, proceeds from gross differentiation (sentences) to finer differentiation (words). This approach can be used (1) as a lead-in to a basal approach, (2) as a teacher-developed method (which would require ingenuity on the teacher's part), or (3) in one of the commercial forms available.

Elementary Word-Identification Skills. The word-identification skills can be approached in several different ways. They can be taught in much the same way as in an analytic basal method. Then the beginning reading word-identification skills could include the following: (1) nucleus words; (2) [phonic elements] such as consonants, consonant blends, consonant digraphs, and so on; (3) structural analysis; and (4) use of context. A slight variation would be to teach consonant letter-sound associations prior to teaching the pupils to read the language-experience charts.

Activities for Reinforcing Associations. The word-sound associations can be made through activities such as the following:

1. Illustrate on the story (or on an adjacent sheet) words and phrases that can be pictured. Anything that is concrete—things and actions—can be drawn by the teacher (or the pupils) or cut out of a magazine and pasted on the story. These pictures are then labeled correctly and serve as word-pronunciation keys.
2. Develop picture dictionaries that contain words (and pictures) used in the stories. These picture dictionaries can be arranged (a) by story, (b) by alphabet, (c) by alphabet within the story. The pupils may illustrate some of the words. Also, pictures can be cut out and pasted in the dictionary.
3. In sum, any of "nail-down" procedures previously discussed can be used.

Basic Materials. A teacher's quest for materials should be limited only by his/her imagination. Few schools will deny teachers materials if they explain why they want them and what they intend to do with them to teach pupils to read. Teachers will want to have available for teaching reading by the language-experience approach the following: (1) a chalkboard, (2) oak tag paper, (3) newsprint paper, (4) duplicating equipment, (5) pencil and paper, (6) felt-tip

---

[4] It is a good idea not to let the stories become too long—two or three sentences at the most for some children. You might like to fashion an occasional story in couplet form.

pens, (7) crayons, (8) chart stand, (9) tape recorders, (10) jack box, (11) headsets, and (12) *Language Master* and cards.

In order to provide opportunities to rehearse the stories, the teacher may record them on cassette tapes and allow the pupils to play them back in small groups or individually. Pupils may wear earphones (headsets) in order not to disturb other members of the class.

Sequence

There is no set sequence for the informal teaching of reading charts. A teacher will want to keep a record of individual and class achievement—the words mastered, the topics covered, and so on—and may also keep a record of words learned according to the phonic elements they contain. This record will provide teachers with words to use when they teach the phonic elements inductively. At some point in the proceedings a portion of the list might look like this:

ch	wh	ai	oo
champion	wheat	tail	football
chicken	what	afraid	look

sh	oy	au	or
Washington	boysenberry	astronaut	orbit
shrimp	ahoy	caught	for

Teaching Procedures

The basic steps for developing one type of language-experience reading chart are as follows:

1. Engage pupils in conversation about the experiences they have had relative to a given topic or occasion.
2. As pupils offer relevant sentences about their experiences, write them on the chalkboard or easel in a suitable sequence.
3. Read the story with the pupils.
4. Help the pupils to memorize the story—through rehearsal with them and/or letting them listen to it on a tape recorder.
5. Read the whole story with the pupils. Point to a line as it is read.
6. Make two copies of the story on oak tag.
7. Cut one copy of the story into sentence strips.
   a. Read the strips.
   b. Let pupils match each sentence strip with the corresponding strip on the intact chart.
   c. Let the pupils rearrange scrambled strips into the correct sequence, using intact chart as the model. Make sure they look at each sentence and say it while looking at it.

8. Cut sentence strips into phrase strips. (Proceed with the matching, rearranging, and association activities as with the sentence strips.)
9. Cut phrase strips into word cards and repeat the above process.
10. Read chart and segments of the chart and note problem words.
11. Make a card for each word taught; scramble the order of cards and test words in isolation. Note problem words.
12. Use nail-down procedures to learn difficult words or phrases.

Note: Throughout these activities the teacher may ask the pupil questions about the whole story and about segments of it. The pupils read segments in response to the questions.

It is possible to teach the reading chart without cutting it into strips. If this is done, more of the question-and-answer work can be covered. Furthermore, when teaching the individual child who progresses well, it may not be necessary to cut up the story. In either case,

1. Place more emphasis on meaningful experiences.

2. Select many words that can be illustrated right on the story page.

3. Take advantage of tape recorders for rehearsal of the story and for recording directions for exercises.

4. Use an instrument such as the *Language Master* for aid in developing associations between printed words and spoken words and between printed phrases and spoken phrases.

Examples of Language-Experience Reading Charts

We visited Grandpa and Grandma in Milwaukee.
They took us to the art show.
We saw paintings and spooky lights.
Then we drove down to the harbor.
We saw a big ship.
The people on it were going to Michigan.
    (By Linda, Katie, and Charlie)

Jill Goes Swimming

My name is Jill.
I like to go to the park to swim.
The lifeguard gave me lessons.
I can swim now so he lets me jump off the board.
Wow! That's neat!
    (By Jill, age 7)

Activities to Emulate. The use of the language experience approach to reading is not limited to stories or to the very first stages of reading. Following are some creative productions and formats that show how art can be combined with reading. In these productions you follow up and *teach* the stories, phrases, and words.

Form 1: Round Things. This production by a seven-year-old girl took place spontaneously one summer day when a little girl just started to draw *round* things. She wanted to know how to spell the words and learn how to read them. These are her original drawings and handwriting.

Form 2: My Book. The following winter this girl and her older sisters and brother received a basketball and hoop for Christmas. Where they live one can play basketball outdoors in January. She produced the following book, which shows a good self-concept. As parents and as teachers we need to be alert to these desires to create. We should allow other children a chance to see these productions and to discuss them. They will be stimulated individually or in small groups to produce similar things that can be shared and learned.

I'm playing
boskaetball.

I'm fishing

I'm playing
foofball.

I'm runaing

I'm Reading.

Form 3: Many people who have a good place to fish consider themselves lucky. And they like to tell their story. Katie's family did not have a boat, but they liked to fish in the Gulf of Mexico and the intercoastal waterways. Katie's production was done originally on a large sheet of white paper (22″ × 16″) and in color. The artwork and story are Katie's; the printing is by her father. Let your pupils draw a picture and then tell you a story about it. Write the story on the paper that has the picture or on a separate sheet that can be affixed to the bottom of the picture.

Are you surprised at Katie's size compared to her mother's size? Katie is the youngest person in the family. Psychologists tell us that drawing oneself bigger than one's parents is a kind of adjustment mechanism that younger children will often use.

Form 4: Illustrated Nursery Rhyme. We teachers can be artists, too. If we make an occasional contribution, we will enter into the spirit of language-experience reading more and do a better job with it.

Directions: (Use a known poem, verse, or couplet. Put diagrams and words on an overhead transparency. Project on a screen and discuss each picture and associated words. Use the last box as programmed learning. Have child cover picture, say word, and then check response with the picture.)

Form 5: Stories on a Topic. As children progress in reading, we can have discussions on a topic that just pops up or one connected with a content area. After a discussion on "How Animals Eat," Renee, a second-grader produced the following story and her own illustration:

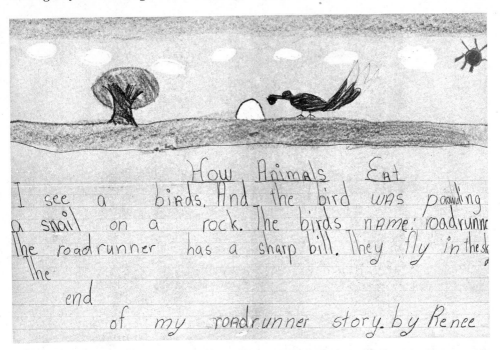

How Animals Eat

I see a birds. And the bird was pounding a snail on a rock. The birds name: roadrunner. The roadrunner has a sharp bill. They fly in the sky. The

end

of my roadrunner story. by Renee

Form 6: Seasonal Charts. We can record phrases pertaining to a particular season or holiday. If we illustrate them, the drawings can help children learn the expressions and use them in stories they dictate or write themselves, depending on the child's ability. Here we have a Thanksgiving chart (not yet illustrated) and an illustrated Christmas chart.

Reading Skill Chart

Thanksgiving Phrases

a neat turkey	watching a football	giving thanks
a piece of pie	game	eating some cran-
watching a parade	eating the food	berries
singing a song	going to church	helping Mother

Some Christmas Words

Christmas tree

angel

music

Form 7: Photograph Illustrated. Take pictures with Polaroid Land camera of, for example, various activities the pupil is engaged in at school or home. Let the pupil tell a story or give a caption for each picture, and put the pictures and stories (or captions) into a little book or display them in some other way agreeable to you and the pupil (Hafner, 1974).

Form 8: Magazine Illustrated. Stories can be thought up on the basis of pictures or the story can be told and pictures sought in magazines. This procedure is especially good for minority groups if you get pictures of these groups from magazines that contain a lot of appropriate pictures (Hafner, 1974).

Form 9: Cartoon Illustrated. Use original cartoons by pupils and/or teachers. Also get comic strips from the newspapers and develop different dialogues, which are pasted over the original dialogue balloons or printed in white space above the cartoon frames. Black out the original dialogue (Hafner, 1974).

Form 10: Branching Out. Couplets, poems, interviews, known songs or poems, events, or stories from other subject matter areas all provide a variety of interesting reading material for the advancing reader. Once again, use cassette tapes for help on the audio and don't be afraid to make colorful illustrations and/or let the pupils make illustrations (Hafner, 1974).

Form 11: Stick Figure Illustrated. Use either a sequence of pictures or a single picture (Hafner, 1974).

The Synthetic Language-Experience Approach

Instead of going from the whole story to the parts and taking advantage of the semantic and syntactic constraints afforded by the sentences in the analytic, the synthetic approach goes from individual words and builds to sentences. The words can be taught as nucleus words by any of the techniques described in this chapter.

The synthetic LEA method works. We designed the following lesson plan for use with a first-grade girl, Nancy, who had previously been unsuccessful in learning to read. The teaching was by an undergraduate student as part of her reading course practicum. This was the first of several lessons. It required several periods to teach. The remaining lessons were of the same order and built upon the first one. Of course, each succeeding lesson had the advantage of more known words, better skills, and the increased confidence of the tutor and the child being taught. It was gratifying to see how well the child progressed in reading. Since that time, this approach has proved to be successful with other pupils as well.

1. Discussion (about where child eats at home).
2. Concrete words.

3. Abstract word "and"

4. Trace over and as she says it.
5. Put it in with other two words and differentiate.
6. Have her draw her chair and table.
7. Write "sentence" under picture.

8. Switch to synthetic/analytic.

9. Trace and say: has   a
10. Differentiate all words: a   and   chair   Nancy   table
11. Substitute words in the first syntactic pattern.
    Nancy has a chair and table.
    Nancy has a plate and fork.
    Nancy has a hamburger and milk.
      (Use word-picture and/or phrase-picture card to teach plate, fork, hamburger and milk.)

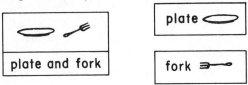

12. Differentiate all words: shuffle word-picture, phrase-picture, and sentence "strips" and test. Review-reteach any unknown material.

13. Develop a new syntactic pattern.

Nancy likes to sit at the table.
Nancy likes to use her plate and fork.
Nancy likes to eat her hamburger and drink her milk.
    (May use context to infer eat and drink. "Nail down" with "know what a word is and isn't" and/or other technique.)

14. Develop a new syntactic pattern; for example:

Noun Phrase	Verb Phrase	Noun Phrase
Nancy	is	happy
Nancy	is	big
She	is	happy and big.

  a. Draw phrase-picture card.

  b. Discuss the picture and the caption.
  c. For the word "is":
    (1) trace and say.
    (2) do "What a word is and isn't."

     it if is his is as it is
  d. Make word-picture cards for "happy" and "big."
  e. Do "What a word is and isn't" for "she."

15. Differentiate all words.
16. Substitute words in the NP-VP-NP pattern and teach.
17. Develop new patterns.

Note: Continue until pupil has learned enough to be placed into another kind of program: analytic language experience, basal, programmed linguistic, or whatever is most suitable.

STRUCTURAL LINGUISTIC METHOD

Characteristic Emphases

Basic Idea. Several reading instruction systems are linguistically oriented. These systems usually incorporate a number of linguistic concepts. The present system, based on structural linguistics, features the control of letter-sound correspondence and the introduction of words by spelling patterns.

The pupils are taught as part of their readiness work the names of the letters of the alphabet. Then in actual reading instruction two kinds of words are taught: those that fit a spelling pattern such as *an* (*fan, can, man*) and those such as *the, is,* and *of* in which the letter-sound correspondence is irregular. In order to provide a meaningful context for the learning of words, they are used in sentences and stories.

Elementary Word-Identification Skills. Some linguists who write reading instruction materials believe that the first step in learning to read is to visually differentiate each letter from other letters and to associate the correct name with each letter. This knowledge can help pupils note differences among words and aid the teacher and pupils in discussing aspects of them.

Words are taught as whole words but they are analyzed for their constituent parts. The words are taught in patterns or in word families. For example, *can, fan,* and *tan* (*-an* family or pattern) may be taught in a lesson and *top, hop,* and *cop* (*-op* pattern) in another. In these pattern words there is consistency in the pronunciation of the consonant sounds and the vowel sounds from word to word: *c* is always pronounced like a *k*, not an *s*, and *f* is always pronounced like an *f* and not like a *v*.

Teach the pupil to examine the meaningful whole words he is learning so that he can see how a word is constructed and how each constituent part of a word is related to the whole word. The linguistic system discussed here emphasizes presenting words that lead gradually to complete familiarity with three important patterns of English spellings:

1. (c)VC—(Consonant) Vowel Consonant: (p)at, (b)at, at.
2. CVCe—Consonant Vowel Consonant, final e: hope, same, time.
3. CVVC—Consonant Vowel Vowel Consonant: rain, coat, seem.

The chief goal of the instruction should be to aid pronunciation, not spelling. Although spelling is an integral part of the present system, it is not necessary for learning to read.

A key aspect of this linguistic-oriented method of reading is the use of the *minimum contrast* to decode words similar in spelling. The words *hat* and *pat,* for example, are different visually in only one respect—in their first letters; the first letter, then, is the point of minimum contrast. A pupil should be taught to take advantage of the identical parts of words and then differentiate the words at the point of minimum contrast. In this way he/she can learn to identify rapidly many words of the same pattern.

Organization for Teaching Reading Skills

Basic Lesson Plan. The linguistic-oriented lesson plan is a systematic, sequential presentation of both spelling pattern words and sight words involving (1) close attention to the construction of the word, (2) much behavior on the part of the pupils—saying the word, spelling it, noting likenesses and differences among words, (3) reading the word in sentences and stories, (4) answering the teacher's questions about the stories, and (5) mastering the material at each step in the sequence. Following is an abbreviated outline of a typical lesson plan in the inchoate stage of reading instruction:

1. Teacher presentation of the first word of a pattern.
2. Pupil behavior with the word.
3. Teacher presentation of the second word of the pattern.
4. Pupil behavior with the word.
5. Introduction of further words and pupil behavior with the words.
6. The teacher's writing of sentences that incorporate the new words.
7. The teacher's writing of a story that incorporates words of the pattern being studied.[5]
8. Teacher questioning to guide the silent reading of each sentence.
9. Teacher and pupil discussion of what has been learned in the story.
10. Children's oral reading of the story.
11. If child has trouble with a word, the teacher's writing on the board of other words that contain the same pattern as the word in question.

Activities for teaching and reinforcing word-sound associations include:

1. Writing practice.
2. Writing names for things pictured on dittoed sheet.
3. Writing in missing letters in words under pictures on duplicated sheet.
4. Seeing likenesses and differences in words through the use of multiway minimum-contrast matrices.
5. Choosing letters to complete words where pictures or phrases are clues.

Role of Sight Words. In order to develop as normal sentence patterns as possible, teach as sight words some of the important function words that are not represented by the regular spelling patterns; for example, *the, of, this, here, from, what.*

Basic Materials. The important materials for teaching a linguistic-oriented reading program are reading texts, teachers' guides, chalkboard, chart paper and easel, duplicating machine, and some special exercises. These materials can be supplemented by using filmstrips, catalogs and magazines, trade books, and picture dictionaries, magnetic board, and alphabet.

Sequence

An involved sequence at this point would not be meaningful or interesting; neither would it represent the spirit of this approach. During the readiness stage the teacher teaches the pupils the names of the letters of the alphabet and continues to develop language skills. In teaching reading he/she teaches words of various patterns, emphasizing the minimum-contrast idea, and teaches a number of function words as sight words. At the same time stories are developed from the words and the pupils are taught to read for meaning.

---

[5] Commercial materials such as the Merrill Linguistic Reading Program will eliminate much preparation.

Teaching Procedures

A typical lesson plan of the rudimentary stages follows:

1. Teacher presentation of the first word of a pattern.
    a. Write the word on the chalkboard or on chart paper, for example,

    man

    b. Say the word while pointing to it.
    c. Spell the word while pointing to the letters.
    d. Use the word in a sentence.
2. Pupil behavior with the word.
    a. The pupils look carefully at the word and say it as they are looking at it.
    b. Pupils say the word and spell it, pointing to each letter as they say that letter.
    c. Pupils make up sentences containing the word.
3. Teacher presentation of the second word of the pattern.
    a. Align the second word, ran, under the first word:

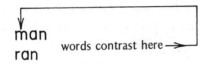

    man
    ran   words contrast here ⟶

    b. Say the second word, ran, as you point to it.
    c. Show how the words differ at the contrast point.
4. Pupil behavior with the word.
    a. Have the pupils say the word and spell it, pointing to each letter as they say the letter.
    b. Have pupils use the word in a sentence.
5. Introduce words three and four, tan and can.
6. Write sentences that incorporate the new words:

The man ran. Joe ran. Joe is tan.

The man can see Joe.

7. Write a story, using some or all of the words the children have learned, making sure to incorporate the words of the new pattern.

Joe is a boy.

Joe has a tan.

The man is in the sun.

Can the man get a tan ?

Yes, the man can get a tan.

8. Ask questions to guide the silent reading of each sentence.
   T: "Who is Joe?"
   P: "Joe is a boy."
   T: "How does Joe look?"
   P: "Joe has a tan."
   T: "Where is the man?"
   P: "The man is in the sun."
   T: "What do we want to know about the man?"
   P: "Can the man get a tan?"
   T: "Can the man really get a tan?"
   P: "Yes, the man can get a tan."
9. Discuss what has been learned in the story.
10. Have the story read orally.
11. If a child has trouble with a word, write on the board other words (that he/she knows) of the pattern involved.

Exercises for Teaching Reading Skills. The following exercises illustrate the types that can be used to advantage when teaching a linguistic-based reading method:

Identifying and Writing Names of Pictured Items on Duplicated Sheets. Explain that the names of the items can be printed under the pictures.

Choosing Letters to Complete Words. Have pupils circle the correct letter in the right-hand column and then write it in the blank. Following are types of items:

1. [Where word alone is the clue] __at   b   z   l
2. [Where picture pattern is the clue] ⊏▨▭▭◯⊐ __at   f   b   m
3. [Where phrase is the clue] ball and __at   c   j   b

Finishing Sentences. Provide pupils with duplicated sheets of incomplete sentences and a list of words to use in completing the sentences. Use one or two sentences as examples so pupils will be sure to understand what they are to do.

1. Sam can _____ . [eat jam and ham]
2. Dan had a _____ . [big pig]
3. Jim did not _____ . [hum]
4. Jip cut _____ . [his lip]
5. Tam is _____ . [in a hut]
6. The cat _____ . [sits on Sal's lap]

Make a list of sight words (that is, ones they know perfectly) to be used in completing the sentences:

jam	eat	lip	on
sits	in	Sal's	lap
hum	a	his	big
pig	ham	and	hut

Scrambled Words. Place scrambled words on a magnetic board. Have a correct model of the sentences in sight. Allow pupils to rearrange the scrambled words so they correspond to the correct model. Have the sentences read as a double check.

1. Correct model: Tad can jump up.   Tim had a fat cat.
2. Scrambled words: daT can jupm up.   Tim had a fta atc.

Scrambled Sentences. A scrambled sentence, using word cards, can be arranged on the chalk ledge or on a mimeographed handout. Have pupils re-arrange the words correctly. Correct answers may be placed on the bottom half of the mimeographed sheet (which is folded while the pupils work). The teacher or the other pupils can judge the correctness of a given pupil's chalk-ledge work.

Examples: 1. Tad a had cat.
          2. Zad had a cat fat.
          3. I hear can a loud sound.

[fold] –[fold]

Answers: 1. Tad had a cat.
         2. Zad had a fat cat.
         3. I can hear a loud sound.

Multiway Minimum-Contrast Matrices.[6] Much practice is needed in making minimum contrasts. Matrices of the following type allow a pupil to make several minimum contrasts on each matrix. The pupils might like to try making

---

[6] We owe a debt of gratitude to Richard Rystrom for the idea of the minimum-contrast matrices.

some of their own matrices; matrix work should provide a lot of fun and learning.

mop	top		rat	hat		fat	hat
mom	tom		ram	ham		fad	had

dim	slim		chat	sat		buck	pluck
did	slid		chap	sap		bum	plum

meat	seat		home	dome		them	hem
meal	seal		hope	dope		then	hen

Effect on Number and Tense of a Change in Word Structure (Variant Endings). In the following exercises it should be pointed out to the pupils that word endings are important and that they often change when we need to express changes in meaning: for example, when referring to two people instead of one, when talking to someone instead of about someone, and when talking about something we did instead of something we are doing.

love	We love to read		sing	I sing.
loves	Jim loves to swim.		sings	Mary sings, too.
loved	We loved our cat.		singing	We like singing.

Effect on Meaning of Change in Word Structure. In adding letters to some words only minor changes in meaning are made; however, a minor change can have a great effect on the meaning:

hat	Do I like to wear my hat?
hate	No, I hate to wear my hat.
hateable	My hat is a hateable thing.

Games to Aid Word Recognition

TITLE: Let's Go Bowling   NAME: Eleanor Brinson
                                            Trigg County, Ky., 1974

OBJECTIVE: After doing this activity, the student will have better command of the basic sight vocabulary for his/her reading level.

MATERIALS: Bowling pins cut from paper and mounted on a board or bulletin board, bowling score sheet, 3 × 5 cards, packaged in groups of ten, with one vocabulary word on each card.

PREPARATION: Two to four players. Score as in regular bowling. Each takes a package of word cards and pronounces ten words. If all are said correctly, a "strike" may be recorded on the score sheet. If any are missed, the player may try again (as in bowling) and if the words are pronounced correctly, a "spare" may be recorded. If neither a "strike" nor a "spare" is made, the number of correct pronunciations is counted. The player with the highest score wins. Packages may be exchanged and/or more packages used as needed.

REFERENCES: All words used are from the vocabulary list of any basal reader.

TITLE: <u>G.I. Joe Game</u>   NAME: <u>Karen Baker</u>
                                                    Trigg County, Ky., 1974

TYPE OF READING ACTIVITY: Game using silent "e" words.

OBJECTIVE: The child will know the word with the silent "e" sound.

MATERIALS: Poster board, note cards, felt markers, glue, manila envelope.

PREPARATION: Draw jeeps, tanks, trucks, and army men on poster board. You might use a color that looks like army green. Cut these out. Make a spinner. Put something like this on it.
  1. You were captured by the enemy.
     Lose 1 turn.
  2. You captured an enemy tank.
  3. You captured an enemy truck.
  4. You captured an enemy jeep.
  5. You captured an enemy soldier.
  6. One of your enemy soldiers escaped.
     Lose one man.
  7. One of your enemy jeeps was taken back by the enemy.
     Lose one jeep.
  8. One of your enemy trucks was taken back by the enemy.
     Lose one truck.
  9. One of your enemy tanks was taken back by the enemy.
     Lose one tank.
  10. Give one of your captured items to another player.

In order to spin the spinner each time, each player must draw a word card from the pile and correctly pronounce the word to take his turn. If a player cannot say the word then he/she must give the word to the next player. If none of the players can say the word, then they all must forfeit an enemy item.

The winner is the one with the most captured items when all the cards have been drawn.

Manila envelope is for storing.

WORD RECOGNITION—FILM PRODUCTION:

Directions: Children enjoy making their own instructional film including their new words. You are able to purchase blank rolls of 35-mm film for the filmstrip projector. On the film, children can print their new words and include their drawings. With special colored marking pencils the child can print the word and include a picture to help with the word meaning. Later, the film can be projected for all to

see. If desired, the film projection can be made on the chalkboard where the child
can write the word in chalk.

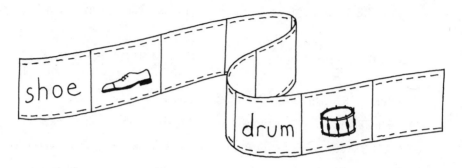

SUMMARY

Pupils can learn to read by a number of methods. Several commonly used
methods featuring direct teaching by the teacher along with a number of strategies, techniques, and games are presented in this chapter. In order for any of
these methods to be optimally successful, the teacher must apply a number of
teaching principles involving pacing the materials to each pupil's ability and
present achievement, teaching for mastery, guiding children in the use of meaning and syntactic cues in addition to phonic cues during reading, practicing of
many correct responses during any given day, practicing for fluent reading to
facilitate meaning development, and providing continued language development.

In many basal methods used today children are taught letter-name or letter-
sound associations and then they are taught to identify words. These nucleus
words are taught by a variety of strategies. Phonic elements can be taught inductively or deductively and applications can be made by comparing a new
word containing a particular element with a known (nucleus) word containing
the same element.

The steps in the basal reading lesson plans are usually (1) preparation for
reading, (2) reading the story (for enjoyment, practice in perception, and
application of comprehension skills), (3) further application of skills guided
by the teacher, and (4) related activities.

The analytic language-experience approach involves stimulating pupils to use
language to relate their experiences, writing down those experiences on charts
for them, and then guiding the pupils in reading and rereading the chart stories
in ways that enable them to read sentences, then phrases, and finally the words.
It is important to remember that use of the language-experience approach is
not limited to the initial stages of reading. This chapter includes some creative
productions and formats that show how art can be combined with reading.

In the language-experience approach the word-identification skills can be
taught in a number of ways, including the inductive approach. Phonic elements
can be taught before, concurrently, or after a beginning is made in teaching the

reading of some stories. However, one of the reasons language experience is used is that it can be used with pupils who have auditory discrimination problems and, consequently, some problems in learning phonic elements.

The analytic language-experience approach, if expertly done, can stand alone as a method of beginning reading instruction. It can be used, also, either as an introduction to or support program for a basal method.

The synthetic language-experience approach features going from individual words to building sentences. It is a good method for the teacher who can think on his/her feet.

The next method presented in the chapter is based on structural linguistics. It features the control of letter-sound correspondence and the introduction of reading vocabulary by spelling patterns. Regardless of the reader's attitude toward linguistics, it is an approach that is widely used in various reading programs; therefore, the reader will want to know something about it.

The lesson plan for the structural linguistics-oriented method is a systematic, sequential presentation of both spelling-pattern words and nucleus words. A typical lesson in the rudimentary stages involves much work on the part of the pupils and teacher and many responses on the part of the pupils.

LEARNING ACTIVITIES

1. Locate a child who is having trouble in identifying words and teach him/her using nail-down strategies. Do not forget to use sentence context in conjunction with the strategies. Keep a log of what you did, the results, and the child's reactions. Report your findings to your classmates or fellow teachers. (In this and succeeding activities do not forget the illustrated phrases for teaching abstract function words.)

2. Observe a teacher using a directed reading lesson in a classroom or on videotape. According to what you have learned so far, what were the strengths of his/her teaching? What would you have done differently that might add to the effectiveness of the lesson?

3. Develop a reading lesson, say, according to a basal plan, for a two- or three-page college-level reading selection and teach it to a group of classmates in your reading methods class.

4. Arrange to teach a reading lesson to a group of children. Use games as needed. Then teach the lesson and report on your experience.

5. If possible, arrange to see videotapes of lessons taught by members of previous reading methods classes and/or members of your reading methods class. Comment on the value of this experience.

6. Arrange to teach two or three language-experience lessons to a child who could profit from them. Report on the experience.

7. Construct some reading games; get them ready for use.

STUDY QUESTIONS

1. What psychological principles does one apply in order to do the best job of teaching reading?

2. Explain in some detail the formula for continuous progress in learning to read.

3. What are the characteristic emphases in basal reading methods?

4. What is done in each step of a basal plan? Explain the purpose of these activities.

5. List some activities for teaching word-sound associations.

6. Explain what nucleus words are.

7. List each nail-down word-identification strategy and state the special importance of each one. (Don't forget the illustrated phrases used to teach abstract function words.)

8. What is the rationale underlying the illustrated phrases used to teach the abstract function words?

9. What are the advantages of the analytic language-experience approach to teaching initial reading acquisition?

10. What aspects of the synthetic language-experience approach jibe with the psychological principles set forth early in the chapter?

11. What are the characteristic emphases in the structural linguistic method?

RECOMMENDED READING

AU, KATHRYN HU-PEI. "Using the Experience-Text-Relationship Method with Minority Children." *Reading Teacher,* 32 (6) (March 1979) 677.

AUKERMAN, ROBERT C. *Approaches to Beginning Reading.* New York: John Wiley & Sons, Inc., 1971.

BURNS, PAUL C. and BETTY D. ROE. *Teaching Reading in Today's Elementary Schools.* Skokie, Ill.: Rand McNally & Company, 1977, Chap. 7.

COOPER, CHARLES R. and A. R. PETROSKY. "A Psycholinguistic View of the Fluent Reading Process." *Journal of Reading,* 20 (3) (December 1976), 184–207.

CRAMER, RONALD L. "Dialectology—A Case for Language Experience." *Reading Teacher,* 25 (1) (October 1971), 33–39.

GIBSON, ELEANOR and HARRY LEVIN. *The Psychology of Reading.* Cambridge: Massachusetts Institute of Technology Press, 1975, Chap. 9.

HITTLEMAN, D. R. *Developmental Reading: A Psycholinguistic Perspective.* Skokie, Ill.: Rand McNally & Company, 1978, Chap. 7.

LUCAS, M. S. and HARRY SINGER. "Dialect in Relation to Oral Reading Achievement: Recoding, Encoding or Merely a Code?" *Journal of Reading Behavior,* 7 (2) (Summer 1975), 137–148.

LUNDSTEEN, SARA W. "On Developmental Relations Between Language-Learning and Reading." *Elementary School Journal,* 77 (3) (January 1977) 192–203.

MACGINITIE, WALTER. "Difficulty With Logical Operations." *Reading Teacher,* 29 (4) (January 1976), 371–375.

SMITH, FRANK. "Making Sense of Reading—and of Reading Instruction." *Harvard Educational Review,* 47 (3) (August 1977), 386–395.

SMITH, R. J. and D. D. JOHNSON. *Teaching Children to Read.* Reading, Mass.: Addison-Wesley Publishing Co., Inc., 1976, Chaps. 5 and 6.

VEATCH, JEANETTE and others. *Key Words to Reading: The Language-Experience Approach Begins.* Columbus, O.: Charles E. Merrill Publishing Company, 1973.

WANAT, STANLEY F. "Relations Between Language and Vision." In H. Singer and R

Ruddell (Eds.). *Theoretical Models and Processes of Reading.* 2nd ed. Newark, Del.: International Reading Association, 1976.

WIESENDANGER, KATHERINE DAVIS and ELLEN DAVIS BIRLEM. "Adapting Language Experience to Reading for Bilingual Pupils." *Reading Teacher,* 32 (6) (March 1979) 671–673.

WILSON, LORRAINE. "City Kids: A Multilingual Experience-based Program in Australia." *Reading Teacher,* 32 (6) (March 1979), 674–676.

REFERENCES

DIACK, HUNTER. *Reading and the Psychology of Perception.* New York: Philosophical Library, 1960.

HAFNER, LAWRENCE E. "Teaching the Nonreader to Read." In L. E Hafner (Ed.). *Improving Reading in Middle and Secondary Schools.* 2nd ed. New York: Macmillan Publishing Co., Inc., 1974, 448–461.

——. *Developmental Reading in Middle and Secondary Schools: Foundations, Strategies, and Skills for Teaching.* New York: Macmillan Publishing Co., Inc., 1977, Chap. 21.

MILLER, HARRY. *Programmed Educational Techniques in Reading.* Richmond, Va.: Kindern, Inc. Educational Materials, 1974.

PALMER, B. C. and L. E. HAFNER. "Black Students Get an Edge in Reading." *Reading Horizons,* 19 (4) (Summer 1979), 324–328.

SMITH, EDWIN H., C. GLENNON ROWELL, and LAWRENCE E. HAFNER. *The Sound Reading Program.* Waco, Texas: Education Achievement Corporation, 1972.

TRIGG COUNTY, KENTUCKY SCHOOLS. *Teacher Made Materials: Vocabulary.* 1974.

CHAPTER 4

Strategies for Teaching
Independent Word-Identification Skills

OBJECTIVES

As a result of thoroughly processing the material in this chapter the reader should be able to state/explain the following:

1. *Name the independent word-identification tools and tell how they are used.*
2. *Define specialized terms such as:*
   a. *Phoneme*
   b. *Grapheme*
   c. *Phonic element*
   d. *Utility of grapheme-phoneme associations*
   e. *Phonograms*
3. *Considerations when pacing the introduction of word-identification elements and skills for pupils to learn.*
4. *The skills that foster independent word identification.*
5. *The strategies for teaching independent word-identification skills.*
6. *Linguists' views about the nature of the syllable.*
7. *A word analysis system based on the teaching of numerous phonograms.*
8. *Principles of teaching phonograms.*
9. *Groff's guidelines for the teaching of syllabication.*
10. *Several games for teaching independent word-identification skills.*

In order to read, a person must be able to identify the pronunciation and the meaning of words in context. When a pupil is confronted with the word *machinery,* for example, he/she must be able to identify the pronunciation /mə-shēn'-ər-ē/. Pupils must particularly identify the meaning of the word as it is used in a phrase or sentence: "*Machinery* is used to manufacture type-writers." A different meaning for the word is implied in, "Smith got his political machinery into action early." Context affects meaning. Identifying the pronunciation means converting print to speech; this conversion process is called *decoding*.

Pupils know the meaning of most of the words they encounter in the beginning stages of reading. Therefore, the big task is to decode the words and do so readily enough so that the resulting chain of words is fluent and intelligible. As pupils begin to read more widely, they will meet words whose meanings are unknown to them. They will look for clues to meaning within the word and the sentence context; when this approach fails they may consult the dictionary.

Because decoding a word in the reading acquisition stages is almost tantamount to identifying its meaning, the term *word-identification* will be used as a generic word for the first unlocking or decoding of the pronunciation of a word. A goal of reading instruction is to teach pupils how to use certain tools that will help them to identify the pronunciations and meanings of words independently.

BASIC INDEPENDENT WORD-IDENTIFICATION TOOLS

The following tools are used in various combinations to decode independently or to identify word parts and whole words: (1) structural analysis, (2) phonics, (3) visual analysis, (4) context (clues), and (5) the dictionary.

Structural Analysis. Structural analysis is a process of looking at words to locate known parts that may facilitate identification of the words: syllables, (*matt-er, doc-tor*),[1] root words (*read-*er, *hope-*ful), prefixes (*un-*able, *inter-*change), suffixes (success-*ful*, help-*less*), and variant endings (read*ing*, brave*ly*, cap*s*, like*d*, and so on). Structural analysis may be used in conjunction with phonics, visual analysis, and context clues in order to identify a word.

Phonics. Phonics is associating a letter or combination of letters with one or more sounds and applying such knowledge (always in conjunction with context clues) to identify words. For example, students learn to say the sound at the beginning of *food* and *fine* when they see *ph*, or the sound in the words *toy* and *boy* when they see *oy*. When children know how to say *oy* and *toy* and *boy*, they have learned to make the *association* between the printed form and the spoken form. They may need to make more than one association for *ea* and then choose the sound on the basis of the other letters in the word and/or the context. For example, in *heal* /hēl/, the *l* is a cue that *ea* is to be pronounced /ē/. In *head* /hed/, the *h* and the *d* are cues that *ea* is to be pronounced /e/ rather than /ē/.

Visual Analysis. Visual analysis can be considered a general skill of looking for whatever visual cues are available: structural, phonic, distinguishing features, comparing a word with a known word in the context that has one or more similar elements, and the like.

---

[1] Groff (1971) suggests a broad concept of what constitutes a syllable.

Context Clues. The words surrounding a given word are the context. This context can provide a clue to the meaning and the pronunciation of that word. Take this sentence, for example: "I'd like a cup of Mocha—no sugar." Those people who drink coffee are pretty sure that Mocha is a kind of coffee; "cup of," "no sugar" in this instance were context clues to the meaning of *Mocha.*

Context clues can be used in conjunction with partial pronunciation to help complete the pronunciation; for example, a pupil pronounces the first syllable of the word *hospital—hos—*and then takes into consideration the meaning of the context of the sentence in which it appears in order to determine what the word is: "Sandra was badly hurt so they took her to the *hos*pital." Success in using context is predicated on the principle that a child can read for meaning only if he/she (1) is correctly placed in reading level, (2) is taught to demand meaning, and (3) reads fluently enough to gather and build meaning.

The Dictionary. Too often the dictionary is merely a book some people refer to occasionally to help settle an argument: How do you spell *cenobite*? How should it be pronounced? What does it mean? Those who turn to the dictionary at least are using some standard in order to come to a reasonable solution. One should think of a dictionary as a useful tool to help in developing and maintaining accurate communication. A person who learns to use a dictionary well and finds it useful will be more likely to continue using it than the person who does not have such experiences. Dictionary usage is discussed in Chapter 5.

BASIC CONCEPTS

Nucleus Words. Nucleus words are those that a pupil has identified and can now recognize readily. These nucleus words are learned by methods discussed in Chapter 3. Teacher and pupils may use nucleus words as the basis for teaching phonic and structural elements of words inductively.

Phonemes. The smallest meaningful sound units of speech are *phonemes.* Spoken words are made up of phonemes. The word *it* has two phonemes: /i/ /t/. The word *dough* also has two phonemes: /d/ /ō/.

Grapheme. A grapheme is a unit of writing used to represent a phoneme. The two phonemes of *it* are represented by the two graphemes ⟨i⟩ ⟨t⟩. In dough the graphemes are ⟨d⟩ ⟨ough⟩.

Phonemic Options. A grapheme may represent more than one phoneme; we then speak of phonemic options. An example follows:

Grapheme	Phonemic Options	Examples	
	/ch/	chop	chew
	/k/	choir	orchestra
⟨ch⟩	/sh/	chateau	chemise
	/k̲/	Bach	Loch

Graphemic Options. A phoneme may be spelled in a number of ways; different graphemes may represent a particular phoneme. For example, some graphemic options of /ō/ are ⟨o, oe, ow, o-e, ough⟩.

Auditory Blending. If a person sounds, that is, speaks, the following separately to someone—/f/ /i/ /sh/—and asks him/her to tell what word is formed when the sounds are "run together" or blended in the same order as presented, and he/she does it successfully by saying /fish/, it is because he/she blended the phonemes. This skill is useful for synthesizing phonic-elements in order to identify a given word independently.

Syllabication. Breaking words into syllables is known as syllabication. It may help a pupil to (1) find known segments such as roots and affixes (prefixes and suffixes), (2) spot familiar phonic elements, and (3) determine phonograms (members of a word family) such as -ake, -ing, -ick, and -ong.

Utility of Grapheme-Phoneme Generalizations. How useful are the generalizations about phonic elements? What is their utility? If a particular grapheme represents a certain phoneme in only 10 per cent of the words containing the grapheme, that generalization is said to be not very useful. A grapheme-phoneme generalization of 50 per cent utility is much more useful because it will hold true half of the time; if a phonemic option takes care of the other half of the cases, one or the other phonemic option will be correct and the modified generalization (with phonemic options) will have 100 per cent utility. Remember that one who reads meaningfully always uses the context as a corrective device.

Inductive Teaching

The way to be convinced that there are many tall buildings in Manhattan is to drive around Manhattan and see them. In making an inductive generalization one notes the attribute or element that is common to a set of things and then generalizes about the things in terms of their common attributes. One is going from particulars to a generalization about them. What kind of generalization can you make about your classmates in terms of the color of their hair, the type of footwear they have on, their affability?

One can use this learning phenomenon in teaching phonic elements. After a pupil has learned words such as *like, the, ride, bed, see, orange, tree, this, can,* and *that,* one arranges three of the words so as to bring out the phonic element that they have in common:

> the
> this
> that

The teacher then leads pupils to note that these words look alike ⟨th⟩ and also sound alike /th/ at the beginning, and with some guiding "teacher talk" gets pupils to associate the grapheme with the phoneme it represents. This is teaching a generalization inductively—from the particulars to the general(ization).

Deductive Teaching

The usual concept of deductive teaching in word analysis is, state a rule and give examples of it. Then ask pupils to state the rule and give further examples to see if they understand it.

OUTLINE OF WORD-IDENTIFICATION SKILLS

Following is an outline of the specific skills taught in the word-identification (readiness, initial reading, and independent word-identification) programs of a number of reading instruction series. The outline assumes that except for the basic consonants and vowels the phonic elements will be taught after a certain number of nucleus words have been taught to the pupils. Whether the consonant is taught as a *name*, for example, b → /be̅/, f → /ef/ or *sound*, such as b → /b/, f → /f/ is left to the discretion of materials authors and/or the teachers. A similar problem relates to the teaching of vowels grapheme-phoneme associations: which will be taught first, glided [long] or unglided [short] vowels?

1. Readiness instruction.
   a. Auditory discrimination.
      (1) Hearing likenesses and differences in words.
         (a) Beginning parts.
         (b) Middle parts.
         (c) Ending parts.
      (2) Hearing rhyming sounds in words.
   b. Visual discrimination.
      (1) Seeing likenesses and differences in letters.
      (2) Selecting a letter to match a model or given letter.
   c. Context clues (oral language).
      (1) Demanding meaning from spoken sentences.
      (2) Being able to provide the missing last word in a spoken sentence.
      (3) Listening for clues in a spoken sentence that will help in determining the meaning and/or pronunciation of a previously unknown word.
   d. Auditory segmentation.
   e. Auditory blending.
   f. Phonic elements.
      (1) Consonants, b, c, d, f, g . . . z.
      (2) Vowels, a, e, i, o, u, (y).
2. Initial reading instruction (reading acquisition).
   a. Nucleus words taught by "nail down" methods.
      (1) Word-picture association.
      (2) Language Master or other card reader.
      (3) Part-whole comparison.
      (4) Knowing what a word is and is not.
      (5) Tracing a word while saying it.
      (6) Illustrated rhyming phrases.
      (7) Illustrated phrases to teach functional (relational) terms.

   b. Nucleus words taught by methods using context and partial graphic cues (partial pronunciation).
   c. Checking derived pronunciation and meaning against the context.
3. Independent word identification.
   a. Structural (morphemic and syllabic) analysis.
      (1) Noting variant endings s, ed, and ing and determining their function.
      (2) Noting other endings such as ly, est, 's and determining their function.
      (3) Noting compound words and identifying them.
      (4) Identifying root words.
      (5) Identifying useful prefixes and suffixes.
      (6) Dividing words into syllables as a possible aid to identifying them.
         (a) Closed syllables
         (b) Open syllables
      (7) Identifying word families such as -ake, -ing, -ink.
   b. Phonic elements analysis.[2]
      (1) Consonants.
      (2) Vowels.
         (a) Long (glided) sounds.
         (b) Short (unglided) sounds.[3]
      (3) Consonant blends (bl, br, pl, st).
      (4) Consonant digraphs (two letters representing one sound as ch, ph, sh, th, wh, ck, ps).
         (a) Sample phonemic options: ch → /ch/ cherry, /k/ choir, /sh/chemise, /k/ Bach and th → /th/ this, them (voiced) /th/ thanks, throw (unvoiced).
      (5) Diphthongs /difthoŋz/ or vowel sound blends (oi, oy, ou, (out), ow (how).
         (a) The phonemic option /ə/ in double and /ō/ in row, mow are not really diphthongs.
      (6) Vowel digraphs (ai, ay, ə, oa, ea, oo, au, ew, ough, eigh).
         (a) Phonemic options for ea are /ē/ meat, seal and /e/ head, bread.
         (b) Phonemic options for oo are /ü/ moon, boot and /u̇/ look, book.
         (c) Phonemic options for au are /ȯ/ auto and /a/ laugh.
         (d) Phonemic options for ew are /ü/ news (midwestern) and /yü/ few, news (southern).
         (e) Phonemic options for ough are

/ō/ dough, though	/o̤/ thought, brought
/ü/ through	/au̇/ (diphthong) bough.

         (f) Phonemic options for eigh are /ī/ height, sleight and /ā/ weigh, freight.
      (7) Murmur diphthongs (ar, er, ir, or, ur).
         (a) Phonemic options include

ar --- /är/ carnal, ark	or --- /ȯr/ for; /ər/ clamor
er --- /ər/ her, certain	ur --- /ər/ turn, urban.
ir --- /ər/ fir, cirque	

         (b) This is also called the r controller principle.

___

[2] Although most of the illustrations for teaching phonics involve inductive procedures, remember that deductive methods and those analogous to "nail down" methods may also be used.

[3] Long and short sounds are difficult for children to understand. Some new materials use the terms *glided* and *unglided* to describe these sounds. In a glided (long) sound the jaw moves and the tongue glides from one position to another. In unglided (short) vowel production there is little or no movement of jaw or tongue.

(8) Miscellaneous items.
    (a) The r controller (see above).
    (b) The l controller: In many words the a followed by l or ll is pronounced /ö/: alternate, ball, almost, malt, hall.
    (c) The w controller: In many words the a followed by w is pronounced /ö/: aw, awl, craw, law, maw.
    (d) The hard and soft c and g: c and g followed by a, o, or u often receive the hard /c/ and /g/ sounds, respectively.

cap, can	gas, gambol
cot, collier	got, golf
cup, culinary	gull, gumption

    c and g followed by e, i, or y often receive the soft /s/ and /j/ sounds, respectively.

cent, ceiling	gentleman, gentian
cinabar	gist, gill (unit of measurement)
cypress, cynosure	gym, gyrfalcon

c. Use of the glossary.
    (1) Knowing the value of using a glossary.
    (2) Knowing alphabetical order.
    (3) Using diacritical marks.
    (4) Selecting correct meaning for the context.
d. Use of the dictionary.
    (1) Transferring glossary skills.
    (2) Knowing alphabetical order.
    (3) Using diacritical marks.
    (4) Using key words if diacritical marks are not memorized.
    (5) Using guide words.
    (6) Selecting the meaning to fit the reading context.

TEACHING INDEPENDENT WORD-IDENTIFICATION SKILLS

Teaching Phonics

Consonants. Inductive teaching of a phonic element involves going from the particular elements in nucleus words to the generalization about the phoneme associated with the grapheme that the words have in common. Much auditory discrimination, auditory segmentation, and visual discrimination work should have preceded (in the readiness period and onward) the teaching of phonics. Following is an exercise on the visual-auditory perception of a consonant in the initial position of words. This paradigm can be used to teach other elements, also.

    T: (Write in a column on the chalkboard, chart paper, or overhead transparency paper known nucleus words containing the phonic element to be taught.)

ride   **rip**

rain   **round**

T: "Let's read the words together."
T and P: "Ride – rain – rip – round."
T: "Now you say the first two words."
P: "Ride – rain."
T: "Do ride and rain begin with the same sound or different sounds?"
P: "Same."
T: "Now say the next two words softly to yourself."
P: "Rip – round."
T: "Do these words all sound the same or different at the beginning?"
P: "Same."
T: "Let's take a close look at the beginning of the words. [Teacher points to beginning letter of each word.] "What can we say about the way they look at the beginning?"
P: "They have the same letter" or "They all begin with r-r [sound]."
T: [You may ask the pupils what letter is used to designate the r-r sound.]
P: "_____."
T: "These words all begin with the letter r. I need four people to come to the chalkboard. Each person will draw a line under one r."
P: "_____."
T: "Who can write an r right here?" [Pointing to space at top of the column.]
P: "_____."
T: "What kind of rule can we make about pronouncing words that begin with ⟨r⟩?"
P: "_____" (Accept any response that makes sense.)
T: "Who can give us other words that start with ⟨r⟩ (or with /r/?)" [Write these words on the chalkboard.]

Phonic Element Substitution: Initial Consonant. A valuable skill for identifying words utilizes known words and known phonic elements; this skill is known as phonic element substitution and will be illustrated now, using initial consonants. Two patterns that serve somewhat different purposes will illustrate the possibilities of this skill.

Alternative 1: If the word *hot* is known and the pupils have associated the correct sounds with the following consonants—*c, d, g,* and *l*—by substituting these consonants for the *h* in *hot* the following words can be identified: *cot, dot, got,* and *lot.*

T: "Today we are going to do some magic. I am going to write this word [hot] on the board."

hot

T: "What is this word?"
P: "Hot."
T: "Now I am going to change it to a different word. [Erase h and substitute c.] What is the word now?"
P: "Cot."
T: "Now I will change it to _____." [Erase c and substitute d.]
P: "Dot."

T: "Let's put these words into sentences." [Write on the chalkboard and have read]:

I can sleep on a <u>cot</u>.

I sleep a <u>lot</u>.

T: [Continue by developing the words <u>got</u> and <u>dot</u> in like manner.]

Alternative 2: The first approach emphasized the use of the latter part of the word—*ot*—which remained constant while the initial consonant changed. Alternative 2 uses the same initial consonant for several words while the remaining part of the word changes.

T: [Sensitize the children to the initial consonant <u>p</u> by arranging several known nucleus words in a column:

pot

pin

penny

Have the words pronounced and elicit the fact that the words look alike at the beginning and sound alike at the beginning. The letter <u>p</u> may be underlined for emphasis. Then place known nucleus words in a column and have them pronounced:

can

sat

hill

let

Remember, you have sensitized the pupils to the sound associated with the letter <u>p</u>.]

T: "Now watch what I do. I am erasing this letter [c in can] and writing the letter <u>p</u> in its place. What is this word [pointing to <u>pan</u>]?"

P: "Pan."

T: "What is the next word?"

P: "Sat."

T: "Watch me erase the first letter and write <u>p</u> in its place. What is the word now?"

P: "Pat."

T: [Continue in like manner to develop the words <u>pill</u> and <u>pet</u>.]

Note: (1) The words one develops will depend upon the particular nucleus vocabulary one has developed up to this point. (2) If the pupils don't know the names or sounds represented by the letters one may refer to them by saying "this letter."

Key Objects for Consonants. A ready reference to refresh the memory for the sound of consonants is the chart on page 106, which can be drawn and posted in a convenient place:

b _____   k _____   **6** s _____

c _____   l _____   t _____

d _____   m _____   v _____

f _____   n _____   w _____

g _____   p _____   y _____

j _____   r _____

Vowels. This pattern for teaching long [glided] vowels can also be used to teach short [unglided] vowels. To teach seeing and hearing the long [glided] *a*:

T: [Write on the chalkboard these sight words:]

came   say   rain   late

T: "Pronounce these words."
P: "_____."
T: "Let's take a very close look at these words. One letter is in all these words. What letter is it?"
P: "A."

T: "Right. The letter is a. When a sounds like its name, we call it long [glided] a."

T: "Let's see if you can hear the long [glided] a sound in some words. Johnny, will you read these words? When you hear Johnny say a word with a long [glided] a sound, raise your hand."

J : "Way – hand – play – tame – farm."

Making a Long [Glided] a Chart. Have pupils state several words that they can already recognize, each of which contains a letter *a* that is a long *a.* The following words, illustrative of the type children will give, may be written on a piece of oak tag.

cake

make
say
came

Select as a key word for the top of the chart a word that represents something concrete, such as *cake.* (A similar activity can be used to illustrate short [unglided] vowel words.)

Consonant Blends. Remember that when we develop a rule or generalization on the basis of particulars, we are doing inductive teaching.

T: [Write green and ground on the chalkboard.]

green

ground

T: "Please say these words for me."

P : "_____."

T: "Listen as I say these words again: green, ground. How many sounds does this part [underlining gr] have?"

P : "_____."

T: [If the pupils have trouble, say, "Gound." "What sound was missing?"]

T: "Tell me other words that begin with these two sounds." [Then write on the chalkboard several sentences that contain a known word with gr and a new word containing gr and let the pupils read the sentences. For example: known: green, ground. unknown: grass, grows.]

Look at the pretty green grass.

The green grass grows on the ground.

Vowel Digraphs. There are a number of ways to teach any phonic element. Vowel digraphs, like other phonic elements, can be taught inductively: sight words containing the element are arranged in a column, and the common sound (phoneme) and the common letters (graphemes) are elicited through observation and discussion. Then the teacher leads the pupils into formulating the rule.

To refresh the memory, these graphemes are examples of vowel digraphs: *oa, ai, ea, ee, ough*. Rather than our giving the rule about vowel digraphs at this point, try to discover it for yourself by examining these columns of words, saying the words in each column, noticing the like graphemes and trying to generate the rule for pronouncing the vowel digraphs.

oak	pail	eat	see	ought
coat	rain	heal	bee	brought
foam	mail	bean	fee	thought

Five important points to remember: (1) Use known words. (2) Arrange the words in a column so that the common element will stand out. (3) Have the pupils say the words in a column in order to hear the common phoneme. (4) Have them inspect the words visually to see the common graphemes, e.g., *oa*. (5) Through observation and discussion lead the pupils to formulate the rule, which may be expressed in their own words.

In addition to the patterns given for teaching pupils to identify phonic elements and words, one should provide practice exercises to help develop firmer knowledge of how these elements function in words.

[Draw the following diagram on the chalkboard:

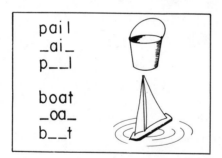

After discussing with the pupils the function of ai and oa in the helping words pail and boat, show them how to write ai in the appropriate blank to make pail and oa in the blank to make boat. Have the pupils read each sentence and fill in the blanks to make the correct word in each sentence.]

1. He walked in the r _ _ n and got wet.
2. He did not put on his c _ _ t.
3. See the pretty _ _ k tree.
4. A g _ _ t has horns.
5. The water went down the dr _ _ n.
6. The man put the m _ _ l in the m _ _ lbox.

Consonant Digraphs. Remember that consonant digraphs are not blends. The sound of *ph* in telephone is *not* a blend of the *p* in *put* and the *h* in *hello*. The sounds represented by the digraphs are rather stable except for the *ch*. In beginning reading most of the words containing *ch* will sound as they do in *cherry* and *chicken.* Remember, the other patterns we have given may be adapted for use in teaching the consonant digraphs. Following are some new patterns, the first for finding the consonant digraph *ch.*

> T: [Place on the chalkboard in random order a number of words that the pupils have learned as nucleus words, including several words that contain the ch as it sounds in cherry.]
>
> T: "I am going to write two letters (ch) on the chalkboard. I want several people to come to the chalkboard to find words which have these letters in them." [Call the pupils to the chalkboard.] "When you find these letters, draw a line under them—like this." [Illustrate.]
>
> P: "_____."
>
> T: "Can you think of other words we have read that begin with 'c-h'?"
>
> P: "_____." [As the pupils respond, put the words in a column and draw a line under the ch.]
>
> T: "If we wanted to write the word choose (or some other word that begins like choose), what would the first two letters be?"

Developing the Consonant Digraph Chart. One can build a consonant digraph chart. After teaching a consonant digraph, place a drawing of an object that begins with that digraph on the chart. Next to it write the consonant digraph. Following is a sample chart:

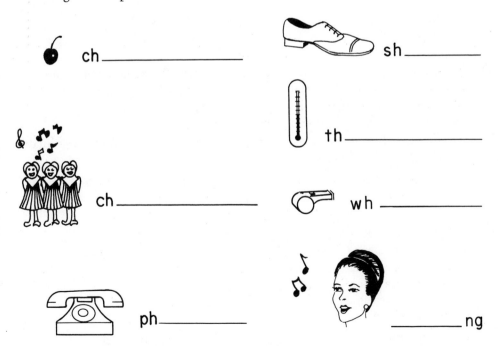

Diphthongs. A diphthong is a vowel blend; for example, one hears two vowel sounds in these diphthongs: in *oy* for *boy* ($\bar{o}\text{-}\bar{e}$ or $\dot{o}\text{-}\bar{e}$, depending on one's dialect), *oi* as in *oil*, *ou* as in *out*, and *ow* as in *howl*.

Diphthongs can be taught inductively, as can other phonic elements. Remember that a minimum of two elements is necessary to develop a phonics generalization inductively. It might be a good idea to develop early the generalization that *ou* sounds as it does in words such as *out, found, house*, and *around*, so that the pupils have good command of this skill before they are introduced to words containing *ou* in which the *ou* is pronounced differently. Exceptions can be taught by nail-down methods. Of course, with the presentation of problems of these kinds, we can see the value of teaching pupils to demand meaning from the printed page, to combine partial pronunciation with context to "unlock" words.

Using Known Words to Unlock Unknown Words. Two of the first words taught in many reading series are *house* and *round*. After these words are learned, one can arrange them in a column of two words—

h<u>ou</u>se
r<u>ou</u>nd

and develop the generalization that *ou* in many words sounds as it does in *house* and *round*. The next time a word (such as *found*) containing the diphthong *ou* is presented, it can be paired with *house* in this manner:

h<u>ou</u>se
f<u>ou</u>nd

Discuss the pronunciation of the word *house*. Elicit the sound of *ou*. Point out, or ask how the two words are alike. Since the consonant elements—*f, n, d*—are regular, the average pupil with adequate auditory and visual abilities should not have too much trouble in unlocking the new word.

Single-Element Emphasis Using Related Sentence Context. A meaningful drill may be constructed as follows:

> Directions: Here are some words you have read. Read each sentence. Put the right word in each blank.
>
> ab<u>ou</u>t   house   f<u>ou</u>nd   <u>ou</u>t   r<u>ou</u>nd   s<u>ou</u>nd   mouse
>
> 1. We went to the old _____.
> 2. Do you know what we _____?
> 3. We found a little _____.
> 4. It made a funny _____.
> 5. The mouse ran _____.
> 6. And we ran _____.

Final *e* Principle. There are several ways of teaching pupils that adding an *e* to a one-syllable word such as *hop, pal*, and *cut* changes these short-vowel-sound words to ones with long vowel sounds, *hope, pale,* and *cute.* An exercise for finding the rule:

> T: "Here are some words that you know." [Teacher writes two or more pairs of words such as the following.]

not   hop

note   hope

> T: "Let's pronounce these sets of words." [Point.]
> T and P: "not, note; hop, hope."
> T: "How are these words at the bottom [indicating note and hope] different from the words right above them?" [Indicate not and hop.]
> P: "Bottom ones have e."
> T: "How do they sound different?"
> P: "Have long o sound." or "They get the ō sound."
> T: "What rule can you make up about words like note and hope?"
> P: "_____."

An alternate approach would be to place the short-vowel-sound words in one column and the long-vowel-sound words in another column:

I	II
can	cane
mat	mate
man	mane

> T: [Develop the generalization that the words in column I have the short vowel sound, those in column II have the long sound. Then write the following words in a column.]

gal

hat

rate

> T: "How do I change the word gal to gale?"
> P: "Add an e after the l." or "Put e after gal."
> T: "How do I change hat to hate?"
> P: [Let the pupils demonstrate how to do it.]
> T: "How do I change rate to rat?"
> P: "Take the e away."

Note: Perception of words, as perception of anything in the world, is done (in one sense) as a figure-ground problem. Consider the previous sentence; when looking at the word *anything,* all the other words in the sentence are ground or background and the word *anything* is figure. We interpret the figure in terms of ground. If a person doubts this, he should consider what kind of sense a person would get for the word *ground* in the sentence in question if he did not consider the context (or "ground") of the sentence. For this reason, words studied in exercises often should be placed in sentence context, at least toward the end of the exercise. For example, in this exercise phonics and context skills are combined in a meaningful perception exercise:

Directions: In each sentence choose the word that makes sense in the sentence.

1. She is a pretty _____.
   gale   gal

2. The cat ran after the _____.
   rat   rate

3. He put his _____ on his head.
   hat   hate

Follow-up Activity for "Final e" Principle

⟨i-e⟩ → /ī/

Step 1. Use a <u>word wheel</u> that contains words such as <u>hop, can, fin</u>; they are changed to <u>hope, cane,</u> and <u>fine</u> when they come to the ⟨e⟩ on the <u>outer wheel</u>. Have students note the rule.

Step 2. Follow-up game: Read and discuss.

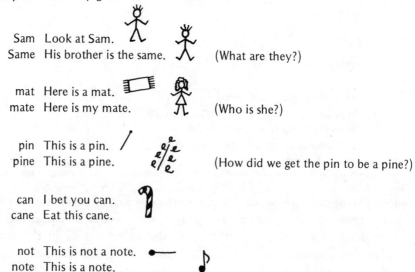

Sam Look at Sam.
Same His brother is the same.   (What are they?)

mat Here is a mat.
mate Here is my mate.   (Who is she?)

pin This is a pin.
pine This is a pine.   (How did we get the pin to be a pine?)

can I bet you can.
cane Eat this cane.

not This is not a note.
note This is a note.

hop | I hop in a garden.
hope | I hope to find a carrot. (What am I?)

fin | I have a fin.
fine | I look fine. (What am I?)

Murmur Diphthongs. The vowel-*r* combinations tend to be confusing enough so that pupils may pronounce *or* in place of *er*, but if they are always reading for meaning they should be able to adjust the sound to *er*. For example, in the sentence "The baker sold me some rolls," even if they pronounced the second word /bākŏr/, they should be able to correct it by the time they get to the end of the sentence.

Following is a pool of common words used in beginning reading that contain murmur diphthongs:

ar	er	ir	ur	or
car	mother	bird	burn	for
farm	her	birthday	turn	horn
far	after	girl	Saturday	torn
barn	farmer	first	turtle	morning
park	Father	circus	turkey	horse

A bright child who does well in auditory and visual discrimination can learn a phonic element inductively on the basis of two words that contain the element. Another child may do better if the inductive generalization is based on more words containing the element.

Coloring the Phonic Element. To add interest to an inductive generalization exercise use colored chalk to make the element more distinctive and bring it out as figure against the ground of the rest of the word.

Magnetic Chalkboard Exercise. A fun exercise that can help develop flexibility of perception is the following one, which utilizes phonic-element substitution. It can be used with one or two elements that have been learned well (*ea* and *ar*, for example) and one that has just been learned (*or*, for example).

T: [Write the following sentence on the magnetic chalkboard in letters that are the same size as the magnetic letters that you will use.]

Would you like to eat a barn?

P: "_____."
T: [Place the magnetic letters *or* over the *ar* in barn.] "Now read the question and answer it."
P: "_____."
T: [Now substitute *ea* in the word and ask for a response.]
P: "_____."

T: [Write the word <u>barn</u> on the chalkboard.]

barn

T: "What is this word?"
P: "Barn."
T: "Who can use this word in a sentence?"
P: "_____."
T: [Write out the sentence, spelling it <u>bean</u>.] "O.K., that's fine." [Wait for someone to correct and then place <u>ar</u> in the word to make the correction.]
T: [You can continue this type of exercise using sets of words such as <u>far, for</u> and <u>park, pork, peak</u>.]

Key Objects Chart for Murmur Diphthongs. Charts such as the following may be used to teach murmur diphthongs:

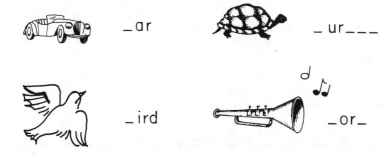

Further Vowel Digraphs. (*au, ew, ie, $\overline{oo}$, oo,* and *aw*). Remember that a number of phonic elements can be pronounced in more than one way. We have discussed the vowel digraph *ea* as pronounced with a long $\overline{e}$ (*eat, heat*) and as pronounced with a short *e* (*head, bread*). Fortunately, pupils can learn that if the one pronunciation of a new word containing such an element does not sound correct, they can use the alternate pronunciation. The same option applies to special vowel combinations such as *ie, oo,* and *ew*. Following are words that contain special vowel combinations:

/ī/ ie	/ē/ ie	/ȯ/ au	/ȯ/ aw	/ü/ oo	/ů/ oo	/yü/ ew	/ü/ ew
pie	believe	auto	saw	moon	look		
lie	field	saucer	aw	food	book	mew	new
tie	chief	daughter	bawl	stool	foot	few	grew
die	shield	cause	jaw	boo	good		flew
		haul	crawl	cool	took		blew
		taught	lawn	boot	cook		drew

Teaching Vowel Combinations Through Use of Rhyming Couplets. Simple rhymes may be used to teach *oo* /ü/ and other combinations:

T: [Write on the chalkboard couplets such as the following.]

A spook said, "Boo,"
And I said, "Boo-hoo."

T: "Let's say this little rhyme together."
T and P: "_____."
T: "Which words rhyme?"
P: "Boo and hoo" [or Boo and boo-hoo].
T: "How are boo and hoo alike?"
P: "_____."
T: "What part says /ü/?"
P: "The two o's" [or pupils may point].
T: "Let's put several /ü/s on the chalkboard."

   oo

   oo

   oo

"How can we make too out of the first /ü/?"
P: "Put t in front of it."
T: "What would you like to make out of the next /ü/?"
P: "_____."
T: "What would you like to make out of the next /ü/?" [It could be something like boo or moon or food.]

Key Objects Chart for Selected Vowel Digraphs. The objects chart is another useful teaching device:

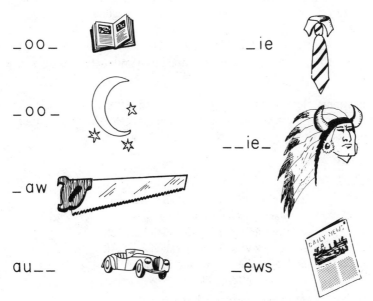

_oo_
_oo_
_aw
au__

_ie
__ie_
_ews

Note: Begin the chart when you teach the first vowel digraph combination. Make sure your pupils associate the sound with the object. They should understand that the dashes indicate missing parts. One could write *saw* and say, "*Aw* is the important part here so we will erase the *s* and put this mark (−) in its place." When children come to words containing such an element, check up on their ability to use the chart. You may need to help them make use of it; it cannot be assumed children will know how to use a chart or will use it just because the teacher made it.

   Teaching *c* **and** *g*. The sounds of *c* and *g* may be taught with the following exercises.

   Building a c *and* g *Chart*. Place a piece of oak tag on a chalkboard, a wall, or an easel. Using the headings and categories that follow, add words from the pupils' reading vocabulary. As a word is added, comment on whether it has a soft *c* ("s") or a hard *c* ("k"), a soft *g* ("j") or a hard *g*. When you have the minimum two (required for making inductive generalizations) in a cell, elicit the fact of visual and auditory similarity at the focal points and help the pupils develop the rule.

c /s/	g /j/	c /k/	g /g/
cent	gem	can	game
cell	gentle	cat	gas
century	gelatin	calf	gallon
city	giant	cone	got
circle	ginger(bread)	cold	gone
Cindy	giraffe	cousin	gold
(bi)cycle	gypsy	cut	gum
Cynthia	gym	cub	guess
cypress	gyp	cuff	gully

   A More Advanced c *and* g *Exercise*. The following exercise should be attempted after the pupils have some familiarity with the hard and soft *c* and *g* concept.

   Directions: Here are sentences with missing letters. The missing letters are c and a vowel or g and a vowel; for example, circle, gold. Cover the answer column. Each time you write your answer, check to see if you were correct.

Answer
Column

1. gi	1. A great big man is called a _ _ ant.
2. ci	2. Many people live in the _ _ ty.
3. cy	3. Boys and girls like to ride bi _ _ cles.
4. ca	4. A very young cow is called a _ _ lf.
5. co	5. Ice cream _ _ nes taste good.
6. gu	6. Some children like to chew _ _ m.
7. cu	7. A baby bear is called a _ _ b.
8. gy	8. We played basketball at the _ _ m.
9. ge	9. My friend has a _ _ ntle kitten.
10. ci, cu	10. We saw clowns and acrobats at the _ _ r _ _ s.

11. ce   11. You can buy an apple for ten _ _ nts.
12. giga   12. A man who is eight feet tall is _ _ _ _ ntic.

Teaching Structural Analysis Skills: Morphemic and Syllabic Analysis

One aids a child's reading achievement by teaching him/her to analyze the structure of a word for pronunciation units and meaning units. Structural analysis skills may be useful in beginning reading; consequently, they may be taught along with phonetic analysis skills early in the child's reading instruction program. Some of the first structural (morphemic) analysis skills are (1) identifying new words formed by addition of affixes and variant endings to root words, (2) identifying compound words, (3) identifying comparison forms of adjectives, and (4) identifying the root in a word.

Identifying New Words Formed by Addition of Special Endings. Although the meanings of words are only slightly altered by the minor modifications that occur when letters such as *s, ed,* and *ing* are added to words to form new words, the perception problems produced are of enough consequence so that direct instruction in perceiving such modified words is necessary. Instruction in these rudimentary forms is generally provided in the first year of reading instruction.

*Adding Variant Endings (*s, ed, ing, er) *to a Known Root Word.* Although the analytic approach is generally based on inductive teaching of phonic and structural elements (and some elements are not taught until they have appeared in a large number of words), structural elements such as *s, ed,* and *ing* can be introduced simply, without much fanfare.

> T: "Did you ever see men building a house (or building)? They make rooms and they put on a roof. They keep adding things to the house. You can add letters to a word, too. You know the word that I am writing on the board?"

cap

> P: "Cap."
> T: "Do you know what letter I must add right here so it will be the word caps?"
> P: "_____." [If the children do not respond with an s, write on the board several known words that end with s and have them pronounced.]
> T: "What sound do we have at the end of the word?"
> P: "/s/"
> T: "What letter do we use for the sound /s/?"
> P: "S."
> T: [Write on the chalkboard the following sentence]:

I have three cap.

> T: "How do you like this sentence?" [Continue this sort of activity, which requires the children to perceive, to think, and to make responses.]

Note: In doing exercises of this sort one can vary the conduct of the exercise according to such factors as the sophistication of the learners and the types of responses they make during the exercise. Also, the preceding exercise could be illustrated by drawing pictures of the objects to show one object or more than one object according to whether one is using the word *cap* or *caps*. Flexibility and imagination are imperative in teaching any reading skill lesson.

*Changing and Adding Endings (*ies*).* At the next level children are taught to read words with elements such as the following added: *y, er* (green*er*, loud*ly*), *es* (changing *y* to *ie* and adding *s* (hurry, hurr*ies*), or *d* (hurr*ied*).

> T: [Write one preliminary set and three other sets of sentences on the chalkboard. One known word in each set will be the word that will be modified. Discuss the sentences and the differences in the endings of the words. Guide the children in selecting the correct word for each context and in adding the appropriate endings.]

y   ies

Jack can hurr<u>y</u>   hurr<u>y</u>

See how he hurr<u>ies</u>   hurr<u>ies</u>

worr<u>y</u>   worr<u>ies</u>

Jean worr___ about her lost dog.   worr___

Don't worr___ about that.   worr___

la<u>dy</u>   la<u>dies</u>

A little old lad___ crossed the street.   lad___

Two young lad___ helped her.   lad___

Note: Similar exercises can be used to develop the comparison forms of adjectives: *er, est* (green, greener, greenest). Attention must be given to both the form and the meaning of such variations.

Prefixes. Often certain prefixes represent a particular level of sophistication. For example, the prefix *un* is more common at the primary grades than *inter* and *al*. Even if certain words containing *inter* might be heard and used by primary children, the real meaning of the deeper concept of words such as *interstate* might be rather difficult. What does *interstate* refer to besides a big four-lane highway?

> Level 1. Grades 2^2 to 3^2 for typical child: <u>un</u>, <u>im</u>, <u>in</u>.
> Level 2. Grades 3^1 or 3^2: <u>re</u>, <u>be</u>, <u>dis</u>.
> Level 3. Grade 4: <u>a</u>, <u>con</u>, <u>pre</u>, <u>ad</u>, <u>re</u>, <u>pro</u>, <u>sur</u>, <u>non</u>, <u>anti</u>, <u>de</u>.
> Level 4. Grade 5: <u>al</u>, <u>com</u>, <u>de</u>, <u>ex</u>, <u>inter</u>, <u>mis</u>, <u>tele</u>.
> Level 5. Grade 6: <u>em</u>, <u>fore</u>, <u>semi</u>, <u>trans</u>.

The goal in teaching prefixes is to make pupils aware of the fact that prefixes modify the meanings of words. The basic emphasis will be on the use in oral and written context of many words containing prefixes. The meaning of prefixes is not an end in itself and the rote memorizing of their meanings must be shunned. Developing the concept of what *semi* means by studying in context over a period of time many words that contain this prefix is a much superior method. Above all, make such words a part of the daily conversations and discussions. Remember the *living* language.

Teaching a Prefix (Level 4). The following is an example of a method that may be used for teaching level-4 pupils the prefix *tele*.

T: [Place on the chalkboard several sentences containing words that have been used in class and that contain the prefix tele.]

We enjoy watching <u>tele</u>vision.

The governor called father on the <u>tele</u>phone.

The man in Iowa received a <u>tele</u>gram from his friend in Oregon.

T: [In regard to the first sentence, bring out the fact that television allows us to see something that is produced far away. In regard to the second sentence develop the idea that by means of the telephone we can hear things that are far away. In regard to the third sentence develop the point that we can read some printed material that has been sent from far away. Then draw attention to the common prefix in the words and the common meaning employed in each sentence.]

T: [If the pupils do not make the connection, discuss the sentences again and as you comment on the words in question write down appropriate clues such as the following] :

write: <u>tele</u> – vision

as you say: "far" "see"

write: <u>tele</u> – phone

as you say: "far" "sound"

write: <u>tele</u> – gram

as you say: "far" "writing"

Teaching a Prefix (Level 1). Here is a sample lesson for teaching the prefix *un* at level 1.

T: "Here is Joe. He is feeling very good today. We say he is happy."

happy Joe

T: "Here is Jan. She does not have a good feeling. She is not happy; she is _____."

unhappy Jan

P: "Unhappy."

T: "Listen. The word unhappy has a part that happy does not have: happy, un-happy. Which word has the extra part un?"

P: "Unhappy."

T: "Look at the word happy and then at the word unhappy. Where is the thing we add to happy to make it say unhappy?"

P: [Points to it.]

T: "What does that say?"

P: "Un."

T: "Unhappy means not happy. Unlucky means not lucky. What does un mean?"

P: "Not."

T: "Here are some sentences on the board. Find which word fits best in a sentence and draw a line under it:"

Tie your shoes. They are [tied / untied

Ruth won a pony. Ruth is [lucky / unlucky

Ruth likes ponies. So she is [happy / unhappy

Jerry did not win a pony. Jerry is [lucky / unlucky

P: [Pupils respond.]
T: [When children are finished tell them to find the un-type words that they under-lined and have them circle un in each case.]

Suffixes. One cannot teach the meaning of every suffix to every child. More likely one will teach the child to identify the form of the suffix and through repeated exposure to a variety of words containing a given suffix teach the general sense of the suffix to him/her. The real test of whether a person is succeeding in teaching a given suffix is the ability of pupils to use in appropriate context words containing that suffix.

Pupils are more likely to encounter given suffixes in their content area and recreatory reading before they encounter them in basal reading.

Level 1. Grades 2^3 to 3^2: ish, ly, ful, al.
Level 2. Grades 3^2 to 4: est, less, ion, scion, tion, ity, ty.
Level 3. Grade 4: able, ible, ish, ment, ive, ness, ward, ous, ious, ent, ure, ern, ese.
Level 4. Grade 5 or 6: ary, tory, ic, ship, ist, ence, ance, en, an, ian, n.
Level 5. Grade 6 or 7: ant, atory, dom, ical, ize, ling, teen, age, eer.
Level 6. Grade 7 or 8: cle, acle, icle, cule, id, ose, some, tude, itude, ule, wright.

Teaching Suffixes (Level 3). Pull from meaningful contexts that the pupils have read several sentences containing the element (in this case the suffix *ish*) that you are going to teach:

T: [Write the sentences on the chalkboard.]

The self<u>ish</u> boy would not share his candy with his friends.

The fool<u>ish</u> girl rode her wagon down the steep hill.

The man who stepped from the space ship has a green<u>ish</u> looking face.

T: "Which part of the first sentence explains what <u>selfish</u> means?"
P: "'Would not share.'"
T: "Can you use the word <u>selfish</u> in another sentence?"
P: "_____."
T: [If a particular child is not clear about the meaning of <u>selfish</u>, ask him to tell in his own words what <u>selfish</u> means or ask him to use it in an original sentence.]
P: "_____."
T: [Proceed in a similar manner with the remaining two sentences.]
T: [Next develop the meaning of <u>ish</u> by giving the pupils a chance to recognize its meaning from among several foils.] "On the board (or on your worksheet) is a

two-part sentence. The second part will mean the same as the first if you underline the correct word."

$$\text{She was girl\underline{ish}; She was} \begin{bmatrix} \text{by} \\ \text{near} \\ \text{like} \end{bmatrix} \text{a girl.}$$

P: "Like."
T: "Yes. You can write the sentence in several ways:"

She was girl<u>ish</u>.

She was girl-<u>like</u>.

She was <u>like</u> a girl.

She acted <u>like</u> a girl.

T: "What do you think <u>ish</u> means?"
P: "_____."
T: [Proceed in a similar manner to discuss <u>foolish</u> and <u>greenish</u>. Do not go into all the detail if the pupils seem to be grasping the concept readily. There should be little trouble in developing the pronunciation of this suffix since the <u>sh</u> is already a very common phonic element.]

Syllabication. Words have as many syllables as they have vowel sounds. Breaking a word into its component syllables is called syllabication. Children can be taught to syllabicate two- and three-syllable words fairly readily. Syllabication may be an aid to pronouncing words if it helps people recognize a known syllable or if it aids a person by isolating a unit that can be sounded out.

Let us again remind the reader that the various phonic and syllabication skills must be used in conjunction with an unrelenting emphasis on meaning. Many of the failures in the use of phonic elements, morphemic analysis, and syllabication analysis are caused by an overemphasis on the value of using them singly or even in combination without a strong emphasis on context/meaning.

The illustrations that we give for the syllabication rules will not extend beyond three syllables. Beyond that point there is too great a load put on a youngster's auditory memory and ability to read fluently. Also, in longer words (more than three syllables), if the youngster cannot figure out the pronunciation (and meaning) after determining the first two or three syllables, he/she may not have had the word in his/her speaking or hearing vocabulary anyway. Then there might be a need to ask someone else to help with the pronunciation and/or meaning or to consult a dictionary.

All of the following syllabication rules, except for rule 1, have high utility; rule 1 has only about 50 per cent utility.

1. V-CV: When there is one consonant between two vowels, divide before the

consonant:

    la-dy

    mo-tor

  2. VC-CV: When two consonants are located between vowels, divide between the consonants:

    pic-nic

    cap-tain

    Exceptions:

      twin consonants: dinn-er[4]   happ-en

      consonant blends: con-stant   a-spects

      consonant digraphs: rich-er

  3. V-Cle: When a vowel is followed by a consonant + *le,* divide after the vowel: ta-ble Bi-ble

  4. VCC-le: When a vowel is followed by twin consonants + *le,* divide after the twin consonants: grapp-le hobb-le

  5. P-R-S: Prefixes, (some) root words, and suffixes form syllables of their own: pre-judge full-ness

Inductive Patterns for Teaching Syllabication Principles

    V-CV Principle.

T: "We have had fun counting syllables in spoken words. We know that there are as many syllables in a word as there are vowel _____."

P: "Sounds."

T: "We can look at a printed word and break it into syllables (or parts). Watch how I divide these words into syllables and see if you can tell me how I did it."

(Write three or four words that have the V-CV element and then divide them into syllables.)

        ba-by

        so-da

        mo-tor

T: "What rule did I use?" or "I divided them the same. In what way are they the same?

P: _____.

You will get various kinds of responses. Accept any responses that are correct. You may need to "work" this situation a bit. For example, draw a box around the v-cv parts and write V-CV above the column. One may prefer to shade this section very lightly with colored chalk rather than draw a box around it. Experiment.

V-CV

ba-by

so-da

mo-tor

Then give the pupils some words to divide.

---

[4] Some reading specialists suggest dividing before the consonants. One doesn't split twin consonants, because they represent *one* phoneme, not two phonemes.

Since you would use similar paradigms for the other principles, we will not go through each one separately, but leave that to your imagination.

Note: We will illustrate a *deductive* pattern:

> T: "I would like to give you a rule about dividing words with twin consonants. Here it is: 'When a vowel is followed by twin consonants plus *le,* divide after the twin consonants.' Like this."
>
> grapp-le
> hobb-le

You will want to give your pupils a chance to differentially apply these rules, so give them words that follow several principles and have them identify which words follow which principles. At times you may want to provide headings for the pupils and have them place the words under the correct headings.

Open and Closed Syllables. A syllable that ends with a consonant is closed; one that ends with a vowel is open. The vowel sounds in accented closed syllables are pronounced with the short sound: /a, e, i, ä, e/ for ⟨a, e, i, o, and u⟩, respectively.

The vowel sounds in accented open syllables are pronounced with the long sounds: /ā, ē, ī, ō, and yü/ for a, e, i, o, and u, respectively: bā-by vē-to sō-da

Note: The problem is that it is most difficult for a pupil to know whether the syllable is accented or not. Although there are exceptions, you might have the pupil assign the schwa sound /ə/ to a vowel if the short sound or the long sound do not seem right. Many times an unaccented syllable does have a schwa sound.

Pronunciation Rules Vis-a-vis Syllabication

Rule 1: In an accented open syllable or part, the vowel is usually pronounced with the long sound:

la'-dy /lā'-dē/
ma'-ple /mā'-p(ə)l/
ti'-ny /tī'-nē/

Rule 2: In an accented closed syllable, the vowel is usually pronounced with the short sound:

hop' /häp/
slip' /slip/
con'-stant /kän-st ə nt/
dinn'-er /dinn-ər/

Rule 3: In an unaccented syllable, the vowel is often, but not always, pronounced with the schwa sound /ə/.

a-bove' /ə-bev'/
Christ'-mas /kris'-məs/
sex'-es /sek'-səz/

Linguists' Agreement on Several Aspects of the Syllable

Groff (1971) reviewed the research and theory on the syllable and found that linguists agree that the syllable rather than the phoneme is the irreducible unit of speech. Only as they are spoken in syllables do speech sounds come to life.

Nondictionary Systems of Word Analysis

The view set forth by proponents of nondictionary systems of analyzing words is that if you do a good job of teaching phonograms little, if any, attention need be paid to syllabication. There exists a difference of opinion regarding the number of phonograms that should be taught:

Gunderson (1939) pointed out that, not counting words, consonant blends, suffixes and prefixes, one should perhaps teach not more than ten phonograms.

Vail (1969) is against the teaching of syllabication. Rather than teaching syllabication, he teaches the following few phonograms which substitute for any attention that might be given to syllabication:

ef	es	ir	ang	ung	ight
el	ex	ur	eng	ank	ought
em	ar	or	ing	ink	eight
en	er		ong	out	

Jones (1970) favors teaching phonograms. According to Jones and colleagues:

> The stability of the phonogram eliminates much of the tedious teaching of rules. For example, if ite, ate, ike, oat, ain, and air are taught as graphemes demanding an immediate oral response, the deductive teaching of vowel rules can be postponed until a later date when such teaching will not "slow up" the beginner's progress. Of course, I would advocate teaching only one phonemic option per phonogram at first (green, seen, queen, not been).

Joos (1966) notes, "It is a characteristic of English vowels that their sounding is regulated (in most cases) by the letter pattern which follows the vowel. Since the phonogram has the vowel plus its following letter pattern, the reader soon learns to see the entire pattern as a unit. Experience has shown that this is exactly what happens; pupils taught to analyze words into phonograms quickly learn to read sound-symbol patterns and are safely past letter-by-letter perception."

In addition to the Vail list of phonograms, the following list contains many phonograms that can be profitably learned:

an	ee	in	ore
and	eek	ilk	ot
ake	eep	int	ound
ack	ent	oke	un
ank	ike	ook	unk
at	ine	ool	
all	ile	old	
atch		oil	

Support for teaching phonograms comes first from a Wylie and Durrell study (1970) of 230 end-of-year first-graders who showed average intelligence and reading progress. Their findings follow.

1. A whole short-vowel phonogram (-*at*, -*us*) was easier to identify than single vowel letters, where the stimulus is spoken and the response is circling the correct phonogram or letter.

2. Phonograms with long vowels (-*ind*, -*old*) were as easy to identify as short-vowel phonograms (-*ack*, -*ent*, -*ink*, -*un*).

3. Silent e phonograms (-*ate*, -*ease*, -*ike*, -*ome*) were as easy to identify as vowel digraph phonograms (-*oat*, -*ear*).

4. Pupils identified a significantly greater number of short or long vowel phonograms than they did phonograms with other vowel sounds.

5. Pupils identified many more of the phonograms that ended with single consonants than those that ended in two-consonant clusters (blends).

6. High-frequency phonograms—those occurring in more than ten primary grade words—were identified significantly more times than low-frequency phonograms (those found in from five to ten words).

A study by Bennett (1942) showed that of the errors made by 595 readers only 15 percent were on the medial vowel of a word. The medial vowel is often the one with which a phonogram or grapheme begins. If only a relatively few errors are made with retarded readers, the success of the phonogram system can be inferred to be well founded and more likely genuine.

On the basis of his study of the syllable and the research on it, Groff (1971) set forth guidelines on the teaching of syllabication:

Firstly, "Teaching rules that correspond to some selected dictionary syllabication of words is not worth the effort."

Secondly, "Bringing to children's attention an important element of our language, the phenomena of the syllable, can help them in spelling and reading."

1. The teacher should be urged to *experiment* with syllabication procedures different from those dictated by the rules of dictionary syllabication.

2. The teacher can well encourage his/her pupils to divide words for the purposes of spelling and reading as his/her linguistic intuition guides him/her. For example: "If pupils find they need to spell a word such as *factory*, they could rely on their abilities to listen for the sounds of its vowels, and then attach to these sounds the consonant sounds that seem to make up vowel consonant clusters." Some possible results:

       fac-try   fact-ry   fac-tr-y   faktre

For the word *investigate:*

      in-vest-i-gate   in-ves-ti-gate   in-vest-ig-ate

3. We encourage "free wheeling" syllabication by children but do not reject proposals, such as Jones', that children be taught to perceive the recurrent spelling patterns of our language. Note also Otto's (1967) comments on the use of color cues. He believes that color cues might aid perception because of (1) aided perception and increased motivation; (2) the opportunity for cue selec-

tion; (3) greater motivation; and (4) the possibility that color may serve as a vehicle for motivation.[5]

4. The advocates of the language-experience approach to reading and spelling teaching could well use recurrent spelling, phonogram (grapho-phoneme) systems of word analysis.

5. If one had to choose between a linguistic approach (such as Fries') and Jones' phonogram approach, the latter is to be preferred.

6. "None of these recommendations violates the information on the true nature of the syllable." The child's ability when he/she comes to school to recognize and produce crest sounds is the readiness needed to teach him/her to consciously recognize syllables. Also, if the syllable is the basic unit of speech, it should be learned as such in reading.

Systems of word analysis should aid the pupil as greatly as possible in making his/her first or preliminary pronunciation of any familiar word its normal pronunciation. That is, with time the learner will pronounce these words correctly on the first "go-round."

A suggestion for teaching pupils to cope with words where the checked (closed) vowel syllable does not obtain is to introduce to the pupils words such as *go, see, blow, day, cue, few, cow, boy* as open syllables in preparation for reading words such as *ro*bust, *dei*ty, *gra*cious, *py*thon, *po*ssess, *ro*yalty, *row*dy, and so forth.

It would probably be wise to delay teaching the open syllable until after pupils have fairly well established their perception of closed syllables. This situation is complicated by the evidence of Wylie and Durrell (1970) that primary-grade pupils have no more difficulty in decoding free [open] vowels then checked [closed] vowels.

7. More research is needed on the syllable and its usefulness in teaching pupils to read and spell. By rejecting the idea of dictionary syllabication, some of the evidence on the research by Clymer (1963) and others on the utility of phonic generalizations becomes unsatisfactory. Groff, in conclusion, believes that "the rejection of dictionary syllabication for teaching purposes is inevitable."

Games

Presto-Change-O provides practice with words containing silent "e." Cut index cards in two. Write short-vowel words on half the cards and their matching long-vowel silent "e" words on the others. It is helpful to collect ten plastic toys to represent the five short-vowel and the five long-vowel silent "e" sounds. For example, you might use a toy cat for short "a" and a toy ape for long "a." Put toys on the table in the two groups as the game is played. This association of concrete objects with sounds is a big help to some children. Introduce the game by having

---

[5] Groff notes that color cues might provide a better system for explaining or teaching the monogram concept to pupils; it could help the child perceive what he/she is asked to look at.

children choose cards, say the words, and match them. Play the game like *Concentration,* having children match words and use them in a sentence.

—Vail (1976)

Presto-Change-o

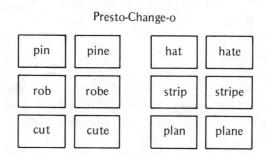

Boiling Boys helps children learn the correct spelling of words using the sound-alike patterns *oi* and *oy.*

On the outside of a manila folder write "Boiling Boys" in bright colors. Tape an index-card pocket on half the inside and divide the other half into two color-coded *oi* and *oy* columns, labeled. Cut index cards in half and write *oi* and *oy* words, color-coded to columns. The color cue, with the sound cue of spelling the word aloud, will help most children remember. Put some blank cards in the pocket for kids to use for additional words.

Sort the word cards and put them in the correct column, spelling each aloud. Then, the words are called as players put markers in correct column. One point for each correct answer.

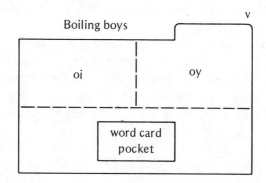

Murder is used to teach correct spelling of sound-alike patterns, *ir, er, or,* and *ur.*

Make the game board as you did for Boiling Boys. Again, color-code word cards to columns on game board, and put blank cards in pocket so that students can add new words.

Players first sort word cards and place in the correct columns. Then one player calls the words while opponent(s) places marker under correct column. One point for each correct answer.

Sample word list: *thirsty, clerk, fur, germ, first, absurd, turn, fern, purpose, curtain, further, burp, purse, circus, bird, shirt, word, worse, turtle, jerk.*

—Vail (1976)

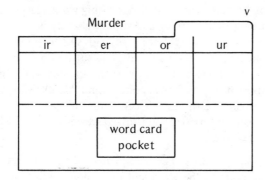

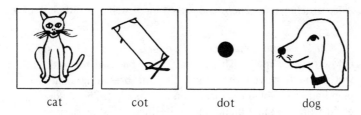

cat cot dot dog

Scrambled Eggs is used to give children practice in word-making.

Use the hollow eggs sold in variety stores at Easter or those that panty hose come in. Taking a child's name, a cheery greeting, or a factual statement, such as "today it is sunny," write it out, then cut the letters apart. Underline *p*'s, *n*'s, *u*'s, *d*'s, and so on, to avoid confusion. Put each group in an egg, shake, and give to a child to make as many words as he can.

—Vail (1976)

Word Exchange. Can you change cat into dog in 3 steps? Yes, cat 1.—cot. 2.—dot 3.—dog. Note that each step changes one letter to form a new word.

Everyone can think up his own word-pairs for a competition in which lowest score wins. However, here are a dozen to get you started. (See if you can equal or beat the par scores shown.)

boy to man in 3. bus to car in 3. cold to warm in 4. girl to wife, 5. walk to ride, 5. head to foot, 5. pond to lake, 5. fast to slow, 6. hide to seek, 6. beer to wine, 6. town to city, 6. rain to snow, 9.

—Jules Leopold

The Root Game teaches knowledge of big words, recognition of root words, meanings of prefixes and suffixes, and structural analysis.

Make a "fat" tree on poster board, with slits to hold tabs. Write prefixes on green tabs, indicating *go* (begin a word), and suffixes on red tabs, indicating *stop*—(end of word). Insert these tabs in the slits. Put root words on index cards. Add some wild cards such as "five bonus points," and "double your score."

Each player in turn draws a card from the root-word card pile, reads the word, and adds as many prefixes and suffixes from the tree as he can. Score a point for each correct word.

Phonograms: Grades Two and Three. Write endings on the chalkboard. The teacher pronounces the word and the children write the number of the ending on their papers.

Example:
1. . . . . ank
2. . . . . ack
3. . . . . ink
4. . . . . ench, and so on.

The teacher says the word *track.* The children write *2* on their papers.
The teacher says *bench,* and the children write *4* on their papers.

—Herr (1977)

Carnival Game: Grades One, Two, and Three. Folders similar to the illustration below may be made. This activity may be used for initial blends or for rhyming words and is played very much like the preceding game. For learning the initial blend an initial blend is placed on each pocket. The children are to find words that begin with the same blend and write them on slips of paper. These slips are placed in the correct pockets. The teacher may duplicate words which the children can cut into strips and place in the right pocket.

—By Betty Rucker
—(Herr 1977)

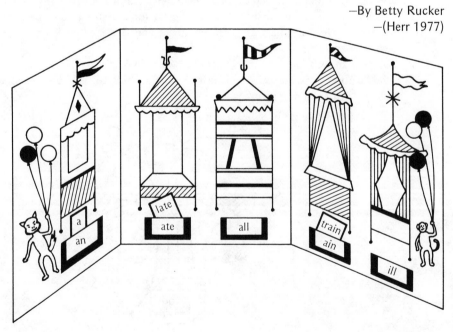

Phonics Bingo: Grades One and Two: A. *Initial Sounds:* Two sheets of 8-by-10-inch cardboard are joined with tape to make a folder. Two-inch squares are marked off. In each square a picture is pasted that begins with the initial sounds you are working with. A folder is prepared for each child, but the pictures are placed in different sequence. The teacher says a word and the children cover the picture of the object that begins like the word the teacher has pronounced. Later, a printed word may be used to show the children and they are to cover the picture of the object that begins like the printed word shown to them. After the children can do this satisfactorily, the markers for covering the picture may have the initial sounds printed on them, and the children place these over the correct pictures. When a child has filled a line, he indicates with some word agreed upon, such as *Bingo* or *Phonics,* and he reads back the sounds he has covered. This may be alternated by placing the initial sound in the squares and showing the pictures in the following illustration.

B. <u>Rhyming Sounds</u>: This is used like the preceding game, except that the rhyming sounds or the endings are used instead of the initial sounds.

C. <u>Long- and Short-Vowel Sounds</u>: This game is used in the second and third grade. Use pictures of objects whose names contain long- and short-vowel sounds. The teacher pronounces a word and the children cover a picture of an object whose name contains that vowel sound. The game is played as described above.

—Herr (1977)

Universal Game can be used to teach phonics rules, spelling, math combinations, synonyms, or just about anything that you like to.

Buy two pieces of plastic cloth, one white and one clear, 30″ × 36″ each. On the white cloth, outline spaces for clue card pockets in the upper lefthand corner. Draw a path, 2½″ wide, marked off in 2½″ intervals, with some loops and bends for variety, and hazards and bonus spaces (see diagram below). Put the clear plastic on top of the white and machine-sew around clue card pockets, the path, space dividers, and postcard pocket at the end. Slit an opening in the clear plastic at the top of each pocket and each space along the path. Fill each space with a 2″ X 2″ path word tag, create clue cards, and insert a post card depicting the game's destination. Find pawns and one die.

To play the game, children roll the die, move the number of spaces shown, and match a card from clue card pocket to the one on that space. For a new game, make new cards and insert in the proper pockets.

Cards, secured with rubber bands, can be stored in shoe boxes, game board rolls up for easy storage. With some imagination, you can adapt this format to teach an infinite number of skills.

—Vail (1976)

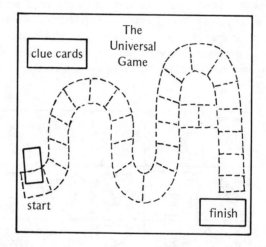

SUMMARY

Nucleus words are those words that a pupil has identified and can now recognize readily. The words have either been taught directly or have been identified through the application of such independent word-identification skills as structural (morphemic and syllabic) analysis, phonics, visual analysis, context (clues), and the dictionary.

It is important to emphasize reading for meaning, using the context in conjunction with other identification skills. Success in using context is based on the principle that one can read for meaning well to the extent that one is correctly placed in reading material, is taught to demand meaning, and reads fluently enough to gather and build meanings.

An aspect of teaching phonic elements is that of teaching phonemic options in order to be flexible in one's approach to identify words independently and increase one's repertoire of skills. The obverse is learning graphemic options, which should transfer to improving spelling skills.

Phonic elements can be taught inductively, deductively, and through analogy. As implied earlier, phonic elements analysis is probably ancillary to the use of context, because meaning is always paramount, both as a strategy and as a goal.

In addition to the formal teaching paradigms, one can develop charts, color particular phonic elements, utilize magnetic and felt letters, and play games in order to teach and reinforce these skills. It is a good idea not to depend on one type of activity, but to have a multi-pronged attack. Furthermore, about the last thing to put a child into is the ordinary workbook or dittoed work sheet, because in teaching word-identification skills one needs both sound and interaction with people as much as possible in order to make grapheme-phoneme associations, clarify various word-identification concepts, and provide guidance as the need for it arises.

Of the structural analysis skills, meaning analysis is probably greatly neglected, especially ongoing, informal analysis of words in the content areas. Syllabic analysis has been treated in two ways—by the dictionary in which words are broken into syllables, and the other in which the syllable rather than the phoneme is viewed as the irreducible unit of speech. The latter view is that if one does a good job of teaching phonograms, little if any attention need be paid to dictionary syllabication. The ideas of several people who prefer to teach phonograms were set forth.

Some guidelines on the teaching of syllabication were delineated. It appears that the rejection of dictionary syllabication (in favor of nondictionary syllabication) is coming to the fore.

LEARNING ACTIVITIES

1. Make a list of phonemic options for several graphemes. Try to determine which option for a given grapheme is most common, least common.

2. Go through an issue of a magazine such as *Newsweek* and *Time* and select sentences that contain words you do not know the meaning or exact pronunciation of. Determine which cues aid you in determining the meaning and pronunciation.

3. Go through the word lists in the first two years of a series and note at which levels words containing given graphemes are introduced. For example:

Phonic Elements	PP[1]	PP[2]	PP[3]	Primer	First Reader	2[1]
ch /ch/				children	each	teacher much choose cherry
th /th/	with	something		thank three	anything both birthday	think threw throw

Such a list can be used as a source of words for inductive teaching of graphones in a particular series. It is especially useful in corrective work.

4. Repeat the procedure used in number three in order to classify by levels vowel digraphs such as *ai, ea /e/, oa,* and the like.

5. Observe some phenomena in your environment. What kinds of inductive generalizations can you develop that you hadn't realized existed? Share some of them with the class.

6. Observe (get data on) some word-identification problems of a child or two, and write a brief report on your findings.

7. Arrange to have a display of games designed to develop word-identification skills. Bring games that are in working order, ready to be used.

STUDY QUESTIONS

1. What does *decoding* mean?
2. What are the independent word-identification tools and how are they used?
3. Define the following terms and give examples of each: (a) Phoneme (b) Grapheme (c) Phonemic options (d) Inductive teaching (e) Deductive teaching (f) Phonics (g) Phonograms
4. Explain the importance of *pacing* in teaching-learning the factors that one must take into consideration when pacing the introduction of word-identification elements and skills for pupils to learn.
5. What are the long vowel sounds? the short vowel sounds?
6. Why is it important to review basic readiness skills in this chapter?
7. What are the structural analysis skills?
8. List the major *kinds* of phonic elements and illustrate each kind.
9. Write out the paradigm for teaching a phonic element inductively.
10. How would you use the "Key Objects for Consonant" chart?
11. Represent the phonemic options of the grapheme ⟨ch⟩ and the grapheme ⟨ough⟩ and give two sample words for each.
12. How would you teach the phonic element *o-e?*
13. Why is it important to use sentence context as a part of independent word-identification exercises?
14. How would you use colored chalk and magnetic letters in exercises designed to teach phonic elements?
15. How does one teach a prefix?
16. Which syllabication rules have high utility?
17. What do linguists say about the nature of the syllable?

RECOMMENDED READING

ARNOLD, RICHARD and J. MILLER. "Reading: Word Recognition Skills." In P. Lamb and R. Arnold. (Eds.). *Reading: Foundations and Instructional Strategies.* Belmont, CA.: Wadsworth, 1976. Chap. 10.

AULLS, MARK W. "Context in Reading: How It May Be Depicted." *Journal of Reading Behavior,* 3 (1970), 61–73.

BAILEY, MILDRED H. "The Utility of Phonic Generalizations in Grades One Through Six." *Reading Teacher,* 20 (5) (February 1967), 413–418.

CASHDAN, A. "Backward Readers—Research on Auditory/Visual Integration." In K. Gardner (Ed.). *Reading Skills: Theory and Practice*. London: United Kingdom Reading Association, 1970.

DIACK, HUNTER. *Reading and the Psychology of Perception*. London: P. Skinner, 1960.

DURKIN, DELORES. "Phonics: Instruction That Needs to Be Improved." *Reading Teacher*, 28 (1974), 152–156.

GIBSON, ELEANOR J. and HARRY LEVIN. *The Psychology of Reading*. Cambridge: The Massachusetts Institute of Technology, 1975. Chaps. 9 and 10.

GROFF, PATRICK. "Fifteen Flaws of Phonics." *Elementary English*, 50 (1973), 35–40.

HAFNER, LAWRENCE E., WENDELL W. WEAVER, and KATHRYN POWELL. "Psychological and Perceptual Correlates of Reading Achievement Among Fourth Graders." *Journal of Reading Behavior*, 2 (4) (Fall 1970), 281–290.

HAFNER, LAWRENCE E. *Developmental Reading in Middle and Secondary Schools*. New York: Macmillan Publishing Co., Inc., 1977. Chaps. 20 and 21.

HITTLEMAN, D. R. *Developmental Reading: A Psycholinguistic Perspective*. Skokie, Ill.: Rand McNally & Company, 1978. Chap. 9.

JOHNSON, T. D. *Reading: Teaching and Learning*. New York: St. Martin's Press, Inc., 1973. Chap. 4.

MOYLE, D. and L. MOYLE. *Modern Innovations in the Teaching of Reading*. London: ULP/UKRA, 1971.

ROBERTS, G. *Reading in the Primary School*. London: Routledge and Kegan Paul, 1969.

SCHELL, LEO M. "Teaching Structural Analysis." *Reading Teacher*, 21 (November 1967), 133–137.

SINGER, HARRY and ROBERT B. RUDDELL, (Eds.). *Theoretical Models and Processes of Reading*. 2nd ed. Newark, Del.: International Reading Association, 1976. (Especially articles by S. J. Samuels, pp. 270–282; J. P. Williams, pp. 283–290; and H. Singer, pp. 302–319).

SPACHE, GEORGE D. and EVELYN B. SPACHE. *Reading in the Elementary School*. 4th ed. Boston: Allyn & Bacon, Inc., 1977. Chap. 11.

ZUCK, L. V. "Some Questions About the Teaching of Vocabulary Rules." *Reading Teacher*, 27 (1974), 583–588.

REFERENCES

BENNETT, A. "An Analysis of Errors in Word Recognition Made by Retarded Readers." *Journal of Educational Psychology*, 33 (January 1942), 25–38.

CLYMER, T. "Utility of Phonic Generalizations in the Primary Grades." *Reading Teacher*, 16 (January 1963), 252–258.

DECHANT, E. "Reading: Psychological Bases." In P. Lamb and R. Arnold (Eds.). *Reading: Foundations and Instructional Strategies*. Belmont, CA: Wadsworth, 1976, 25–59.

FRIES, C. C. *Linguistics and Reading*. New York: Holt, Rinehart and Winston, 1963.

GROFF, P. *The Syllable: Its Nature and Pedagogical Usefulness*. Portland, Oregon: Northwest Regional Educational Laboratory, 1971.

GUNDERSON, A. G. "Simplified Phonics." *Elementary School Journal*, 39 (April 1939), 593–601.

HERR, S. E. *Learning Activities for Reading*. 3rd ed. Dubuque: William C. Brown Company, Publishers, 1976.

JONES, V. W. *Decoding and Learning to Read*. Portland, Oregon: Northwest Regional Educational Laboratory, 1970.

JONES, V. W., G. T. GABRIEL, and L. W. JOOS. *The Phonogram Method: A New Approach to First Grade Reading*. Materials available through Virginia Jones, State University College, Oswego, N.Y. (no date).

JOOS, LOYAL W. "Linguistics for the Dyslexic." In John Money (Ed.). *The Disabled Reader*. Baltimore: Johns Hopkins Press, 1966, 83–92.

LEOPOLD, J. "Car Capers." *This Week Magazine*. May 15, 1966.

VAIL, E. O. *Formula Phonics*. Los Angeles: Lawrence, 1969.

VAIL, P. "Fifteen Reading Games," *Instructor*, 86 (2) (October 1976), 60–62.

WYLIE, R. E. and D. D. DURRELL. "Teaching Vowels Through Phonograms." *Elementary English*, 47 (October 1970), 787–791.

Developing Reading/Reasoning and Organization Skills in Narrative and Expository (Content) Materials

CHAPTER 5

Strategies for Teaching Concepts and Vocabulary

OBJECTIVES

As a result of thoroughly processing the material in this chapter the reader should be able to state/explain the following:

1. *The importance of vocabulary development.*
2. *The four factors upon which the success of a vocabulary development program depends.*
3. *The types of direct experience useful in developing concepts and related vocabulary.*
4. *The meaning of vicarious experience and types of vicarious experience useful in developing concepts and related vocabulary.*
5. *The guidelines and suggestions to keep in mind when planning a program to enhance vocabulary development.*
6. *The means of teaching students to use the various types of context clues to develop meaning and to develop the multiple meanings of given words.*
7. *The teaching of synonyms, antonyms, classification, and analogies.*
8. *Introduction to the study of etymology as an aid in deciphering certain word meanings.*
9. *The principles and strategies used in teaching the uses of a dictionary.*
10. *Exercises for studying specific words.*

The development of vocabulary is a lifetime process. The words we know are a product of all our language experiences. If we have read widely, listened well, sought experiences, and generally been interested in the ideas and activities of our world, we are likely to have rich vocabularies.

The importance of enlarging our students' vocabularies, of making them interested in words, can hardly be overstated. Many studies have shown that vocabulary knowledge undergirds reading comprehension. For example, Hafner and Weaver (1970) and Davis (1944) have shown that word knowledge is the most important factor in reading comprehension in the elementary and secondary school years. Not only are words the medium of daily interaction with our fellows, they are the chief vehicle of all learning, in school and out. The pupils' personalities, their success in school and in most other important activities of their lives, are significantly affected by their ability to communicate their ideas and to understand the ideas of others. Becker (1977) analyzed the research data from the *Follow Through Program.* The "data support the view that vocabulary-concept knowledge is not systematically taught by the schools." The question of importance to teachers is not "Should we provide instruction to enrich vocabularies?" but "How can we best do so?"

Reading authorities are in general agreement that the enrichment of word power requires a systematic developmental reading program emphasizing a variety of language experiences. The success of such a program will depend to a large extent upon four factors:

1. The intellectual capacities and experiential background of the pupils.

2. The amount and quality of the reading and oral language experiences they engage in.

3. The extent of the teacher's genuine interest in and enthusiasm for language and literature.

4. The quality of materials and methods used in language arts instruction.

THE IMPORTANCE OF EXPERIENCE

Words are abstractions of our experiences and observations. We attach a label (a word) to what we see and experience and give meaning to the experience. We can tell natives who have never seen a car all that we know to explain what an automobile is and does, but until they see and ride in one their understanding of *car* will remain vague.[1] If their first experience with a car is a ride in a jeep or truck, from that time forth their referent for the symbol *car* will be that one vehicle they have experienced. If they should see a shiny new Detroit model, they would probably not know what it was or, if told it is a car, they must revise their concept of the word to include this new experience. Children learn in exactly the same way. The words they acquire and the meanings they attach to them come from their experiences. Without experiences words are sterile configurations on paper or meaningless sounds.

Teachers must realize this basic relationship between meaning and experience and strive to provide whatever experiences are needed to deal with concepts that appear. We can do this in two ways—through direct, firsthand experiences or through vicarious experiences.

Direct experiences are probably always valuable to students, but they are

---

[1] Pascual-Leone and Smith (1969) demonstrated that if a word is to be learned the concept for the word should already be known. When students are asked to learn a word by using a dictionary, they will not learn the concept the word represents. To learn the concept the students must have experience with both positive and negative exemplars of the word. This experience may be direct or vicarious.

most valuable as part of a school program when the experience is relevant to meaning problems that the students are having or will soon encounter in their reading. The following types of direct experiences have been used with success:

1. Visit and observe such places as museums, art exhibits, a football stadium; historical sites such as battlefields, monuments or restored homes; local industries and businesses; libraries, a farm, a zoo, a fire station, a dairy; a county or city courthouse or other government service operation.

2. Construct simple science apparatus, simple play equipment, geometric figures, relief maps, models of theaters, homes, bridges, airplanes, and so on.

3. Collect and exhibit rocks, leaves, small animals and insects, farm products, photographs, wild flowers.

4. Demonstrate the effects of light and food on plants; the effects of nutrition on white rats; the use of science equipment; crafts such as pottery making, gemstone polishing, fly tying, wood carving; the function of magnets; plant growth from seeds or bulbs.

5. Assemble and operate a science weather station; a steam engine; an electric motor; a simple computer.

Teachers should be able to add a number of specific activities to this list; every community has possibilities for experiences that are unique to its size, location, and climate and the industries of its people.

Such experiences do not, however, guarantee that concepts will be developed or enriched. The teacher must make students ready for each experience by establishing purposes for it, by introducing them to terms and concepts that the experience should clarify, and by pointing out its value or applicability to meaning problems at hand. The experience should be followed by discussion in which the new concepts, facts, or terms are reviewed and clarified, and some application of them is made.

One first-grade teacher, using direct experience combined with pupil writing, brought in a white mouse, a rabbit, and guinea pigs for her class to observe and discuss. As the children talked about the animals, the teacher recorded their words and phrases on the board, and the children then used them to compose stories about the animal visitors. They consulted picture dictionaries or called upon the teacher for words they did not know. The teacher says that this approach places emphasis upon triggering new concepts, creative expression, and application of skills that had been acquired in previous lessons in reading and language.

Because it is not possible to use firsthand experiences to cope with all meaning problems, teachers must often provide vicarious experiences in the classroom. Motion pictures, filmstrips, models, discussions, stories, and dramatizations are frequently used for this purpose.

One fifth-grade teacher in his planned presentation before the reading of a science lesson on "How Airplanes Fly" began with a description of his personal experiences in flying, followed by a class discussion in which students who had flown contributed. This was followed by a presentation of pictures of airplanes and a demonstration with a model showing how wings provide lift and how the plane is steered. New terms introduced in the discussion and demonstration, such as *propeller, aileron, fuselage, lift, bank, airfoil, stick, aerial, rudder,* were put on the board. The multiple meanings of *stick, bank,* and *lift* were discussed and the appropriate meaning of each word for the lesson was clarified. Students later labeled appropriate parts of the model with some of these terms. After guided reading and discussion of the selection, students constructed simple paper planes and test-flew them in the school yard. The class raised so many questions about why some planes flew better or longer than others that the teacher finally had to call in a pilot friend to "consult" with them. A number of students did voluntary research on aerodynamics, and for weeks afterwards the school yard was filled after school hours with "flyers." These students had no difficulty with the concepts and vocabulary in their lesson.

GUIDING PRINCIPLES

The development of vocabulary involves far more than simply teaching students what a word means; for, as we have suggested, words are not completely static. Their meanings vary, depending upon context, upon the degree of emotional force they carry, or upon whether they are used in a figurative or a literal sense. This variability of meaning is one of the most important notions about words that a teacher can convey. Students must be led to understand that words are delightfully flexible symbols, made precise only by carefully considered placement in a spoken or written context.

In addition to this basic principle of the flexibility of words, the following guidelines and suggestions should be kept in mind when planning a program to enhance vocabulary development:

1. Much vocabulary should be presented in oral contexts, particularly in the primary grades. Meaning problems should be discussed fully in the classroom.

2. Let the students' ability to use new words in class discussions contribute positively to their language grades.

3. Learn all you can about the students' level of performance with meaning skills, their interests, and their specialized vocabulary achievement.

4. Convey the idea that learning about words is useful and fun.

5. Keep a master list of new words children must learn in order to deal with meaning problems in their reading so you can use the words in conversation or discussion with the class.

6. Use concrete examples and direct experiences in developing concepts whenever possible.

7. Discourage empty verbalism and vagueness in language by demonstrating the effects of careless diction in speech and writing. Emphasize the need for the right word.

8. Develop in students a questioning attitude toward what they read and hear. They should be led to see that meaning is not always explicitly given; sometimes it must be wrested from the context.

9. Develop a habitual, almost automatic use of the dictionary and other basic reference works.

10. Teach systematically and directly in contexts new words and concepts students will encounter in their reading.

11. Use imagery as an aid in remembering vocabulary.[2]

12. Make applications of words learned to other print context, some of which you may need to develop.

SPECIFIC SKILLS AND TEACHING PROCEDURES

A comprehensive program on word meanings usually includes some instruction in the following areas:

1. Use of context clues.
2. Multiple meanings.
3. Synonyms and antonyms.
4. Common Latin and Greek roots and affixes.
5. Dictionary use.
6. Denotation and connotation.
7. Figurative language.

These factors vary considerably in their usefulness in the elementary grades. An understanding of the use of context clues, the dictionary, multiple meanings, and synonyms and antonyms is basic and applicable at all instructional levels. Latin and Greek etymology, connotation, and figurative language, on the other hand, have more limited and specialized uses.

Some workbooks, programmed texts, and the like may do a fair job of teaching such skills; and for some students this kind of presentation may be useful. However, the teaching of lessons or units on these skills is often unrelated to the vocabulary problems students are encountering in their reading and seems to have little transfer value. We believe that the most meaningful teaching of all meaning and study skills generally occurs when the need for it arises. When the student reads, "Mr. Morton has only three packages of seed on hand" that is the best time to illustrate the multiple meanings of *hand*. The teacher might give examples of as many other uses of the word as he/she thinks students are likely to meet.

The exercises and suggestions for teaching vocabulary skills included in the rest of this chapter are not intended to exemplify drills or lessons isolated from basal or subject matter reading. They are strategies that should be employed when they can contribute to the meaningful development of needed skills. As it is impossible to include separate exercises for each grade level, the teacher will often have to *adapt* or change a particular exercise to fit the levels of his/her students.

---

[2] The use of imagery can aid vocabulary learning and comprehension. Bull and Wittrock (1973) showed that recall of vocabulary was ensured for children who conceived images related to the vocabulary terms. Compared to group one (children) who copied definitions and group two who read definitions and traced pictures of words, group three, who read definitions *and* drew their own pictures, were superior in recalling the vocabulary items.

CONTEXT CLUES AND MULTIPLE MEANINGS

In the primary grades, where a pupil's listening vocabulary usually far exceeds his reading vocabulary, pupils are taught to seek clues to the identity (pronunciation) of an unknown word by examining the meaning of the words around it. In the sentence "We went to the top floor of the store on the *elevator,*" pupils may have to identify *elevator* by considering the meaning of all the sentences preceding the word. Assuming that they have seen an elevator and remember it, they should have no difficulty identifying the word. They may identify it as *escalator* if they can apply no phonic skills; but we would still consider the identification a meaningful use of context clues.

Our concern in this section is the use of context clues to aid in determining the possible meaning of a word the pupil may never have encountered, one which is not in his/her hearing vocabulary. If the student has had considerable experience and guidance in using context aids to identify words, he/she should be easily led to see the value of the same kind of clues to discover meaning.

If teachers follow the plan of the direct reading lesson, they have an excellent opportunity to teach context clues each time they introduce new words before the reading. The word *frantic,* for example, in a story in a current fifth-grade reader, might be presented first in a sentence: "Our family became *frantic* when Bobby did not get home from the woods by dark." The students might first be led to identify the word through structural and phonic analysis (dividing it into two closed syllables with short vowels) and then be asked to guess its possible meaning by examining the rest of the sentence. They may guess that it means "angry," "worried," "frightened," or "upset," all of which fit the context. After recording their suggestions, the teacher can direct them to test their guesses with a dictionary or simply tell them its meaning. More appropriately for this particular word, he/she might direct them to read the story, pause when they find the word, and note how the meaning is affected by the total paragraph in which it occurs.

Drills and exercises on context clues are not necessary for all students. Many discover and use them long before any direct instruction is given. For some students, however, lessons and exercises, after instruction on the common types of context clues, are helpful. We recommend that at least the following common types be introduced.

Contrasting elements:

1. Although the juice was supposed to be sweet, it was too tart to drink.
2. Jack is not very smart, but his brother is quite bright.
3. Bill and I disagree about home design. I want mine to be simple and plain, but he wants his to be ornate.

What are the key words, that alert as to the contrasts or opposites? (1, although; 2, but; 3, disagree, but.)

Explanatory words and phrases:

1. The igloo, a dome-shaped hut built of ice blocks, was surprisingly warm inside.
2. The butcher sold giblets—hearts, livers, and gizzards—for eighty-six cents a pound.
3. Wandering around our streets in filthy, ragged pants and no shoes, the boy looked like a ragamuffin.

Clues from the reader's knowledge and experience:

1. After sitting two hours, we all began to fidget.
2. As soon as the cowboy sat astride the horse, it began to buck.
3. The tractor mower cut one wide swath across the hayfield and then broke down.

Clues from larger contexts:

June and I both began blushing as several people stopped to watch us. What at first seemed a simple matter of untangling my watchband from her hair became a painful puzzle. Each time I thought it was free and tried to pull away June "ouched" and said it was still caught. As the crowd of onlookers got larger, our faces grew redder.

Though there are many examples in each reading assignment that can be used to illustrate the importance of multiple meanings, occasional exercises may also be useful.

Explain how the meaning of the key word differs in each sentence.

BANK

1. Fred put his savings in the bank.
2. My father was using the boat, so we fished from the bank.
3. He made a long bank shot to win the game.
4. The plane banked to avoid the thunderhead.

CAST

1. I caught a bass on the first cast.
2. Jim's leg is in a cast.
3. The play has a large cast.
4. His face has a strange pale cast.

The use of "cloze" passages is another way to develop context as well as other comprehension skills. A "cloze" paragraph is one in which one word is omitted at regular intervals. For example, every tenth word might be omitted to be supplied by the reader. Depending upon the type of exercise, the student may supply any word to fit the context, or may have words provided from which to choose the appropriate one. In the sample portion of a cloze paragraph that follows, the pupil must supply every fourth word, by choosing one from the numbered options that corresponds to the number in the blank.

When Alec Thomas 1 to the county 2 with his father 3 exhibit his bull, 4 had no inkling 5 the adventure which 6 him. Alec was 7 forward to seeing 8 carnival and taking 9 ride on the 10 wheel. He did not 11 his bull to 12 any prizes, but 13 father thought he 14 learn some useful 15 about cattle raising.

1. a. rode
   b. goes
   c. went
   d. came

2. a. seat
   b. court
   c. fair
   d. sale

3. a. and
   b. to
   c. of
   d. for

4. a. he
   b. we
   c. they
   d. I

5. a. of
   b. for
   c. to
   d. what

6. a. finds
   b. catches
   c. might
   d. awaited

7. a. seeing
   b. doing
   c. looking
   d. going

8. a. those
   b. whose
   c. some
   d. the

9. a. that
   b. a
   c. him
   d. place

10. a. big
    b. water
    c. Ferris
    d. Wilbur

11. a. feel
    b. want
    c. expect
    d. care

12. a. lose
    b. stamp
    c. catch
    d. win

13. a. their
    b. his
    c. my
    d. our

14. a. should
    b. might
    c. did
    d. often

15. a. spots
    b. ways
    c. helps
    d. things

When such an exercise is followed by a discussion and examination of the words selected, teachers may discover useful facts about their students' general language problems.

SYNONYMS AND ANTONYMS

Occasional attention to words that are related through their similar or opposite meanings is one way for students to learn specific words and remember them better, because one known word may act as a cue for the recall of others related to it. The study of synonyms also enables students to see how fine distinctions in meaning may be determined by a writer's choice of one particular word rather than one of its synonyms. For example, students might be asked to consider possible reasons that the writer of the following sentence chose the italicized word in preference to one of the synonyms given: "The Russian army began *retreating* toward Stalingrad." What change would be made in the meaning of the sentence if each of these words replaced *retreating*?

(a) withdrawing, (b) retiring, (c) departing

Such an exercise emphasizes the real value of knowing many words. The more we know, the more accurately we can think and express our thoughts.

In the following "opposites" exercise devised by Trisha Franklin, the teacher would do well to work directly with the pupils. The following steps can be taken: (1) give the students several examples of opposites, (2) ask them for examples, (3) distribute copies of the exercise to the students, (4) show them how to do the example, (5) do another example with the students if necessary, (6) discuss the responses in order to clarify concepts. (Students may use some of the words in sentences.)

Opposites

Look at the word that is underlined. Find a word in the same row that is opposite in meaning; circle the word.

Example: high: hot   up   (low)   sad

1. up: down   above   sky   air
2. go: fast   stop   move   take
3. light: day   dark   white   sun
4. inside: on   above   outside   under
5. morning: light   night   sleep

The following exercises are also useful for practice with antonyms, synonyms, and analogies.

Exercise A. From these words choose the antonym of the underlined word in each sentence and put its number in the blank space.

1. synthetic   2. thrive   3. refreshed   4. ignite
1. We were exhausted by the long walk back to camp. _____
2. How many men were needed to extinguish the blaze? _____
3. We thought the dress was made of some natural fibers. _____
4. Tobacco plants fail in cool, dry climates. _____

When use of such exercises is to teach and not to test, it is best to work with small numbers of sentences and include no more test words than there are sentences.

Exercise B. Read each sentence and note the underlined word. From the group of words corresponding to the number of the sentence, choose the one that you think is closest in meaning to the underlined word. Be prepared to explain your choice.

1. After the game and the fight that followed we were all weak and confused.
2. The enemy planes never reached their vital target.
3. Mr. Steele bought an entire block of seats for the show.
4. Put your numbers in the blank space before each sentence.
1. (a) puzzled, (b) bewildered.
2. (a) essential, (b) important.
3. (a) section, (b) form.
4. (a) unfinished, (b) expressionless, (c) empty.

Vocabulary Games

Synonyms Game. Directions: Several students can play this game. First prepare on 3 X 5 cards words for your students. Place the numbers, 1, 2, or 3 on each.

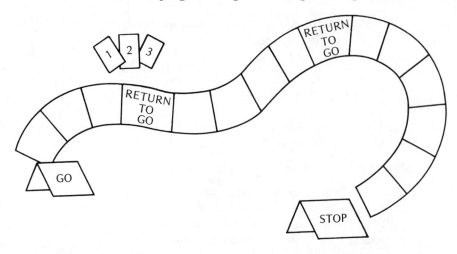

Next prepare a game board as shown above. The first student selects a card from the pile and gives a synonym. If correct he/she can move the number of squares as indicated on the card. Watch for the hazards. If you land here you must return to the beginning.

The first to reach stop is the winner.

—Harry Miller

Antonym-o. Directions: Prepare a list of words and their antonyms. Type these in two horizontal columns. Fill in the remaining spaces on the line with random letters. The student is to find the word and its antonym and circle them.

```
A   B  (H   O   T)  T   C   Y   C   H   L   M   P  (C   O   L   D)  Z   Y   X   B

B   T  (W   A   L   K)  C   S   H   Y   M   N   I   Q  (R   U   N)  Y   Z   C   M

C   Z   H   E   R   E   M   Y   G   K   L   M   T   H   E   R   E   P   Q   C   Z
```

Complete the exercise as shown above.

—Harry Miller

Facial Expressions. Ask child to imitate your facial expressions—*happy, sad, angry*—and together discuss synonyms for these words. Put all the words on cards; then have child pick a card, say its word, and try to make the appropriate facial expression.

—*Instructor* (April 1979)

CLASSIFICATION

A concept is a generalized idea about a set of features that several things may have in common. Let us look at the features that X_1 and X_2 have in common; they will be described in terms of a feature list.

	walls	roof	floor	windows	lights	cabinets	bedrooms	kitchen	living room	bathroom
X_1	✓	✓	✓	✓	✓	✓	✓	✓		✓
X_2	✓	✓	✓	✓	✓		✓	✓	✓	

The set of features that X_1 and X_2 have in common suggest the concept that we call dwelling. If we looked at more of the features, we might find that one is a house and the other an apartment, or perhaps they are both houses. The point is that any concept can be described as a set of features.

Although children learn concepts gradually, over a period of time, without developing formal feature lists, they obviously have a store of some kind of informal feature lists or concepts and labels for many of these concepts.

Let us look at some more examples. The common physical elements and characteristics of *cat*, for example, are claws, whiskers, good night vision, "meow," carnivorous, and so forth (Hafner, 1977). Other concepts—here related and in ascending order from concrete to abstract—are orange, citrus, fruit, food, commodity, things. Tree, intelligence, hunger, love, justice and the like are further examples of labeled concepts.

When we organize concepts into some kind of relationship such as categories, we are classifying. In doing this, one is developing parts of meaning hierarchies. Figure 5-1 shows parts of an abstraction ladder and a meaning hierarchy.

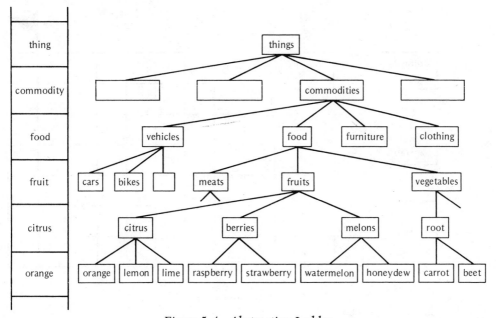

Figure 5-1. Abstraction Ladder.

The foregoing discussion is related to the concepts of vocabulary and general information, both extremely important to communication, especially to reading. At this point, let us offer some classification exercises as aids in developing vocabulary. Toward the end of the chapter there are several classification activities listed under "Health."

Plant and Harvest with Catalogs

Cultivate children's remedial reading skills (1–8) with manipulatives made from old seed and plant catalogs. Create individual and small-group activities tailored to their needs. The following examples will get you started *A-B-C order*—Cut out 10 vegetable names, laminate, and cut apart. Children practice alphabetizing and finding pictures to illustrate each word. *Visual discrimination*—On bottom of paper, paste various-shaped flower cutouts (circle, square, rectangle, and so on). At top, outline shapes. Laminate and cut out flower shapes. Students match cutouts to outlines. *Stop and think*—Use pictures of fruits and vegetables and an outlined tree and ground. Students answer the question, Where do these grow? *Likenesses or differences*—Paste a variety of vegetables on paper. Ask children to name each vegetable, colors, tactile differences, taste sensations. Try puzzles, classification, vocabulary builders.

—Marilyn Karns

Games

Vocabulary—Capture the Flag. <u>Directions</u>: Students are to supply the proper words that fill in the squares to reach the top and capture the flag.

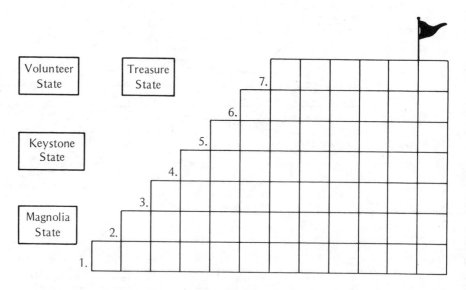

1. The state that is known as the Keystone State.
2. The Magnolia State.
3. The Golden State.

4. The Volunteer State.
5. The state known for its production of oil.
6. The state whose capital is Albany.
7. The state that is most northern.

—Harry Miller

Analogies. We offer the following teaching strategies as practical means of showing students how to think in developing relationships. The teacher needs to be involved in directing teaching, not running off work sheets that are then handed to students with directions to "do these." One way of handling these paradigms is to put each paradigm on a transparency and then, through discussion and demonstration, develop the relationships and fill in the missing pieces. Under the exercise "showing connections," have students hold large cards containing the needed words and have them move forward, as necessary, to labeled spots on the floor—*S* for same and *O* for opposite.

Work in analogies is predicated on much previous direct teaching and related exercises and games on synonyms, antonyms, and classification.

Directions for the teacher are implicit in the strategies. The key idea is for teacher and students to *discuss the paradigms and relationships.* You do these analogies strategies whenever previous work in synonyms, antonyms, and classification tell you the students are ready for analogies.

Some Kinds of Relationships

SIMILARITY:

1. Set up problem
   happy is to glad as mean is to _____ .
   good   bad   smile

2. Picture someone who is

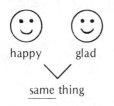

happy   glad

same thing

3. Show(ing) connections:
   a. Discuss in order to get at relationships.

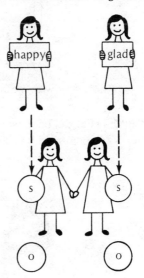

b. Move to ⓢ and hold hands.

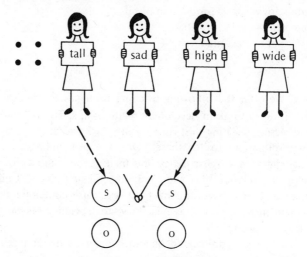

4. Now find the word that is the <u>same</u> as **mean.**

a.

mean   good?   bad?   smile?

b. Another way.

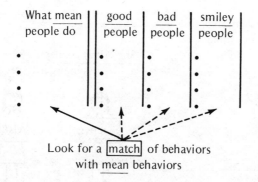

What <u>mean</u> people do	good people	bad people	smiley people

Look for a ⟨match⟩ of behaviors
with <u>mean</u> behaviors

OPPOSITES: can be shown spatially/numerically.
<u>rich</u> is to <u>poor</u> as <u>old</u> is to short, sour, young.

bright is to dim as <u>open</u> is to wide, closed, wet.

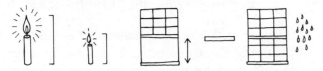

SUBORDINATION:

1. Get "connection" first.
   (orange, robin, bass): fish :: <u>pine</u>: tree
2. **Pine** is a kind of **tree**
3. What is a kind of **fish**.
   orange?   no
   robin?   no
   bass?   yes

SUPERORDINATION:
Bird: robin :: furniture: _____ (car, window, chair).

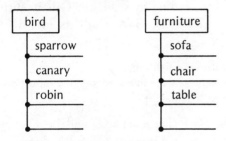

Whole-Part Relationship
Arm : hand :: leg : _____ (foot, finger, toe).

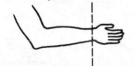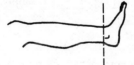

ETYMOLOGY

A group of college juniors and seniors in one of our classes was recently stumped when asked the meaning of the word *dyslexia,* which had been written on the board. They were indignant, claiming that, out of context, they had no clues to its meaning. In a discussion that followed it became evident that many of the students knew the meaning of the stem *lex* from the Greek *lexis* ("relating to words"). They recalled this after the words *lexical, lexicon,* and *lexicographer* were put on the board. The prefix *dys-* or *dis-* ("no," "not") was also well known. Now, they suggested that the word *dyslexia* must mean literally "no words" or "without words." They were unable to suggest why they had to be forced to apply what they already knew in order to induce the word's meaning.

There is little doubt that knowledge of the meanings of common Latin and Greek stems and affixes is useful throughout life. Undoubtedly it can be. The problem of their use, as evidenced by the experience just described, is that there is often very little transfer from drills on etymology to its practical application to unlock words when reading.

We believe that, to be effective, the learning of these elements should be accomplished over a relatively long period with frequent review and application exercises.

The first affixes students encounter are the prefixes *in-* (*im-*), *re-*, *un-*, and *dis-*. As these begin to appear in their reading material, they should be discussed and their meanings clarified. Later, as more difficult words containing them appear, formal exercises with the prefixes will be helpful. The following exercise on *dis-*, one of the more ubiquitous prefixes, uses words in context to allow students to infer the meaning.

Present the following sentences for reading by students. Call attention to the underlined words with the similar elements. Have students identify the root words without the prefixes.

1. Scientists disagree about the cause of lightning.
2. My father was displeased when he saw the low grades on my report card.
3. Our teacher disapproves of rough games.

Ask the students how the meaning of the sentences will be changed if the prefixes are left off the words. Have pupils complete the following:

When added to a word the prefix dis- causes the word to take on its
_____ **opposite** _____ meaning. The prefix dis- often means
_____ **not** _____ .

Using these words, illustrate that *dis-* is often just a negative prefix to which no single general meaning can be attached. Have pupils identify the root words and discuss the meaning when the prefix is included and when it is omitted.

1. The police captured the bandits and disarmed them.
2. My room is always disorderly.
3. The smoke discolored the building.

Additional example words: disappear, disgrace, dislike, disband, dishonest, disobey.

In the blank space put a word containing the prefix dis- that has the same meaning as the word or phrase following the sentence:
1. As we watch, the sun will _____ over the horizon. (go out of sight)
2. We were afraid the spilled water might _____ the beauty of the painting. (mar the figure or appearance)

3. The judge showed proper _____ in refusing the prosecuting
attorney's bribe. (lack of self-interest)
Use each of the following in one good sentence: disunity, displace, disfavor, dismay.
Use the dictionary if necessary.

Other prefixes and suffixes can be taught in a similar manner so long as the
students have some words in their vocabulary containing the affix to be taught.
Like all inductive teaching, this pattern builds upon what the student knows,
putting stress on inferential thinking.

After several common prefixes and suffixes have been presented, students
may be benefited by grouping them on the basis of meaning similarities.

Prefixes that reverse the meaning of the root word:

dis-: disagree, dislike.
de-: defrost.
un-: unable, uncertain.
im-, in-: inactive, impossible.

Prefixes that intensify the meaning of the root word:

ad-, ac-: accelerate.
ex-: exalt, exuberant.
com-, con-: confide, complete.
ultra-: ultraconfident, ultramodern.

Suffixes meaning "full of"; "having," "characterized by":

-able, -ible: edible, moveable.
-y: gloomy, sleepy.
-ous: curious, furious.
-ed: bearded, slanted.

Suffixes meaning "state or condition of"; "act of":

-age: bondage, leakage.
-ance: tolerance, maintenance.
-ism: realism, criticism.
-ment: replacement, fulfillment.

After any Latin or Greek form has been learned, deductive exercises become
a challenge:[3]

If arche means "chief" or "beginning," what do the following words mean?

1. archangel _____

2. architect[4]_____

3. archrival _____

---

[3] You may say, "Only my gifted students can learn this." Try some of these ideas with other students,
too. See what happens.
[4] *Tect* comes from a Greek word meaning "weaver" or "maker."

4. archbishop _____

5. archetype _____

If duc (duct) means "to lead" what do these words mean? (Note the prefixes you have learned.)

1. reduce _____

2. deduce _____

3. induce _____

4. conduct _____

Latin forms often found in elementary and middle school materials include the following:

cap, cept ("take"): capable, capture, concept.
dict ("say"): dictate, diction, edict.
dis ("apart; not"): disarm, dislodge, discover.
duc, duct ("lead"): conduct, educate, product.
mit, miss ("send"): admit, commit, missile.
port ("carry"): deport, portable, report.
pel, puls ("drive"): compel, pulse, expel.
pre ("before"): precede, preface, precaution, prelude.
pro ("forward"): procede, produce, prologue.
scrib, script ("write"): script, scripture, inscribe.
spect, spic ("look"): spectacles, inspect, conspicuous.
sub ("under"): submerge, subside, subject.
super ("above"): supernatural, superb, superior.
tain, ten ("hold"): retain, contain, tent.
trans ("across," "over"): transfer, transport, transcontinental.
uni ("one"): uniform, unity, union.

Common Greek forms are as follows:

auto ("self"): automobile, automatic, autobiography.
bio ("life"): biology, biography, biotic.
chrono ("time"): chronicle, chronic, synchronize.
gram, graph ("write"): diagram, telegram, phonograph.
log ("science," "speech"): biology, monologue, geology.
micro ("small"): microbe, microscope, microphone.
mono ("one"): monologue, monoplane, monocle.
pan ("all"): Pan-American, panorama, panacea.
phon ("sound"): gramophone, telephone, phonic.
syn, sym ("together"): synonym, symphony, synopsis.
tele ("far"): telegraph, television, telephone.

Games

Vocabulary—Word Clusters. Directions: Select a word part that has a specific meaning. Now find as many words as you can that include this word part.

Example:	*Meaning:*	
phobia	fear	
acro	high places	_____acro_____ phobia *fear of high places?*
xeno	outsiders	_____phobia_____
photo	light	_____phobia_____

Now try <u>mania</u>.

| pyro | mania | _____ |
| klepto | mania | _____ |

—Harry Miller

Having students make a card file or keep a notebook of the elements they learn may provide a useful reference and a source for review.

USING A DICTIONARY FOR MEANING

Many college and high school teachers complain that their students do not voluntarily use the dictionary, that few of them own a good dictionary, and that fewer still carry and consult one regularly. (In one of our college English classes it was discovered that three students out of twenty-six owned a quality dictionary, and none of the three who owned one had brought his to class.) This seemingly widespread attitude toward the dictionary by upper-level students has led us to conclude that instruction on the dictionary and its use is not adequately stressed at any level, that students are not developing, or at least not sustaining, the dictionary habit. Although students may have once been required to use a dictionary regularly, as they reach the upper levels, they have felt no personal need to do so.

As the dictionary is an invaluable tool, indeed, the most basic meaning resource a student has at his disposal, we urge that renewed emphasis be given to it at all grade levels.

For students to become real dictionary users, three requirements must be met:

1. Students must learn to use a dictionary efficiently.

2. They must discover what value a dictionary has to improve their skills, what its strengths and limitations are.

3. They must have a need to use it, preferably every day in every grade. It is the general neglect of the last of these three requirements that has resulted in widespread disuse of the dictionary by otherwise able students.

Sequence of Skills in Dictionary Training.

In the primary grades the dictionary is introduced as a valuable aid to word identification. Pupils begin with picture dictionaries and progress gradually into standard beginning dictionaries. In the lower grades the foundation is laid for efficient dictionary use. Pupils learn what a dictionary is; they learn the alphabetical arrangement and the use of the guide words. They practice locating words quickly and efficiently, and they learn to use the diacritical markings and respelling to pronounce a word correctly. Some incidental teaching of the dictionary as an aid to meaning may be carried on in the second grade, particularly with more able pupils.

In the third grade systematic instruction usually begins on using the dictionary as a source of word meanings. Pupils must learn the contents and arrangement of word entries, and they should discover that the dictionary contains such things as biographical and geographical entries, as well as the definitions of words. They should learn that the correct choice of a word's meaning from the dictionary entry depends upon the context from which the word is taken.

By the time students reach the middle grades they should own a dictionary that the school recommends and be able to answer the following questions about it:

1. If you do not know the sound of a letter with a particular diacritical mark, where can you find out?
2. What sections of the front matter may help you use the dictionary efficiently?
3. What is the order of arrangement of the definitions? (Oldest meaning first, or the most common meaning first?)
4. How and where does your dictionary indicate the origin of a word?
5. How does it indicate if a word is still considered foreign?
6. What do the supplements or appendixes contain?

Tinker and McCullough (1968) advise teachers to be certain of three factors in order to teach the dictionary successfully: (1) that students are ready before the dictionary is taught as a meaning resource; (2) that students use the dictionary to satisfy a real need to know what a word means; (3) that students use a quality dictionary appropriate for their level.

Encouraging Dictionary Use

After a student has learned *how* to use a dictionary, the real challenge to the teacher begins—to get him to use it. Mortimer Adler once suggested that one reason students and adults do not use the dictionary is that they seldom read anything beyond their level of literary competence. The things they do read do not send them to the dictionary for help. Besides, when a student is reading dull, uninteresting material, he is not likely to care enough about the meaning of a word to bother looking it up.

Teachers should ask themselves, "Under what conditions do I look up words in a dictionary?" If they do not use it often, can they expect their students to do so? A student's attitude toward the dictionary, as toward reading in general, may be a near mirror image of the teacher's. Teachers must, then, communicate a high regard for the dictionary by their example. A dictionary should be a standard fixture on the teacher's desk, and he/she should use it frequently in the students' presence, even if he/she has to contrive reasons to do so.

Although many texts and workbooks provide exercises for dictionary training, they are usually aimed at teaching some facet of dictionary make-up. To this end they may be quite useful, but encouraging regular and voluntary use of the dictionary cannot be done with exercises. The following practices may be helpful:

1. See that pupils keep a dictionary *open* on their desks as they read. This alone may provide incentive to look up a troublesome word.

2. When pupils ask about a word, do not say simply, "Look it up." Ask them to examine the context for clues first and tell what they think it might mean. Then ask them to verify guesses with the dictionary, being certain that they get the right meaning for the context they are reading. The pupil is not just looking to see what a word means but is looking to see what a writer means by the word.

3. See that pupils read some challenging material each day in which they must encounter some unknown words. This may be a newspaper, magazine, or content material as well as the basal reader.

4. Make it a practice to use an occasional word in a discussion or story-telling session that you are sure the pupils will have to look up.

The following advice to pupils about looking up a word may be helpful:

1. Take time to examine several different meanings of any word you look up. If you can see the meaning relationships, you may remember more about the word.
2. Examine the information about the word's origin and etymology. You may find something interesting enough to make the word easy to remember and you may reinforce your learning of word parts.
3. Check the pronunciation. If you don't know how the word sounds, you may not recognize it when you hear it again. Sounding it to yourself several times may also help anchor it in your memory.

Vocabulary—Word Hunt. Directions: Prepare a cigar box by covering it in a colorful, interesting way. Cut a rectangular opening at the top so 3 X 5 cards can be inserted. Place the box along with the note cards at a corner of the room. The students are asked to seek out new words. As they encounter new words they are asked to record the word and its meaning on the note card (include their name) and insert the card in the box.

Each Friday afternoon, the teacher can open the box and record the new words students have identified.

It is well to review the list periodically.

GARGOYLE

DENOTATION AND CONNOTATION

Our written and spoken communications abound with words and expressions that suggest as well as denote meaning. This suggested meaning or emotional coloring of a word we call *connotation*. A word's connotation may be pleasant or unpleasant; it may be, as Hayakawa (1964) has termed it, a "snarl" or a "purr" word. A word develops connotations through our association of it with some referent—thing, condition, or idea—that we consider desirable or undesirable, pleasant or unpleasant. Typically, we respond favorably to words like *mother, baby, flag, patriotism,* and *ambition,* but unfavorably to *mother-in-law, brat, red, gang, death,* or *opportunist.* As our reactions to words such as these are purely personal and subjective, depending on our experience with them, we cannot possibly measure or specify the connotation; but there is little doubt that a high percentage of our everyday reading and conversation is highly connotative.

By the time they enter school most children have discovered that whoever said "Sticks and stones may break my bones but names will never hurt me" did not really know much about words. To be called a "sissy," a "crybaby," or a "mama's boy" can often hurt worse than a stick. In the primary grades, discussion of this power of words to affect us emotionally may not only lay the foundation for later interpretive reading, it may help soften some verbal blows.

Though there is little significant use of connotation in primary reading materials—with the exception of an occasional poem—teachers can begin to work with what is present, both in speech and writing. The first-grader can respond to, "How do spiders make you feel?" or "What does the word *snake* make you feel?" "Would you rather be called a 'chicken' or an 'eagle'? Why?"

As students progress through the grades, their reading material begins to contain more figurative and connotative expressions, and these can be discussed in the classroom. Newspapers and magazines have many examples of colored words that can be brought into the classroom and discussed.

As students enter the upper middle school grades they can begin to deal with more sophisticated matters of connotation. The reaction aroused by characters' names, for example, can be discussed: "What does the name 'Ulgine Barrows' suggest?" (Ugly? Crude?) "In this story, does the hero's name, Rocky Martin, suggest anything about his character?" What are some of the words in this story that add to its scary qualities?" ("thunder," "weird," "clanking chains," and so on.)

More mature students in the upper middle school grades may enjoy "conjugating" some connotative words in the fashion of Bertrand Russell's facetious and famous pattern: "I am firm. You are obstinate. He is a pig-headed fool." Provide them with some samples such as "I am plump. You are overweight. He is fat." or "I am slender. You are skinny. He is a bean pole." Students catch on quickly to this exercise and seem to take a sort of malicious delight from finding insulting words. Start them with some phrases like these to "conjugate":

"I am a genius." "I am an athletic champion." "I am swift." "I am beautiful (handsome)." "I am graceful." "I am clever." "I am an unusual person."

Euphemisms

A euphemism is a word used to supplant another word that is felt by its user to have unpleasant emotional connotations. Thus we often hear *memorial gardens* in place of *cemetery, pass away* instead of *die, rest room* or *lounge* instead of *toilet* (which is itself a euphemism). Although upper middle school pupils will encounter few meaning problems connected with euphemisms, the concept is a fascinating one, worth being introduced and discussed. (For more thorough analysis of connotation and euphemism see S. I. Hayakawa, *Language in Thought and Action* (New York: Harcourt Brace Jovanovich, Inc., 1964).

FIGURES OF SPEECH

An examination of several third-grade basal readers turned up these figures of speech:

Sings sweetly as a bird.
Father's face was like a thundercloud.
The laughter was like sunshine in the house.
A bed like a rock.
Eyes looked like saucers.

It is possible that many students would not understand these figures unless they come from homes where figurative expressions are commonly used in everyday speech or occur in stories that are read to them. Even then some of these expressions may prove difficult and should be discussed by the teacher when the students confront them.

One effective way to deal with figures of speech is by asking questions about them that will clarify their meaning:

"This sentence says that Father's face was like a thundercloud. How can a person's face be like a thundercloud? What is a thundercloud like? Would Father's face be smiling? What has happened to make Father's face like a thundercloud?"

"Would you like to sleep on a bed that was like a rock? Why not?"

"What do you think the author meant when he said the laughter was like sunshine in the house? What do you like about sunshine? Do you like to laugh or hear someone else laugh? Does it give you a 'warm' feeling?"

Students are likely to encounter figures of speech in content materials at every level. The following figures are examples of types found in many social studies texts:

> Individuals are merely cogs in the nation's machinery.
> China was bottled up.
> Germany's attack on Poland was the last straw.
> Austria was an easy prize for Hitler.
> The hydrogen bomb may yet prove to be another Frankenstein's monster.

With the exception of the allusion to Frankenstein's monster, these figures can be dealt with in the same manner as those from the basal readers, with questions to point up the meaning of the comparisons.

The problem of understanding allusions is slightly different from that of other figures, for their meaning derives from knowing the characteristics of the person or thing alluded to. In these sentences, for example, "He was the Hank Aaron of bowling" or "He had the strength of Hercules," if the student knows that Hank Aaron was a great baseball player or that Hercules was a mythological character of supernatural strength, the meaning is clear. If he does not, then, the statements mean nothing. The teacher's job, then, when allusions appear, is to provide the necessary background information to give them meaning. This may be done by sending students to the source of the allusion or, if that is not practical, by describing its relevant characteristics.

The objective of teaching figures of speech in the elementary grades is to help pupils understand what they mean or suggest. The teaching of figures as special poetic devices should be reserved for the middle school where the technical aspects of poetry are being studied. There is no value for purposes of understanding what they read in having students learn to classify figures as simile, metaphor, hyperbole, or personification.

STUDYING SPECIFIC WORDS

The teaching of specific words becomes necessary as students read content materials. Technical terms and other words unique to each discipline should be taught before a given reading selection because the students' understanding of it will depend upon knowing their meaning. There is little point in giving them a vocabulary list after the reading of a selection, as many textbooks have done in the past.

A desirable way to deal with such specific words would be for all teachers to follow the pattern for introducing new words used in a directed-reading lesson, as described in Chapters 3 and 8. This practice will not only build the general vocabulary, it will help students comprehend material that is the basis of the instructional program.

No matter how thoroughly the teacher presents new words before the reading, students will still find words that will baffle them. This is a necessary challenge. The teacher should encourage students to follow some regular procedure when this happens:

1. Examine the context carefully for clues.
2. Look for known stems, prefixes, or suffixes.
3. If you are still uncertain about the word's meaning, make an educated guess and consult your dictionary.
4. If you are still in doubt about which dictionary meaning fits the context, ask the teacher.

A piece of oak tag with these steps printed on it might be kept in view as a reminder of the procedure.

Specific Words Out of Context

Teachers are aware that the least meaningful way to develop a good vocabulary is through memorizing the meanings of isolated words. Words taken at random from a dictionary or workbook each day are not remembered very long. We rarely encounter them again or use them in our conversation. But the study of certain types of words out of context can be both meaningful and fun—even when no immediate practical value is apparent. For example, students are fascinated by the study of their names. Eugene is pleased to discover that his name means "well-born," Arthur that his means "noble," Lawrence that his means "crowned with laurels."

Teachers can provide words with interesting origins for students to look up, such as *sandwich, tantalize, harlequin,* and *sinister.* Each of these and a myriad others like them can provide material for excellent discussions that may give students a new regard for words. In one fifth-grade class where an enthusiastic teacher introduced the study of word origins, the class began a competition to see who could turn up the funniest word origin. Several students began collecting unusual word origins as a hobby.

Degree of Meaning

Students' writing and reading may be improved by seeing how words can take on varying degrees of meaning, from general and abstract to specific and concrete. They may be led to see how many of the words we use to describe everyday situations and feelings are so general as to be almost without meaning. (What do we mean by *awful, interesting, fine, nice,* and *good?*) We can demonstrate the difference between general and specific words by showing students a pattern like this:

General	Less General	Specific	More Specific
Athlete	A ball player	A baseball player for Grover School	Clyde Krantz
Pupil	A fourth-grader	A fourth-grade boy in Miss Cooper's room at Braw School	My cousin, Elmer Stump
Criminal	Thief	Pickpocket	The man who stole my watch

Provide some for students to try:

General	Less General	Specific	More Specific
Food	(A vegetable)	(A green, leafy veg-etable	(Cabbage)
Creature	(An insect)	(A small green bug)	(A grasshopper)
Store			
Vehicle			
Person			
Interesting place			

Examining ambiguity in written or spoken contexts is another way to emphasize the importance of the right word:

Exercise. What two different things might each of these sentences mean?

1. He looked over the old wall.
2. Tom is outside drinking in the fresh air.
3. He pulled on the dumb waiter.
4. The natives are having the missionary for dinner.

Exercise. How many meanings can you give for these phrases?

1. Some dirty horse thieves.
2. A pretty little girls school.
3. The fine little boys car.
4. The funny book salesman.

Puns and Malapropisms

A malapropism is a wrong word that sounds somewhat like the correct one for the context in which it occurs. Its effect is often humorous, and the use of malapropisms has come to be a standard device for many comedians. The error is named for Mrs. Malaprop, a character in Sheridan's play *The Rivals*, who constantly used absurdly inappropriate words, for example, "as headstrong as an *allegory* on the Nile" (alligator).

A pun is a deliberate play upon the multiple meanings of a word to achieve a humorous effect, as in the case of the two old ladies who leaned from a window of their neighboring homes each day to argue. They could never agree because they argued from different *premises*.

Puns and malapropisms can be introduced in the middle grades for the sheer delight they can bring. In addition, because their humorous effect depends totally upon the meaning of one or more sentences, students must attend to the context to appreciate them. Puns depend upon context for their effect and also upon one's knowing the multiple meanings of the word played upon.

Many puns and malapropisms may come from the students' writing and conversation. When they can be enjoyed without bringing embarrassment, they may be shared with the class.

Students may also find pleasure in looking for malapropisms in such examples as these:

1. The dirty hobo was arrested for fragrancy.
   (vagrancy)
2. I got galluses on my hands from chopping wood.
   (calluses)
3. We'll meet here at one o'clock; let's simonize our watches.
   (synchronize)
4. This early machine gun was known as a cackling gun.
   (Gatling)
5. The North defeated the South in the silver war.
   (civil)

Here are a few examples of puns:

1. Needless to say, I can't sew for you.
2. The "Cemetery Affair" had an earthy plot.
3. The musician borrowed money from the king and gave him a grace note in return.
4. Little ghosts like to eat spook-etti-Os.

Colorful and Descriptive Words

Another useful exercise with specific words is to give students practice finding or using colorful descriptive words. Calling their attention to good description in their reading material is one way to do this. Another is to have them search occasionally for adjectives and other descriptive words of particular kinds, for example, words describing sense impressions:

1. Sight: foggy, hazy, muddy, shadowy, flashy, inky.
2. Smell: rancid, moldy, pungent, sickening, stenchy.
3. Sound: creaky, clatter, clank, click, hiss, pop, whir.
4. Taste: sour, bitter, sweet, salty, biting, sugary, bland.
5. Touch: rough, velvety, soft, downy, gritty, tingly, clammy.

It will become clear to any teacher who introduces much study of such matters as euphemisms, puns, malapropisms, ambiguity, and specific and general words that students must be motivated by the pleasure or challenge that such study brings. The study of specific words can be deadly when it is sheer busy work. In the hands of a teacher with imagination it can be the beginning of an intrinsic love of language that may lead some students to the pleasant agony of such professions as writing, editing, or even teaching.

Music

TITLE: "Music Grade One" NAME: Mildred Anne Jones
  Trigg County, Ky.

TYPE OF READING ACTIVITY: Music vocabulary for use in their areas in between music classes.

OBJECTIVES: 1. To continue the vocabulary introduced during regularly scheduled music classes. 2. By the end of the year we would hope they had perceived (thought), reacted (felt), produced (by using all concepts), analyzed, and evaluated simple music plus had given a value to music of all types.

MATERIALS: A. Each chart is made from construction paper of many different colors and shades.
B. Each word has a picture dealing with the word or the printed word on each sheet. Dry mark was used for the words to appear large and easy to see. Small pictures were sometimes used along with the words.
C. Each task chart is laminated.
D. There are two sets of task charts, one for ITA classes and one for traditional first grades.

Note. Instead of laminating, you may use heavy cardboard.

There is a music vocabulary list for first grade. At the end of one year each child should be able to understand and use these words during music class or in conversation with others. Our first grades have 40 minutes of music per week.

A tape recording goes along with each set of charts. I used classical and "pop" music for examples, and wrote my own script.

Science

TITLE: "Dinosaur Game"   NAME: Geneva Guinn
                                               Trigg County, Ky.

TYPE OF READING ACTIVITY: Vocabulary-Science (Dinosaur names)

OBJECTIVE: To help the student recognize dinosaur names and pictures.

MATERIALS: Pictures of dinosaurs (tear up two dime store books), names of dinosaurs, construction paper, magic marker, laminator.

PREPARATION: Glue pictures of dinosaurs on cards 4 X 6 (cut up construction paper) and write names of dinosaurs on other cards. Decorate backs of cards. Write directions. Laminate.
Directions: Four may play. The dealer shuffles the cards and deals them, face down, six to each player. The dealer then calls from a particular player for the NAME card to match a PICTURE card in his hand. If he gets a match, he lays them down, and calls again until he fails to get a match. The player on his left then calls and the game proceeds as with the dealer calling.

Mathematics

TITLE: "Math Puzzle"   NAME: Mavis F. Wolfe
                                                   Trigg County, Ky.

TYPE OF MATH ACTIVITY: Puzzle.

OBJECTIVE: Learning the meanings and usage of math words.

MATERIALS: Ditto sheet and pencils.

PREPARATION: Give each child a duplicated crossword puzzle sheet to fill in
               with answers going across and down. Each word that is used in
               this puzzle has been used and explained in working previous
               problems.

               Across 2. A number to be added to another.
                      3. The number subtracted from.
                      5. The answer to an addition problem.
                      6. The answer you get when one number is multiplied
                         by another.
                      8. If you know the number subtracted, and the re-
                         mainder, to find the missing minuend you _____.
                      9. What is left when a smaller number is subtracted from
                         a larger one?

               Down 1. The number subtracted.
                     2. To get the sum of two numbers.
                     4. An answer to a division problem.
                     7. The number you divide by.

TITLE: "What Am I?"   NAME: Mavis F. Wolfe

TYPE OF MATH ACTIVITY: Vocabulary Game.

OBJECTIVE: Knowing the meaning of the words and recognizing the dif-
               ferent parts of the problem by matching the correct mathe-
               matical terms to the right position in the problem.

MATERIALS: Ditto sheet and pencil.

PREPARATION: Prepare a ditto sheet of words and problems. Circle the parts
               of the problem students are to match the words to, as:

               divisor
               minuend   43   48   121   83   ⑥⑤
               product   -⑮   +24   ⑦)847   ×6   -31
               subtrahend 28   ⑦②   ④⑨⑧   34
               sum

Social Studies

TITLE: "Social Scramble"   NAME: August J. Pisa
                                                   Trigg County, Ky.

TYPE OF ACTIVITY: Social studies words, definitions, and pictures.

OBJECTIVE: The student will be able to correlate the correct word, defini-
                  tion, and picture into a natural order from a scrambled form.

MATERIALS: Peg-board hooks, magic marker, rubber cement, tag board,
                  laminating material, felt tip pen, old history books.

PREPARATION: 1. Cut pictures from books.
                  2. Paste pictures to tag board or index cards (6 X 9).
                  3. Write word on another card of same color.
                  4. Write definition on another card of same color.
                  5. Place 3 hooks across board and make 6 rows of hooks.
                  6. Place 6 pictures and 6 words, and 6 definitions on board in
                     mixed order.
                  7. Student will correct the board by putting picture-word-
                     definition in a row.
                  8. Time will be kept to see how fast they can be arranged.
                  9. Score will be kept on a bar graph.

TITLE: "Bingo"   NAME: August J. Pisa

TYPE OF ACTIVITY: Social studies words and definitions.

OBJECTIVE: The student will be able to name a word after hearing the
                  correct definition.

MATERIALS: Tag board or index cards (6 X 9), ruler, laminating material,
                  felt tip pen.

PREPARATION: 1. Section off cards into 25 blocks to resemble bingo cards.
                  2. Put in a free space.
                  3. Put words from flash cards into the remaining 24 boxes.
                  4. Laminate.

                  A. Students will cover the correct word when the definition is
                     read. The first student to get 5 in a row, as in regular bingo,
                     wins.
                  B. Score will be kept on bar graphs on a pre- and post-test
                     basis.
                  C. With the graphs the student will also learn to work and read
                     them, benefiting his knowledge of graphs along with his
                     social studies word knowledge.

TITLE: "Flash Cards."   NAME: August J. Pisa

TYPE OF ACTIVITY: Social studies words and definitions.

OBJECTIVE: The child will learn to recognize and define the different words in the social studies book.

MATERIALS: Tag board or index cards (6 X 9), magic marker, felt tip pen.

PREPARATION: 1. Write word on front of card (in large letters).
2. Write definition on reverse side of card, for example,
legislature. . . . . .the law making body
boycott. . . . . .refuse to buy goods

A. Have individual flash downs.
B. Have group flash downs, seeing which team can answer the most.
C. The flash cards can be used for a dual purpose by making bingo cards with the same words.

HEALTH

TITLE: "Go Eat"   NAME: Mrs. Da Fayne Stunson
Trigg County, Ky.

TYPE OF READING ACTIVITY: Vocabulary.

OBJECTIVE: The child is to pair up like pictures of foods according to categories. The game is played like "Go Fish."

MATERIALS: Pictures of foods, tag board.

PREPARATION: Identical copies of food categories are needed. Cut out and glue to tag board. Laminate.

TITLE: Smorgasbord Restaurant   NAME: Mrs. Da Fayne Stunson

TYPE OF READING ACTIVITY: Vocabulary.

OBJECTIVE: The child is to select commonly eaten foods served at breakfast, lunch, and dinner by looking at pictures of foods that have been arranged on a table for his choosing when a meal is announced.

MATERIALS: Pictures of foods, paper plates, paper knives, paper forks, paper spoons, paper napkins, and paper cups, construction paper, and tag board.

PREPARATION: Cut out, glue to tag board, and laminate pictures of the following foods: meats, vegetables, fruits, breads, beverages, salads, soups, sandwiches, cereals, and desserts. (The loose pictures from the lotto or food bingo games may be used here.)

Trace and cut out on construction paper single-line drawings of knives, forks, spoons, plates, and napkins. Laminate and cut out. Real cups may be used.

TITLE: "Food Categories"   NAME: Mrs. Da Fayne Stunson

TYPE OF READING ACTIVITY: Vocabulary.

OBJECTIVE: After naming and discussing each picture the child is to sort pictures of foods according to category or type. This can be varied by letting him/her sort foods according to category and meal served. The pupil is to use complete sentences in the following manner: This is an (a) _____. It is a _____. It is eaten at _____.

MATERIALS: Pictures of foods. (Can use small lotto or bingo game pictures.) Tag board.

PREPARATION: Cut out, glue to tag board, laminate, cut out.

TITLE: "Food Lotto Cards"   NAME: Mrs. Da Fayne Stunson

TYPE OF READING ACTIVITY: Vocabulary.

OBJECTIVE: The child is to match like categories of foods presented on small cards with pictures on lotto cards.

MATERIALS: 5 X 7" tag board cards. Pictures of foods.

PREPARATION: Glue six pictures of different types of foods to a card and laminate. Glue separate pictures to tag board and use for matching. Laminate and cut up.

TITLE: "Food Bingo Cards"   NAME: Mrs. Da Fayne Stunson

TYPE OF READING ACTIVITY: Vocabulary.

OBJECTIVE: The child is to listen and cover with pictures the type of food described by the teacher. When four pictures have been covered on the card in any direction the child says "Food Bingo" and wins the game. This can be varied by using word cards with the types of foods printed in ITA and TO. Vocabulary words taught are meat, vegetable, fruit, beverage, bread, dessert, soup, salad, sandwich, and cereal.

WIDE READING

So many authorities have emphasized the value of wide reading as the best way to enlarge the vocabulary that there seems little point in belaboring the matter. It is obvious that most of the words we have learned since we entered school we learned from reading. The more we have read, the better our vocabularies.

The point teachers often raise about the necessity for wide reading is that by the time a child reaches the upper-middle school grades, if his vocabulary is poor, he does not want to read. So we have what appears to be a vicious circle: to build his vocabulary a pupil should read, but he does not read because his vocabulary is poor.

There is no simple answer for this problem. As we have pointed out, vocabulary building is a long-term process, even for able readers. For those who have fallen behind, it is quite formidable. The steps we recommend for keeping students in the learning situation are quite simple in exposition, time-consuming, and difficult in actual practice:

1. Begin developmental or remedial instruction at the pupil's instructional reading level. Teach him/her any basic skills he/she lacks. Make it possible for him/her to read without undue effort.

2. Provide recreational materials that are high in interest but low enough in difficulty that vocabulary problems are not discouraging.

3. Parents and teachers must find means to motivate the pupil to read. This must be a cooperative effort. If the pupil is allowed to watch television excessively, for example, the teacher can do little to motivate recreational reading.

Additional suggestions for developing reading interests can be found in Chapter 9.

SUMMARY

We have urged in this chapter that instruction to enrich the pupils' vocabulary be an integral part of the developmental and content-area reading programs. Without proper introduction to new concepts and words that they will encounter, and without instruction on basic and generally applicable skills, the pupils' total comprehension will suffer. Determining meaning will become for them a matter of trial and error. Reading will be an onerous task.

In the program we have recommended, vocabulary development is enhanced by providing the necessary experiences, actual or vicarious, to give concrete meanings to words and concepts. We have emphasized the particular importance of teaching, in advance of reading, unknown words or technical terms and of developing interest to promote wide reading.

A number of suggestions and systematic exercises were recommended for teaching the use of context clues, the use of the dictionary, multiple meanings, figurative and connotative language, etymology, synonyms and antonyms, classification, and analogies. Finally, we suggested more informal introduction of euphemisms, puns, malapropisms, and specific words of several kinds.

Three related goals of vocabulary training were implied in the framework of the instructional patterns and recommendations in this chapter:

1. Enable students to deal with immediate meaning problems in their school reading through various types of informal and incidental teaching.

2. Teach skills such as the use of context clues, the dictionary, and etymology to give pupils independent means to determine meaning in all their reading, now and in the future.

3. Imbue students with an understanding of and respect for the language and its powerful potential to affect our lives.

In essence, we agree with Russell (1961) that "A vocabulary building program is a service program, not so valuable for its own sake as for its contribution to other abilities and personal development."

LEARNING ACTIVITIES

1. Visit a classroom and note the strengths and weaknesses in vocabulary instruction. Comment on how the instruction could be improved.

2. Plan a field trip with students of a particular grade level. Select a topic, a place to visit, the pre-trip activities, observation guidelines, post-trip discussion, and culminating activities such as construction of a model, student reports, writing of a play, and so forth.

3. Plan a specific demonstration on a certain topic in science, art, health, and the like. Plan pre-demonstration work—discussion, reading, audio-visual presentations, and so forth. Follow up with discussion, adding vocabulary and illustrations to an illustrated dictionary.

4. Find several students in a class who can use some help in learning vocabulary. Select the methods of your choice and teach a number of words that they want to learn or need to learn.

5. Select a group of students and a segment of reading material from one of their content area textbooks and then plan a presentation in which new key terms are taught to these students, utilizing selected strategies from this chapter.

STUDY QUESTIONS

1. How important is vocabulary development?

2. What are the four factors upon which the success of a vocabulary development program depends?

3. How are words and experiences related?

4. What types of direct experience are useful in developing concepts and related vocabulary?

5. What must be done to guarantee that concepts will be developed or enriched?

6. Explain the meaning of vicarious experience and the types of vicarious experience useful in developing concepts and related vocabulary.

7. Which guidelines and suggestions should we keep in mind when planning a program to enhance vocabulary development?

8. Please explain the principle of variability of meanings.

9. How does one teach students to use the various types of context clues to develop meaning?
10. How can one develop the multiple meanings of given words?
11. How does one teach synonyms and antonyms?
12. Explain how to teach students to classify concepts/vocabulary.
13. Explain how one can effectively teach students to think and understand analogies.
14. How can one introduce students to the study of etymology?
15. What are the principles and strategies used in teaching the use of a dictionary?
16. Explain the difference between denotation and connotation.
17. What value is there in studying figures of speech?
18. Explain exercises for studying "specific words."
19. What are some specific games/exercises for teaching content vocabulary?
20. Comment on the recommended steps for keeping students in the learning situation.

RECOMMENDED READING

CRISCUOLO, NICHOLAS D. "Effective Approaches for Motivating Children to Read." *Reading Teacher,* 32 (5) (February 1979), 543–546.
DUNLAP, WILLIAM P. and MARTHA BROWN MCKNIGHT. "Vocabulary Translations for Conceptualizing Math Word Problems." *Reading Teacher,* 32 (2) (November 1978), 183–189.
FOX, PATRICIA L. "Reading As a Whole Brain Function." *Reading Teacher,* 33 (1) (October 1979).
FARR, ROGER and NANCY ROSER. *Teaching a Child to Read.* New York: Harcourt Brace Jovanovich, 1979. Chapter 6.
GILLET, JEAN WALLACE and M. JANE KITA. "Words, Kids and Categories." *Reading Teacher,* 32 (5) (February 1979), 538–542.
RANSOM, GRAYCE A. *Preparing to Teach Reading.* Boston: Little, Brown and Company, 1978. Chapter 8.
RICO, GABRIELE L. "Reading for Non-Literal Meaning." In E. W. Eisner (Ed.). *Reading, the Arts, and the Creation of Meaning.* Reston, Va.: National Art Education Association, 1978.
VAUGHAN, SALLY, SHARON CRAWLEY, and LEE MOUNTAIN. "A Multiple-Modality Approach to Word Study: Vocabulary Scavenger Hunts." *Reading Teacher,* 32 (4) (January 1979), 434–437.
VOIGT, SHARON. "It's All Greek to Me." *Reading Teacher,* 31 (4) (January 1978), 420–422.

REFERENCES

BECKER, W. C. "Teaching Reading and Language to the Disadvantaged—What We Have Learned From Field Research." *Harvard Educational Review,* 47 (1977), 518–543.
BROWN, JAMES I. *Efficient Reading.* Lexington, Mass.: D. C. Heath & Company, 1952, p. 118.
BULL, BRITTA L. and MERL C. WITTROCK. "Imagery in the Learning of Verbal Definitions." *British Journal of Educational Psychology,* 43 (3) (November 1973), 289–293.
DAVIS, FRED B. "Fundamental Factors of Comprehension in Reading." *Psychometrika,* 9 (3) (1944), 185–197.

HAFNER, LAWRENCE E. and WENDELL W. WEAVER. "Psychological and Perceptual Correlates of Reading Achievement Among Fourth Graders." *Journal of Reading Behavior,* 2 (1970), 281–290.

HAYAKAWA, S. I. *Language in Thought and Action.* 2nd ed. New York: Harcourt Brace Jovanovich, 1964.

KARNS, MARILYN. "Plant and Harvest With Catalogs." *Instructor,* (April 1979), p. 60.

MILLER, HARRY. *Reading Games.* Monroe, La. Miller Publishing Co., 1974.

PASCUAL-LEONE, JUAN and JUNE SMITH. "The Encoding and Decoding of Symbols by Children: A New Experimental Paradigm and a Neo-Piagetian Model." *Journal of Experimental Child Psychology,* 8 (2) (October 1969), 328–355.

RUSSELL, DAVID H. *Children Learn to Read.* 2nd ed. New York: John Wiley & Sons, Inc., 1961.

SPACHE, GEORGE D. and EVELYN B. SPACHE. *Reading in the Elementary School.* 4th ed. Boston: Allyn & Bacon, Inc., 1977.

TINKER, MILES and CONSTANCE MCCULLOUGH. *Teaching Elementary Reading.* New York: Appleton-Century-Crofts, 1968.

TRIGG COUNTY, KENTUCKY ELEMENTARY AND MIDDLE SCHOOL TEACHERS. *Vocabulary.* Triggs County Schools, Mr. Tom Vinson, Superintendent, 1974.

VAIL, PRISCILLA. "Reading Games You Can Adapt to Any Level." *Instructor,* 86 (2) (October 1976), 60–62.

CHAPTER 6
Strategies for Developing Comprehension and Study Skills

OBJECTIVES:

Following study of this chapter, the reader should be able to:

1. *Describe pupil responses that evidence varying degrees of comprehension.*
2. *State general guidelines for developing study-meaning skills.*
3. *Describe the steps in teaching a directed reading-thinking lesson.*
4. *Construct exercises for reading-thinking activities in the primary grades.*
5. *Construct questions that call for reader-responses of four different types: literal, interpretive, critical, and creative.*
6. *Construct sentence analysis and main idea exercises.*
7. *Teach students to make logical analyses of relationships in reading test selections.*
8. *Describe the organization and reference skills and construct exercises for teaching and practice.*
9. *Explain the purpose and operation of the SQ3R technique.*
10. *Describe activities for developing meaning skills in several content areas.*
11. *Define interpretation, translation, and extrapolation.*
12. *Explain what comprehension is.*

WHAT IS "COMPREHENSION"?

Reading is an act of communication, a *thinking process* in which ideas, facts, and feelings are transmitted from a writer to a reader through the medium of language symbols. Like conversation, reading is a two-way communication. The good reader is not a passive receptor; he is able to feel, interpret, question, and reject, as well as digest, information. In short, he is able to respond both rationally and emotionally to what he reads. It is this facet of reading that has led some authors to speak of it as an art as well as a skill. This ability to respond meaningfully to language, broadly referred to as *comprehension,* is, at once, the most important aspect of teaching reading and the most difficult to analyze and describe.

Despite the recent efforts of linguists, psychologists, and reading specialists to discover more adequate descriptions, definitions, and models of the comprehension process, much is still unknown about how it takes place; for, as a thought process it is neither observable nor demonstrable. Hence, conclusions about comprehension must be based largely upon observations of what a reader says or does during or, most often, following reading. It is upon this sort of behavior in the form of pupils' answers to questions, their comments and discussions, or their test performance that teachers must rely as a means to diagnose comprehension problems.

An interesting theoretical description of the fundamentals of comprehension has come recently from the linguists. In their view, deriving meaning from the printed page is basically a matter of listening internally to the language, of identifying the meaning of familiar words in familiar structural patterns. As language is primarily speech, the first step in reading is to decode the written symbols into familiar sounds, what reading teachers call word identification. If the units of sound are accurately associated with lexical meanings (referents, ideas, and so on), and if they are related to each other in an arrangement (syntax) familiar to the reader, the utterance may become meaningful. Perceiving meaning requires an awareness—usually gained through wide experience with the language—of both lexical and structural meaning.

Although this theoretical description of reading may leave unanswered many questions about more complex comprehension problems, such as critical evaluation or the perception of irony, it has important implications for teachers. It reminds them that a reader not only derives meaning from the words he/she reads but also brings meaning to them. He must, to be a successful reader, be able to relate some fundamental experience with language sounds and with the referents and ideas they represent to the symbols that the teacher is introducing. At any level, the efficiency of a reader's comprehension depends upon a multitude of complex factors: word-identification skills, experience and vocabulary, familiarity with the spoken language, ability to perceive relationships, intelligence, and the like. In the midst of all these abstract and little-known factors that affect comprehension, it is almost ironic to realize that one's comprehension may be thwarted by so small a matter as failing to note a comma, a negative word, a signal word, or the antecedent of a pronoun.

It is our intent in this chapter to consider those matters related to comprehension that are of practical concern to the elementary teacher. To do so it is first necessary to clarify several terms that are commonly used in the literature in describing meaning skills.

The word *comprehension,* in its broadest sense, refers to one's ability to understand, to grasp with the intellect. Much of the literature in reading subdivides comprehension into three categories: literal comprehension, interpretation, and critical reaction, referring respectively to the act of perceiving the literal, denotative meaning of a selection, to the act of perceiving implied meanings, and to the ability to make judgments about the accuracy, intent, or merit of a selection. Despite the abstractness of these terms, they are useful to distinguish, generally, certain types of meaning problems that confront pupils. We should keep in mind, however, that the factors underlying these processes are little known and not specifically defined.

EVIDENCE OF COMPREHENSION

Teachers are generally aware that they cannot be certain that pupils have understood a passage simply because they can read it aloud with reasonable facility; many efficient word-callers fail to understand what they read. Nor can a teacher feel assured that pupils have comprehended because they have been able to regurgitate names, dates, or other facts from materials they have read. There are apparently several levels or degrees of comprehension, and it is not reasonable on the basis of little evidence to say of a pupil, "He understands what he reads." The wise teacher will withhold judgment about a pupil's comprehension until he/she has a chance to observe responses in a number of different reading situations.

The following list includes some of the basic types of behaviors that reflect comprehension. Although some effort has been made to list them in sequence, in order of simple to complex, so little is known about some of these processes that decisions about the arrangement had to be arbitrary.

Comprehension has taken place in some degree when pupils can

1. Answer questions of fact and detail on the material that they have read.
2. Follow directions or accurately perform some actions described in the material.
3. Recall and describe in their own words what they have read.
4. Recount the sequence of events in a narrative.
5. Discriminate the significant from the insignificant details.
6. Describe the relationship of illustrations, examples, or anecdotes, and so on to the points they are intended to clarify.
7. Identify the topic sentences, main ideas, and thesis statements in exposition.
8. Describe the relationship of the content read to other content in the same or in a related area.
9. Specify accurate, independent conclusions and inferences from expository material.
10. Describe the organizational pattern of expository selections—time, space, cause-effect, and so on.
11. Describe the connotations and other implied meanings in literary materials.
12. Describe the tone or mood of a selection.
13. Identify the author's implied motives or purposes.

14. Identify symbolism, figurative language, and other subtle language devices and describe their function.

15. Compare, using a two-column paradigm, how similar concepts are the same and how they are different.

In a study by Davis (1968) of skills basic to the ability to comprehend, knowledge of word meanings and ability to draw inferences were found to be the most significant factors. These two components of the comprehension process, along with the ability to follow the structure of a passage and to find the answers to specific questions, appear to undergird the more complex comprehension behaviors.

GENERAL RECOMMENDATIONS FOR TEACHING COMPREHENSION SKILLS

Over the years, teachers and researchers have observed that pupil comprehension is enhanced when certain guidelines, principles, and techniques are given careful and systematic attention in the classroom. These factors and the teaching approaches they foster are applicable at all instructional levels if the teacher understands the underlying assumptions.

Materials

Unquestionably the best material for teaching comprehension and study skills is content textbooks, articles, essays, or other expository material that meets three conditions:

1. Material serving as the vehicle for teaching meaning and study skills should contain subject matter that is an integral part of the content course. (When a student learns content as he learns the skill, the activity becomes more meaningful and relevant.)

2. The material must be written at the appropriate level of difficulty for the instructional reading level of the student.

3. The type of skill being taught must often determine the kind of material used. (Outlining, for example, cannot be done on narrative material. Science material is usually inappropriate for teaching figurative language, connotation, or other interpretive reading skills.)

When content materials of enough variety to meet these requirements are not available, the teacher has no choice but to turn to workbooks or other commercially prepared materials. There are some excellent materials available and, if used judiciously (following the guidelines here listed), they may do an adequate job. Two particularly good materials for the intermediate and middle school levels are Joseph C. Gainsburg's *Advanced Skills in Reading* (Macmillan Publishing Co., Inc.,) and Nila B. Smith's *Be a Better Reader* (Prentice-Hall, Inc.,). Both of these are available on several different instructional levels.

Guidelines for Developing Study-Meaning Skills

Karlin (1964) has specified several important guidelines for teaching comprehension skills:

1. Select content that has no meaning problems other than those on which practice is intended.
2. Teach only one skill in each lesson.
3. For best results, teach each skill when the need for it arises.
4. Teach skills in sequence.

The last of these points deserves special consideration by the teacher, especially when he is preparing his own material to teach skills. This guideline reminds the teacher to reflect, not only on the final skills-mastery desired, but on all the prerequisite skills that must be mastered. If for example, a student is poor in outlining, he may also be poor in identifying significant details, determining topics and main ideas, or perceiving relationships, skills upon which outlining ability must depend.

However, at another stage of development we recommend selecting a segment of reading material and guiding the students in "mining" it for all that it is worth by taking the following steps: clarifying concepts, developing literal comprehension, developing inferential comprehension, and, finally, drawing conclusions.

The Directed Reading-Thinking Approach (DRTA)

The "directed-reading" lesson, sometimes called a "developmental" lesson pattern, is a teaching plan followed by most basic readers and also recommended for content teaching as a technique to stimulate thoughtful reading. Such a lesson generally includes the steps contained in the following outline, varying slightly depending upon the series:

1. *Readiness.* Provide for background, introduce new words and concepts, establish purposes for reading.
2. *Guided Reading.* Pupils read silently, guided by specific purposes set forth by the teacher or mutually agreed upon by teacher and students.
3. *Discussion and Clarification.* Following reading, the material is discussed with particular reference to the pre-established purposes. Emphasis is upon interpretive rather than literal understanding. Some oral rereading may be done to clarify or prove points.
4. *Skill Instruction.* Word-analysis, meaning, reference, or some other skill relevant to the material is taught.
5. *Enrichment.* Pupils are encouraged or directed to wax creative or scholarly. Drawing, sculpture, model building, creative writing, or research grow out of the previously read material or the discussion that followed.

Two aspects of this plan are particularly important for the encouragement of thoughtful reading—the readiness and discussion phases.

The Readiness Phase

In the readiness phase pupils are prepared for the reading by activities that stimulate them to reason about, recall, or extend their background of experiences related to the story or subject matter they are about to read. The teacher may use slides, motion pictures, an experiment, a field trip, an experience of his/her own, a poem—almost anything he/she can conceive—to stimulate pupil contributions and involvement.

In conjunction with this thought-stimulation, difficult concepts and new words not clarified by the selection should be introduced and either clarified or "hypothesized" about by the pupils. As Stauffer (1969) has argued, the practice of simply giving pupils the definitions of words or concepts before the reading denies them a chance to reason about them, to attempt to wrest the meaning from the context on their own. His concern that the readiness activities of a reading lesson are often mechanical, nonthinking ones appears justified in view of the directions in many basic reader manuals.

Finally, the purpose setting before reading should grow out of the preliminary discussion of background. When pupils become involved in the discussion, they will raise their own questions and suggest directions that the reading should take. Purpose setting becomes, then, a mutual undertaking in which the teacher guides and stimulates rather than dictates. Nothing could be more meaningless to pupils than to be told to "Read this passage to enjoy it."

One of the more fruitful practices accompanying this preparatory phase of a lesson is that of eliciting predictions or "hypotheses" from the students. Pupils who become involved enough in the preliminary discussion to draw tentative conclusions, to guess how the author may deal with a subject or problem, become truly purposeful readers. They become obligated to find out how valid their own guesses or predictions were.

The following sample of teacher comments illustrates how a teacher might introduce an essay and include these steps:

Abdul of Pakistan

Today we are going to read an essay in the form of a letter from a boy in Pakistan. Here is Pakistan on the map. Does anyone know anything about this country? Can you predict from looking at the map what its weather might be like? All right, we'll see after we read the story whether you are right or not.

The boy who writes this letter is an orphan. His and his sister's life are considerably different from yours. If I tell you that Pakistan is a very poor country, can you guess some of the ways these children's lives are different from yours? [List ideas on the board and ask other leading questions, if necessary.]

Look now at the first picture on page 88. What does it reveal about the boy? [Thin, dressed in rags, hauling water.] What is the thing wrapped around his head? Well, we'll see if the story tells us what it is and why he wears it. Any other comments on the picture? Does what the boy is doing [hauling water] tell you anything about the way he lives? What do you suppose is the function of that little mud hut he is going into? [His home.] We'll see.

Well, from all the things you have "supposed" about these two children, how do you think this letter might sound?

Let's read now and see how right we were in our guesses. I'd like you to look for one other thing also: What problems might this boy and his sister have that we have overlooked? Go ahead now and read it silently.

Discussion and Clarification

The kind of questions teachers ask has a decided effect upon the kind of thinking pupils do. If the teacher's questions are typically of fact and detail, calling for a feeding back of literal information, pupils will read for that purpose. If questions demand thought, if they go beyond the literal, seek main ideas, demand conclusions, many pupils will gradually learn to read for those puposes also. Thus, the "right question" becomes one of the most important devices to enhance comprehension.

Types of Questions

Questions asked of pupils following reading may be of four types:

1. *Literal*—questions that call for answers based on information explicitly stated in the selection.
2. *Interpretive*—questions that require the reader to use past experience and knowledge to draw inferences from the facts of the selection.
3. *Critical*—questions that call for evaluations or judgments about the content, its style, or purposes.
4. *Creative*—questions that call for contributions of new or additional information from the reader.

Questions calling for interpretation, critical or creative reaction can only be answered if the pupils have grasped the facts of a selection; thus, there may be no need to ask literal questions at all.

The following questions are based on the selection "Abdul of Pakistan":

Interpretation: 1. How might Abdul and his sister's lives be different if they lived here in our town?

Interpretation: 2. What sort of health problems might these children have?

Interpretation: 3. You concluded that the tone of the letter was hopeful. What has Abdul to be hopeful about?

Interpretation: 4. What kind of person is Abdul? What words would you use to describe him? Why?

Interpretation: 5. What does Abdul have to look forward to?

Critical reaction: 6. What is Abdul's motive in writing this letter? to inform? to gain sympathy? to get money?

Creative: 7. How well do you think you would get along if you had to change places with these children?

Creative: 8. Would you find it hard to answer his letter describing the way you live? Why?

Creative: 9. Can you think of some things to tell Abdul which might make his life safer or better?

Creative: 10. Does anyone know anything about the United States' relations with Pakistan? Do we have Peace Corps workers there? How can we find out?

Notice that these questions use the content merely as a stimulus, a jumping-off point into areas that require inferences, perceiving relationships, drawing conclusions, and making judgments. And an answer to one such question is likely to raise another question of the same type; discussion is stimulated as pupils get ideas to share. It is important, however, to have pupils answer some *questions in writing.* Only in this way can the teacher truly sample the thinking of every pupil. During a discussion, the teacher knows only that one pupil has comprehended well enough to answer the question. How many others cannot?

That such questions can be constructed from the simplest sort of material is illustrated by the following examples:

Custard Recipe

Beat slightly six egg yolks. Add ½ cup of sugar and a dash of salt. Scald and stir in slowly 2 cups of milk. Place the mixture over a very slow fire. Stir it constantly. Take care that it does not boil. Strain and cool the custard. Chill it thoroughly. Serves 4.

Literal: How many eggs are used to make the custard? How should the milk be stirred in? What should be done to the milk first?

Interpretive: Why do you think it should be cooked over a slow fire? Why not pour the milk in all at once? How can you tell the difference between an egg yolk beaten 'slightly' and one beaten 'well'?

Critical: Would this recipe make a firm or soft custard? Why? Is this recipe an economical one?

Creative: Suppose you add 3 eggs too many. How can you correct the error? What can you do with the extra egg whites? Can you suggest a way to enhance the flavor with some additional ingredients?

Math Problem

It takes a man 2 hours to drive a distance of 100 miles. If he averages 60 miles an hour in the country and 30 miles an hour in each city he passes through, how great a part of the trip does he spend in the country?

Literal: What are you asked to find in this problem? What pertinent information is given?

Interpretive: Assign a variable to the unknown quantity.

Critical: Does this seem to be a practical problem to you? Why?

Creative: Can you think of another practical problem which can be solved by the same method? Can you think of some alternative method of solution? Illustrate your solution to the problem graphically.

Narrative Selection

Strong Bow rode into the valley. The sun, directly overhead, beat down with increasing fury. The Black Toe chief was very tired. The raid had not been successful. One third of his men had been killed. Six mounted braves trailed close behind their chief. Small puffs of dust arose from the horses' hooves, and their manes lay motionless against their wet sides.

The chief was very sad. He was returning to his village in disgrace. He had no booty. He had no scalps. Slowly the small band headed home toward the mountains. As the sun sank behind the mountain range, they were still far from their loved ones. The chief decided to stop for the night. The men and horses needed rest.

In fact, this would be the final resting place for some of the unlucky warriors.

Literal: How many braves were returning with chief Strong Bow? Why were they sad?

Interpretive: What time of day is it? How many braves started the raid? What was the weather like? What direction were they going?

Critical: Is this selection sympathetic to Strong Bow? What makes you think so?

Creative: Do you know of any other exploits of Strong Bow? Can you describe possible reasons for the failure of his raid? How do you suppose he is going to lose even more braves?

A reading problem-solving activity that students enjoy is that provided by tricky questions such as these:

1. Do they have a Fourth of July in England?
2. I went to bed at eight o'clock in the evening and set the alarm to get up at nine in the morning. How many hours of sleep would this allow me?
3. Some months have thirty days; some have thirty-one. How many months have twenty-eight?
4. How many animals of each species did Moses take aboard the ark?
5. If you had only one match and entered a dark room where there was an oil lamp, an oil heater, and some kindling wood, which would you light first?
6. If your doctor gave you three pills and told you to take one every half hour, how long would they last?
7. Divide 30 by ½. Add 10. What is the answer?
8. A farmer had 17 sheep. All but nine died. How many did he have left?
9. Take two apples from three apples. What do you have?
10. A man built a house with four sides. Each side has a southern exposure. A bear wanders by. What color is the bear?
11. An archeologist digging in a Roman ruin discovered a coin dated 78 BC. He rushed off to announce his find. Suddenly he stopped, tossed the coin away, and went back to work. Why?
12. The electricity is off in your neighborhood. It is night and you have no form of light. You must finish dressing in the darkness. In a drawer are 10 pairs of

socks, 5 black and 5 white. How many socks must you take out of the drawer to be certain of having a matching pair?
(Answers on the last page of this text.)

TECHNIQUES FOR DEVELOPING COMPREHENSION SKILLS

Kindergarten and Primary Grades

Reading and listening comprehension involve thinking with language in response to language stimuli. In the lower grades before and during the time pupils are acquiring skills in word identification, when their hearing vocabularies are better than their reading vocabularies, teachers must not neglect the need for a variety of experiences that demand reasoning. As Spache (1964) has pointed out, higher types of thinking do not appear spontaneously. Pupils will exert only the minimum amount of thinking effort required to accomplish a task. If the teacher is satisfied with mere word calling or the feeding back of a few specific details, pupils will do little more than that. The following activities are aimed at requiring pupils to respond thoughtfully to oral and written language.

Silly Sayings. Kindergarten or primary pupils can be challenged to think by the teacher presentation—orally in lower levels and in writing at higher ones—of statements that are illogical or nonsensical in some way. The pupils must identify the "problem" and correct it or explain it; for example, in "The farmer took the grain out to feed his barn," pupils must not only recognize that *barn* makes no sense in the context, but they should tell why and perhaps suggest some words—cow, horse, sheep—that would fit. The teacher should always ask after presenting the statement, "Why is it silly?" The humorous element in silly sayings makes them especially enjoyable to primary children.

The following examples of "silly sayings" should give the teacher ideas for making up others:

1. There are two sparrows swimming in that tree.
2. I always use greens to hang pictures on the wall.
3. I like ice cream with telephones over it.
4. Guess how many peanuts I have and I'll give you all three.

After practice with silly sayings in which one or two key words must be identified, the teacher can progress to slightly more complicated ones, such as non sequiturs:

1. His ears were cold so he put on his shoes.
2. If your head hurts, smile.
3. Close your eyes and the rain will stop.

The ever-popular "little silly" jokes can be useful in this kind of thinking exercise:

Voice on phone: I'm sorry I woke you up.
The silly: Oh, that's all right. I had to get up and answer the phone anyway.

Longer stories with nonsensical conclusions can also be read to pupils for both pleasure and analysis:

> One day a very high Chinese judge was walking along and he noticed that he was limping. He was not lame or hurt. Why did he limp? His leg didn't even hurt. So he looked down at his feet.
>
> Right away he saw what was the matter. His shoes didn't match. One was a fine boot with a rather high heel. The other was less dressy—and flat.
>
> So he told the clerk who attended him to go home and hurry back with the right shoe.
>
> The clerk rushed off but in a few minutes came back empty-handed. "It is no use to change your shoes," he said sadly. "The pair at home are just like these."

This and many similar useful stories and riddles can be found in Maria Leach's *Noodles, Nitwits, and Numskulls*.[1]

Contingency Games. Orally presented contingency games can serve a similar end in the kindergarten. The pupil must listen thoughtfully to the teacher's statements and respond if they apply to him or her:

1. If you are five years old, raise your hand.
2. If you have black hair, scratch your head.
3. If you like ice cream, smile.
4. If you like stories about animals, hop like a rabbit.
5. If you are left-handed, raise your left hand.
6. If your eyes are blue, hold up three fingers.

Such contingency statements can also be used with pupils who can read by having them printed on a transparency[2] or chart for pupils to read silently and respond to as the teacher reveals or points to each statement. Pupils who are either unable to understand the statement or are having difficulty with the words will be quickly identified.

Interrupted Sentences. An exercise appropriate for any grade level is the presentation of sentences or paragraphs with words or phrases that do not belong:

1. I like to see the Christmas Easter Bunny.
2. The tiger eats popcorn meat.
3. The snow melted and the hungry water ran down the hill.
4. Jack Columbus discovered America in 1492.

Riddles. Like the previous exercises, riddles appear to be more play than learning; nevertheless, they stimulate thought as pupils read them or as the teacher presents them orally, depending upon the level of the pupils. The cumulative riddle can be written on a transparency and revealed one line at a time. Pupils' guesses as each clue is revealed should be discussed briefly as to

---

[1] Maria Leach, *Noodles, Nitwits, and Numskulls* (Cleveland: William Collins & World Publishing Co., Inc., 1961).

[2] For projection onto a screen.

their reasonableness. The following are appropriate for the kindergarten or first grade:

I have a face.
There are numbers on my face.
My hands are on my face.
I tell time.
What am I? [clock, watch.]

I am a sailor.
I fight.
I smoke a pipe.
I eat spinach.
My girl friend's name is Olive.
Who am I? [Popeye.]

I have a tongue.
I have holes on top.
There is a string in the holes.
The string is tied in a bow.
Put me on your feet and run. [Shoe.]

The classical and the joke riddle may also be used now and then to stimulate thinking:

What is it that nobody wants but wouldn't give up if he had it? [A bald head.]
What should you keep after you have given it to someone? [Your word.]
What did the earth say when it rained? [If this keeps up my name is mud.]
Why do birds fly south? [Because it's too far to walk.]

Read and Pantomime. In the first and second grades, strips can be prepared with instructions for some activity written on them. Each can be prepared making provision for the reading ability of each pupil. Classmates are to guess what the pupil is doing:

Comb your hair.
Pull in a long rope.
Pick flowers and put them
  in a basket.
Pass a football.
Open a window.
Bandage your finger.

Rock a baby.
Bat a ball.
Sew on a button.
Blow up a balloon.
Pick up a slippery, slimy snake.
Take a shower.

Portions of a reading selection can also be designed on cards and pupils allowed to draw and pantomime the action.

Noting Details. Pupils must be able to identify the important details in a reading selection before they can proceed to drawing conclusions or determining main ideas. The following exercises require a variety of different types of detailed reading:

1. Type out general descriptions of items pictured in a catalog, keeping the language appropriate for the abilities of the pupils. Cut out the pictures and have individual pupils match each picture with its description.

2. Provide pupils with a list of words either individually or on the board.

After they have read a selection, they are to choose words from the list that describe a character, setting, or incident they have read about. Whenever possible, the words on the list provided by the teacher might be synonymous of the words used in the story, in order that vocabulary might be extended.

3. After reading and/or observing an experiment in science, the pupils may be asked to provide significant details in answer to questions like the following:

>   1. What was the subject of the experiment? [Friction.]
>   2. What action was performed? [A marble was rolled from a wooden surface onto a piece of carpet.]
>   3. What was the effect observed? [The marble slowed down when it struck the carpet.]
>   4. What was the cause? [Greater friction when the marble hit the carpet.]

4. Prepare questions or directions like the following, which can be slipped into a pocket chart from time to time.

>   1. Stand up and put your arms up as high as you can.
>   2. Put your books away now.
>   3. Get out your notebooks.
>   4. Has the school bus come yet?

Place the oak tag strip into the chart and point to it as you direct pupils to read it and do as directed. Sometimes a pupil's name can be slipped into the chart beside a specific direction or question:

> Mark Lewis, please bring me your paper.
> _____, please close the door.
> _____, please read the thermometer for us.
> _____, please collect the workbooks.

5. Cereal boxes are fascinating pieces of reading material that no primary teacher should overlook. With the help of your pupils acquire as many different empty boxes as possible. Almost everything on the box may become a topic for discussion or material for an exercise in noting details and following directions: Pupils can be asked to read and recount the procedures for acquiring the box-top offers; discuss the meaning of the illustrations; research the meaning of *protein* or *niacin;* compare the number of ounces in the different brands; follow the steps in making bran muffins; work the puzzle, follow the maze; set up the cutouts, or follow the directions to put together the model.

One teacher who tried cereal boxes in her second-grade class warned of the lasting effects. She and her pupils are avid cereal-box readers, both at home and at the market. Every few weeks one of her pupils brings in the "revised edition" of corn flakes.

6. Tricks and stunts are also appealing materials for practice with details. Many boys will concentrate diligently to be able to perform a simple trick to fool their friends. Simple tricks can be found in many books on magic but will

probably have to be rewritten and simplified for the primary students. The following is a teacher's simplification of a trick done for some third-graders:

> Tell your friend that you are going to rub a penny into your elbow and make it disappear.
> Hold the penny in your left hand.
> Bend your right arm at the elbow, placing your right fist close to your right shoulder, the elbow pointing down toward the floor.
> With your left hand place the penny against your right arm just above the elbow and begin to rub it in a circle as though you were trying to rub it into your arm.
> Drop the penny, pick it up, and begin rubbing it again.
> Drop the penny a second time, and, as you say something about the penny being slippery, reach down with the right hand, pick it up, and return the right fist containing the penny to your shoulder again.
> Place the left hand back on the arm and begin rubbing as if the penny were there. In a moment, remove the left hand and show the penny gone.
> It's easy to slip the penny down your shirt collar, if you did not borrow it from your friend.

Picture Comprehension. Even before pupils can read, pictures offer a wealth of opportunities for stimulating the drawing of conclusions. The picture in the preprimer or readiness book showing the two children playing with their dog, for example, can be used by the pupils to answer such questions as "How old do you think the boy in this picture is?" "Is he older or younger than the girl?" (clue from their relative sizes); "What time of year is it in the picture?" (clues in the vegetation, clothing); "Are the children in the city or the country?" (clues in the surroundings).

Prior to the reading of a selection, either in content material or narrative, the pictures and illustrations can often serve as a stimulus to get pupils to try predicting outcomes, hypothesize about the nature of the content, and set up expectancy clues in preparation for new words or new concepts they may encounter.

Surveying pictures and illustrations before reading may be the spark to ignite a good "readiness" discussion and whet some otherwise lethargic curiosities. It is a practice that should become a habit as pupils begin to encounter more content materials.

Sentence Analysis. In order to lead students eventually to the critical skill of identifying main ideas of paragraphs or longer selections, it may first be useful to provide practices in identifying significant details in sentences:

> "When Phalanx fell into the creek, he splashed the icy water on Prunella and Corina, who ran away screaming."
>
> 1. What did Phalanx do?
> 2. What might have caused Phalanx to do this?
> 3. What did the girls do? Why?

Having students reduce elaborate sentences to bare elements by crossing out words provides practice in selecting significant elements in a sentence.

"Phalanx emptied the box ~~containing a thick ball~~ of ~~red, wiggling~~ worms on his sister's ~~new pink~~ bedspread."

"Prunella slipped ~~quietly~~ into Phalanx's ~~upstairs~~ bedroom and squeezed a full, ~~giant-size~~ tube of ~~green~~ toothpaste onto his ~~new red~~ sheets."

Additional practice on this skill can be provided by having students reduce the meaning of several sentences to one summary sentence:

"Phalanx sat on the floor at the side of his bed. He had a surprised look on his face. He had never slipped out of bed before. Prunella stood in the door laughing."

Summary: Prunella laughed at the look on Phalanx's face when he slid out of bed to the floor.

Main Ideas. Poor readers often develop such a habit of looking for details that they become lost over reading tasks that require them to derive general impressions or identify the gist of a selection. This difficulty is a natural outgrowth of reading purposes, expressed or implied by the teacher, directing pupils to answer specific questions of fact and detail. To counteract this effect many of the purposes specified by the teacher should direct the pupils to identify the topics and main ideas:

1. Read (or listen to) this short story to supply a title.
2. Read this paragraph and decide what word appears in it more than any other. (ants)
3. The paragraph talks mostly about (a) ants as workers, (b) the food of ants, (c) the home of ants.

In order to demonstrate to pupils the thinking processes involved in identifying and organizing details and main ideas, it is useful occasionally to review and organize a small, previously studied body of information in the manner of an experience story. With their books closed the pupils are called upon to tell the teacher any facts they can recall about the subject. The teacher writes their contributions on the chalkboard or overhead transparency. After the facts have been listed, the group, through discussion, arranges them in some logical order that they determine. A third-grade class, after studying the section in one current social studies textbook on the Indians of the Amazon rain forest, might contribute a list like the following:

1. The Indians are hunters. They kill wild pigs and monkeys.
2. They mostly eat a root called manioc. It is poison.
3. The women wash the root and that takes away the poison.
4. The men use poison on their arrows and blowgun darts.
5. They make hats out of parrots' and beetles' wings.
6. They grow some food—pumpkins, yams, and corn.
7. They get fruit from the forest trees.
8. The men catch fish and turtles.
9. They might get bitten by a piranha; they can bite your hand off.
10. The Indians like living in the forest and don't want to move anywhere else.

By calling the pupils' attention to the key terms in the sentences, the teacher guides them in providing topics under which to group their facts. Topics for the list here might be "Food the Indians Raise," and "Food the Indians Get from the Forest." No matter what topics they provide some of the details are likely to be difficult to place (as with the contributions about the "hats" or "piranhas"). The ability to distinguish significant from insignificant details, however, will be improved when pupils are led to see what makes a detail relevant or irrelevant to the topic.

The final step in the exercise would be a return to the textbook. Here the pupils can see how the author arranged his details, what details they overlooked, and how the author was able to fit in details that they seemed to feel were irrelevant.

A variation of this exercise would be to provide the pupils with details and allow them to hypothesize the titles, headings, or topics.

Sentence Building. Sentence building combines practice in reading with an exercise to develop an awareness of English syntax. On the chalkboard or a transparency the teacher prints words in lists under numbered headings (if names of form classes have been studied, the terms can be used as headings also):

1 (Determiners)	2 (Adjectives)	3 (Nouns)	4 (Verbs)	5 (Adverbs or Prep. Phrases)
the	dopey	boy	ran	from the roof
a	angry	girl	dived	into the alley
an	spooky	clown	waved	across the river
one	happy	teacher	swam	happily
every	weird	coach	floated	quietly
that	excited	flea	jumped	in the sandbox
each	smiling	dinosaur	stumbled	from the class

One pupil is called upon to choose any word from column 1 and read it aloud; another pupil chooses a word from column 2 and reads it; the next pupil chooses one from column 3; thus, five pupils will put together a sentence. The teacher can provide for individual differences by assigning pupils to choose from columns containing words they can identify. Even the weakest pupils can probably identify one of the words from column 1, for example. Even with short lists such as these, so many combinations are possible that each pupil should get several chances to choose and read a word.

After practice with reading words from a list the teacher has supplied, each pupil may be assigned to choose a word of his/her own that would fit under a particular number (form class). For example, if the teacher directs the pupil to choose a word which would fit in column 2, he/she must choose an adjective, whether he/she knows what an adjective is or not. In this way pupils' knowledge of parts of speech, which may be largely intuitive, can be employed to teach them "about" parts of speech and sentence structure. The pupil who is attempting to choose a word to fit in column 2 may have to be shown by the teacher how to check the correctness of a choice by trying it in a slot where *happy* or one of the other adjectives will fit.

In lower grades, pupils greatly enjoy a variation of this activity in which the teacher prints the words on cards that can be hung by string around the pupil's neck. The first time this is done the teacher can pass out the cards at random and then call up one pupil from each of the form classes. He/she might first let these five students, with the help of their classmates, arrange themselves into a sentence that is read aloud by the group observing. Next, five more "pupil-words" come forward and arrange a new sentence.

Soon each pupil who comes forward must point to a classmate in the group who can come forward and fit into his/her position. The pupil whose word is a verb must look over the rest of the class and point out another verb, say the word, and have the designated pupil come up to be a part of the next sentence.

Another factor can soon be added in the form of "floater" words such as *only* or *somehow* that can be put at various places in the sentence and still "make sense." Once the teacher tries this activity, he/she will see numerous possibilities for both reading activities and language study. Students will quickly demonstrate their knowledge of syntax by suggesting more complex combinations with more modifiers, transitive verbs with objects, and conjunctions.

Comprehension Exercises for the Middle Grades and Middle School

There is a greater need for instruction in study and meaning skills in grades beyond the third because the amount of expository material pupils read at school begins to increase rapidly at this point. Guidance in the reading skills necessary for good comprehension of content materials must become an integral part of reading instruction. One major weakness in the reading programs of many schools is the separation of reading from the subject matter studies as if they were unrelated. Teachers in the content areas must constantly remind themselves that when they teach math, or science, or health that they are still teaching (or should be teaching) basic reading skills.

Main Ideas. The ability to identify main ideas remains fundamental to effective content reading in the middle school, and the exercises illustrated for the primary levels may be adapted to these grades. Some additional exercises appropriate for use in the content areas follow:

1. Which statement does not relate to the topic sentence?

   Topic sentence: Shoes are made largely by machines.

   a. Leather is cut out by machines into the shapes for the different parts of shoes.
   b. Some parts of the shoes are tacked together by machines.
   c. Machines with strong needles sew other parts together.
   d. Leather gloves are also sewn by the machines.

2. Read the following sentences.
   a. If burning fireworks or other materials contain boron, the flame will be green.
   b. If they contain sodium, the light will be yellow.
   c. Calcium produces a red light.

   Which of the following topics are those sentences most closely related to?

   a. Fireworks burn with different colors.
   b. Certain chemicals burn with a particular color.
   c. Chemists often burn material to test it.

3. Read the following paragraph and choose the best topic sentence from the three choices that follow.

   Snow falls in some parts of Alaska when the temperature is 50 degrees below zero. In Eastern Siberia snow has fallen in temperatures of 40 below, and in that part of Siberia that has recorded temperatures of 94 below, snow has fallen.

   a. Is it ever too cold to snow?
   b. Siberia is the coldest place in the world.
   c. Cold weather makes it difficult to live in Siberia.

The construction of a "main-idea outline" is useful both as a review of content and a device to teach organization and main idea skills. This outline is constructed by following a pattern similar to the following in organizing one or more related paragraphs:

Topic: **Snow and Temperature**

Component facts: **Snowflakes form at about 32 degrees Fahrenheit or slightly below.**
At lower temperatures, snow falls in the form of ice spicules.

(Main idea:)   **It snows even in such places as Alaska and Siberia.**
It may get too cold for snow to fall in flakes, but it never gets too cold to snow.

The following activities may also be helpful:

1. Pupils construct topic sentences on subjects suggested by the teacher. (This is a useful adjunct to paragraph writing.)
2. Pupils provide major headings for outlines after being provided with subheadings.
3. Pupils write headlines for proposed articles about school events.
4. Pupils do research to locate facts to support conclusions provided by the teacher.
5. Pupils formulate main idea statements for teacher's lecture, which provides only details.

Analysis of Relationships in Reading Test Selections

Some time ago a fifth-grader named Katie brought home the copy of the *Weekly Reader Diagnostic Silent Reading Test* she had taken at school. Her father was somewhat perturbed at the results, for she had missed 26 of 54 items. He was determined to find out what and how Katie was thinking and how he could help her analyze the material so as to make the correct responses on the items she had missed. Following are two selections, the child's responses, and the analyses.

Selection 1

In 1912 the city of Tokyo, Japan, presented our capital city with many Japanese cherry trees. They were planted near the river in Potomac Park. These trees are unusual for they do not *bear* any cherries. They are grown only for their blossoms.

Each year thousands of people come to see the clouds of pink and white blossoms. Visitors can see the Jefferson Memorial and the cherry trees reflected in the waters of the Tidal Basin.

a. The cherry blossoms help make our capital
   □ different   □ busy
   □ good   ☑ popular
b. To most people these cherry trees would not be
   ☑ pretty   □ healthy
   □ useful   □ colorful
c. The BEST title for this story is:
   ☑ Beauty Near Potomac Park
   □ Pink-and-White Cherry Blossoms
   □ Waters of the Tidal Basin
   □ Cherry Trees in Our Capital City
d. In line three the word *bear* means
   ☑ produce   □ bring
   □ present   □ give

Analysis. Following are the steps in the analysis.

1. Katie was asked to read the selection orally to determine if there were any word recognition problems. Oral reading was all right except she pronounced Potomac as /pätəmat'ik/ and tidal as /tid'əl/.

2. She had missed item *b* by answering *pretty* instead of *useful*.
   Steps in the analysis:
   a. Katie was asked to tell what blossoms were.
      (She responded correctly.)
   b. Then she was asked, "What would 'clouds of pink blossoms be'?"
      (No response.)
   c. "Do you often see many clouds when you look in the air?"
      ("Yes. Oh, like fluffy bunches of blossoms!")

    d. "What one word in the question did you overlook?"
       ("Not.")
    e. Then it was established that if a cherry tree did *not bear* any cherries it
       would not be considered "useful."
       (She knew the meaning of the word *bear* in this context.)
  3. Katie had missed item *c* by answering "Beauty Near Potomac Park."
    a. She evidently forgot that the first paragraph stated, "*near* the *river* in
       Potomac Park."
    b. Katie was asked to go through the selection and see what it talks about
       most: "Katie, go through the selection and count how many times it
       says:

Katie's response

1) "cherry trees"	"three"
2) characteristics of cherry trees:	
"looks like"	"two"
"function" "what they	
'do'"	"one"
"pronouns and synonyms	
of cherry (trees)"	"three"

    c. Then Washington, D.C. and capital city were related to features of it:
      1) Potomac Park
        (cherries)
      2) Jefferson Memorial
      3) river
      Putting this all together, Katie could see the relationships involved
      and develop the correct answer.

We conclude that key tasks in teaching comprehension are to work on concepts and vocabulary and to demonstrate through interacting with the student and material the use of inductive and deductive processes to help children see relationships. We need to teach this directly. We must help pupils make logical analyses of cognitive [meaning] relationships. This process involves more than just asking questions. Let us examine another example.

Selection 2

    When a long freight train goes by, you realize that the cars come from every corner of the country. You see such names as Sante Fe, Soo Line, Chicago & Northwestern, Norfolk & Western, and Union Pacific.

    How do the owners know where their cars are? A close *check* is kept on their location. However, this job is a big one. Each day thousands of freight cars are loaded or unloaded, added to or removed from strings of cars. As soon as the freight cars enter a railroad yard, they are spotted and a report is made. No matter where a certain car is or how far it goes, the owners know where it is.

a. Companies send freight over great
  ☐ lands   ☑ distances
  ☐ tracks   ☐ cars

b. In most railroad yards freight cars are
  ☑ rearranged   ☐ stored away
  ☐ sent back   ☐ repaired

c. The BEST title for this story is:
  ☐ Watching Freight Cars Go By
  ☑ Long Strings of Freight Cars
  ☐ Knowing the Location of Freight Cars
  ☐ The Owners of Freight Trains

d. In line four, *check* means
  ☐ control   ☐ count
  ☐ mark   ☑ watch

Katie had missed the BEST title for this story by selecting "Long Strings of Freight Cars" instead of "Knowing the Location of Freight Cars."

Analysis.

Katie was helped when her father started reading through the selection for clues to *location:*

Katie

Sentence #1 says, "You realize that cars come from every corner of the country." "What makes you realize, Katie?"

"All the cars."

Sentence #2: "What in sentence 2 resembles something in sentence 1?"

"You see."

Paragraph 2: "What are words in paragraph 2 that have to do with *seeing* or *information*?"

(She missed "know")
  "close check"
(missed "location")
  "spotted"
  "report"
  "know"

"Now, what is the correct answer, Katie?"

"Knowing the Location
  of Freight Cars"

Format for Vocabulary and Comprehension Development Through Expository Selections

One must begin early to teach students to read expository material. Following is a sample lesson plan that can be used by the teacher directly and as a guide for the construction of lesson plans. The teacher will need to interact with the students and the material in order to guide the thinking of the students. Those who do not are only testing; the goal is teaching that results in increased vocabulary and comprehension proficiency.

Lesson Plan for a Selection About Bees

1. Vocabulary development.

   a. Labeling.

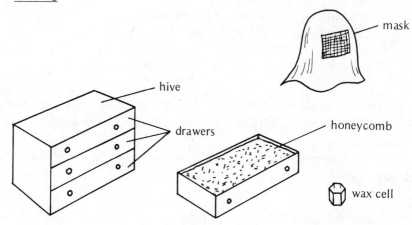

   b. Definitions.

      (1) hive [hīv] Home of bees; contains drawers.
      (2) honeycomb [hə-nē-kōm] Where bees store their honey.
      (3) container [kən-tā-nər] It holds something; A cup is a container; so is a can.
      (4) sting [stiŋ] When a bee bites you.

   c. Words in context.

      (1) Bees live in hives.
      (2) Hives contain drawers.
      (3) Bees build honeycombs in the drawers.
      (4) Each wax cell in the honeycomb can hold honey.
      (5) When a bee stings you, it hurts.

   d. Vocabulary check.

      (1) The place where bees live _____.   A. cell
      (2) Made up of many wax cells _____.   B. sting
      (3) Things you can slide in and   C. honeycomb
          out of hives _____.   D. drawers
      (4) Made out of wax; it holds honey _____.   E. hive
      (5) Put it on head so bee can not sting it _____.   F. mask

2. Reading the selection.

   a. Read silently and answer the question.

      (1) What job does the bee have?

b. Read silently to answer a question on each paragraph.

(1) (Paragraph 1) Where do bees put the honey they make?
(2) (Paragraph 2) On what do the bees make their honeycomb?
(3) (Paragraph 3) (a) What forms on the body of bees when they eat honey?
(b) Where do the bees get the honey (nectar)? (Inferential)
(4) (Paragraph 4) What would happen to the beekeeper if he did not wear a mask and he moved fast?

Bees have two <u>main</u> jobs. They make honey and they build honeycombs. The honey they make is stored in these honeycombs.

Where do bees work? They work in hives. Each hive contains several drawers, and each drawer has several frames. The bees build their honeycombs on these frames.

After the bees eat a lot of honey, wax forms on their bodies. They use this wax to make wax cells or containers. Each honeycomb is made up of many of these wax cells. The bees fill the cells with honey.

When a honeycomb is full, the beekeeper takes it out. He has to move slowly or the bees will sting him. So the beekeeper plays it safe by wearing masks and gloves so the bees cannot sting him.

3. <u>Seeing and naming</u> (vocabulary review).

a. <u>Directions</u>: Write the correct word(s) on each card below.

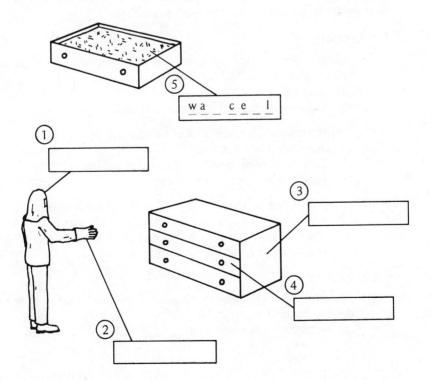

4. Developing the basic ideas.

   a. Finding a sentence with the same meaning. Put the answer in the blank to the right.

     (1) Bees lives in homes called hives.   _____
        (a) Hives are the homes of bees.
        (b) Bees lives in homes.

     (2) Bees build honeycombs on frames.   _____
        (a) Honeycombs which bees build are put on frames.
        (b) Frames are what bees build on honeycombs.

     (3) Each honeycomb has many wax cells.   _____
        (a) Honeycombs are part of wax cells.
        (b) Many wax cells together are a honeycomb.

     (4) Bees put honey in cells.   _____
        (a) Cells have honey in them.
        (b) Honey in cells is placed there by bees.

     (5) Bees sting the beekeeper if he moves fast.   _____
        (a) When the beekeeper moves slowly, the bees sting him.
        (b) The bees will not sting the beekeeper if he moves slowly.

     (6) The bees cannot sting him if he wears mask and gloves.   _____
        (a) Masks and gloves keep him safe.
        (b) If he wears masks and gloves, he will be stung.

5. Building the main idea. (Allow the student to refer to the selection as needed. As always, when teaching you often need to mediate.)

   a. Paragraph one.

     (1) Sentence one says that bees have two main jobs. Those who have jobs do things. What are the "do" words in sentence two?
        (a) working.
        (b) build . made up of . make . frames.

     (2) Which sentence is the main idea of paragraph one?
        (a) Bees make honeycombs.
        (b) Both honeycombs and honey are made by bees.
        (c) Bees make honey and store honey.

Note: The student is now in the process of analyzing the meanings so that he/she will be able to build the key ideas of each paragraph and, in turn, the main idea of the story. At the end of the analysis of paragraphs he/she will be asked to select the best title for the story.

   b. Paragraph two.

     (1) The sentences. (The student will need to go back into the paragraph and develop his answer.)
        (a) Sentence 1 asks where bees _____.

(b) Sentence 2 tells where they work.
(c) Sentence 3 tells how the hives are _____ .
(d) Sentence 4 tells where the bees build their _____ .

(2) Which sentence is the main idea of paragraph 2? _____ .
   (a) Honeycomb tastes good.
   (b) Hives contain several drawers.
   (c) Bees work in hives, putting honey into honeycombs.

c. Paragraph three.

(1) Three sentences tell about something being made by bees. The "make" word in sentence one is <u>forms.</u> In sentence two it is <u>make,</u> and in sentence three it is <u>made up.</u> What do they make? _____ .

(2) Which sentence is the main idea of paragraph three?
   (a) Bees make honeycomb from wax that forms on their bodies.
   (b) Bees put honey into wax cells.
   (c) Bees eat honey.

d. Paragraph four.

(1) We get the main idea of a paragraph by finding out a) <u>who</u> does the most or is talked about or b) what is being done the most.

(2) <u>Who</u> does the paragraph talk about the most? Look at the two following lists before you answer.

beekeeper words:	bee words:
beekeeper	
He	bees
him	
beekeeper	bees
him	

(3) <u>What</u> is being done the most? (I've already picked out what is being done the most. The student can read the paragraph to check out my selection.)

beekeeper:	bees:
takes	
move	sting
plays it safe	
wearing	sting

(4) The last sentence is mostly about the _____ and what he does.

(5) The main idea of the paragraph is
   (a) How the beekeeper safely removes honeycomb.
   (b) What the beekeeper wears while he works with bees.
   (c) How bees sting.

6. Selecting the best title for the story.

Directions: Pick the title that tells best what the story is about:

a. Where Bees Work.

b. Putting Honey in Glass Jars.

c. Honey: Its Makers and Its Takers.

d. The Beekeeper.

Note: It may be necessary to allow the student to read the story again before he/she can select the best title.

Organization Skills. The pupils' ability to understand and remember what they read is enhanced if they are able to perceive the author's organization and if they can reproduce the essence of the material in a form that depicts its sequence and points out relationships. Summarizing, outlining, and note-taking are skills that assist pupils in visualizing organizational patterns and provide them with tools for later review.

It is important to recognize that teaching pupils to outline, take notes, or summarize is not the same as teaching comprehension. Comprehension must come *before* one is able to outline or summarize with real effectiveness. Thus, the teacher must recognize skills requisite to the production of these tools, particularly the ability to identify main ideas, significant details, and their relationships.

Instruction in the organization skills aims at developing the abilities to:

1. Follow the order and sequence in narrative and descriptive material.
2. Classify and group topics.
3. Depict the relationship of details and topics in outline form.
4. Summarize succinctly.
5. Take and organize notes effectively.

The following exercises aim at developing these abilities.

Following a Sequence of Events. After reading a narrative, extract a list of events and direct the pupils to arrange them in proper sequence without looking back at the content:

_____ Arnold gave the old man all his money.

_____ Arnold's mother gave him money to buy lunch.

_____ As the sun came up Arnold left for town.

_____ An old man ran after Arnold.

_____ Arnold was worried about what his mother would say.

Storytelling and the recounting of actual events provide practice with sequence as do experiences with scientific experiments, how-to activities, and recipes that require following directions in proper order.

Classifying and Grouping Topics. In the lower grades it is a common practice to provide pupils with objects or pictures to be sorted into groups. At upper levels similar practice can be provided by presenting disarranged topic outlines for the pupils to put in proper order. The two samples that follow are of a type that can be adapted to most grade levels:

pineapples	horses
bananas	animals bearing live young
fruit	frogs
cold weather fruit	alligators
strawberries	animals
apples	pigs
lemons	animals that lay eggs
oranges	turtles
warm weather fruit	cows
pears	chickens
peaches	cats

Formal Outlining. The skill of outlining is merely an extension and refinement of the ability to classify and group topics to depict their relationships. Instruction to teach formal outlining might well begin with exercises like the previous one, accompanied by an explanation from the teacher as he/she assigns Roman numerals, capitals, and numbers to the topics and subtopics.

After pupils have read a well-organized selection, guide them in the determination of major headings for a formal outline;

I. Ants live in highly organized colonies.
II. . . .
III. . . .

As their understanding of the process and the mechanics increases, the pupils can be directed to fill in more and more detail in skeleton outlines provided by the teacher until finally the entire job can be left to them.

Summarizing. Summarizing, like classifying and outlining, requires a pupil to select, evaluate, and record information in a useful form for review. Although summarizing does not require the learning of formal conventions as does outlining, it does require considerable practice in reducing large segments of facts, details, and main ideas into concise and inclusive statements. Obviously, pupils' total verbal competence will greatly affect their ability to write a good summary.

One exercise is recommended for teaching summarizing: Require pupils to attempt summarizing often, providing the best possible guidance. Have them try to tell what a story was about in one or two sentences. Have the best summaries read to the class and explain why they are good. Provide positive criticism of weak summaries, and give general pointers to the group on summary writing, such as explaining that summaries omit anecdotes, examples, and illustrations. Occasionally have a competition to see who can most adequately summarize a paragraph or section in the fewest words. Frequent guided practice with summary writing will pay dividends in many other areas of language development.

Location Skills. The trend in education toward independent and self-directed study makes it vital that pupils learn to use basic reference tools efficiently. They should be taught and should be required often to use a table of contents, an index, library card catalog, *Readers' Guide,* and such basic reference tools as an encyclopedia and an almanac.

Perhaps more than any other study skill, the location skills should be taught when the need for their use arises. There is ample opportunity in every grade beyond the third for individual or small group research, which should create the need. No special commercial materials are necessary; pupils should be surrounded by the reference tools they must learn to use. The most effective teaching of location skills occurs when one pupil or a small group asks the teacher, "How can we find out . . .?" It is particularly important at that moment for the teacher to remember that guided learning is much more efficient than trial and error. He should not be tempted to say, "Why don't you go hunt? See how well you can do before you ask me."

Keeping the following points in mind should improve the effectiveness of instruction on location skills:

1. Use guided discovery whenever possible in teaching the use of a reference tool. With the resource before them, ask the pupils questions that will enable them to draw conclusions about its use. For example, after turning to an index entry, the pupils might be asked to look at a number of entries on the page to guess how the index is arranged (if they have had experience with alphabetical order in a dictionary, they will recognize it here). Ask them to guess what the relationship is between the words in boldface type and those beside or beneath it with different page numbers. After their hypotheses are made, allow them to verify by attempting to locate several items.

2. Explain any necessary terms, abbreviations, or special features of a resource tool, but don't bog down with meaningless drill on nonfunctional tasks such as memorizing the subjects designated by Dewey Decimal numbers.

3. Whenever possible, take pupils directly to the tool rather than providing a workbook page or a transparency illustration. Go with pupils in small groups to the library and introduce catalog cards inductively as you do with any other reference tool.

4. Give meaningful assignments that will require enough use of the various reference tools to improve and maintain pupils' location skills.

Using Pictorial Aids. Teaching pupils to read a map, chart, diagram, graph, or any other illustrative device is little different from teaching location skills. Beyond the general comprehension skills necessary for reading prose, successful use of pictorial aids is largely dependent upon two factors: (1) an understanding of the purpose or function of the device—knowing, for example, that a pie graph illustrates vividly and concretely the uses of certain fractional parts of a whole; and (2) a knowledge of the conventions or specialized symbols necessary to understand the aid, as in knowing the directional orientation of a map.

Because pupils can read and comprehend the printed matter in a textbook the teacher should not therefore assume that they will also be able to understand its pictorial aids. It is entirely possible that pupils may be able to understand the language in their social studies textbook but be unable to interpret a particular chart or graph accompanying it. Teachers must not only teach general principles associated with comprehension of the various pictorial aids, they should also try to locate and remedy weaknesses in understanding each new pictorial aid that pupils encounter.

As maps are one of the more common pictorial aids, some specific suggestions for teaching map reading may serve as an illustration and guide for teaching pupils to use other pictorial aids.

Maps in textbooks seldom depict areas with which children are familiar; hence, as a concept, "mapping" may mean nothing to lower-grade pupils. It is wise then to introduce the concept by actually mapping areas they know, gradually expanding the size and scope of maps to illustrate their value in the depiction of unfamiliar areas. Eventually the pupils must be led to see that a map is a "picture" by which one can determine, without actually ever seeing the area represented, sizes, distances, altitudes, directions, and a number of other characteristics.

The following is a list of activities for introducing and teaching the concept of "mapping" in the lower grades:

1. On chart or butcher paper make a large sketch of the classroom, illustrating only the placement of such fixtures as windows, doors, and closets. Provide cutouts of the other furnishings and have pupils in small groups take turns in placing them to show the actual classroom arrangement and to show other ways the classroom furnishings might be placed.

2. Present a large diagram of the school, labeling only the pupils' location. Provide other labels for pupils to place on rooms with which they are familiar, such as the library, principal's office, auditorium, water fountains, rest rooms, gymnasium, and cafeteria. By working with this sketch on the floor, show the importance of orienting the map in the proper direction. Direction of turns in the corridors could also be labeled.

3. On a sketch of the area of the community surrounding the school, have the pupils locate their homes and other well-known reference points such as a shopping center, post office, churches, or park. Distances and directions should be discussed in whatever terms the pupils are now able to understand—miles, blocks, steps.

4. Construct a map of an imaginary community, including a simple distance scale in blocks and a compass rose (the traditional symbol on a map to indicate directions). Provide questions such as What direction would you travel to go from the Plunketville School to the park? How far is it? Could you walk that far in an hour? What building is next to the water tower? What building is 12 blocks east of the city hall?

5. Acquire commercially prepared maps of your city, county, and state. Use them as the basis for discussing the conventions and symbols used on most professionally prepared maps.

From this point on, teaching map reading involves explaining more complex devices used to make a map meaningful—the importance of colors, devices for depicting altitudes and topography, the function and use of latitude and longitude lines, and the importance of the legend. As with location skills, the pupils should be led to deduce as much about the reading of maps as possible from studying maps, with as little teacher explanation as is necessary to avoid confusion.

Using Reference Sources

As the need arises pupils should be introduced to efficient use of a table of contents, index, encyclopedia, atlas, and library reference guides. Following a lecture-demonstration of each source, exercises of the following type can be introduced, using the pupils' own textbooks where appropriate:

Index

Bluebirds
    description, 40
    attracting, 40
    birdhouse construction, 29–30
    diet, 41–42
    habitat, 43
    migration, 20–21
    enemies, 43
    song, 41

Where would you look to find the following?

    A picture of a bluebird?
    What to put in your birdfeeder for bluebirds?
    How a bluebird sounds?
    What dangers threaten a bluebird?
    Where bluebirds go in winter?
    Plans for a bluebird house?

Reference Books. To use reference books efficiently pupils must be taught the following skills:

1. Purpose and organization of each reference work.

2. Efficient location skills—alphabetical order, guide words, cross referencing.

3. Ability to determine "topic" words under which desired information can be found.

4. Use of pronunciation keys in dictionaries or glossaries.

5. Ability to interpret map legends, scales, and directions in an atlas or encyclopedia.

The following exercise tests knowledge of source materials:

In what reference book could you find the following information?

Correct pronunciation of *joust*? (dictionary)
Distance from Nashville, Tn. to Tallahassee, Fl.? (atlas)

The largest number of hamburgers eaten by one man?   (Guinness Book of Records)
Cloth out of which first American flag was made?   (encyclopedia)
How to make lye soap?   (encyclopedia, *Foxfire Book*)

Cassidy (1981) describes a four-week inquiry program that teaches gifted students to research independently some area of particular interest to them. This program, which has been implemented successfully with youngsters in grades 3 through 6, can be used in a variety of settings.

SQ3R. The SQ3R (Robinson, 1970) is a somewhat sophisticated yet psychologically sound technique to enhance pupils' understanding and retention of expository material. The following description is a simplification of the approach:

1. Survey. A preview of a chapter is made by reading the title, introduction, summary, examining pictures, maps, or charts, and reading the headings and subheadings.[3] In the absence of separate headings or for a more inclusive survey, topic sentences are read. The survey provides a type of readiness by revealing the nature of the content and the manner of its organization and presentation.

2. Question. As he surveys, the reader frames questions for himself to answer later. As he gains insights into the topic in the survey, he should try to bring his previous knowledge to bear upon it, thinking always in terms of what he already knows and what he needs to know. Many of the author's headings may simply be turned into questions and either written down or kept in mind.[4]

3. Read. The reader returns to the beginning of the chapter or section and begins to read the material carefully, one segment at a time, focusing on finding the answers to his questions and looking for other pertinent information that he did not anticipate through the survey.

4. Recite. As he pauses after each segment on one topic, the reader "tells himself" what he read. He answers the questions and specifies other main points in the material before proceeding to the next section. One may write complete answers or key words, phrases, or drawings needed to recall the whole idea. This "thinking over" the content while reading in short unified sections is one of the most valuable features of the SQ3R.

5. Review. After completing the entire reading assignment, the reader now pulls together loose ends, attempting to make a unified whole out of the separate segments and answers to questions. One reads the question, recites the answer, looking at the notes only when necessary, and then reviews again after several hours, a day, or several days. By delaying this total review until time for class discussion or just prior to an examination, retention may be significantly enhanced.

It is apparent that this is not a technique for primary pupils. It should, however, be introduced and practiced in the upper elementary grades[5] to lay the

---

[3] The summary will help the reader see how the ideas are tied together; it will help one "see the forest."

[4] If questions are provided in the chapter, they may be used.

[5] Donald (1967) found that seventh-graders who were given developmental lessons in applying the SQ3R method to social studies material (in a year-long experimental study) made statistically significantly (.01 level) higher scores—compared to control groups—on social studies tests which required judgment and critical evaluation.

ground work for the kind of concentrated study students are likely to encounter in high school. The *Survey* step, however, can be taught to pupils as low as third grade, and pupils can learn to employ it on narrative as well as expository material.

One major benefit from teaching the SQ3R is that pupils learn that reading and studying are not identical processes, that merely reading an assignment from beginning to end may leave gaps in their knowledge. Learning about this technique should convince them that thinking about the material in a special way before, during, and after the reading is as important as the reading itself.

Comprehension in Content Areas

Many of the suggestions made earlier in this chapter are aimed at improving the pupils' understanding of mathematics, science, and social studies as well as of literary materials. However, an awareness of some of the problems specific to these content areas may make it possible for the teacher to anticipate some problems before they occur.

Mathematics and Science. As pupils begin to encounter written problems in math and the precise exposition of science, their achievement in these areas may be as significantly affected by their ability to comprehend the language peculiar to the discipline as by their computational skills or aptitudes. The following factors are particularly important to the pupils' success in reading mathematical and scientific material.

1. Knowledge of the specialized vocabulary in the disciplines—terms, abbreviations, and symbols.

2. Ability to follow directions and sequential steps in process or procedure descriptions.

3. Ability to paraphrase written problems and specify the details and processes necessary for their solution.

4. Ability to perceive the relationships between the data and conclusions or generalizations in an inductive or deductive organizational pattern.

Much research supports the generalization that vocabulary problems are primary causes of difficulty in the content areas. If the teacher remains alert to possible difficulties with specialized terms, he/she may deal with most comprehension problems effectively. The following activities are directed toward overcoming such problems in math and science reading:

1. Before each new unit or new process is introduced, administer an informal test to determine pupil strengths and weaknesses in the vocabulary necessary for a mastery of the content. Keep a record of who needs more instruction in the areas tested.

2. In vocabulary instruction deal with words in specific contexts—(a) general vocabulary; (b) words with meanings different from their general meaning, such as *root, table, improper, rational*; (c) words with meanings in math or science that are more precise than their general meanings, such as *remainder, mixed,*

opposite, elements, similar; (d) words peculiar to the discipline, such as *subtra-hend, osmosis, ectoskeleton.*

3. Have pupils construct a mathematics and science dictionary, a personal glossary of terms they have learned.

4. Teach the origin and derivation of mathematical and scientific terms. (The word *perimeter* is made up of two Greek forms: *peri-* meaning "around" and *metron* meaning "measure.") It may be helpful to have pupils group words in their dictionary according to similar elements in their make-up, such as peri*meter*, thermo*meter*, speedo*meter*, hydro*meter*.

5. As part of review work, have pupils group terms and symbols with their definitions under process headings, for example:

Multiplication	Combustion
multiplier	ignition
multiplicand	oxidation
product	heat energy
X	ash
times	kindling

6. Demonstrate the manner in which pupils should approach a difficult written problem or an explanation of a difficult scientific process. Write the problem on the board. Read it aloud in its entirety. Reread it slowly, putting vocal stress upon pertinent data. Write down figures or topics as you progress. Discuss the techniques used for the solution in a math problem, emphasizing the verbal clues that revealed the process. Point out the same types of clues in science material that clarify or lead to conclusions.

7. When pupils miss written problems, try to determine whether the failure was a result of a lack of understanding of the mathematical content or a result of some language barrier. A few moments with an individual pupil in which you determine the cause and help him see his weakness by leading him with questions may accomplish more than several sessions of group instruction.

Social Studies. Like mathematics and science, social studies material has numerous vocabulary and concept difficulties. Concepts are particularly troublesome in social studies because of their frequency and because textbook authors seem to underestimate their difficulty. Also troublesome is the fact that many social studies concepts are stated figuratively, like *balance of trade.* The teacher or textbook that discusses *nationalism, economics, capital,* or the like, without adequately clarifying the concepts can expect poor comprehension from many pupils.

Much social studies material in current use is highly condensed. In popular materials like magazines and newspapers particularly, it requires cautious, critical evaluation. The following activities for teaching reading in the social studies are aimed primarily at improving the pupils' awareness of the differences in both language and focus in social studies material:

1. Relate new concepts to pupils' experiences whenever possible. The teacher might lead pupils to a better understanding of *nationalism,* for example, by

first discussing school spirit, pride, family loyalty, or any other related matter that pupils know firsthand.

When it is not possible to relate a concept to their background of experience, provide vicarious experience through discussion, films, photos, or models.

2. Determine the general organization pattern followed in the pupils' textbook and lead them in an analysis of it. Help them answer such questions as the following: Does the book use a chronological order of development? Is there an emphasis upon cause-effect relationships? How extensively does the author use headings and subheadings? How are separate chapters related? How inclusive are the summaries? Does the author provide clues to main points through questions following the chapter?

3. Aid pupils to detect the author's general approach to the subject. Does he emphasize people or events? Is he an objective reporter of facts? How extensively does he interpret events? Does he carefully qualify his conclusions and assumptions? Is he consistent?

4. Require a frequent breakdown of content into premises and conclusions in order to examine their relationships and evaluate the logic.

5. Occasionally extract several of the author's conclusions and present them for the pupils to designate as fact, opinion, or generalization. Have them return to the textbook context to verify their judgment.

6. After a discussion of the techniques of slanting and propaganda, have pupils bring in examples collected from newspapers, magazines, or television.

7. As a basis for an occasional discussion, choose an article from each of several newspapers or newsmagazines that treat the same subject or event from different points of view. Guide the students through an examination of how each position is treated and defended. A comparison of a conservative and a liberal newspaper's analysis of a presidential speech is usually appropriate for students at the upper elementary levels.

8. When social studies material is colorless, a catalog of events enlivened only by an occasional anecdote or political cartoon, pupil interest quickly fades. Perhaps more than in any other content area, social studies needs considerable enrichment, both in the teachers' presentations and in the use of interesting supplementary materials. A classroom library of paperback books, newspapers, magazines, and historical novels is almost a necessity in maintaining the pupils' interest in the social studies.

In our teaching of social studies we should encourage more than a perfunctory reading of material. Higher levels of work—analysis, synthesis, problem solving, and evaluation—are predicated upon the more basic levels of knowledge, comprehension, and application. Such hierarchies, in which successful work at higher cognitive levels is contingent upon success at lower levels, are delineated in *Conditions of Learning* (Gagne, 1975) and *Taxonomy of Educational Objectives* (Bloom, 1956). Bloom has arranged the cognitive domain into six levels of increasing complexity: (1) knowledge, (2) comprehension, (3) application, (4) analysis, (5) synthesis, and (6) evaluation. At this point we are especially concerned with comprehension.

Teachers should develop comprehension exercises based on existing materials. These exercises should stimulate interpretive reading as well as reading at the more literal level.

Understanding at the comprehension level can be achieved in three ways: (1) by translating, (2) by interpreting, and (3) by extrapolating.

Translating. Being able to state something accurately in your own words is a sign of comprehension. Requiring a person to state material in his own words obviates verbalism or using words without understanding their meaning. In order to translate well, a reader must be able to understand figurative language as well as prosaic language.

1. Translate a problem from abstract to more concrete terms (that is, go down the abstraction ladder to the more concrete or specific or tangible examples).

2. Translate a lengthy part of a communication into briefer or more abstract terms. Example:

> "Besides the vineyard, you would see hayfields, pastures, and fields of grain. In smaller patches you would also see vegetable gardens, potato fields, and orchards." (R. M. G.: p. 77.)[6]
>
> This scene can best be described as _____ .
>
> 1. Irrigated
> 2. Agricultural
> 3. Industrial
> 4. Mechanized

3. Translate an abstraction, such as a generalization, by giving an illustration or sample. Example:

> "Bombay is a city of contrasts." (R. M. G.: p. 344.)
>
> Basing your thinking on the main idea in the sentence, you might expect to see (in Bombay):
>
> 1. Many legal agreements to be made.
> 2. Crowded tenement sections and areas of fine residences.
> 3. Many Indian people living there.
> 4. Extreme poverty and many starving people.

Interpretation. In interpretation a person is required to understand the basic ideas in a communication and go a step further to understanding the relationships of those ideas; he must grasp the significance, the point, of the selection he is reading. There are various ways of showing understanding of relationships and so on; one way, according to Bloom (p. 106), is by reordering material by writing a summary.

---

[6] The reading passages which serve as the basis for the exercises are from R. M. Glendinning, *Eurasia* (Boston: Ginn, 1962).

Write a one-sentence summary of the following paragraph:

"Soybeans . . . are used as food for man, and they furnish him with vegetable oil, flour, breakfast foods, and so on. They supply animals with hay and pasture, and they enrich the soil in which they grow by adding needed nitrogen. . . . Soybeans are used in making such products as soap, paints, and varnishes. Plastics and water-proof coatings for cloth are also made from soybeans." (R. M. G.: p. 308.)

Summary: _____

_____

Read the following material carefully. One word is missing. If you really understand the selection, you should be able to supply the missing word.

"Farmers and villagers dig up layers of the peat with long spades. The peat is left in the open to dry out. Then it is used as fuel for cooking and for heating cottages. Peat burns slowly and with a great deal of smoke, but it is cheap. This cheap fuel is very _____ because Ireland has little coal and practically no forests to supply firewood." (R. M. G.: p. 59.)

Answer: _____

Extrapolation. A person extrapolates when he makes inferences, draws conclusions, or predicts outcomes on the basis of some data. Pupils need *much* practice in this skill if they are to acquire the ability and propensity to use it. Discussions should accompany this work in order that the teacher can get some insight into the reasoning processes of his students and provide cues to how the ideas are related.

Read the following segment of material, picture the conditions, and note the effects of the sun's rays. Enter the number of the correct answer in the blank.

". . . the south-facing slopes receive much winter sunshine. The slanting rays of the winter sun strike these south-facing slopes rather directly and bring warmth to this part of the Alps." (R. M. G.: p. 213.)

Therefore, we probably find that _____.

1. Farms of this region have a shorter growing season than some of the surrounding areas.
2. The area is famous as a winter resort.
3. Nothing is planted on these slopes.
4. The summer sun strikes the north-facing slopes rather directly.

Here is another example of extrapolation:

Read the following passage carefully and then carry out the directions.

"Austria is a manufacturing country. Most of the workers in this country of some seven million make a living in the manufacturing industries."

"We have seen that the lack of high-grade coal is a handicap."

"Dams . . . have been built in the mountains of Austria. . . ." (R. M. G.: pp. 179–181.)

In the blank space before each statement make a mark indicating the truth or falsity of the statement according to the following directions.

____A____ if the information given in the preceding passage is sufficient for a judgment that the statement is <u>definitely</u> true.

____B____ if the information given in the passage is sufficient only to indicate that the statement is <u>probably</u> true.

____C____ if the information given in the passage is insufficient to indicate any degree of truth or falsity in the statement.

____D____ if the information given in the passage is sufficient for a judgment that the statement is <u>probably false</u>.

____E____ if the information given in the passage is sufficient for a judgment that the statement is <u>definitely false</u>.

_____ There is scarcely any precipitation in Austria.

_____ Hydroelectric power is generated in Austria.

_____ There is not much agriculture because of the mountains.

_____ Austria imports some coal.

_____ Austria has no resources for generating hydroelectric power.

_____ It is important for Austria to have a source of electric power.

A Note on Interpretation

The ability to read interpretively, to think "beyond" the literal content of a selection is essentially what this entire chapter has focused upon up to this point. We have pointed out also that the pupils' ability to read well interpretively is dependent to a large degree upon their intelligence and their ability to relate their experiences and background of information to the content being read. However, since the pupils' ability to interpret at higher grade levels is significantly affected by good early training and practice with interpretive reading, it is fitting that this chapter close with some suggestions and exercises for improving this most important reading skill in the primary grades:

1. Provide practice in interpretive listening and observing in the readiness stages and in the later primary grades with activities like the following:
   a. Charades and riddles such as those described earlier in which one clue at a time is revealed until a correct conclusion can be drawn.
   b. Pantomimes for which the teacher suggests an activity for each pupil to act out and allows him/her to practice it at home. As each pupil presents a performance to the class, the others try to guess what he/she is doing. (Nursery rhymes lend themselves well to pantomimes.)
   c. Create an imaginary character, "Little Ferd," to use as an example in daily discussions, perhaps creating a hand puppet to provide a focus on his character. Recount some event each day involving Ferd and have pupils talk about how he felt or behaved: "Today Little Ferd was almost hit by a car as he crossed the street. How do you think he felt afterward? Can you think of some things that might have caused this to happen? What might he do the next time he crosses to make sure he will be safe?"

2. Regularly ask questions that will require some particular type of interpretive response from the pupils:
   a. Reasoning from effect to cause. (Accept any good, logical possibilities as answers and also encourage any divergent thinking.)
      (1) Why are cars many different colors?
      (2) Why do people read newspapers?
      (3) Why do you have a name? What would it be like if none of us in this class had a name?
      (4) Why put a bandage on a cut finger?
      (5) Why do we sit at desks rather than stand all day?
      (6) What makes flowers grow?
      (7) Some days it is cloudy and some days it is sunny. Why?
   b. Conclusions about possible effects.
      (1) What would happen if everyone talked at once?
      (2) What would you do if you were lost in a big store?
      (3) What would happen if the bus had a flat tire on the way to school?
      (4) What would happen if it grew so dark we could see nothing in here and we had no lights?
      (5) What would happen if there weren't any sunshine?
      (6) What would happen if no one could walk more than a block?
   c. Problem solving.
      (1) How could you find your way home from a strange town?
      (2) How could you get to the other side of the river without a boat when you can't swim?
      (3) How would you find your way out of a woods?
      (4) How would you help a cat down out of a tree?
      (5) How would you help someone who was unconscious in a burning building?
      (6) How could you get onto the roof without a ladder?
      (7) How could you write something without a pen or pencil?
      (8) How could you find out how high the flagpole is?
      (9) If you were lost in the woods, how could you catch fish or animals to eat?

3. Provide pupils with a conclusion and have them reason about how it might have been determined.
   a. It is going to rain today. (What clues might have led to this statement?)
   b. That bird is going to lay some eggs soon.
   c. Spring is here.
   d. You had jam for breakfast.
   e. He is a happy boy.
   f. He works outdoors most of the time.
   g. That man is a fireman.
   h. She likes school.

4. When pupils begin to read more efficiently in the second and third grades and the content becomes more varied, make it a regular practice to assign a purpose for reading some selections that will focus the pupils' attention on reading to interpret, for example, "Read this story to find out what Bobby did when he found the horse caught in the fence. Decide what else he might have done that would save the horse."

5. After pupils have read a selection be sure to stimulate discussions with interpretation questions. Focus particularly on questions that ask pupils to explain their personal feelings and conclusions and why or how they arrived at them.

6. Interpretation often depends upon connotative use of language. Therefore occasionally focus pupils' attention upon a particular word or phrase that conveys strong emotional coloring. Discuss this effect and how it is achieved, for example, "In this story the author says his feelings as he floated down to earth in his first parachute jump were 'dreamlike.' What could be 'dreamlike' about being in a parachute?"

SUMMARY

This chapter has stressed the need for teachers to view literal comprehension, interpretation, and study skills in reading as being inseparable from achievement in content areas. Reading instruction and subject-matter instruction are not or should not be dichotomized in teachers' minds. Pupils who can and do read content-area materials with good comprehension, who discover how to use basic study skills, are pupils who achieve well.

A number of exercises have been illustrated in this chapter, not so much as prescriptions but as idea-starters, models of types of exercises that can grow out of what pupils already know about their language or out of the content materials they are studying. Particular stress has been put on the need for numerous language-thinking activities in the lower-elementary grades.

Study and comprehension skills are most effectively taught through inductive processes in which the pupils are led by the teacher in a careful examination of the content or skills until individual conclusions are generated. Basic to good teaching of comprehension and study skills is the teacher's constant concern with (1) providing appropriate materials for each child, (2) establishing meaningful purposes for each reading assignment, (3) following reading with questions that teach, (4) guiding the reader in making logical analyses of meaning relationships, and finally, (5) directing thinking skills through good exercises in conjunction with content learning.

Answers to Tricky Questions:

1. Sure, the fourth day of July occurs everywhere. 2. One hour. 3. Every month has twenty-eight days in it. 4. None, Moses didn't build the ark. 5. The match. 6. One hour. 7. Seventy. 8. Nine. 9. You have two apples. 10. White; the house has to be at the North Pole. 11. It was a fake; it couldn't have been dated BC. 12. Three.

LEARNING ACTIVITIES

1. Select a picture in a pre-primer and write five questions requiring pupils to interpret the picture.

2. Select a graph or chart in an elementary content textbook and prepare five questions of interpretation.

3. Select a story in a basal textbook and write a brief statement explaining how you might introduce the selection to a group of students using the DRTA procedure.

4. Using the selection chosen for the preceding activity, write two questions of each type: literal, interpretive, critical, creative.

5. In an elementary textbook in science or social studies, select a unified section of several pages. Write a brief analysis of the meaning problems for pupils in the section. Consider general vocabulary difficulties, technical terms, figures of speech, allusions, concepts, organizational complexity, charts, and the like. Describe how you might help pupils deal with some of the problems you find.

6. Assume that a student in your class has failed to comprehend a selection (could answer only four of ten questions you asked) that he has just been assigned to read silently. You know that his intelligence is high average and that he has no word-identification problems. What might account for this failure? Suggest some ways you might seek to discover the causes of this failure.

7. Obtain some test-type selections and help several students do a "nitty-gritty" analysis as was done with Katie.

STUDY QUESTIONS

1. State in general terms what is meant by the term *reading comprehension.* Compare your definition with that found in one other professional reading textbook.

2. Explain the essential differences in these processes: interpretation, translation, extrapolation, and critical reaction.

3. Explain the purpose of the readiness phase of a DRTA.

4. What related principles and purposes are there in the SQ3R and the DRTA?

5. Explain the importance of helping students do "nitty gritty" logical analyses of test-type selections.

RECOMMENDED READING

DECHANT, EMERALD V. *Improving the Teaching of Reading.* Englewood Cliffs, N.J.: Prentice Hall, Inc., 1964. Chap. 13.

ESGAR, L. P. "Drawing Their Own Conclusions," *The Reading Teacher,* 31 (1978), 494–496.

HAFNER, LAWRENCE E. *Developmental Reading in Middle and Secondary Schools.* New York: Macmillan Publishing Co., Inc., 1977. Chaps. 5, 6, and 7.

HARKER, WILLIAM J. "Teaching Comprehension: A Task Analysis Approach," *The Reading Teacher,* 16 (1973), 379–82.

HARRIS, ALBERT J. *How to Increase Reading Ability,* 7th ed. New York: David McKay Co., Inc. 1980.

HERBER, HAROLD L. *Teaching Reading in Content Areas.* 2nd ed. Englewood Cliffs, N.J.: Prentice-Hall, Inc. 1978.

POTTER, R. L. and C. E. HANNEMANN, "Conscious Comprehension: Reality Reading Through Artifacts," *The Reading Teacher,* 30 (1977), 644–649.

SMITH, FRANK. "The Role of Prediction in Reading." *Elementary English,* 52 (1975), 305–11.

STAUFFER, RUSSELL G. *Directing Reading Maturity as a Cognitive Process.* New York: Harper & Row, Publishers, 1969. Chap. 2.

—— *Directing the Reading-Thinking Process.* New York: Harper & Row, Publishers, 1975.

SULLIVAN, JOAN "Receptive and Critical Reading Develops at All Levels." *The Reading Teacher,* 17 (1974), 796–800.

WEAVER, CONSTANCE. *Psycholinguistics and Reading: From Process to Practice.* Cambridge, MA: Winthrop Publishers, Inc., 1980. Chap. 8.

REFERENCES

BLOOM, BENJAMIN (Ed.). *Taxonomy of Educational Objectives, Handbook I: Cognitive Domain.* New York: David McKay Co., Inc., 1956.

CASSIDY, JACK. "Inquiry Reading for the Gifted." *Reading Teacher,* 35 (1) (October 1981), 17–21.

DAVIS, FREDERICK B. "Research in Comprehension in Reading." *Reading Research Quarterly,* 3(4) (Summer 1968), 499–545.

GAGNE, ROBERT M. *Conditions of Learning.* New York: Holt, Rinehart and Winston, 1975.

GLENDENNING, R. M. *Eurasia.* Lexington, Mass.: Ginn and Company, 1962.

HAFNER, LAWRENCE E. *Developmental Reading in Middle and Secondary Schools.* New York: Macmillan Publishing Co., Inc., 1977. Chap. 6.

KARLIN, ROBERT. *Teaching Elementary Reading.* 2nd ed. New York: Harcourt Brace Jovanovich, Inc., 1975. Chaps. 6 and 7.

ROBINSON, FRANCIS P. *Effective Study.* Rev. ed. New York: Harper & Row, Publishers, 1970.

SPACHE, GEORGE D. and EVELYN B. SPACHE. *Reading in the Elementary School.* 4th ed. Boston: Allyn & Bacon, Inc., 1977.

STAUFFER, RUSSELL G. *Directing Reading Maturity As a Cognitive Process.* New York: Harper & Row, Publishers, 1969.

WEEKLY READER. "Diagnostic Silent Reading Test." Form 5-L, Middletown, CT: Weekly Reader Co., Inc., 1975.

Evaluating Capacity and Achievement and Applying Results to Teaching Children Reading

CHAPTER 7

Using Norm-Referenced Tests and Criterion-Referenced Tests to Evaluate Reading and Capacity

OBJECTIVES

As a result of thoroughly processing the material in this chapter the reader should be able to state/explain the following:

1. *The definition of norm-referenced tests.*
2. *The basic areas for evaluation.*
3. *The steps in the measurement and evaluation process.*
4. *The meaning and determination of capacity for reading.*
5. *The nature, purpose, construction, administration and scoring procedures, and performance criteria for informal silent/oral reading inventories.*
6. *The writing of perceptual readiness tests.*
7. *Usefulness of commercial measures of capacity.*
8. *Construction of informal capacity inventories.*
9. *Important measurable comprehension traits at the elementary and secondary levels.*
10. *The role of verbal reasoning in reading.*
11. *Usefulness of norm-referenced survey reading tests.*
12. *The nature of informal reading inventories compared to norm-referenced reading tests.*
13. *The profiling of test information.*
14. *The difference between norm-referenced tests and criterion-referenced tests.*
15. *The conditions under which norm-referenced testing is useful.*
16. *The writing of behavioral objectives for reading.*
17. *The purposes of the National Assessment Program (NAP).*
18. *The differences between the National Assessment Program and a standardized testing program.*
19. *Measurement of the eight major reading themes by the sample items.*
20. *The major criticisms of skills management systems.*

What skills do Johnny and Amy have for identifying words? How well do they understand what they read? How bright are they? When the teacher administers and scores tests designed to answer such questions, he/she is *measuring* performance.

When the teacher interprets the obtained scores for a specific purpose, he/she is *evaluating* performance. Suppose he/she obtains both achievement scores and capacity scores and then compares Johnny's and Amy's actual achievement with the expected achievement as determined by capacity measures. As the teacher notes and interprets discrepancies between the achievement and capacity scores, he/she is evaluating. Evidently it is necessary both to measure certain kinds of performance and also to evaluate these performances in order to do a good job of teaching.

A teacher must find out how well children read and whether they are reading as well as their capacity scores indicate they should be. Thoughtful parents want their children's achievement to be commensurate with their ability, and the alert teacher will want no less for them. But there are many capacities, skills, talents, and achievements in reading for teachers to measure and evaluate if they are going to help Johnny and Amy.

This section will treat standardized or norm-referenced tests. Generally, these are carefully constructed survey tests of (1) the basic reading skills such as comprehension, vocabulary, word recognition, and (2) the study-reference skills. They are so named because norms are developed against which a given teacher can compare the achievement of his/her pupils. In order to accomplish this standardizing, the test is administered to samples of children who are representative of pupils throughout the country. In that way, given raw scores can be assigned grade placement and percentile equivalents. This chapter also discusses criterion-referenced tests. Use of such competency-based tests helps determine whether or not pupils can accomplish particular reading subskills that are thought to undergird reading skills.

PART ONE: BASIC AREAS FOR EVALUATION

A teacher will measure and make evaluation in several areas.

1. *Capacity.* What are the pupil's basic abilities? Intelligence, language, and so forth.

2. *Reading skills.* How well do the pupils read? How well do they pronounce words? How well do they understand the basic, literal meaning? Do they get the gist of what they read? Do they relate supporting details to the main ideas, and so on? Can they make adequate inferences while reading, that is, can they draw conclusions while they read? Can they read and understand vocabulary?

3. *Word analysis skills.* Do the pupils have the basic skills underlying the ability to learn and use phonics? That is, how do they function in auditory discrimination and visual discrimination tasks? Do they know the important

phonemic options? Can they apply knowledge of phonemic options and context skills to aid word-identification in reading.

4. *Study-reference skills.* Can a pupil apply important reading skills such as getting the main idea and relating the important details to the main idea? Can the pupils shift gears, so to speak, and read for various purposes? Can they locate information? Do they know which resources and skills to use in locating information? Can they select materials pertinent to their reading purposes? Can they evaluate these materials? Finally, can they organize the information that they glean for their particular purposes? (Hafner, 1977.)

Determining the Quality of Evaluating Devices

Validity. A test is valid if it measures what it purports to measure. Any given test should have various kinds of validity. A test has *predictive validity,* for example, if it predicts well scores on some criterion such as another test of its kind or school marks. It has *concurrent validity* if it correlates highly with an accepted test of its kind. A correlation on the order of 0.80 is generally needed to establish concurrent validity. If the test grows out of psychological theory, it has *construct validity.* One such theory states that intelligence is the ability to see relationships and to understand abstract concepts. To have construct validity, according to this theory, an intelligence test would need to have a large proportion of items that require seeing relationships and understanding abstract concepts. *Content validity* is particularly important when considering the validity of achievement tests. To have high content validity, a test should reflect a large portion of the material presented in a course of instruction. A test has *face validity* when it looks as though it tests what it is supposed to test.

Reliability. A test is considered reliable if it yields consistent results. A test must be reliable if it is to be considered valid. However, a test may be reliable and still not be valid. For example, if a person wanted to measure the range of vocabulary in a typical sixth grade and all items were taken from Thorndike's first one thousand words, the test would not be valid even if it yielded consistent results. To be valid it would have to contain an adequate sampling of words from other Thorndike levels (Hafner, 1977).

Steps in the Measurement and Evaluation Process

The steps in the measurement and evaluation process are as follows:

1. Determine what is to be measured and evaluated.

2. Understand the nature of the thing to be measured and evaluated.

3. Note the reliability and validity criteria that experts say tests should meet.

4. Check available tests against the criteria.

5. Study interpretation manuals and technical manuals that accompany the tests, and study reviews of the tests written by competent specialists.[1]

6. Select the test(s).

7. If existing tests do not satisfy reliability and validity criteria described by experts as desirable, choose the test that most nearly satisfies them, or else develop a test.

8. Administer and score the test.

9. Evaluate the results.

10. Apply the findings as a guide to teaching, to placement in self-instructional materials, and so on.[2]

If teachers are to measure and evaluate capacities and achievements and use the results as a basis for preparing and presenting learning experiences, they will need to become acquainted with valid tests that they can administer and interpret. They will need to become familiar enough with various tests to see what they are designed to do and to determine whether, in fact, they do what is claimed for them. For any given test that they consider using, they will ask the question, "For what purpose(s) is this test valid?"

PART TWO: MEASURING CAPACITY FOR READING

What Capacity for Reading Means

If we are going to predict ability to read, obviously we cannot use with non-readers a test that involves reading.[3] Therefore, we will have to use some form of a test called language auding, because language auding relates to verbal comprehension, which is the basic factor in language understanding. It is listening comprehension, and it underlies reading ability. Actually the basic capacity involved is intelligence, and verbal comprehension and performance ability are two basic factors in intelligence.

Verbal comprehension or language auding can be measured in various ways. Of course, the problems, tasks, and questions will be given in an oral form so that reading is not involved. Some basic factors tested are vocabulary, general information, and arithmetic reasoning. When you measure vocabulary you are to some extent measuring a built-in reasoning factor, too, because reasoning processes are used to acquire, retain, and use vocabulary.

The verbal comprehension factor can also be measured by an auditory comprehension test such as the *Durrell Listening Test* (1968–1970) or a teacher-constructed test. For example, one can read a story to the students and then

---

[1] See the latest and previous editions of O. K. Buros, *Mental Measurement Yearbook,* published by Gryphon Press, and available in college libraries.

[2] Commercial, norm-referenced reading survey tests tend to rate pupils somewhat higher than what they can actually achieve.

[3] For average and good readers, reading ability may exceed language auding ability. For example, a sixth-grade girl who obtained a *Slosson Individual Intelligence Test* IQ of 104 earned an IQ of 125 on the *Kuhlman-Anderson Intelligence Test.* The latter test involved much reading.

ask questions on the story. This kind of test can even be used in group situations when the answer is indicated by marking the correct picture out of four or five choices or by marking a category designated by a picture under which a spoken word fits. Auditory comprehension tests, being verbal comprehension tests, are good predictors of reading achievement.

Generally, performance factors do not predict reading nearly so well as verbal factors do, because there is less verbal comprehension involved in performance tasks.[4] However, one performance task correlates well with the total intelligence and reading. That task is Block Design, which measures a visual-spatial factor.

Some people feel that performance or nonlanguage factors show the basic intelligence of a person. They may indicate what might have been had the person had better language stimulation as a child. The fact remains that language factors are the best predictors of reading achievement.

A person with fairly good language ability may still have problems with reading because he or she has not learned to decode words. If there are problems in auditory or visual perception, a person can be handicapped in learning to decode printed symbols. One can try to remedy the perceptual deficits of students who are not reading up to their basic language capacity level. However, research by Cynthia Deutsch (1964) has shown that auditory perception deficits that exist as late as third grade are most difficult to remedy.

The deficits are often in auditory perception, making ordinary phonics approaches to reading acquisition rather inefficacious. One must then use special techniques such as those discussed in the chapters on reading acquisition [Chap. 3] and applications [Chap. 8].

Commercial Auding, Intelligence, and Language Test

The *Durrell Listening-Reading Series* is designed to make possible a comparison of pupils' reading and listening abilities. Its purpose is to ascertain the degree of retardation in reading as compared with capacity for reading as measured by the listening test.

1. *Title: Durrell Listening-Reading Series: Listening.*

2. *Authors:* Donald D. Durrell and Mary T. Hayes.

3. *Publisher:* Harcourt Brace Jovanovich, Inc., New York, 1968–1970.

4. *Grade Levels:* Primary. Also available: Intermediate (grades 3.5–6) and Advanced (grades 7–9).

5. *Areas Tested and How Tested:* Vocabulary listening; sentence listening. (Capacity for reading is measured by these two listening tests.) At the intermediate and advanced levels, the tests measure vocabulary listening and paragraph listening. (1) *Vocabulary listening.* The listening vocabulary is measured by having the pupils listen to a word and then marking their responses in one of three columns. Each column is a category such as *toys, flowers, babies.* If the

---

[4] We are talking about the performance section of the *Wechsler Intelligence Scale for Children* (WISC). Most beginning teachers have not had a course in WISC testing but can take such a course at most colleges.

stimulus word spoken by the examiner is *puppy,* the pupil marks in the column that contains the category *babies.* When the examiner says "ball," the pupil marks in the *toys* column. (2) *Sentence listening.* This test works in a similar manner: Sample categories are "In Space," "Imaginary," and "Inside the Earth." Sample sentences are "The lion wore a crown because he was a king" and "The water main runs under the city streets."

6. *Comments:* (1) The listening (capacity) tests are designed to be used with the reading tests of this series. (2) The manual for the listening and reading tests gives much information regarding the design of the measures, initial research on these tests, the standardization program, validity, reliability, and suggested methods for helping low-achieving readers. (3) The assumption of a positive relationship between listening comprehension and reading comprehension is basically sound. Modality weaknesses (such as poor hearing) in individual cases may cloud the relationship between listening comprehension and reading comprehension. Among good readers from the middle grades and up one can expect to find reading comprehension to be better than listening comprehension; in such cases the listening comprehension test would not provide an effective reading capacity estimate.

COMMERCIAL INTELLIGENCE TESTS

Although total working intelligence is a function of the interaction of pyramidal intelligence—"the potential intelligence attributable to genes and physical development factors up to 25 months"—and functional intelligence—the functional ability of the brain that has been influenced by experience—it is still *measured* intelligence (which is a function of total working intelligence) that correlates the best with reading achievement in the later primary grades and beyond (Hafner 1977). One should try to use appropriate instruments to obtain the best estimates of measured intelligence. Naturally, nonreaders and poor readers should be given intelligence tests that do not require reading.

The Slosson Intelligence Test (SIT).[5]   The *SIT* is an individual test of intelligence that requires minimal training and could be used by the classroom teacher for individual testing. Testing and scoring take from 10 to 30 minutes. The following abilities are purported to be tested by the *SIT:*

1. Language-vocabulary, abstract words, rhymes, definitions, and comprehension of verbal relations.

2. Memory.

3. Conceptual thinking.

4. Reasoning—the perception of logical relations, discrimination ability, and analysis and synthesis.

5. Numerical reasoning.

---

[5] The authors thank Andrea Anderson for the use of her "Critique of the *Slosson Intelligence Test,*" unpublished paper, Florida State University, 1976.

6. Visual-motor-manual dexterity, eye-hand coordination, and perception of spatial relations.

7. Social intelligence.

A number of items in the *SIT* are taken (with permission) from the *Stanford-Binet Individual Test of Intelligence (SB)*. Although the two tests correlate at 0.92, they do not seem to be evaluating the same intellectual functions at the various age levels in the same proportion (Nicholson, 1970). The potential user of the *SIT* must know just what is tested at each age level.

Above the age level 6-10, the *SIT* has no reasoning category and no visual-motor items; the *SB*, on the other hand, increases in percentage of reasoning verbal items above that age. Memory items on the *SIT* also decrease as the age level increases. Therefore, the *SIT* does not produce comparable IQs for certain levels of chronological age and intellectual functioning for the higher intelligence levels (Ritter, et al, 1973).

The *SIT* uses the ratio IQ (MA/CA) rather than the deviation IQ; thus, the IQ is likely to be unstable for a given individual across age levels. Although the *SIT* is less time consuming, it should not be used uncritically as a substitute for the *SB* or the *WISC* (Hammill, 1968-1969).

The Wechsler Intelligence Scale for Children (WISC). This test, developed by David Wechsler, is suitable for most children from ages five to fifteen. The *WISC* uses five verbal subtests and five performance subtests. Subtests and sample items follow:

Verbal Tests

General Information. What color is grass? What do carpenters use to cut a board? Who wrote Tom Sawyer?

Comprehension. Name something we get from the sun. Why should a person not hitchhike?

Arithmetic Reasoning. You have two apples and somebody gives you another apple. How many do you have then? If bananas are two for twenty-five cents, how much would six bananas cost? If two pieces of candy cost 15 cents, how much would a dozen and a half cost?

Similarities. How are a carrot and a beet alike? How are a bicycle and a skate-board alike? How is a needle like a tin pan?

Digit Span. (auditory memory test). Say these numbers after me. 7-2-8 _____; 9-1-4-8-3 _____.

Vocabulary. (an optional test). What is a rose? What does caution mean? What is bauxite?

Performance Tests

Picture Arrangement. A series of scrambled pictures that tell a story when arranged in correct sequence is set before the child. The pupil's task is to arrange them in correct order.

Picture Completion. The task is to identify what is missing in each picture presented.

Block Design. The pupil is required to arrange colored blocks to match given patterns such as the following:

Object Assembly. The pupil is required to put together large, disarranged pieces of a jigsaw puzzle to form a figure of a giraffe or a boy.

Coding A. The pupil is provided with a key and then marks figures such as a star, a cross, and the like with the appropriate marks. The key follows:

Coding B. The numerals 1 through 9 are written in boxes. A symbol is associated with each numeral. The task is to write in the blank box beneath each numeral the correct symbol associated with it according to the key.

Key:

1	2	3	4	5	6	7	8	9
✓	✗	⁒	//	∩	∧	\\\	∪	÷

Task:

2	4	9	3	7	1	5	2	6	8	4	7	5	3	1	6	9

Mazes. The child is required to trace through mazes with a pencil without touching the lines.

Informal Measures of Capacity

The Hafner-Smith Verbal Comprehension Test (See Appendix A). The *HVCT* is an aptitude test that can be used as a mental abilities test; except for a few visual-motor items, it measures what Cattell has termed "crystallized intelligence" and, therefore, is influenced by schooling and home environment. It provides a rather good estimate of crystallized intelligence.

Through the use of this test, verbal comprehension ages ranging from three years to nineteen years and nine months may be obtained. Using the verbal comprehension age as the numerator and the (exact) chronological age as the denominator, one can obtain a verbal comprehension quotient.

The five basic factors measured by the *HSVCT* are the following:

1. Visual-Motor (spatial).
2. Arithmetic Reasoning.

3. Vocabulary.

4. General Information.

5. Providing Superordinates (noting similarities).

These factors are fairly well distributed across the age range, except that Visual-Motor tops out at seven years and Providing Superordinates does not begin until the six-year level.

The Hafner-Jolly Individual Mental Abilities Point Scale (MAPS). (See Appendix A). The *MAPS* is an informal test of mental abilities found useful in determining aptitude for reading. The types of items used in *MAPS* were explained in the previous segment.

The four subtests are as follows:

1. General Information.

2. Auditory Memory Span (Digit Span).

3. Proverbs.

4. Vocabulary.

One can use the scores on the vocabulary subtest to estimate a vocabulary age level. The approximate vocabulary age level of each item is printed in the margin of the test.

Local norms can be built for this scale. Also, comparison of pupils' mental ability scores and total points on this test with the scores of known good and poor readers at certain chronological age levels can lead to the development of reading achievement expectancy patterns. This requires work, but the results are worth it.

Learning Rate Test (LRT). (See Appendix A). At times the test data for certain individuals seem to yield equivocal results as far as using these data to make a clear-cut prediction of success in initial reading acquisition. At that point one can use a learning rate test. The basic thesis for this test is that the best way to tell if a pupil is ready to learn to read is to teach the pupil some words to a mastery criterion and one hour later test him/her to see if he/she can still read all or most of the words. This test has been a real boon to prospective and in-service teachers.

Informal Listening (Auding) Tests

Informal Listening Inventory (ILI). To measure auding one uses the same set of graded passages as in the informal reading inventory.

Description. The ILI consists of a series of stories or story segments, one from each graded reader, several vocabulary items to be defined, and a set of questions—literal and interpretive—for each of the passages. The examiner reads a passage to the pupil and then asks prepared questions. Following this, the examiner asks the pupil to define several words from the selection and a related topic.

Purpose. The informal listening inventory is designed to yield information about the pupil's ability to define words and to understand material that is read to him/her. Basically, it is used to estimate at what level a pupil could read with comprehension if his/her word-identification skills were maximized.

Construction. To prepare a set of stories that will be read to a pupil, use a readability formula to locate passages that are at given levels of difficulty. The levels might be as follows:

	Difficulty Level		Difficulty Level
Preprimer	1.2	4[1]	4.3
3[2]	3.8	9	9.5

Prepare three literal comprehension questions and two interpretation questions for each difficulty level. The literal questions require the pupil to understand directly stated facts or ideas. The interpretation questions require the pupil to make inferences and see relationships among ideas. These points can total 90; the remaining 10 points are accounted for by five vocabulary items that are to be defined, two points for each item correctly defined.

Performance Criterion. The minimum criterion to show that a person understands a selection read to him is 75 per cent correct. The capacity score is comprised of the total of the listening comprehension score and the vocabulary definition score. The highest level at which Cindy can understand a selection read to her and define the words well enough to score at least 75 per cent correct is the level at which she could read if her word-recognition skills were up to par and she had been receiving excellent reading instruction.

Administering and Scoring the Test. There are two approaches:
(1) After determining an *approximate* level by administering the *General Information Test* or the *Vocabulary Test* (appendix A, *Hafner-Jolly Individual Mental Abilities Point Scale*) one can select a correspondingly difficult passage and read it to the pupil.
(2) Administer the ILI after administering the informal reading inventory. Select the level above the level at which the pupil failed to meet the criteria for instructional reading performance. In either case, read the selection to the child (after establishing rapport) and ask him/her the corresponding questions. Total the correct points. Seventy-five per cent correct on the questions is a passing mark; that is, it meets the criterion set to show one understands listening material at that level.

To check your understanding, determine Cindy's capacity level if she makes the following scores on the capacity (auding plus vocabulary definition) test:

Level	Score (Per Cent)
Seventh grade	79
Sixth grade	85
Fifth grade	94

Cindy's capacity level, as determined by this type of capacity test, is seventh grade.

Informal Capacity Inventories

Listening Comprehension. The listening comprehension test is used as the basis for the capacity test of the informal reading inventory.[6] It can be applied to content areas as well as to basal reading material. For example, here are two comprehension and two interpretation questions that can be asked a child following a section of a fifth-grade social studies text[7] read to him/her on the topic "How the New World Was Discovered":
Comprehension:

1. When the seamen returned, what did they do with their valuable goods?
2. What was another name for the Atlantic Ocean in Columbus' time?

Interpretation:

1. Why could the goods brought from the Far East bring such high prices when sold in Europe?
2. Who traveled through cooler waters, Cabot or Columbus?

Bear in mind that interpretation questions are characterized by the fact that they call for the listener or reader to draw inferences, to read between the lines.

Several abilities important to success in reading can be assessed on an informal basis: Command of general information, auditory memory span, vocabulary, visual discrimination, and interpreting proverbs. Such a test, except for the visual discrimination section, can be administered orally so that it does not require reading.

Local norms can be built for such tests. Comparison of the patterns of children on these tests with the patterns of their scores on reading tests can lead to the development of reading expectancy patterns.

General Information Test. Develop a set of questions over a wide range of topics that vary in difficulty from very easy to very hard. Arrange the questions in order of difficulty. Explain to the pupil that you are going to ask him/her questions about many different things. Write his/her responses in the space after the question. Allow one point for each correct response.
Examples of questions:

1. Name one of the colors of the United States flag.
2. What is a canoe?

Auditory Memory-Span Test. The most direct and common way of measuring auditory memory span is to say several numbers at one-second intervals and ask the pupil being tested to repeat what was said. There are two sets of numbers for each of eight items. If the pupil fails the first, say the second set

---

[6] Complete inventories are found in Appendix A.

[7] Selection from *Your Country and Mine* by G. S. Brown, published by Ginn.

and let him/her repeat them. In the easiest set there are two numbers. In the most difficult set there are nine numbers. The pupil's score is the highest number of digits correctly repeated. For example, if the last item he/she gets correct is item B (below), the score is three.

> A. 4-2   B. 7-3-5   C. 6-2-7-1
>   5-9   4-7-1   3-9-8-4

To more nearly approximate standardized auditory memory span tests, the pupil, after completing a performance on the total series of numbers, can be given similar sets of numbers (beginning with two numbers) and asked to repeat them backwards. If given 3-7, he/she is to say 7-3. Total score would be the score for regular (or forward) repetitions plus the score for backward repetitions.

Vocabulary Test. Word knowledge is a basic ability in reading. To build a vocabulary test go through a dictionary and choose from every tenth or twenty-fifth page (depending upon how many words are needed and how big the dictionary is) the *n*th word, for example, the fifth word, on the page. Arrange in order from easy to difficult the words of the list that have been compiled. In trying out the test on pupils, rearrange the items in accordance with the actual difficulty discovered through testing. For example, results for five words might be as follows:

Words	Percentage of Pupils Who Answer Items Correctly
cat	95
obsequious	2
rattle	70
coniferous	20
proud	40

Then rearrange the words in your revised test in order of increasing difficulty:

1. cat
2. rattle
3. proud
4. coniferous
5. obsequious

Allow two points when a pupil shows a good grasp of the meaning of a word. Allow one point for each minimally correct response. Then compile a list of responses that are considered to be correct (indicating two-point responses and one-point responses) so that scoring will be consistent.

Proverbs Test. The ability to interpret proverbs is a subtest found in a number of excellent intelligence tests. Most pupils will probably not begin to understand proverbs very well until intermediate and upper-elementary grades. Nevertheless, the proverbs subtest is included in the mental ability test because ability varies from child to child. The proverbs in this test are figurative expressions and are interpreted at a general level. Literal renditions are not credited. Examples of proverbs:

1. A bird in the hand is worth two in the bush.
2. Don't count your chickens before they are hatched.

The Spache Diagnostic Reading Scales (Listening), developed by George D. Spache, consists of 11 written passages that range in difficulty from primer to eighth reader/listener level. The capacity level score is obtained by reading passages to the pupil, asking questions about the material, and determining the percentage correct for each passage. The minimum percentage correct for the capacity level is 60 per cent comprehension, although most experts in the field have established minimums of 70 to 75 per cent correct.

Reading Readiness Tests. (See the appropriate section in Chapter 2.)

Converting Raw Scores to Grade Placement Scores

The following table shows how the scores on our vocabulary, information, and auditory digit span (auditory memory) tests in the testing appendix can be converted to grade placement scores.

Table 7–1. Conversion Tables for Changing Raw Scores to Grade Placement Scores

Vocabulary				Information		Auditory Digit Span	
Raw Score*	Grade Placement	Raw Score	Grade Placement	Raw Score	Grade Placement	Raw Score	Grade Placement
47	10.0						
46	9.5	31	4.9	22	—	14	—
45	9.0	30	4.6	21	—	13	—
44	8.6	29	4.3	20	10.0	12	—
43	8.0	28	4.0	19	9.0	11	8.7
42	7.7	27	3.7	18	8.0	10	5.7
41	7.5	26	3.4	17	7.0	9	4.0
40	7.2	25	3.1	16	6.7	8	2.0
39	7.0	24	2.9	15	6.4	7	1.5
38	6.8	23	2.6	14	6.0	6	1.0
37	6.6	22	2.3	13	5.3	5	—
36	6.3	21	2.0	12	4.5	4	—
35	6.0	20	1.7	11	3.7	3	—
34	5.8	19	1.3	10	3.0	2	—
33	5.5	18	1.0	9	2.4	1	—
32	5.2	17	—	8	1.7	0	—
		16	—	7	1.0		
				6	—		

*Where two points are given for an excellent response and one point for a minimum response to a vocabulary item.
Source: Based on tables from the manual for the *Wechsler Intelligence Scale for Children.*

In the appendix where the individually administered vocabulary test beginning with the words *apple* and *lamp* is found, you will also find the approximate vocabulary age level for each item. It is important to remember when
crediting a person for responses to the vocabulary items to give two points only
for excellent responses. This is particularly true when counting raw score for
entry into the table.

Informal Measures of Perceptual Readiness

The nature of these tests will be explained here. The complete tests can be
found in Appendix A.

Visual Discrimination Tests. Being able to make visual discriminations is
necessary to success in reading. Usually a test requiring a pupil to discriminate
visually among letters or among words is given when the teacher feels the pupil
is going to have some success at the task. A pupil who cannot discriminate
among words probably will have trouble in learning phonic elements and
nucleus words. In giving these readiness tests, one will generally work several
examples with the pupil before proceeding.

Word Discrimination: Different. The pupil is presented an array of three
printed words, two of which are identical and one of which is different. He/she
is instructed to underline or circle the word that is different from the other
two.

Examples:

A.	cat	cat	bee
B.	shop	chock	shop

The tasks increase in difficulty so that one is able to determine whether the
pupil can make fine discriminations as well as gross ones.

Auditory Discrimination Tests. These tests involve the ability to discriminate
beginning sounds, middle sounds, and ending [rhyming] sounds. The pupil who
has trouble with auditory discrimination tasks may find it difficult to learn
phonic elements (grapheme-phoneme relationships). The tests in Appendix
A are self-explanatory.

Auditory Segmentation Test. This test combines Elkonin's idea of segmentation of sounds with Durrell's and Murphy's idea of hearing the separate sounds
in spoken words. Say a word to the pupil and ask him/her to say the separate
sounds. Then ask the pupil if a given sound is in the word. Or the examiner
may say a word and ask the pupil to add a given sound and say the resulting
word or to subtract a sound and say the resulting word.

Examples:

A. (1) Stimulus: /man/ Expected response: /m/ /a/ /n/
   (2) Question: Is there a /m/ sound in man?
                 Is there an /a/ sound in man?
                 Is there a /n/ sound in man?

B. (1) Stimulus: /päp/ Expected response: /p/ /ä/ /p/
   (2) Question: Is there a /p/ sound in <u>pop</u>?
      Is there a /j/ sound in <u>pop</u>? (nonexemplar)

C.   Stimulus: "Say <u>ground</u>." Expected response: <u>ground</u>
    "Now say it without the /g/." Expected response: <u>round</u>

D.   Stimulus: "Say <u>lake</u>." Expected response: <u>lake</u>
    "Now say it with an /f/ at the beginning." Expected response:
    <u>flake</u>[8]

Auditory Blending Test. We have thought for years that auditory blending is an important skill for reading; recent research has confirmed this belief. The pupil who can sound out letters of a word but cannot blend these sounds to produce the whole word cannot independently identify polysyllabic words, especially if he/she is a nonfluent reader who understands little of what he/she reads.

When administering the test, read the sounds using the pupil's dialect: if the pupil pronounces ⟨of⟩ as /əv/, pronounce it /əv/, and not /äv/.

Auditory Memory Test. The most direct and accepted way of measuring auditory memory is to use the digit span test: say several numbers at one-second intervals and ask the pupil being tested to repeat what was said. In this test there are two sets of numbers for each of eight items. In the easiest set there are two numbers (digits). In the most difficult set there are nine digits. There are also eight items for the backward repetition, for example, the examiner says 7–1 and the pupil says 1–7. Total score is the highest number of digits repeated correctly forward plus the highest number of digits repeated correctly backward.

Letter Association Tests. Letter association can be construed in two ways—knowing the typical speech sounds associated with letters and knowing the names generally associated with letters.

Knowledge of Typical Speech Sounds. The ability to give the phonemes such as /m/ for ⟨m⟩—rather than the name /em/— transfers more directly to reading. After all, when we read the word ⟨mint⟩, for example, we say /mint/, not /emint/. When a vowel is presented, any of the typical phonemes associated with it can be accepted as a correct answer; the same is true of consonants such as ⟨c⟩ and ⟨g⟩.

Knowledge of Names. The ability to name letters is helpful in referring to parts of the printed word. As with the speech sounds test, present a random array of ten letters as in the letter knowledge subtest in the *Hafner Quick Phonics Test.* For a complete test, use our test in Appendix A that utilizes all 26 letters.

---

[8] Rosner (1973) has written an auditory segmentation test that he has also standardized. However, we have not included such a test in Appendix A.

PART 3. EVALUATING READING ACHIEVEMENT

Commercial Reading Tests

For a number of years theoreticians, practitioners, and theoretician-practitioners have tried to determine what people need to do to read well and comprehend fully, particularly in order to answer the variety of questions that can be asked.

One problem that has puzzled theoreticians over the years is the identification of particular reading abilities. Berg (1973) states, "Before a reading test can claim to measure some particular ability in reading, the existence of that ability must first be demonstrated by an appropriate statistical analysis." Lennon (1962) suggested that only four factors could be measured reliably:
  1. A general verbal factor (word knowledge).
  2. Comprehension of explicitly stated materials.
  3. Comprehension of implicit or latent meaning.
  4. Appreciation.

Schreiner and colleagues (1969), using experimental tests, attempted to identify measurable comprehension traits among fifth-grade pupils in several Iowa schools. They found only four factors to be statistically definable for diagnostic purposes:
  1. Speed of reading.
  2. Listening comprehension.
  3. Verbal reasoning (classification of words).
  4. Speed of noting details.

They found the following factors to be highly correlated with Verbal Reasoning (VR):

Paragraph Meaning (PM), 0.92.   Information (I), 0.89.

Cause and Effect (CE), 0.88.   Main Ideas (MI), 0.82.

Hafner (1978) analyzed these results and explained the role of verbal reasoning (classification of words) in these results. In brief, Verbal Reasoning was a classification task, but Hafner found that the items measuring each of the highly related factors could be analyzed to show that they all called for knowledge of meanings and ability to determine within the stem or passage and between stem, passage and correct answer the following kinds of relationships:
  1. Shared attribute relationship (R_{SA}).
  2. Shared component parts relationship (R_{SCP}).
  3. Shared function relationships (R_{SF}).

In more familiar terms, running throughout the items for VR, PM, CE, I, and MI (in addition to R_{SA}) were the following kinds of paradigmatic relationships: whole-part, part-whole, coordinate, opposite, and synonymic, all of which the reader had to determine in order to answer the various items correctly.

At the twelfth-grade level, using a different test (*Davis Reading Test*), asking some different kinds of questions, and using a special statistical analysis, Davis

(1968) found five skills to be significantly independent; the skills and the percentage that each contributed to the variation[9] in scores follow:

Reading Skill	Percentage of Variance Accounted For
1. Memory for word meanings	32
2. Drawing inferences from content	20
3. Following the structure of a passage	14
4. Recognizing a writer's purpose, attitude, tone, and mood	11
5. Finding answers to questions explicitly or in paraphrase	10

Standardized Reading Survey Tests

Survey tests are designed to measure reading achievement in such key areas as vocabulary and (paragraph) comprehension. In the upper-elementary or middle school years additional tests are available for evaluating the ability to read efficiently, skim and scan, locate information, and recognize the tone and mood of a passage and so forth.

1. *Title:* SRA Achievement Series: Reading.

2. *Authors:* L. P. Thorpe, D. W. Lefever, and R. A. Naslund.

3. *Publisher:* Science Research Associates, Chicago, 1968.

4. *Grade Levels:* 1–9.

5. *Areas Tested:* Grades 1–2.5, verbal-pictorial association, language perception, comprehension, vocabulary (composite). Grades 2–4, comprehension, vocabulary (composite). Grades 4–9, comprehension, vocabulary (composite).

6. *Comments:* Guthrie (Buros, 1972) was not enamored of the inclusion of the language perception subtest because it does not contribute to the function of the test as a reading test.

The comprehension tests at all levels are commendable, according to Guthrie, because "the passages are interesting and the multiple-choice questions require a broad range of skills such as recall, inference, and the identification of central themes. Most admirable is the exclusion of vocabulary items from this subtest." For reasons stated in his review, Guthrie finds the vocabulary subtests (actually a vocabulary in context format) questionable.

1. *Title:* Iowa Silent Reading Tests.

2. *Coordinating Editor:* Roger Farr.

3. *Publisher:* Harcourt Brace Jovanovich, Inc., New York, 1972.

4. *Grade Levels:* Level 1: upper elementary, basic adult. Level 2: high school, community college, other post-high school groups. Level 3: college-bound high school, college, professional groups.

5. *Areas Tested and How Tested:* Vocabulary, reading comprehension,

---

[9] The nonerror variation or variance in scores.

directed reading, part A–locating information; part B–skimming and scanning; and reading efficiency in Levels 1 and 2; vocabulary, reading comprehension, and reading efficiency in Level 3.

6. *Comments:* The revision of this test has been so extensive that it bears little relation to its predecessor. For example, the poetry test has been dropped, the directed reading test uses a different set and format, a general vocabulary test has been substituted for the four content-area vocabulary tests, and the thorough treatment on the use of the index has been replaced. The test user should consult the publisher's technical manual to obtain further information about the rationale for the test, its validity and reliability, and how it should be used (Hafner, 1977).

1. *Title: Metropolitan Achievement Tests: Reading.*

2. *Authors:* Irving H. Balow, Roger Farr, Thomas P. Hogan, George A. Prescott (senior author).

3. *Publisher:* Psychological Corporation, New York, 1978, 1979.

4. *Grade Levels:* Preprimer, K.5, primer, K.5–1.4, primary 1, 1.5–2.4, primary 2, 2.5–3.4, elementary 3.5–4.9, intermediate, 5.0–6.9 (also two advanced tests).

5. *Areas Tested:* Phonics, sight vocabulary (word recognition), auditory and visual discrimination, letter recognition, vocabulary in context, and reading comprehension are emphasized from beginning levels through the elementary level. At the intermediate and advanced levels the emphasized areas are vocabulary in context, skimming and scanning, rate of comprehension, and reading comprehension.

6. *Comments:* Students who take the typical reading tests of word recognition, vocabulary (in context), and reading comprehension can have their results reported in terms of grade placement scores and percentiles.

Students who take the criterion-referenced tests of subreading skills can have their results reported in terms of percentage of items passed on each test.

1. *Title: Durrell Reading Test.*

2. *Authors:* Donald D. Durrell and Mary T. Hayes.

3. *Publisher:* Harcourt Brace Jovanovich, New York, 1969.

4. *Grade Levels:* Primary, grades 1–3.5; intermediate, grades 3.5–6; advanced, grades 7–9.

5. *Areas Tested:* Vocabulary and sentence reading (comprehension).

6. *Comments:* At the primary level, the vocabulary test requires the child to relate a word to one of three categories in a cluster. Each (category) word or words at the top of the columns is illustrated as well as printed. The sentence reading test is organized in the same manner. Obviously there is no paragraph comprehension test.

At higher levels there is a paragraph comprehension test. The pupil reads a passage and then marks statements about the passage as True, False, or Not Given. These tests appear to be excellent, and they fit the meaning hierarchy theory espoused by the authors.

7. *Examples of the Vocabulary Test* (not actual items):

	Parts of a tree	Fruits	Time
1. today	—	—	—
2. hour	—	—	—
3. orange	—	—	—
4. branch	—	—	—
5. plum	—	—	—
6. leaf	—	—	—

Individual Survey Reading Tests

1. *Title:* *Analytical Reading Inventory (ARI).*
2. *Authors:* Mary L. Woods and Alden J. Moe.
3. *Publisher:* Charles E. Merrill, Columbus, O., 1977.
4. *Grade Levels:* Primer through sixth grade, word recognition; primer through ninth grade, comprehension.
5. *Areas Tested:* Word recognition and comprehension.
6. *Comments:* The readability levels of the *ARI* are controlled for all three forms of the test; that is, the primer comprehension is at 1.5 readability level, grade level selection one is 1.7; two is 2.5, and so forth. There was a concerted attempt to make the questions passage-dependent. The questions were designed to measure six aspects of comprehension:

    a. main idea
    b. factual
    c. terminology
    d. cause and effect
    e. inferential
    f. conclusion

The criteria used to determine the three reading levels (and the listening level) are those traditionally used in informal reading inventories; the authors gave a rationale for the practice.

	Percentage Correct	
Level	*Oral Reading*	*Comprehension-Interpretation*
Independent	99[10]	90
Instructional	95	75
Frustration	less than 90	about 50
Listening Capacity	—	75

1. *Title:* *Standard Reading Inventory.*
2. *Author:* Robert A. McCracken.

---

[10] That is, no more than one uncorrected pronunciation in each 100 words.

3. *Publisher:* Klamath Printing Co., Klamath, Oregon, 1966.

4. *Grade Levels:* 1–6 (11 reading levels, preprimer to grade 7).

5. *Scores:* Reading levels obtained: (1) independent, (2) minimum instructional, (3) maximum instructional, (4) frustration.

6. *Areas Tested:* Vocabulary in isolation, vocabulary in context, oral word recognition errors, total oral errors, recall after oral reading, recall after silent reading, total comprehension, oral speed, silent speed.

7. *Comments:* The content of the tests is based on three basal series; the tests are deemed to have content validity. Also, these tests are more reliable than teacher-made IRIs would generally be. Robinson (Buros, 1972) asks whether the test actually furnishes diagnostic information about oral reading errors when the scoring is quantitative rather than qualitative. Furthermore, he states that the "scoring of oral errors seems needlessly complex and confusing." "The test's major contribution is in providing more information . . . about the process of reading as opposed to the product normally measured by group standardized silent reading tests." It can be used as a rough, semi-diagnostic tool to learn more about a particular reader and how he/she reads certain kinds of material.

Norm-Referenced Study-Referenced Skills Tests

Biologists and psychologists claim that people use only a small fraction of their brain power. What keeps them from using more? Lack of efficient, effective methods of acquiring and organizing information for immediate and later use is a prime deterrent to fuller utilization of brain power.

The schools can do much to develop the necessary skills and attitudes needed to locate, select, evaluate, and organize information efficiently and effectively. In fact, if the schools do not teach these skills, they usually are not learned. At best, people might learn them on their own, but only after much effort and the wasting of precious years.

The reading-study skills measured by the *Iowa Tests of Basic Skills—Work-Study Skills* are reading maps, reading graphs and tables, and knowing of and using reference materials. Although these skills are important, they represent only a fraction of those needed in reading-study situations.

1. *Title: Iowa Tests of Basic Skills—Work-Study Skills.*

2. *Authors:* E. F. Lindquist, A. N. Hieronymus.

3. *Publisher:* Houghton Mifflin Company, Boston, 1955.

4. *Grade Levels:* 3–9.

5. *Areas Tested:* (1) map reading, (2) reading graphs and tables, (3) knowledge and use of reference materials.

6. *Comments:* (1) Curricular materials were studied as an aid in developing the test. (2) Work-study skills scores can be shown in a profile along with other scores from the *Iowa Tests of Basic Skills* coordinated achievement series; the profile makes it possible to see strengths and weaknesses in a pupil's performance. (3) Mastery of work-study skills is important to academic achieve-

ment. These skills can be developed in conjunction with activity in the various subjects in the elementary classroom.

Much of the measurement and evaluation of these reading-study skills needs to be done on an informal basis because (1) norm-referenced instruments that could measure a large number of the skills are not available and (2) the informal instruments measuring more of the skills can be designed by the teacher for use with specific textbooks that pupils use. Informal criterion-referenced reference-study skills tests will be discussed in Part 4 of this chapter.

INFORMAL READING INVENTORIES [IRI]

An informal inventory is a listing of a person's educational skills that is developed by a teacher for specific, limited use. Such inventories, rather than calling on people to recognize a response, generally require them to produce a response. In a word-recognition test, one pronounces words from graded lists. In a silent/oral reading test, one reads a selection silently and answers questions about the selection by producing answers, and then reads the selection aloud so that the examiner can check on one's ability to pronounce words in context. In a reference-study skills test, one also produces answers in demonstrating one's ability to (1) use a table of contents and index, (2) interpret graphs, and (3) summarize and outline material. The immediate emphasis in this section will be on silent/oral reading inventories.

The selections that individuals read in performing silent/oral reading tasks can be narrative (literary or story) selections from a reader or they can be expository segments from a content area. Reference-study skills inventories are based on expository materials. At any rate, one should not rely on results of narrative (IRIs) for placement in expository materials; use expository materials.

Silent/oral reading inventories can be used to ascertain a pupil's dynamics of thinking, his/her reasoning processes. You may ask the pupil at times what leads him/her to make a certain response, where the information is on which he/she based the response, and/or what additional information he/she may have brought in to make an interpretation.

Such reading inventories can be used for instructional placement. By setting certain performance criteria it can be ascertained if a pupil reads well enough to be instructed at fifth-grade level or if he/she should be instructed, say, at third-grade level.

Performance on the inventories can be checked to see the pupil's particular strengths and weaknesses in reading skills performance. You may determine, for example, that a pupil can do a good job of contextual oral reading at the fourth-grade level, but only answer correctly half of the literal comprehension and none of the interpretation questions after silent reading. When you give such a child a graded word list to read (word recognition in isolation), you may find that he/she reads at the fifth-grade level. If you use the results of the latter test alone for instructional placement, you will place him/her in material that is too difficult. It is most important to notice a real weakness in interpretation and work to improve that area. The results of such testing can be studied to determine which children have the same weaknesses (on the same levels) so that, where possible, group instruction can be given to correct the deficiencies.

Finally, the records of such measurement, evaluation, and teaching should be passed on to the next teacher to facilitate accurate instructional placement and continued growth in reading. Of course, the material that is passed on should be of a qualitative, dynamic nature as well a quantitative one. Also, the accuracy depends on the degree of content validity and test reliability.

When the scores from a standardized reading test are used to determine the instructional level for reading, one too often finds the student placed at a level where the material is much too difficult. Independent observations reveal that the frustration level obtained by the silent/oral reading inventory is often found to coincide with the reading grade as determined by a standardized reading test that utilizes a recognition response mode. When one considers this information plus the fact that we can discover more about the quality of responses and the means used to produce the responses, it is reasonable to conclude that results of the silent/oral reading inventory are better to use in determining the level of placement as well as the relative emphases to place on certain skills.

Informal Silent/Oral Reading Inventories

Description. The informal silent/oral reading inventory consists of a series of stories or story segments, one from each reader of a reading series, and a set of questions for each of the stories. The student reads a selection silently[11] and answers several comprehension and interpretation questions posed by the teacher. Then the student reads the same selection orally and the examiner notes pronunciation errors on a duplicate copy of the story. The copy is double-spaced to make the reading easier and to facilitate marking errors.

Purpose. The informal silent/oral reading inventory is designed to yield information about the pupil's ability to understand what he/she is reading and to pronounce the material correctly. One should also note the fluency of reading. If reading is halting, the student may not be able to tie the parts of a sentence or paragraph(s) together in order to determine meaning. This is a very important point. Other basic purposes of the inventory are to determine the level of materials to use in ongoing reading instruction and to evaluate the quality of responses and the processes used to develop these responses.

Construction. To prepare a set of stories that the pupil will read, first determine the readability of selections by using a readability formula or graph so that you will have selections at approximately the following readability levels:

---

[11] Brecht (1977) conducted a study to determine whether the IRI test passages should be read silently or orally first. He concluded that to get the best measure of a child's instructional reading level, we must allow him/her to read the selection silently first, a practice we have long advocated.

1.2	1.5	1.8	2.3	2.8	3.3	3.8	4.3	4.8
5.5	6.5	7.5	8.5	9.5 (and higher if needed).

For each story deleted, duplicate a segment of 100 to 200 or more words. On the duplicated copy of the story the examiner marks the errors that the pupil makes during oral reading. Also duplicate on a separate sheet the two to four literal comprehension questions and the two or three interpretation questions that will be used to determine a student's understanding after reading the selection(s) silently. After each question place the correct answer(s) in parentheses as well as the number of points given for a completely correct response and partial credits for partially correct responses.

Of course, the interpretation questions require the student to make inferences, see relationships, and draw conclusions. One must be forewarned that one uses processes to obtain products. When the main idea is a product that can be obtained because it is directly stated and requires relatively simple processes, then we say literal comprehension is involved. Or it can be indirectly stated or hinted at so that one needs to use inferential processes such as inductive reasoning, deductive reasoning, or analogy to develop the product or main idea. The same holds true for details and conclusions. A conclusion may be very directly stated or one may have to infer it.

We must also note that a "why" question is not automatically an interpretation question (the answer to it may be directly stated). Nor is a "what" question always merely a literal comprehension question. One may have to infer the answer by using the reasoning processes of induction, deduction, and analogy.

Five or ten vocabulary words in sentence context and of appropriate difficulty may also be listed for the student to define. The terms selected should be related to the topic of the reading selection and should be definable. A rule of thumb might be to select about two thirds of the items from the selection and about one third that are closely related to the topic and of a difficulty level commensurate with that of the reading selection. One may include the vocabulary test as part of the silent/oral reading inventory, in which case it would comprise 10 per cent of the test, or one may compute a separate vocabulary-in-context score and convert it to a per cent rating.

Administering the Test. After determining an approximate reading level by administering the *Hafner Quick Reading Test* and subtracting roughly one grade level from the result, use the resultant figure as an estimate of the reading level selection you will first present to the student. Then develop an interest in the selection you are asking him/her to read. Next have the student read the selection silently and then ask him/her the literal comprehension and the interpretation questions. Allow the student to reinspect the material to determine answers. Kender and Rubenstein (1977) determined that pupils should be allowed to reread, that is, reinspect, the selection as necessary before answering the question(s). High-ability fourth-graders scored 23 per cent higher by reinspection than by recall; low-ability fourth-graders scored 20 per cent higher by reinspection. We advocate the reinspection method. Note the responses. Then ask the pupil to read the selection orally; note errors in pronunciation according to the "Code for Checking Oral Errors." Finally, if you are doing the vocabulary-in-context test, you may do it at this time.

One should always be sensitive to the child's performance and obvious feelings about it. If the student is not doing well and is showing signs of frustration, drop to a level at which you think he/she will do well. Do not wait too long into the testing situation before you do that or you may not get his/her cooperation even after you give him/her an appropriate reading selection.

Scoring the Test. Determine the word-recognition accuracy by dividing the number of errors by the number of words in the reading selection. Subtract this quotient from 100; the result is the percentage of accuracy in oral reading. Compute the percentage correct in comprehension by totaling the points. Partial credits may be given for certain items. A separate score may be determined for vocabulary or you may include it in the total score. In the latter case, 90 per cent of the items would be literal comprehension-interpretation (60 per cent literal comprehension, 30 per cent interpretation) and ten per cent vocabulary.

Performance Criteria for Informal Reading Tests. For the silent reading test— the comprehension-interpretation phase—and the oral reading test there are several levels that must be determined: the instructional level, the independent level, and the frustration level. (You don't actively seek the frustration level, but it may occur during testing.) Basically, one wants to discover the student's reading instruction level. Whatever the materials used for reading, the teacher wants to know which level book to use for effective instruction. Remember, too, that the alert teacher will also want to know which level content area text(s) the student can handle and will take appropriate steps to find out.

Performance Criteria for Silent/Oral Reading Tests. The same three levels must be determined for the silent/oral reading tests: the independent level, the instructional level, and the frustration level. Basically, one wants to discover the student's instructional level for reading instruction. If a teacher is using a "basal" reader for instructional purposes, he/she wants to know which level book to use. If he/she is using a content area text for expository instruction, a teacher will determine instructional level by similar procedures.

As explained previously, it is important to determine a person's capacity level; that is, the level at which he/she could be performing if not encumbered by word-recognition problems and the like. Procedures for determining the capacity level were treated earlier in the chapter.

Instructional Level. To determine at what level day-to-day reading instruction should be carried on, have the child read selections from an informal inventory (silent/oral) and check his/her comprehension-interpretation score and oral reading score. Minimum criteria percentages for these two facets of reading are oral reading, 95 per cent correct, and comprehension-interpretation, 75 per cent correct.

What is Sandy's instructional level if she makes these scores?

Selection Level	Oral Reading %	Comprehension-Interpretation %
Fourth grade	80	63
Third grade	95	78
Second grade	98	90

By applying the criteria of having to score at least 95 per cent correct in oral pronunciation and 75 per cent in comprehension, we ascertain Sandy's instructional level to be third grade, because that is the highest level at which she scored at least 95 per cent correct in oral pronunciation and at least 75 per cent in literal comprehension-interpretation.

Independent Level. At what level can a pupil read on his/her own, make very few pronunciation errors, understand most of what he/she reads, and feel rather confident about the whole process? Our pupil should manifest these behaviors at the level in which he/she scores at least 98 per cent on oral reading (pronunciation) and at least 90 per cent in comprehension-interpretation on reading a selection. This level of good, confident achievement is called the independent level.

Frustration Level. When a lower level of performance—50 per cent or less in comprehension and 90 per cent or less in oral pronunciation—blocks learning and exploration and appears to bother the child, that performance represents the child's frustration level. Often a pupil who is reading on his/her frustration level will exhibit behaviors that indicate difficulty and associated frustration: moving lips, pointing with the finger, restlessness, and so on. (However, it is not necessarily wrong for beginning readers to point with their fingers.)

What is Franklin's *frustration* level under the following circumstances?

Per Cent Correct

Reading Level	Frustration Behavior	Oral Reading	Comprehension-Interpretation	Interest	Learning
Sixth grade	yes	80	45	low	not much
Fifth grade	no	90	65	average	some
Fourth grade	no	95	80	high	yes
Second grade	no	98	92	high	yes

For the particular pieces of material used, sixth grade appears to be a real frustration level for Franklin.

Let's use these data, then, to determine Franklin's independent reading level and his instructional reading level. He meets the independent level criteria (98 per cent oral and 90 per cent comprehension) at the second-grade level and the instructional level criteria (95 per cent oral and 75 per cent comprehension) at the fourth-grade level.

Exploration Level. A pupil's exploration level is that at which he/she is reading the material well enough to learn something and to enjoy the reading. For example, a child in the primary grades might be particularly fond of reading an encyclopedia of history. By no means could the child be expected to pronounce 98 per cent of the words accurately or understand 90 per cent of the content. However, he/she might understand the material well enough so that concepts could be gained and interest held. To deprive a child of such a golden opportunity to explore because his/her "independent" level at this age is at fifth or sixth grade is not right.

Code for Checking Oral Errors. As the pupil reads the selection, the examiner notes on the duplicated copy of the selection mispronunciations, omissions, substitutions, insertions, repetitions, and inversions of word order. Each of these mistakes counts as one error.

1. *Supplying Word.* After a pupil pauses for five seconds, apparently unable to pronounce a word, or after ten seconds of attempting to pronounce it, supply the word and put a check mark ($\sqrt{}$) over it.

2. *Mispronunciation.* Underline the word and write the child's pronunciation above the word. Example:

> *pray*
> freight [1 error]

3. *Partial Mispronunciation.* Example:

> *phone*
> telegram [1 error]

4. *Omission.* Circle omitted elements. Example:

> (ma)jesty [1 error]
>
> fast (as a) jet [1 error]

5. *Insertions:* The insertion of an element into a word counts as an error. Example:

> *gest*
> The big cars were moving along [1 error]

The insertion of a word or several words counts as one error. Example:

> *very nice*
> The little girl received a present. [1 error]

6. *Substitution.* If one word is replaced by a substitution of a word or words, count it as one error. Example:

> *moon*
> The sun shone. [1 error]
>
> *were not*
> The boys had much fun. [1 error]

If two words are replaced it counts as one error. Example:

Now is the time. [1 error]

Help the little girl. [1 error]

7. *Repetitions.* Underline the repeated word or words with a wavy line. Example:

The teacher will tell you what to do. [Don't count the error even though you note it.]

Thank you for helping me. [Don't count.]

8. *Inversions of Word Order.* Mark as follows:

This is it. [1 error]

The man was happy to be home. [1 error]

Cognitive Taxonomy IRI. Frazier and Caldwell (1977) constructed a test for second- and third-grade pupils that related to content suitable for primary grades, conformed in part to standard objective test format, and consisted of questions from the first four levels of Bloom's cognitive taxonomy: knowledge, comprehension, application, and analysis. Higher-level questions were as difficult to write as they were for the children to answer. The test included multiple-choice and open-end items. The percentage of pupils who passed various item types were as follows: knowledge, 81; comprehension, 68; application, 66; analysis, 37.

Group Reading Inventory

Classroom teachers often have difficulty in obtaining tests that they can use as they see fit. Therefore, we are including in the testing appendix a group inventory developed by the senior author (Hafner, 1977). At this point we will discuss only the Silent Reading Test: word recognition, (RL 1–5.0)[12] and comprehension (RL 1–16[+]), and vocabulary, RL 1–13, added since the 1977 version.

1. *Title: The Hafner Comprehensive Group Reading Inventory.*
2. *Author:* Lawrence E. Hafner.
3. *Publisher:* Originally published in Hafner (1977); published in the present volume by permission of the author and the publisher. (New York: Macmillan Publishing Co., Inc., 1977 and 1982).
4. *Reading Levels:* Prereading through college level. (The very brightest students in grade 8 will need some of the upper regions of the comprehension test.)
5. *Areas Tested:* B. Silent Reading:[13] word recognition, (RL 1–5.0); compre-

---

[12] Expanded from 3.0 to 5.0.
[13] The comprehension test is difficult more by dint of semantic complexity than syntactic complexity.

hension (RL 1–16+), and vocabulary (RL 1–13). Supplemental individual tests: *Hafner Quick Reading Test: Expanded Version* (RL 1–13) and *Hafner Quick Phonics Test.*

6. *Comments:* "These tests cover a wide range of skills and levels of difficulty. The upper levels of the comprehension test are quite difficult. The comprehension test uses a cloze, multiple-choice format. The tests use a multiple-choice format and have the ordinary advantages and disadvantages of tests of this kind" (Hafner, 1977).

INFORMAL READING AND INDEPENDENT WORD IDENTIFICATION SKILLS TESTS

Reading Tests

Word Recognition Tests. The ability to read words can be tested by having the pupil read graded word lists and/or read contextual material, as in an informal reading inventory, and noting percentage of words correctly pronounced.

Hafner Quick Reading Test: Expanded Version (HQRT). See Appendix A. The *HQRT* correlates highly with standardized word recognition tests and markedly with reading comprehension tests; of course, students generally obtain a higher grade level placement on word recognition tests than they do on reading comprehension tests. That is to be expected because teaching word recognition is emphasized more than teaching reading comprehension. It yields the correct level for ability to read words in isolation. There are 13 levels to this test, grade 1 through college, with ten words at each level.

Reading Comprehension Tests. There are many ways of measuring reading comprehension. We have provided in Appendix A the *Hafner Multilevel Reading Test,* which is the reading comprehension test of the *Hafner Comprehensive Group Reading Inventory* discussed in this chapter. The complete test is found in Appendix A.[14] For any given way of measuring comprehension there are proponents and opponents. Some of the ways of measuring and examples of these ways follow:

1. *Passage plus questions*
   a. Teacher-made IRIs (geared to specific instructional material).
   b. Commercial IRIs (representative instructional material).
   c. Commercial norm-referenced tests.

2. *Cloze passages*
   a. Teacher-made cloze passages (based on specific instructional material).
   b. Teacher-made cloze passages (geared to representative instructional material).

---

[14] This group reading inventory is not presented in the appendix as a unit. Subtests of the inventory are placed under the appropriate skill headings.

3. *Cloze passages plus multiple-choice response array*

a. Teacher-made cloze test.

b. *Hafner Multilevel Reading Test* (See Appendix A; "normed" by correlating with existing standardized tests).

Independent Word-Identification Skills Tests

Graphones (Phonic Elements) Tests. The *Hafner Quick Phonics Test (HQPT)* contains a number of subtests with ten randomly selected phonic elements per subtest. The *HQPT* is useful as a screening device. It can be found in Appendix A.

The following elements are tested in the *HQPT—Revised*:

LN-C: Letter Names-Consonants.
LN-V: Letter Names-Vowels.
L-TSS: Letters-Typical Speech Sounds.
CB: Consonant Blends.
CD: Consonant Digraphs (Phonemic options).
VC: Vowel Clusters (Phonemic options, 3 groups).
OC: Other Combinations.

READING PROFILES

Reading Capacity and Performance

A person's potential for reading achievement should be measured, evaluated, and recorded on a profile such as the one seen in Table 7–2. If the scores are converted to grade placement, entry into the profile can be made from the left-hand column—grade placement. If the scores are converted to age placement, entry can be made in the right-hand column.

For example, if a pupil obtains a vocabulary comprehension score that has a grade placement equivalent of 4.3, follow the column down to 4.0–4.4. Move to the right (to the columns of dots under *vocabulary*). If a standardized test was used, circle the dot under *S*. If an informal test was used, circle the dot under *I*. A comparable age placement can be obtained by going to the far right column and reading the corresponding age, which will be the vocabulary-comprehension age.

Enter the name of the test in the appropriate place beneath the profile.

PART 4. CRITERION-REFERENCED INVENTORIES

Many years ago Thorndike (1913) recommended the use of a testing procedure that set forth certain objectives for students to achieve. However, the common method of testing had been to test students on a poorly defined set of skills and then compare a student's achievement with other students'

Name _____ Birthdate _____ Chronological Age _____
Grade _____ Date _____

Table 7-2. Reading Capacity and Performance Profile

	Capacity								Performance				
	Language and Conceptual					Perceptual			Reading				
				Intell.			Seq. Mem.	Mem.			Comprehension		
Grade Placement	*Listen. Comp.*	*Vocab. Comp.*	*Gen'l. Info.*		*Verbal Comprehension*	*Aud. Blend.*	*Aud.*	*Vis.*	*Word Recog.*	*Level*	*Accuracy*		*Age Placement*
	S* I†	S I	S I		S I	S I	S I	S I	S I	S₁ S₂ I₁ I₂ S			
13.0+	.	.	.	.	.	.	.		.	.			18.3+
12.0-12.9	.	.	.	.	.	.	.		.	.			17.3-18.2
11.0-11.9	.	.	.	.	.	.	.		.	.			16.3-17.2
10.0-10.9	.	.	.	.	.	.	.		.	.			15.8-16.2
9.0- 9.9	.	.	.	.	.	.	.		.	.			14.3-15.2
8.5- 8.9	.	.	.	.	.	.	.		.	.			13.8-14.2
8.0- 8.4	.	.	.	.	.	.	.		.	.			13.3-13.7
7.5- 7.9	.	.	.	.	.	.	.		.	.			12.8-13.2
7.0- 7.4	.	.	.	.	.	.	.		.	.			12.3-12.7

11.8-12.2
11.3-11.7
10.8-11.2
10.3-10.7
9.8-10.2
9.3- 9.7
8.8- 9.2
8.3- 8.7
7.8- 8.2
7.3- 7.7
6.8- 7.2
6.3- 6.7

6.5- 6.9
6.0- 6.4
5.5- 5.9
5.0- 5.4
4.5- 4.9
4.0- 4.4
3.5- 3.9
3.0- 3.4
2.5- 2.9
2.0- 2.4
1.5- 1.9
1.0- 1.4

Names of Tests Used:

Listening Comprehension _____
Vocabulary Comprehension _____
General Information _____
Word Recognition _____
Comprehension Level _____
Comprehension Accuracy _____

Intelligence _____
Auditory Blending _____
Auditory-Sequential Memory _____
(auditory digit span test)
Visual-Sequential Memory _____
Verbal Comprehension _____

*S = Standardized Test †I = Informal Test

249

achievement. Such norm-referenced tests, as ordinarily used, are not especially useful for determining how students are achieving specific curriculum
objectives.

Norm-referenced tests tell how one person performs compared to another
person or group of persons and how a group performs compared to another group. They reveal how students are doing generally in reading skills
but not how they are attaining specific objectives in a reading curriculum.

What is needed is a better system of monitoring what teachers are doing and
of determining the exact information students know and the particular behaviors they can perform. The public wants to know exactly what students
know and do not know. A grade of A or D or a percentile rating on a test does
not tell what a person knows or can do. *Criterion-referenced tests* are needed
to provide certain kinds of information needed by teachers and the public.

"A criterion-referenced test is one that is deliberately constructed to yield
measurements that are directly interpretable in terms of specified performance
standards" (Glaser, 1970). These tests measure attainment of specified instructional objectives. Such objectives are spelled out before instruction begins, and
each objective specifies what must be done to show mastery of it. These objectives are ostensibly set up in a hierarchy. A given level in a hierarchy has
prerequisites and is also requisite to the succeeding level.

Notice the difference between an ordinary reading objective (ORO) and a
behaviorally stated reading objective (BSRO):

> ORO: Has a sight word vocabulary of 100 to 170 words.
> BSRO: Given a maximum two-second exposure per word, the pupil is able to
> recognize the first 133 words from the Kucera-Francis list.
> ORO: Chooses appropriate meaning of multiple meaning words.
> BSRO: Given a multiple-meaning word in varied contexts, the pupil is able to
> choose the meaning appropriate to the context. (The pupil chooses the appropriate
> given definition of spring for each of the following contexts: "The lion was about
> to spring." "We had a drink at the spring." "The violets bloom in the Spring."
> (From the Wisconsin Design for Reading Skill Development (Otto and Askov,
> 1970).

What might prove to be useful, then, is a program of criterion-referenced
achievement tests. The *Wisconsin Design,* among others, provides such tests.
It will be mentioned again in the present chapter.

ASSUMPTIONS

The Need to Know CRT and Subject Matter

People who work in the field of criterion-referenced testing must know subject matter well enough to work in a specific field and/or recognize and use an
expert in that area.

CRT Is Important

Criterion-referenced testing is, in truth, important. It is used to measure attainment of particular performance standards in mastery learning, performance contracting, and the like. It can be a good way of monitoring the performance of pupils vis-a-vis the curricula in the various subject matter and skills areas.

Limitations/Unresolved Questions in CRT

Good Tests Cannot Overcome Poor Objectives. A test item designed to evaluate accomplishment of a reading objective, for example, will not be satisfactory if the objective is not valid. An objective, in turn, cannot be valid if it is grounded in poor theory and/or is otherwise poorly designed.

Can CR Tests Measure Complex Domains Adequately? Complex domains such as reading comprehension cannot be measured adequately by tests constructed by individuals or groups of individuals who do not understand both reading comprehension theory and test construction.

Is There Enough Control of or Consideration of Semantic Content? There probably is not enough control of semantic content in either NRTs or CRTs. More consideration of the level, complexity, and nature of semantic content must go into the development of CR tests.

What Is the Problem With One-Time Demonstration of Mastery-Stated Objectives? One-time demonstration of objectives may overshadow attention to objectives that involve long-term retention and transfer of what is learned to higher-level skills (Otto, 1973).

Is "Small" Necessarily Propaedeutic to Big? It cannot be assumed that because a learning unit is small it is necessarily prerequisite to learning a larger unit that contains it. For example, one doesn't necessarily have to know phonic elements before one can read words.

Can Teachers Get Bogged Down With Record Keeping? The need for extensive record keeping by teachers in addition to their myriad existing duties has spawned some negative attitudes. Poorly planned assessment programs, especially those that are not carefully thought out and pilot-tested in terms of time requirements for record keeping, do not help education. Also, when poor management systems are a part of CRT, then not enough time remains for teachers to do their planning and teaching. Furthermore, overemphasis on the simple readiness and reading skills, with resultant self-satisfaction on the part of testing personnel that something is really being accomplished, means there may be too great a chance that the skills requiring higher-level thinking by both teacher and students will be sorely neglected.

Both Criterion-Referenced and Norm-Referenced Tests May Be Used. We have already shown that CRT is useful. NRT is useful under the following conditions:

1. When correlations among various educational and capacity factors are desired.

2. When the relative standing of a pupil vis-a-vis other pupils is desired.

3. When the goal is to show gain in achievement stated in various kinds of standard scores or grade placement scores.

4. When scores for various acceptance (into programs or educational institutions) and placement purposes are needed.

Usual Indices of Validity and Reliability Are Not Applicable. Obviously, content validity is necessary. But the type of validity that depends upon a percentage of certain kinds of pupils passing given items is not appropriate in CR testing.

Cox (1971) states, "Test items answered correctly by all examinees or no examinee will have difficulty levels of 1.00 and 0.00, respectively, and cannot discriminate in the usual sense between those scoring high and low on the total test."

One can determine items useful for pretest diagnosis by subtracting the percentage of pupils who pass an item on a pretest from the percentage who passed it on the post-test. (It is assumed that the larger the difference, the more valid the item.)

The question of the theoretical validity of an item (which we raised earlier) is still a specter. For example, in reading comprehension, one not only tests the ability to obtain a product such as the main idea but also measures the two ways by which this product can be obtained: the ability to identify a clearly stated main idea, and the ability to use inferential reasoning processes to develop the main idea. The former is literal comprehension and the latter is interpretation.

NATURE OF INSTRUCTIONAL OBJECTIVES

Traits Desired in the Individual Instructed. Garvin (1971) points out that "a statement of instructional objectives must specify the desired final state of the trait or traits involved within the individual instructed. This may be the maximum level of which he is capable or it may be desired that he attain some predetermined level of this trait." He gives the following examples:

1. Any task in which the public safety is involved must be performed at a specifically high level: landing an airliner at O'Hare airport, or compounding a prescription.

2. Mediocre performance that can be remedied might be acceptable in areas such as cooking, house painting, and spelling.

3. Ineptness or minimum performance might be accepted in golfing, acting, and writing poetry, particularly on an amateur basis.

Four Kinds of Instructional Objectives. Briggs (1970) lists four kinds of instructional objectives that one needs to develop when designing performance-based instruction: (1) lifelong objective, (2) end-of-course objective, (3) unit objective, and (4) specific behavioral objective. He illustrates these for a theme in science:

Lifelong Objective. The student will be able to give an intelligent informal, social discussion of future environmental needs for survival of astronauts on a two-month mission, in terms of hazards to be overcome (radiation, zero gravity, oxygen, cold), and to suggest principles used in designing the protective environment.

End-of-course Objective. At the conclusion of instruction on each behavioral objective pertaining to topics such as friction, gravity, force, work, the student will be able to write a theme showing the application of each principle learned in each topic if used in designing a space vehicle life support environment.

Unit Objective. The student can use the concepts of gravity and force to compute physical work load abilities of men at zero gravity.

Specific Behavioral Objective. Given five problems in which the student must compute the force required by men working at tasks at zero gravity, given the force at sea level, the student will show all formulas used correctly, and must miss the correct values by no more than five per cent in four of the five problem tasks.

Mager (1962) described three formal criteria for writing behavioral objectives:
1. *Given what,* the
2. *Student does what*
3. *How well.*

Did the specific behavioral objective in science meet all three criteria?

What Constitutes a Meaningful Instructional Objective (IO) Criterion?

We have just discussed important types of objectives and the three formal criteria for a behavioral objective. Garvin (1971) makes the following important points about what constitutes a meaningful IO criterion:

1. One can set an entering level of competence for it. (For example, prior to teaching graphones inductively, one might require of a pupil a specified level of performance in auditory discrimination, ability to read nucleus words, and ability to understand simple paragraphs.)

2. It arises from tasks performed outside the classroom but is not independent of the capabilities displayed within the classroom.

   a. An arbitrary standard of performance specified by the instructor is not a criterion; for example, requiring a student to diagram four out of five selected sentences correctly is not a meaningful criterion.

   b. Requiring a correct diagnosis from a standard set of symptoms is an example of a meaningful criterion.

3. It must lie within the range of capabilities of those (capabilities) available to perform the task involved. For example,

   a. There is no point in demanding great reading speed for entry into grade 3.

   b. One would not rate all piano students against a Horowitz recording.

4. Behavioral objectives must specify the behaviors involved. (See the example here of the specific science behavioral objective and Mager's three formal criteria for writing behavioral objectives.)

Variety of Teaching-Learning Methods. The following paradigm is not meant to be exhaustive nor are the elements under a given heading to be used to the exclusion of other elements; often they are used in an integrated manner. For a given project or task, several methods may be used, various processes called upon, and a number of products result.

Methods/Delivery Systems	Processes	Products
independent reading	associate	associations
guided reading questions	differentiate	concepts
programmed learning	manipulate	rules
directed reading lessons	rearrange	facts
lecture	build	main ideas and
lecture-discussion	memorize	supporting ideas
illustrated lecture	recall	generalizations
movies	develop literal	conclusions
	meanings	
slides	interpret:	relationships
	deduce	
audio tapes	induce	directions
radio	develop analogies	object
television	criticize	
demonstrations	apply	
field trips	solve a problem	
posing a problem	analyze	
	compare	
	contrast	
	relate	
	synthesize	
	evaluate	

Variety of Correct Answers at Analysis and Synthesis Levels. Let us point out just a few situations in which there can be more than one correct answer or product:

Writing a letter.	Writing a report.
Writing a story.	Planning a picnic.
"Doing" a bulletin board.	Planning a budget.
Publishing a class newspaper.	Painting a portrait.
Designing a reading lesson.	Making a mockup of a
Planning a budget.	shopping plaza and park.
Composing a hymn.	

CRITERION-REFERENCED TESTS

Sample Reading Assessment Items

The following sample reading assessment items were designed by the authors to give the reader an idea of how such items can be constructed. Later in the chapter we will present items from the national reading assessment testing program.

Rhyming Words. Examiner: "Look at the three boxes on the page. Point to the first box. Now I am going to say two words. If they rhyme, put an X in the first box: tall, bell."

Now point to the second box. "If the next two words rhyme, put an X in the box: rain, pain."

Now point to the last box. "If the next two words rhyme, put an X in the last box: cat, sat."

1. ☐   2. ☐   3. ☐

Root Words. Examiner: "Look at the three words on the page. The first word is swimming. Draw a line under the root word in each of these words:

swimming   pitches   walks

Differentiating Beginning Consonant Phonemes. Examiner: "Look at the four pictures on the page. I will say the names of the pictures. One word does not start with the same sound as the others. Put an X under the picture of the word that does not start like the others: boy, ball, pin, bus."

Consonant Digraph(eme)-phoneme Relationship. Examiner: "I am going to say the three words that are on the page. In each word there are two letters that stand for one sound. Draw a circle around the two letters in each word that stand for one sound: chap, clash, with":

chap   clash   with

Reading a Map. Examiner: "On this page you will find a portion of a map and a key. Study the map and key carefully and then answer the six questions beneath the map."

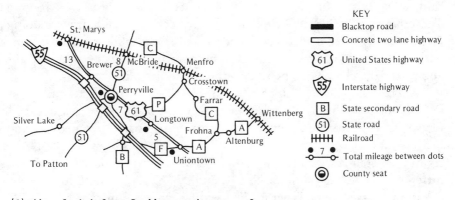

(1) How far is it from St. Marys to Longtown? _____

(2) What road runs from Perryville to McBride? _____

(3) How are McBride and Wittenberg most directly connected? _____

(4) What town is the county seat? _____

(5) What road parallels highway 61? _____

(6) I dentify the road that connects Uniontown and Wittenberg. _____

Listening: Short-term Memory for Details (requiring translation). (This could be made a reading test entirely by giving the students ten seconds to read the selection and then having them turn the page to the response section. Another way is to project the ditty on a screen for ten seconds.) Examiner: "Listen carefully to the verse I read and then turn to the next page. Write a + after the true statements and a 0 after the false statements:

Jim Trim could eat no brim.
His wife could eat no perch.
And so between the two, you see,
They ate a lot of red snapper.

(1) Mrs. Trim could not eat perch. _____

(2) Jim Trim could eat brim. _____

(3) Mr. and Mrs. Trim ate red snapper. _____

National Assessment Program (NAP)

A national assessment program was devised to inform the public more adequately what educational progress is being made and where the critical problems exist on which greater attention and effort must be concentrated, and to get intelligent backing for the discussions needed to use resources effectively so as to produce the greatest results (Tyler, 1974).

Prior to the NAP there were no comprehensive and dependable data about the educational attainments of our citizens. Consequently, Tyler points out, the schools have been criticized by those who had no evidence to support their claims. The press and the public were unable to correctly interpret the results of norm-referenced testing, the major type of testing prior to NAP. By definition, in most schools, 50 per cent of the children were not up to grade level. The press continually reported that 50 per cent of children were doing poorly in school. The tests were designed to distribute children in a normal curve pattern, but use of a percentile system in norming tests perpetuated the myths about half the class being behind in their schoolwork.

The NAP has been designed to sample those things that pupils should be learning in the schools and also the percentage of pupils who are learning them (Tyler, 1974). Norm-referenced tests are not designed to measure and report progress in that way. There are seven key distinctions between the NAP and the traditional standardized testing programs used in the majority of schools. These differences have been summarized by Finley (1974) in the following table.

National Assessment Program in Reading. In planning for the NAP/Reading Assessment it was assumed that the information gathered would help anyone interested in reading. The assessment is done in terms of reading themes or

Table 7–3. Characteristics of the National Assessment Program as
Compared with Traditional Standardized Testing Programs

National Assessment Program	*Standardized Testing Program*
1. National Assessment exercises measure how well students as a group achieve desirable goals.	Standardized tests compare students with the average performance of other students.
2. The time allotted to a given learning area ranges from six to eight hours each.	The time allotted to a given subject ranges from about 30 minutes to 70 minutes each.
3. National Assessment administers exercises to groups no larger than 12 and to individuals by interview.	Standardized tests are generally administered to total classes or groups of classes in a central location.
4. Exercises use a wide variety of stimuli and approaches often requiring the student to perform or to provide the correct response rather than just recognize it.	Test items are generally confined to that paper-and-pencil variety which can be scored by machine.
5. Exercises are prepared for the "high," the "average," and the "low" ability students.	Items are aimed at the "average" child.
6. Total scores, which reflect the number of students who got the correct answer, are given to each exercise. People do not receive total scores.	Total scores reflect the number of correct answers a student gives.
7. Results are reported on an exercise-by-exercise basis.	Results are reported in relation to a standardization group.

skill areas. For example, the theme called *Written Directions* requires one to read directions that are message-imparting materials telling how to do something. The theme *Inferences from Passages* "requires that a respondent derive a conclusion not stated in the passage but which might logically be expected to follow from the organization of the information in the passage." The sample items from Gadway (1972) measure eight major reading themes.

Sample Items Measuring Eight Major Reading Themes

AGE LEVEL:	9	13
RELEASE NO:	106	106
PACKAGE-EXERCISE NOS:	3–16	4–5
OBJECTIVE:	I B	
THEME:	1. Understanding Word Meanings	
	B. In Context	
IDENTICAL OR SIMILAR PASSAGES:	None	

MODE OF ADMINISTRATION:	Group Directions - Tape recorded Stem - Read by respondent Response - Written by respondent

TIME OF ADMINISTRATION:	Age 9: 1½ minutes Age 13: ¾ minute

COPYRIGHT REQUIREMENT:	No

People who run zoos sometimes put signs on animal cages to tell what the animals are like or where they come from. If you went to a zoo and saw these four signs on different cages, which one would tell you that there is a dangerous animal inside the cage? Fill in the oval beside the correct sign.

⊂⊃ Inside this cage is one of the smallest animals found in America.

⊂⊃ Inside this cage is an extremely ferocious animal.

⊂⊃ Inside this cage is an animal that sleeps all the time.

⊂⊃ Inside this cage is a rare type of eagle—one of the few left in the world.

⊂⊃ I don't know

AGE LEVEL:	9	13
RELEASE NO:	210	210
PACKAGE-EXERCISE NOS:	5-6	6-4
OBJECTIVE:	I B2	

THEME:	2. Reading and Visual Aids
	   A. Interpreting Drawings and
	      Pictures	

IDENTICAL OR SIMILAR PASSAGES:	None	
MODE OF ADMINISTRATION:	Group Directions - Tape recorded Stem - Read by respondent Response - Written by respondent	

TIME OF ADMINISTRATION:	Age 9:	1½ minutes
	Age 13:	¾ minute
COPYRIGHT REQUIREMENT:	No	
AGE LEVEL:	13	17
RELEASE NO:	309	309
PACKAGE-EXERCISE NOS:	4–4	9–7
OBJECTIVE:	II A3	

THEME: 3. Following Written Directions
                A. Understanding Written
                    Directions

IDENTICAL OR SIMILAR PASSAGES:		
	Age 13:	3–9(sim), 2–2(sim)
	Age 17:	7–10(sim), 8–3(sim)
	Adult:	2–6(sim)

MODE OF ADMINISTRATION: Group
                Directions - Tape recorded
                Stem - Read by respondent
                Response - Written by respondent

TIME OF ADMINISTRATION:	Age 13:	1½ minutes
	Age 17:	1½ minutes

COPYRIGHT REQUIREMENT: Editors of Better Homes and Gardens,
                Bread Cookbook. Copyright, 1963,
                by Meredith Publishing Company.

Director of Publications
Better Homes and Gardens Books
Meredith Corporation
1716 Locust Street
Des Moines, Iowa 50303

Look at the picture and fill in the oval beside the sentence which tells BEST what the drawing shows.

o   The boy has two dogs on a leash.

o   The boy is walking behind his dog.

o   The dog on the leash has spots on it.

o   The dog sitting down has spots on it.

o   I don't know.

Here is a recipe for making muffins. Read the recipe and answer the question which follows it.

ENGLISH MUFFINS

1 package active dry yeast
½ cup warm water
1 ½ cups milk, scalded
2 tablespoons sugar
2 teaspoons salt
¼ cup shortening
5 ¾ to 6 cups sifted all-purpose flour

Soften yeast in water. Combine next 4 ingredients; cool to lukewarm. Stir in 2 cups flour; beat well. Add yeast; mix. Add enough of remaining flour to make a moderately stiff dough. Turn out on a lightly floured surface; knead till smooth (8 to 10 minutes). Place in lightly greased bowl, turning dough once. Cover; let rise till double (1 ¼ hours).

After softening the yeast in the water, what 4 ingredients are combined next?

o   Scalded milk, sugar, salt, shortening

o   Yeast, warm water, scalded milk, sugar

o   2 cups flour, scalded milk, sugar, salt

o   2 cups flour, warm water, scalded milk, sugar

o   None of the above.

o   I don't know.

AGE LEVEL:	9	13
RELEASE NO:	408	408
PACKAGE-EXERCISE NOS:	7-3	13-2
OBJECTIVE:	III C3(2)	
THEME:	4. Reading and Reference Materials	
	A. Knowledge of Sources	

IDENTICAL OR SIMILAR PASSAGES:	None

MODE OF ADMINISTRATION:	Group
	Directions - Tape recorded
	Stem - Read by respondent
	Response - Written by respondent

TIME OF ADMINISTRATION:	Age 9:	1 minute
	Age 13:	¾ minute

COPYRIGHT REQUIREMENT:	No

Read the question and fill in the oval beside the correct answer.

If you had to tell your class about windmills, which of these would be the BEST book to use?

○   An atlas

○   A dictionary

○   An encyclopedia

○   The Yellow Pages in the telephone book

○   I don't know.

AGE LEVEL:	9

RELEASE NO:	A. 50101
	B. 70301
	C. 70302

PACKAGE-EXERCISE NO:	1–7

OBJECTIVE:	A. I CIb
	B. IV A
	C. IV B2

THEME:	A. 5. Reading for Significant Facts
	A. Recognizing Factual Information
	B. 7. Reading and Drawing Inferences
	B. Drawing Inferences from Information Given plus Additional Knowledge
	C. 7. Reading and Drawing Inferences
	A. Drawing Inferences from Information Given

IDENTICAL OR SIMILAR PASSAGES:	None

MODE OF ADMINISTRATION: Group
                                              Directions - Tape recorded
                                              Stem - Read by respondent
                                              Response - Written by respondent

TIME OF ADMINISTRATION: 4 minutes

COPYRIGHT REQUIREMENT: Dawson, Elwell, Zollinger, and
                                              Johnson, Language for Daily Use,
                                              Book 4. Published by Harcourt Brace
                                              Jovanovich, Inc.

                                              Rights and Permissions
                                              Harcourt Brace Jovanovich, Inc.
                                              757 Third Avenue
                                              New York, New York 10017

Read the story and answer the questions below. You may look back to this page
if you wish.

Mr. Popper was a house painter, but what he really wanted to do was travel to
the South Pole. When he wrote to Admiral Drake at the South Pole, telling him
how funny he thought penguins were, he never expected to get an answer. But
Admiral Drake did answer. He sent Mr. Popper a live penguin!

Can you imagine having a penguin for a pet? Mr. Popper named his penguin
Captain Cook and made him a home in the refrigerator.

It was not long, however, before Captain Cook became so lonely that he would
not eat. The keeper of a large aquarium sent Mr. Popper another penguin, named
Greta, who was lonely too. To take care of the two penguins, Mr. Popper had a
refrigeration plant installed in the cellar. Before long Greta and Captain Cook had
ten baby penguins.

Although the Poppers became very fond of the penguins, the birds caused many
problems. The problems they caused make a very funny story.

A. Which of the following is true of Admiral Drake?

    o He made refrigerators.

    o He was at the North Pole.

    o He wanted a penguin for a pet.

    o He had a girl friend named Greta.

    o He sent a penguin in answer to Mr. Popper's letter.

    o I don't know.

B. Why did Mr. Popper make Captain Cook's home in the refrigerator?

○ Penguins like milk.

○ Captain Cook was lonely.

○ Captain Cook liked to eat.

○ Penguins live in cold places.

○ Captain Cook had always lived in a refrigerator.

○ I don't know.

C. What is generally true about penguins?

○ They like to live alone.

○ They like painted houses.

○ They live in refrigerators.

○ They are difficult pets to care for.

○ They make excellent pets for city dwellers.

○ I don't know.

AGE LEVEL:	9	13
RELEASE NO:	618	618
PACKAGE-EXERCISE NOS:	9-4	12-15
OBJECTIVE:	IV A	
THEME:	6. Reading for Main Ideas and Organization B. Reading to Discover Organization	
IDENTICAL OR SIMILAR PASSAGES:	None	
MODE OF ADMINISTRATION:	Group Directions - Tape recorded Stem - Read by respondent Response - Written by respondent	
TIME OF ADMINISTRATION:	Age 9: 1½ minutes Age 13: 1¼ minutes	
COPYRIGHT REQUIREMENT:	No	

Read the two stories and answer the question which follows them.

Story 1

A handsome prince was riding his horse in the woods. He saw a dragon chasing a beautiful princess. The prince killed the dragon. The prince and the princess were then married.

Story 2

Mary was taking a boat ride on a lake. The boat tipped over. Mary was about to drown when a young man jumped in the lake and saved her.

If Story 2 ends like Story 1, what would happen next in story 2?

○ A prince would kill a dragon.

○ The young man would become a prince.

○ Mary and the young man would get married.

○ The king would give the young man some money.

○ I don't know.

AGE LEVEL:	9
RELEASE NO:	726
PACKAGE-EXERCISE NO:	8–5
OBJECTIVE:	IV A

THEME:	7. Reading and Drawing Inferences
	   B. Drawing Inferences from
	      Information Given plus
	      Additional Knowledge

IDENTICAL OR SIMILAR PASSAGES:	Age 9: 9–15, 7–2
MODE OF ADMINISTRATION:	Group Directions - Tape recorded Stem - Read by respondent Response - Written by respondent
TIME OF ADMINISTRATION:	1¾ minutes
COPYRIGHT REQUIREMENT:	No

Read the story and answer the question that follows it.

Christmas was only a few days away. The wind was strong and cold. The walks were covered with snow. The downtown streets were crowded with people. Their faces were hidden by many packages as they went in one store after another. They all tried to move faster as they looked at the clock.

What were most of the people probably doing?

○ Window-shopping

○ Waiting for a bus

○ Last-minute shopping

○ Looking at decorations

○ Talking to Santa Claus

○ I don't know.

AGE LEVEL:	7	13
RELEASE NO:	804	804
PACKAGE-EXERCISE NOS:	3–3	1–11
OBJECTIVE:	II C2	
THEME:	8. Critical Reading B. Recognizing Mood and Tone	
IDENTICAL OR SIMILAR PASSAGES:	Age 9: 1–3, 2–15, 4–8 Age 13: 2–13	

MODE OF ADMINISTRATION:	Group
	    Directions - Tape recorded
	    Stem - Read by respondent
	    Response - Written by respondent	

TIME OF ADMINISTRATION:	Age 9: 2 minutes Age 13: 1¼ minutes	
COPYRIGHT REQUIREMENT:	No	

Read the story and complete the sentence which follows it.

The wind whistled woefully as it wound its way through the nearly leafless trees. The pale yellow moon cast eerie shadows as it slipped in and out from behind the clouds like a blinking flashlight. Strange figures could be seen dashing and darting through the streets. Ghosts, goblins—what could they be? What do they want? Whom have they come to haunt? Beware . . .

The mood or feeling of this story is

○ amusing.   ○ gay.   ○ sad.

○ frightening.   ○ ridiculous.   ○ I don't know.

Skills Management Systems for Reading Instruction

The Wisconsin Design for Reading Skill Development, D–6. The Wisconsin Design has four main purposes:

1. To identify and describe behaviorally the skills that appear to be essential to competence in reading.

2. To assess the individual pupil's skill development status.

3. To manage instruction of children with different skill development needs.

4. To monitor each pupil's progress.

The SOBAR (System for Objectives-Based Assessment-Reading). Greene (1977) reviewed the SOBAR materials and found the whole package to be elegant but unnecessary.

Johnson and Pearson (1975) criticized skills management sytems (SMS) as instruments of accountability. The commercially available and locally developed systems with which they were familiar shared these components: (1) a sequentially ordered set of behavioral objectives for the various reading skills monitored by the system, (2) a set of subtests for measuring the objectives, (3) rules for deciding what level of achievement constitutes mastery of each objective, (4) a resource file listing specific workbook pages, ditto masters, and the like to use in providing instruction, and (5) a method of reporting to teachers which pupils have or have not mastered which skills.

Johnson and Pearson do not favor these systems for the following reasons:

1. They are psycholinguistically naive.

2. They are inappropriate applications of engineering rationality.

3. There is precious little evidence to support the existence of separate skills, let alone separate skills that can be placed into a sequence or hierarchy.

4. There does not seem to be evidence that subtest performance is related to any generally accepted measure of a real reading task.

In sum, they contend that SMSs do not provide a reasonable framework for establishing an accountability system for teaching reading.

SUMMARY

Teachers are interested in measuring reading achievement and capacity for achievement. Evaluation of the achievement is made in terms of capacity for reading and the goals of reading. The quality of measuring devices should be determined in terms of validity and reliability.

To determine capacity for reading, one should use a test with nonreaders and poor readers that does not involve reading. Generally, individual intelligence tests and auditory comprehension tests are capacity tests that meet that criterion.

The teacher will want to use informal inventories to evaluate reading performance. The main purpose of giving IRIs is to ascertain a pupil's instructional reading level.

Directions for constructing, administering, scoring, and interpreting IRIs are detailed in the chapter. It is important to note again that the most valid method of administering the IRI allows the student to reinspect the reading material in order to develop the answer. In this way, understanding and memory are not confounded. Some practitioners, however, will prefer not to allow reinspection.

Also included in the chapter are directions for constructing informal capacity tests—a point-scale intelligence test and an auditory comprehension test. Several commercial capacity tests are also discussed.

Criterion-referenced tests are designed to measure attainment of specified instructional objectives that are set up in a hierarchy. Criterion-referenced testing is important because it is used to measure attainment of particular performance standards in mastery learning, performance contracting, and the like.

There are real limitations and unresolved questions in CRT that must be taken into consideration before embracing testing programs or embarking on a project of writing CRT items. To be successful in writing behavioral objectives, one must not only know content and theory but must meet three formal criteria for writing such objectives: (1) Given what, (2) the student does what, (3) how well.

The National Assessment Program (NAP) was devised to keep the public adequately informed about critical educational problems and progress made in rectifying them, and to get intelligent backing so as to produce the greatest results. Specifically, the NAP has been designed to sample those things that pupils should be learning in the schools and the percentage of pupils who are learning them.

LEARNING ACTIVITIES

1. Construct a set of informal reading inventories, using the suggestions given in this chapter.

2. Construct a set of informal listening inventories, using the suggestions given in this chapter.

3. Construct several capacity subtests of intelligence according to the suggestions given in this chapter.

4. Obtain copies of criterion-referenced reading tests and the manuals that accompany them. Discuss them in terms of the following:
   a. Validity.
   b. Administration and scoring time.
   c. Record keeping.
   d. Hierarchy of skills.
Then list the strengths and weaknesses of the tests as *you* see them.

5. Read reviews of these tests in the most recent edition of Buros' *Mental Measurements Yearbook* and journal articles. What are the strengths and weaknesses of the tests according to the testing and reading specialists? In the main, paraphrase your answers.

6. Administer segments of criterion-referenced reading tests to (a) elementary school pupils, (b) middle school students, (c) college students or other adults. To what extent do the higher-level reading skills seem to be dependent upon success in the lower-level skills such as the readiness skills (for students reading, say, at the lower-grade levels) and independent word-identification skills? Are adults adept at using independent word-identification skills?

7. Look for newspaper and magazine articles on criterion-referenced testing. What problems are being raised? What assumptions are being made? What would be the results if the recommendations in the articles were carried out? Would they be good for education? Explain.

8. Select an area of reading and write several criterion-referenced test items.

9. What do the latest findings on the NAP in reading portend for education?

10. Select several paragraphs of reading material and explain the relationships among the facts.

11. Select several National Assessment Program reading objectives and explain the abilities needed to accomplish them. Use paragraphs, questions, and the like to make your explanation more effective. You may use the NAP items if needed.

12. Why would you be careful about using the kinds of skills management systems discussed at the end of the chapter?

STUDY QUESTIONS

1. What is the difference between measurement and evaluation?

2. Under what conditions is one concerned about the following kinds of validity: (a) predictive, (b) concurrent, (c) construct, (d) content?

3. How can a person be more sure of doing a good job of measuring and evaluating?

4. What does capacity for reading mean? Elaborate.

5. How can one determine capacity for reading?

6. Why are informal inventories important?

7. Discuss the nature, purpose, construction, administration, scoring procedures, and performance criteria for informal silent/oral reading inventories.

8. How does one construct informal capacity inventories?

9. Which commercial inventories of capacity might be useful?

10. How does one construct an informal listening inventory?

11. What are some important measurable comprehension traits at the elementary and secondary levels? Explain.

12. Discuss the role of verbal reasoning in reading.

13. Explain the strengths and weaknesses of several norm-referenced survey reading tests.

14. Under what conditions would you use (commercial) individual survey reading tests. Explain the strengths and weaknesses of several such tests.

15. What are some good reasons for using informal reading inventories rather than norm-referenced reading tests?

16. What are criterion-referenced tests?

17. Explain how an ordinary reading objective differs from a behaviorally stated reading objective.

18. Under what conditions is norm-referenced testing useful?

19. How does the NAP differ from a standardized testing program?

RECOMMENDED READING

BURNS, P. C. and B. D. ROE. *Teaching Reading in Today's Elementary Schools*. Skokie, Ill.: Rand McNally & Company, 1980. Chap. 11.

CLARK, C. H. "Assessing Free Recall." *Reading Teacher*, 35 (4) (January 1982), 434–439.

CUNNINGHAM, P. M. "Match Informal Evaluation to Your Teaching Practices." *Reading Teacher*, 31 (1) (October 1977), 51–59.

HAUPT, E. J. "Writing and Using Literal Comprehension Questions." *Reading Teacher*, 31 (2) (November 1977), 193–199.

KARLSEN, B. "Reading: Assessment and Diagnosis of Abilities." In P. Lamb and R. Arnold (Eds.). *Reading: Foundations and Instructional Strategies*. Second Edition. Belmont, CA: Wadsworth Publishing Co., Inc. 1980.

LAPP, D. and R. J. TIERNEY. "Reading Scores of American Nine-Year-Olds: NAEP's Tests." *Reading Teacher*, 30 (7) (April 1977), 756–760.

MacGINITIE, W. H. "What Are We Testing?" In W. H. MacGinitie (Ed.). (See following.)

MacGINITIE, W. H. (Ed.) *Assessment Problems in Reading*. Newark, Del.: International Reading Association, 1973.

PAGE, W. D. and K. L. CARSON. "The Process of Observing Oral Reading Scores." *Reading Horizons*, 15 (3) (Spring 1975), 147–150.

PIKULSKI, J. J. "Criterion-Referenced Measures for Clinical Evaluation." *Reading World*, 14 (1974), 116–128.

POPHAM, W. J. *Educational Evaluation*. Englewood Cliffs, N.J.: Prentice-Hall, Inc., 1975.

SMITH, J. M., D. E. P. SMITH, and J. R. BRINK. *Criterion-Referenced Tests for Reading and Writing*. Two Volumes. New York: Academic Press, Inc., 1977.

SPACHE, G. D. and E. B. SPACHE. *Reading in the Elementary School*. 4th ed. Boston: Allyn & Bacon, Inc., 1976, 337–355.

STAUFFER, R. G., J. C. ABRAMS, and J. J. PIKULSKI. *Diagnosis, Correction and Prevention of Reading Disabilities*. New York: Harper & Row, Publisher, 1978. Chap. 5.

VENEZKY, R. L. "NAEP–Should We Kill the Messenger Who Brings Bad News?" *Reading Teacher*, 30 (7) (April 1977), 750–755.

REFERENCES

BERG, P. C. "Evaluating Reading Abilities." In W. H. MacGinitie (Ed.). *Assessment Problems in Reading*. Newark, Del.: International Reading Association, 1973.

BRECHT, R. D. "Testing Format and Instructional Level With the Informal Reading Inventory." *Reading Teacher*, 31 (1) (October 1977), 57–59.

BRIGGS, L. *A Handbook of Procedures for the Design of Instruction*. Pittsburgh: American Institutes for Research, 1970.

BUROS, O. K. (Ed.). *Seventh Mental Measurements Yearbook*. Highland Park, N.J.: Gryphon Press, 1972.

—— *Eighth Mental Measurements Yearbook*. Highland Park, N.J.: Gryphon Press, 1978.

COX, R. C. "Evaluative Aspects of Criterion-Referenced Measures." In W. J. Popham (Ed.) (See following.)

DAVIS, F. B. "Research in Comprehension in Reading." *Reading Research Quarterly*, 3 (4) (Summer 1968), 499–545.

DEUTSCH, C. P. "Auditory Discrimination and Learning: Social Factors." *Merrill-Palmer Quarterly of Behavior and Development*, 10 (1964), 277–296.

FINLEY, C. J. "Not Just Another Standardized Test." In R. W. Tyler and R. M. Wolf (Eds.). (See following.)

FRAZIER, K. and E. CALDWELL. "Testing Higher Cognitive Skills in Young Children." *Reading Teacher.* 30 (5) (February 1977), 475–478.

GADWAY, C. J. (National Assessment of Educational Progress) *Preliminary Report 02-R-00, Reading Summary.* Denver: Education Commission of the States, 1972.

GADWAY, C. J. (NAEP) *Report 02-R-20, Reading: Released Exercises 1970–71 Assessment.* Denver: Education Commission of the States, 1973.

GARVIN, A. D. "The Applicability of Criterion-Referenced Measurement by Content Area and Level." In W. J. Popham (Ed.). (See following.)

GLASER, R. (Ed.). *Criterion-Referenced Measurements.* Englewood Cliffs, N.J.: Educational Technology Publications, 1971.

GREENE, F. "Review of SOBAR." *Reading Teacher,* 30 (7) (April 1977), 822–823.

HAFNER, L. E. Unpublished study. Florida State University, 1978.

—— *Developmental Reading in Middle and Secondary Schools: Foundations, Strategies, and Skills for Teaching.* New York: Macmillan Publishing Co., Inc., 1977.

HAMMILL, D. "The Slosson Intelligence Test as a Quick Estimate of Mental Ability." *Journal of School Psychology,* 7 (4) (1968–1969), 33–37.

JOHNSON, D. D. and P. D. PEARSON. "Skills Management Systems: A Critique." *Reading Teacher,* 28 (8) (May 1975), 757–764.

KENDER, J. P. and H. RUBENSTEIN. "Recall Versus Reinspection in IRI Comprehension Tests." *Reading Teacher,* 30 (7) (April 1977), 776–779.

MAGER, R. F. *Preparing Instructional Objectives.* Palo Alto, CA: Fearon, 1962.

NICHOLSON, C. L. "Analysis of Functions of the SIT." *Perceptual and Motor Skills* (October 1970), 627–631.

OTTO, W. "Evaluating Instruments for Assessing Needs and Growth in Reading." In W. H. MacGinitie (Ed.) *Assessment Problems in Reading.* Newark, Del.: International Reading Association, 1973.

POPHAM, W. J. *Educational Evaluation.* Englewood Cliffs, N.J.: Prentice-Hall, Inc., 1975.

SCHREINER, R. L., A. N. HIERONYMUS, and R. FORSYTH. "Differential Measurement of Reading Abilities at the Elementary School Level." In *Reading Research Quarterly,* 5 (Fall 1969), 184–199.

SMITH, J. M., D. E. P. SMITH, and J. R. BRINK. *Criterion-Referenced Tests for Reading and Writing.* Two Volumes. New York: Academic Press, Inc., 1977.

SPACHE, G. D. and E. P. SPACHE. *Reading in the Elementary School.* 4th ed. Boston: Allyn & Bacon, Inc., 1977, 337–355.

STAUFFER, R. G., J. C. ABRAMS, and J. J. PIKULSKI. *Diagnosis, Correction, and Prevention of Reading Disabilities.* New York: Harper & Row, Publishers, 1978. Chap. 5.

THORNDIKE, E. L. *An Introduction to the Theory of Mental and Social Measurements.* New York: Teachers College, Columbia University, 1913.

TYLER, R. W. and R. M. WOLF (Eds.). *Crucial Issues in Testing.* Berkeley: McCutchan Publishing Corp., 1974.

CHAPTER 8

Applying Evaluation and Teaching Strategies in the Schools

OBJECTIVES

As a result of thoroughly processing the material in this chapter and doing the suggested practicum the reader should be able to do the following:

1. *Use the Diagnosis-Development Flow Chart as an aid in diagnosing several students' capacity for reading and their reading achievement.*
2. *Carefully study the diagnostic data, prescribe instructional strategies, and develop the strategies.*
3. *Use the various formats for teaching reading lessons.*
4. *Perform the suggested practicum with elementary students in the schools.*
5. *Write a diagnosis-development report on your practicum.*

This chapter explains how to do diagnostic teaching of reading. The diagnostic segment focuses attention on informal tests of reading achievement, of aptitude for reading, and on administration, scoring, and interpretation of these tests. To aid in this procedure a test manual is included.

The correction/development segment emphasizes utilizing the diagnostic results to plan reading instruction. Several types of lesson plans will be explained. Also included is a complete case study done by an undergraduate student under our direction.

In order for prospective teachers to learn how to diagnose and teach, we have them administer a series of tests to students and, using the information obtained, plan instruction and then teach these students in small groups or individually. The tests used are included in Appendix A.

PART ONE: THE LOGISTICS OF DIAGNOSIS

Diagnosis-Development Flow Chart

When we place the students from our reading methods classes in the schools to do their reading practicum work, we require them to diagnose the capacity and the reading achievement of several pupils and to plan instruction on the basis of their findings. The use of our diagnosis-development flow chart is a great aid in sorting out the steps in the procedure. In practice one may not necessarily enter where it says ENTER, but we generally have our students enter at that point on the chart.

The Flow Chart (FC) may seem difficult, but it is much easier to explain the steps to take by visual means than by giving them orally; actually we do both. The following explanatory notes should prove helpful:

A. Progression.
    1. The general progression, beginning with readiness tests, is as follows:
        a. Readiness (Select the ones you want to use).
        b. Word recognition.
        c. Comprehension.
        d. Phonics (Capacity is skipped until later).
B. Diagnostic Steps.
    1. Administer *readiness* tests. (They are readily scored as you go along.)
    2. Administer the *word recognition* test and score immediately.
        a. Then check the diamond-shaped figure on the Flow Chart beneath the word recognition test.
            (1) If the student *cannot* read (response of *no*), follow the arrow to the box that suggests checking up on the readiness results.
            (2) If the student *can* read (response of *yes*), choose one of the options for a reading comprehension test. (There is a blank box for you to list another test of your choice.)
    3. Now you check the readiness tests to see basically how the person did on the auditory discrimination (A.D.) test and the visual discrimination (V.D.) test. Then check again to see how he/she did in word recognition and comprehension.
    4. Next you have four options. The two on the left have to do with students who *can* read.
        a. Box 1 tells you that if the student does well on auditory discrimination and can read, you can go ahead and give the phonics test and then remedy deficit areas. (Remediation generally takes place within the context of a complete reading lesson.)
        b. Box 2 states that if the student did not do well in auditory but can read, you should proceed to remedy any deficit areas in word recognition and reading comprehension. (One can also teach the student lessons designed to remedy auditory deficiencies. One should also take into consideration auditory segmentation deficiencies.)
        c. Boxes 3 and 4 have to do with students who cannot read.
            (1) Do you want to know if the student can learn to recognize words? Give the *Learning Rate Test.* If the student is successful on that test, you have options:
                (a) If you like the Language-Experience Approach, use that to teach reading acquisition (beginning reading.)

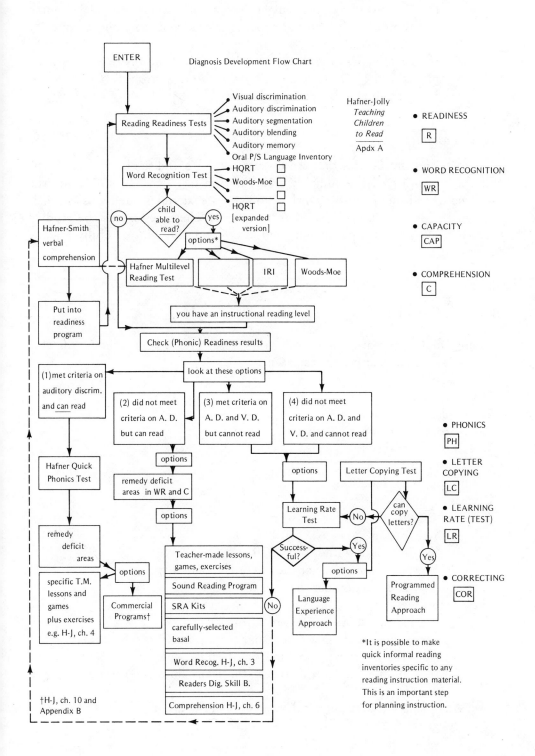

Diagnosis Development Flow Chart

ENTER

Reading Readiness Tests
- Visual discrimination
- Auditory discrimination
- Auditory segmentation
- Auditory blending
- Auditory memory
- Oral P/S Language Inventory

Hafner-Jolly
Teaching Children to Read
Apdx A

Word Recognition Test
- HQRT ☐
- Woods-Moe ☐
- ———— ☐
- HQRT ☐ [expanded version]

child able to read? — no / yes

options*

Hafner Multilevel Reading Test | IRI | Woods-Moe

Hafner-Smith verbal comprehension

Put into readiness program

you have an instructional reading level

Check (Phonic) Readiness results

look at these options

(1) met criteria on auditory discrim. and can read

(2) did not meet criteria on A. D. but can read

(3) met criteria on A. D. and V. D. but cannot read

(4) did not meet criteria on A. D. and V. D. and cannot read

Hafner Quick Phonics Test

options

remedy deficit areas in WR and C

options

remedy deficit areas

specific T.M. lessons and games plus exercises e.g. H-J, ch. 4

options

Commercial Programs†

options

Learning Rate Test

Letter Copying Test

can copy letters? — No / Yes

Successful? — Yes / No

Teacher-made lessons, games, exercises

Sound Reading Program

SRA Kits

carefully-selected basal

Word Recog. H-J, ch. 3

Readers Dig. Skill B.

Comprehension H-J, ch. 6

options

Language Experience Approach

Programmed Reading Approach

- READINESS
  R
- WORD RECOGNITION
  WR
- CAPACITY
  CAP
- COMPREHENSION
  C
- PHONICS
  PH
- LETTER COPYING
  LC
- LEARNING RATE (TEST)
  LR
- CORRECTING
  COR

*It is possible to make quick informal reading inventories specific to any reading instruction material. This is an important step for planning instruction.

†H-J, ch. 10 and Appendix B

273

(b) If you think you might like to use a programmed reading approach, give a letter-copying test. (See if the student can copy some letters.)

(2) If the student is *not* successful on the *Learning Rate Test,* administer the *Hafner-Smith Verbal Comprehension Test* in order to find out about his/her mental ability.

Testing Manual

The tests and inventories that are discussed in this and the previous chapter, with the exception of the auditory segmentation test (Rosner, 1973) and the visual sequential memory test (Kirk, 1968), and that our students use in their work in the schools are found in Appendix A. These tests must be studied *prior to* reading the testing manual *and in conjunction with* carefully reading the manual.

READINESS TESTS

A. Where Obtained: Hafner and Jolly, the present text, Appendix A (see also Chap. 7) or other sources as indicated.
B. The Tests:
   1. Visual Discrimination.
   2. Visual Sequential Memory.
   3. Auditory Discrimination (rhyming).
   4. Auditory Memory (also called Auditory Digit Span).
   5. Auditory Blending.
   6. Auditory Segmentation.
C. Discussion by Tests.
   1. *Visual Discrimination.*
      a. Administration.
         (1) See directions with test, p. 370.
         (2) You may want to print these words in larger type.
      b. Scoring: add the number that are correct.
      c. Recording.
         (1) Record raw score on Record Form.
         (2) Compute percentage correct and record on Record Form.
         (3) Note if score meets the criterion of 70 per cent.
         (4) If it does, place a + between the slant lines: /+/; if not, place a 0: /0/.
      d. Analyzing data: If person does not meet the criterion, there are several things that need to be done.
         (1) Check vision.
            (a) Nearpoint vision (Telebinocular device) or Titmus Vision Test.

(You may need to have this testing done by a qualified reading specialist.)

(b) Acuity.

(2) Check maturity level.

(a) Intelligence test results.

(b) Piagetian level.[1]

(c) Quality of visual discrimination instruction that has been given.

2. *Visual Sequential Memory.* This is a subtest of the *Illinois Test of Psycholinguistic Abilities* (ITPA) by Kirk and McCarthy (1968). Visual Sequential Memory is the "ability to reproduce sequences of nonmeaningful figures from memory." Special training is required to administer and interpret the test. However, we wanted to make you aware of the test.

3. *Auditory Discrimination.*

a. Administration.

(1) See directions with the test, Rhyming test, p. 371.

(2) You will be seated slightly in back of the examinee so that he cannot see your lips, or else he may get the right answer in the wrong way.

b. Scoring.

(1) Count the number correct.

c. Recording.

(1) Record raw score on the Record Form.

(2) Compute percentage correct and record on the Record Form.

(3) Note whether score meets the criterion of 70 per cent.

(4) If the score meets the criterion, place a + between the slash marks; otherwise mark a 0.

d. Analyzing Data: If the person does not meet the criterion of 70 per cent correct and he is in the first or second grade, corrective instruction should be started. See the readiness chapter in the present text. If the person is in the third grade, corrective instruction in auditory discrimination may be instituted, but the prognosis for improvement is not too good.

4. *Auditory Memory* (Auditory Digit Span).

a. Administration.

(1) See directions with the test, p. 394. Be sure to read the digits at the rate of one per second.

(2) This test is not valid unless it is administered in a quiet place, free from distractions.

b. Scoring.

(1) See directions with the test.

(2) Count the highest number of digits repeated correctly forward—5-8-1-4 is 4 digits—and add to highest number repeated correctly backward—2-9-4 is 3 digits—and add: 4 + 3 = 7.

---

[1] Our undergraduate students learn how to obtain these levels in another course.

(3) To convert raw score to Reading Grade Placement, consult Table 7–1 in chapter seven of the present text. In our example a Raw Score of 7 converts to a grade placement of 1.5.
  c. Recording.
    (1) Record the raw score and grade placement on the Record Form.
5. *Auditory Blending*
  a. Administration.
    (1) See directions with the test.
  b. Scoring.
    (1) See directions with the test.
  c. Recording.
    (1) Record raw score on the Record Form.
    (2) Compute percentage correct and record on Record Form.
    (3) If the percentage meets the criterion, place a + between the slash marks; otherwise mark a 0.
6. *Auditory Segmentation.* One can construct his or her own test of auditory segmentation from the instructions given earlier in this chapter and then develop some norms or guidelines. However, it would be easier to use the test developed by Rosner (1973).

LETTER KNOWLEDGE TEST

A. Choice of tests:
  1. Full test (26 letters), in Appendix A.
  2. Abbreviated test (15 letters), Test 1 of *Hafner Quick Phonics Test,* Appendix A.
    a. Administration: See appropriate directions.
    b. Scoring.
      (1) Write down items missed.
      (2) Count number of items correct.
      (3) Compute percentage correct: number correct divided by number of items on test.
    c. Recording.
      (1) Record in appropriate places on the Record Form raw score, percentage correct, and items missed.
    d. Analyzing data: Ability to learn letter names is one indicator of ability to learn words. Letter names not known should be taught using concrete mediating methods and devices.

CAPACITY TESTS

1. *Hafner-Smith Verbal Comprehension Test* (a basic learning aptitude test).
  a. Administration
    (1) Materials needed:

  (a) The questions or items (Appendix A).

  (b) A response sheet for each person who is tested (Appendix A).

  (c) The examiner records responses on the response sheet.

(2) Obtain all pertinent information—name, birthday—and record on response sheet.

(3) Determining the starting point.

  (a) If you think the subject has *average* ability, start one year and a half below his/her chronological age.

  (b) If you think the subject has *below* average ability, start two and a half years below his/her chronological age.

  (c) If you think the subject is quite a bit above average, start a year to a year and a half above his/her chronological age.

  (d) If the subject gets the first four items (from starting point) correct, you can assume correct on all items up to that point.

b. Scoring.

(1) An item is scored as 3 (months), 2, or 1, depending upon the completeness of the response.

(2) Write down the responses.

(3) The last item correct before a miss is the Basal Verbal Age; for example:

$$
\begin{array}{l}
\text{5--0 } \underline{3} \text{ (3)} \\
\text{5--3 } \overline{3} \text{ (3)} \\
\text{5--6 } \overline{3} \text{ (3)} \\
\text{5--9 } \overline{3} \text{ (3)} \\
\text{6--0 } \overline{3} \text{ (3)} \\
\text{6--3 } \overline{1} \text{ (3)} \\
\text{6--6 } \overline{3} \text{ (3)} \\
\text{6--9 } \overline{0} \text{ (3)} \\
\text{7--0 } 3 \text{ (3)} \\
\text{7--3 } 0 \text{ (3)} \\
\text{7--6 } 0 \text{ (3)} \\
\text{7--9 } \overline{0} \text{ (3)} \\
\text{8--0 } \overline{0} \text{ (3)}
\end{array}
$$

Basal Verbal Age (next to the 6–0 line)

(4) Stop when 4 items in a row are missed.

(5) To the Basal Verbal Age of 6–0, one adds one month credit (from the 6–3 level), 3 months' credit (from the 6–6 level) and 3 months' credit (from the 7–0 level):

Basal Verbal Age	6–0
Additional Credits	1
	3
	3
Verbal Comprehension Age	6–7

This may also be converted to Reading Grade Placement; see Table 7–2.

(6) To determine Verbal Comprehension Quotient, divide the Verbal

Comprehension Age by the Chronological Age. Assuming a Chronological Age of 6-0 and a Verbal Comprehension Age of 6-7, we compute: (First convert years and months to months)

$$VCQ = \frac{VCA}{CA} \times 100$$

$$= \frac{79}{72} \times 100$$

$$= 1.10 \times 100$$

$$= \underline{110}$$

c. Recording.
(1) Record Verbal Comprehension Grade Placement (VCGC), Verbal Comprehension Age (VCA), and Verbal Comprehension Quotient (VCQ) in appropriate places on the Record Form.
d. Analyzing data.
(1) Theoretically a person should be able to read "up to" his capacity. This expectation is predicated upon good perceptual ability, excellent teaching, good motivation, and the like.
(2) A VCQ between 90 and 100 is average; however, 110 is much greater than 90 because 110 borders on bright, whereas 90 borders on dull.

2. *Listening Comprehension.* Listening comprehension as a capacity test is predicated upon the idea that what a person can hear and understand puts a limit on the difficulty of language and ideas that he can process while reading. So one's Listening Comprehension Age is at once a facilitator and a limiter. Listening comprehension test materials are obtained by using the paragraphs of the Informal Reading Inventory (IRI) or commercial inventory.
a. Administration.
(1) Take the (reading) selection that is one level above the instructional level obtained when administering the IRI and read the selection to the subject. Immediately following this reading, ask the subject the questions.
(2) Record the subject's responses.
b. Scoring.
(1) Score the responses according to the predetermined answers or criteria. Partial credit may be given.
(2) Add the points the subject obtained for the selection.
(3) The criterion is 75 per cent correct.
(4) If the subject scores above 75 per cent, read the next highest selection.
c. Recording.
(1) Record on the Record Form the highest-level listening grade placement at which the subject meets the criterion of 75 per cent.

d. Analyzing data.
   (1) The Listening Comprehension Grade Placement (or age) can be interpreted in the light of the Verbal Comprehension Grade Placement (or Age).
   (2) The LC Grade Placement and the VC Grade Placement may be averaged and the average grade placement considered a more realistic estimation of ability.

READING TESTS

1. *Word Recognition:* Hafner Quick Reading Test–Expanded Version (HQRT–EV). There are 13 reading grade levels to this test, ten items at each reading grade level. The results give a quick estimate of the level at which the subject can read words. Since words were selected that at the upper levels are hard to "sound out," it is more likely that when a subject pronounces a word correctly he knows what it means. Therefore, this test should not yield scores as inflated as those on other oral reading tests. The results of this test are used as a guide for entering the Informal Reading Inventory (IRI). Enter one to two grade levels below the HQRT–EV grade placement. This test (HQRT–EV) can be found in Appendix A.
   a. Administration.
      (1) Directions are found with the test.
      (2) Start at level one and have subject read across the page. Mark incorrect responses. Stop when the subject misses four consecutive items.
      (3) For older subjects for whom the examiner has no idea of ability, one can have them read down the first column until a word is missed. Then drop one whole level below that level and have him read across. For example:

      The person misses the first word in the second row of level 6. Go back to the second row of level five and have the subject read across. Continue.

   b. Scoring.
      (1) Count as correct all accurate pronunciations. For example, *linear* must be pronounced as /lin'-ē-er/, not /lin-ēr/, to be counted as correct. If in doubt, have the subject tell you (without giving him or her the correct pronunciation) what the word means. If he/she can tell you what it means, count it correct regardless of pronunciation.
      (2) Add number correct.
      (3) Compute Reading Grade Placement according to this formula:

$$\text{R. Gr. Pl.} = \frac{\text{Number correct}}{10} + 1.$$

For example:

number correct = 33

$$R. \ Gr. \ Pl. = \left(\frac{33}{10}\right) + 1$$

$$= 3.3 + 1$$

$$= \underline{4.3}$$

c. Recording.
  (1) Record the raw score and reading grade placement on the Record Form.
d. Analyzing the data.
  (1) The results tell the examiner at which level a person can pronounce words accurately.
  (2) Words in context are usually easier to pronounce than words in isolation.
  (3) A person will usually score higher on a word recognition test such as the HQRT–EV than on a test of paragraph comprehension requiring the answering of literal comprehension and interpretation questions.
  (4) The results on the HQRT–EV can be used to estimate level of entry into an Informal Reading Inventory. Enter one or two grade levels below the HQRT–EV Grade Placement. Use your judgment.
2. *(Paragraph) Comprehension:* Informal Reading Inventory (IRI). Explanation of the IRI is given in Chapter 7 of the present text by Hafner and Jolly. (A new type of scoring can be found in Hafner's 1977 text). The IRI is designed to measure oral reading or pronunciation and comprehension.
  a. Administration.
    (1) See directions in the present text (or in Hafner's 1977 text).
    (2) Silent reading of a selection and answering of the questions are done before the oral reading of the selection.
    (3) The examiner will mark errors according to the "Code for Marking Oral Errors" in the present text (or in Hafner's 1977 text).
  b. Scoring.
    (1) Note directions on IRI selections.
  c. Recording.
    (1) Record the instructional reading levels on the Record Form.
  d. Analyzing the data.
    (1) One is interested mainly in the instructional reading level.
    (2) One can note the type of pronunciation errors and compare them with the results on the *Hafner Quick Phonics Test.*
3. *Hafner Multilevel Reading Test (HMRT).* The range of reading difficulty in this test is grade 1 through college. One may use the results of either

the HQRT–EV or the Reading Vocabulary Test to estimate where one should start. The other procedure is to let the students start at the beginning, since the various levels are related to a basic theme.

a. Administration: Directions are found with the test (Appendix A). The subjects may be allowed to work as many items as they wish. No time limit, but 30 minutes of working time is usually more than enough.

b. Scoring: See Answer Key. One point per item correct.

c. Recording: Record the raw score and reading grade placement on the Record Form.

d. Analyzing the data: The results tell one at which level the subject can read narrative text with understanding.

KNOWLEDGE OF PHONEMIC OPTIONS

There are many instances when a grapheme represents more than one phoneme. Students should learn these phonemic options. The following test samples many such options.

1. Hafner Quick Phonics Test.
   a. Administration.
      (1) See directions on the test.
      (2) See marked copy to understand how to mark the phonemic options. For example:

th /th/	ch /ch/
th /th/	ch /k /
	ch /sh/

In the examples, /th/ is voiceless, /th/ is voiced. Thus, when a subject says /th/ you indicate by marking /th/ after th.

When a person looks at ch and says /ch/, write /ch/ after one of the ch's; it doesn't matter which one. Discontinue when it is obvious the person is not doing well.

   b. Scoring.
      (1) Count the number correct in each section and record in the numerators in the right-hand column.
      (2) Determine the percentage for each section and put them in the correct place on the left-hand side of the page.
      (3) Profile the results on the Pupil Profile. Connect the results.
   c. Recording.
      (1) Record items correct and items missed on the Record Form.
   d. Analyzing data.
      (1) Note weak areas and select grapheme-phoneme associations that are to be taught in the near future.
      (2) Work these options into your lesson plans.

Record Form

Name _____   Birthdate _____

Grade Placement _____   C.A. _____

School _____   Examiner _____

Date of Testing _____

READINESS

Score (Per Cent)		Criterion
_____	Visual Discrimination	70% / /
_____	Letter Names-Consonants	80% / /
_____	Letter Names-Vowels	80% / /
_____	Auditory Discrimination	70% / /
_____	Auditory Blending	70% / /
_____	Auditory Segmentation	70% / /

		Gr. Pl.	Age	
_____	Auditory Memory	_____	_____	/ /
_____	Visual Sequential Memory	_____	_____	/ /

CAPACITY

Score

_____ – *Learning Rate Test _____ %

Hafner-Smith Verbal Comprehension Test

Verbal Age (V.A.) _____

Verbal Grade Placement _____

Verbal Quotient _____

READING

Word Recognition (Oral Reading)

Score		Grade Placement
_____	Hafner Quick Reading Test	_____
_____	Woods-Moe Reading Test	_____
_____	% Informal Reading Inventory	_____
_____	_____	_____

(Paragraph) Comprehension

Score		Grade Placement
	Woods-Moe Reading Test	_____
_____	Hafner Multilevel Reading Test	_____
_____	% Informal Reading Inventory	_____
_____	_____	_____

Phonics (Grapheme-Phoneme Associations)
Hafner Quick Phonics Test

Intelligence

Mental Age (M.A.) _____

Mental Grade Placement _____

Intelligence Quotient _____

Listening Comprehension

Listening Age _____

Listening Grade Placement _____

Listening Quotient _____

Individual Mental Abilities
Point Scale

Total Points _____

Oral P/S Language Inventory

Raw Score _____

Rating _____

Percent Correct		Known	Unknown
	Letters - typical speech sounds		
_____	Vowels		
_____	Consonants		
_____	Consonant Blends		
_____	Consonant Digraphs		
_____	Vowel Clusters		
_____	group 1		
_____	group 2		
_____	group 3		
_____	Other Combinations		

*Number of words correct on post-test one hour later is placed in the numerator. The number taught and tested is placed in the denominator. For example, 4 correct/5 taught = $5\overline{)4}$ = 80 per cent.

PART TWO: STUDYING THE DIAGNOSTIC DATA AND PRESCRIBING INSTRUCTION

We want to emphasize meaningful instruction rather than the fragmented instruction that has grown, in part, from aspects of the criterion-referenced testing movement. Therefore, most reading instruction will be integrated with the reading of narrative and/or expository selections. The selections will be a vehicle for instruction: the pupils will usually enjoy the selections and the teacher can use them as the basis for meaningful reading instruction. Following are some steps to take in studying diagnostic data and prescribing meaningful reading instruction in which the teacher teaches.

1. Look carefully at the diagnostic data that you have recorded on the Record Form and determine the following:
   a. The instructional reading level.
   b. Relative strengths and weaknesses in capacity and reading achievement.
   c. Specific weaknesses in
      (1) Nucleus words.[2]
      (2) Vocabulary.
      (3) Structural analysis.
      (4) Phonetic analysis.
      (5) Comprehension.
2. Select reading materials at the student's instructional level.
3. Select an appropriate teaching format:
   a. *Basic,* such as the format used to teach the "Freckles" story.
   b. *Comprehensive,* such as the format used in teaching the "Oxygen" story; this format may also be used with expository material.
   c. *Paraphrase-cloze.*
   d. *Basal* (see reading acquisition chapter).
   e. *Expository,* such as the format used in teaching the selection on beehives.
4. In each lesson, "slot" in at appropriate points in the lesson structure teaching-learning activities—exercises and games, and so forth for rectifying skill weaknesses. Where existing lesson plans such as those in basal readers are used, modify the skill exercises to make them appropriate for the particular pupil(s). For example, if the phonics exercises are designed to teach ⟨ph⟩ → /f/ and your pupils know that phonic element but are having trouble with ⟨oa⟩ → /ō/, then develop or modify your exercise to teach that phonic element. This will also entail changing illustrative or practice sentences, but some of them can be elicited from the pupils and written on the chalkboard as needed.
5. Teach the appropriate number of lessons to rectify deficiencies in the various skill areas. (Students in methods courses will be under certain time constraints.) Also remember that one lesson may take two sessions. You should make provision for review lessons as appropriate.

---

[2] Once you get into graded material, you can look at the next lesson you will teach and pull out words you think may cause the pupils difficulty in addition to the new words given in the lesson and pretest the pupils on the words to see if you will need to make special provisions to teach any of those words also.

6. Keep a log of what you are trying to accomplish, what happened during the lesson, and how you need to modify your approach in order to accomplish your goals.

7. Write your diagnostic-developmental (or corrections) report, using the outline provided.

Structural Guide for Report Writing: Reading

1.0 Introduction.
1.1 Situation.
1.1.1 The classroom.
1.1.2 Types of materials for teaching reading.
1.1.3 Apparent emphasis on reading.
1.2 Obtaining the children to work with.
1.3 Existing data on pupil(s).
2.0 Diagnostic Results.
2.1 Organized data on each child: perceptual abilities, capacity, reading achievement, other data.
2.2 Clarifying and evaluative comment.
3.0 Plans for Reading Development/Correction.
3.1 What you plan to do and why (relate to diagnostic test results, principles of learning, and so forth).
3.2 Lesson plans: identify existing plans you used and how you modified them and plans that you wrote.
3.3 Log: what happened in the lesson and why; how you plan to modify instruction where necessary.
4.0 Indications of Progress and Recommendations for Continued Instruction.
5.0 Summary of Experiences and Evaluation of Experience.

PART THREE: LESSON FORMATS AND LESSON PLANS

Formats for Teaching Reading Lessons: Outlines of Formats Explained in Chapter Three

Please refer to chapter 3 and review the following formats: basal reader approach; analytic language experience approach; and the synthetic language experience approach.

Outlines of New Formats to Be Presented in This Chapter

5.0 Comprehensive Reading Lesson (illustrated with the "Oxygen" story).
5.1 Readiness.
5.1.1 Develop background and new concepts.
5.1.2 Teach new vocabulary.
5.1.3 Meaningful review.
5.2 Guided reading.
5.2.1 Motivating, guiding questions.
5.2.2 Silent reading and answering of motivating question.

5.3 Teaching comprehension.

5.3.1 Ask pertinent questions to bring out relationships in the story and provide cues to aid the pupils in seeing those relationships.

5.3.2 Develop further nuances of meaning of vocabulary and of ideas in the story.

5.3.3 Guide pupils' reactions to ideas in the story and seek further implications and applications.

5.4 Teach other reading skills such as vocabulary and independent word identification.

5.4.1 Utilize appropriate exercises and discussion in active teaching.

5.4.2 Utilize appropriate games.

6.0 Regular corrective reading lesson (illustrated in this chapter with the "Freckles" story).

6.1 Preparation (readiness).

6.1.1 Develop background and new concepts.

6.1.2 Develop vocabulary.

6.1.3 Use new vocabulary in a game format.

6.1.4 Vocabulary/concept check.

6.2 Read the story (options).[3]

6.2.1 Silent reading to enjoy the story.

6.2.2 Teach comprehension skills through guided analytical reading.

6.3 Improve specific reading skills (teach in the specific area or areas in which the pupils are having difficulty).

6.3.1 Teach a graphone inductively, build words, and use words in context.

6.3.2 Teach a structural element, build words, and use words in context.

6.3.3 Teach comprehension strategies.

6.3.4 Teach problem nucleus words including function words.

7.0 Paraphrase-cloze forms (especially good for comprehension work).

7.1 Objectives.

7.2 Materials needed.

7.3 Preparation.

7.3.1 Pretest.

7.3.2 Teach unknown words to mastery criterion.

7.4 Read the selection, using one of several means.

7.5 Make sure the pupils understand the selection thoroughly.

7.6 Have pupils read a paraphrased-cloze version of the selection and fill in the blanks in order to check on their comprehension.

Paraphrase/Cloze Procedure Lesson Outline

1.0 Objectives.

2.0 Materials.*

---

[3] Comprehension check and teaching (particularly if comprehension is a problem) is a possibility. Use one or a combination of the following written formats and allow the reader to reinspect the text: 1) free response items, 2) completion items, 3) multiple-choice items. (Of course, one takes into consideration the maturity of the readers.) After the responses are checked, provide appropriate cues to help pupils see the relationships among ideas so that they may then answer the questions correctly. (See comprehension chapter for analysis of the *Weekly Reader* test passages.)

* List the materials you are going to use. Be specific. At times you may want to write your own reading selection. Control readability by checking your writing against a readability formula. State the readability of the selection.

3.0 Preparation.†
3.1 Pretest of Concepts and/or Words.
3.2 Teach Unknown Words to Mastery Criterion.
4.0 Read Selection.
4.1 Options.
4.1.1 Teacher reads story to student(s).
4.1.2 Story is on cassette tape (may need to use "beeps" to show where sentences end).
4.1.3 Children read silently, then aloud.
4.1.4 Students read in response to guided questions.
4.1.5 Continue.
   5.0 Selection Paraphrased and in Cloze Form (Delete every seventh word of the paraphrased version).
   6.0 Deleted Words Placed in Alphabetical Order. (They are placed here for reference, such as help in spelling.)
   7.0 Student Replaces Deleted Words.
   8.0 Experience Story (related topic).

Story

A mama sometimes calls her children honey. Do you know why? Honey is sweet. She thinks her children are sweet, too.

How do bees make honey? Bees fly to flowers. They get nectar from flowers. The bee can change the nectar into sweet honey.

The bees fly back to their homes. Their homes have little containers. The bees put the honey into these containers.

People make cookies and cakes from honey. You can put honey on bread and eat it. It is very good.

Cloze
Comprehension:

New words	nectar	know
	container	honey

Selection Paraphrased and in Clozed Form (Delete Every Seventh Word)

Did your mama ever call you _____? Are you sweet? Honey is very _____. Mamas like their children and think _____ are sweet.

What makes honey? Bees _____ honey. They make their honey from _____. They get the nectar from nice _____. The bees can change nectar into _____. This honey is sweet. The bees _____ the honey into little containers. People _____ good things from honey. Are you _____ of honey?

---

† Anticipate problem words. Pretest. Teach unknown words by using nail-down methods (suggested in the reading acquisition chapter of the present text). If the student knows enough word-identification skills for the particular word(s) involved, he may be guided in sounding out the word(s).

Words in Alphabetical Order

flowers	made	nectar	they
honey	make	put	
honey	make	sweet	

Sample Reading Lesson Plans

Comprehensive Reading Lesson Plan for Teaching an Expository Selection on "Oxygen"

1. <u>Readiness.</u>
    a. <u>Background.</u>
        (1) Did you know that you are a magician?
        (2) About 14 times a minute you change something into something else— and you can't even see it.
        (3) If you did not do this, you would not live very long. What am I talking about? (Bring out the idea that the air we breathe is necessary to life and that an important element in air is <u>oxygen</u>. Also make the point that in the process of breathing we use up oxygen; oxygen is changed in our bodies so that what we breathe out /exhale/ is another kind of gas called <u>carbon dioxide</u>. Write these two words on the board as you are talking.)
    b. <u>New concepts</u>: oxygen, carbon dioxide, inhalator, oxygen tent, nitrogen, suffocation.
        (1) How many of you have ever watched the television show "Emergency"?
        (2) What do the <u>paramedics</u> do when a person has a heart attack and has trouble breathing or has been <u>suffocating</u> or choking from smoke? (Elicit the fact that inhalators containing oxygen are used to revive these heart attack and smoke inhalation victims. You may write the responses on the chalkboard.)
        (3) After the paramedics get these victims to the hospital, the doctors and nurses provide further tests and treatment. Often they place clear plastic material over the patient's bed and pump oxygen into this special <u>oxygen tent</u>. In this way the patient's heart does not have to work so hard to get enough oxygen.
        (4) The air that we breathe is made up of oxygen and nitrogen. In every five liters of air that we breathe, one liter of oxygen is mixed with four liters of another gas called <u>nitrogen</u>.
    c. <u>New words.</u>
        1. Check/develop <u>pronunciation and meaning</u> (Chart A).
           Discuss each definition to bring out the meaning of the underlined word. (The charts should be placed on large sheets of paper and taped to a wall or chalkboard.)
           <u>oxygen</u> /äk-si-jin/ a gas in the air that we breathe in (inhale).
           <u>carbon dioxide</u> /kär-bən dī-äk-sīd/ a gas in the air that we breathe out (exhale).
           <u>inhalator</u> /in-hā-lə-tər/ a machine that pumps oxygen into a person's lungs.

oxygen tent /äk-si-jin tent/ used in hospitals to help heart attack patients.
suffocation /sə-fə-kā-shən/ choking, not getting enough air into one's
    lungs.
2.   Words in context.
     Teacher and/or students read the sentences, and students answer the
     questions.

Words in Context (Chart B)

(1) I do magic when I breathe in oxygen and change it to something
     else. I need oxygen to stay alive.
Q.   What important thing do you do to stay alive?
(2) I change oxygen to carbon dioxide inside my body.
Q.   Do you breathe out (exhale) oxygen or carbon dioxide?
(3) If a person does not get enough oxygen, he or she will choke. Such
     choking is called suffocation.
Q.   What is another name for choking from lack of air?
(4) Paramedics on emergency squads carry medical equipment with
     them. They are trained to give special first aid.
Q.   Do you happen to know what kinds of equipment paramedics use?

3.   Picture dictionary.
     Point out that one may refer to the picture dictionary for the meaning of
     certain words if one has trouble while reading.
4.   More words in context.
     Read and discuss the sentences. After each sentence is read, try to
     develop the meaning of the word as it is used in the story. Let students
     help as much as possible.

More Words in Context (Chart C)

(1) Air is about 79 per cent nitrogen and 21 per cent oxygen.
Q.   Is nitrogen usually a liquid or a gas?
(2) Paramedics use inhalators to give oxygen to people who are suffoca-
     ting from smoke or from lack of oxygen.
Q.   This is a deep thought question: Do you think the heart works
     harder or takes it a little easier as the inhalator is putting oxygen
     into the lungs?
(3) In hospitals heart attack victims are put under oxygen tents.
Q.   Do you know why heart attack victims are put under oxygen tents?
     Explain.

5.   Review.
     (a) Chart A: Find the word for a machine that puts oxygen directly into
          a person's lungs. Point to it and read it.
     (b) Chart A. Find the word that means somebody who is trained to give
          emergency medical treatment.
     (c) Chart B: Find the sentences that tell what happens to a person who
          does not get the oxygen he or she needs. Read the sentences, please.

(d) Chart B: Find the sentence that tells what oxygen becomes in our body.

(e) Chart C: Find the sentence that tells where doctors in hospitals put heart attack victims.

2. Guided Silent Reading and Rereading.
   a. Setting the purpose for silent reading.
      (1) Show a picture of some people exercising—jogging or biking. Ask the students what is needed to do these things. ("Oxygen" is the expected response. You may need to give additional clues.)
      (2) We are going to read about this substance to see if it really is magic(al).
   b. Students read to answer the motivating question.
   c. Guided analytical rereading.
      (Students read to answer the questions that follow. One needs to call on the "average" readers as well as on the better readers. If the material is too difficult for a given group, don't use it with them. Guide the students to see the relationships involved in developing answers.)
      (1) Paragraph one tells which substances are important for life. Which one do we need all the time? (In order to help the students to see the importance of oxygen, you may need to help them combine the idea that we could not live more than a few minutes without oxygen with the idea that we breathe it in (inhale it) about 14 times a minute.)
      (2) In your own words tell us what sentence three says. (You may need to help your students convert the first clause from the passive voice to the active voice: "We need food and water . . . ." The second part may involve the students knowing the antecedent for the pronoun "them." Have them substitute words until they get the right fit if they have trouble.)
      (3) Now you will verify sentence four in paragraph one. (Clock students for a minute as they count how many times they inhale during that time. You might determine the average number of times for a sample of students who seem to be breathing normally.)
      (4) What qualities does oxygen have? or What is oxygen like? or What does something have to be to be oxygen? (You might list these on the board as they are given by the students.)
      (5) Read sentence six in paragraph two. What happens when a person blows out a match?
      (6) Why doesn't the supply of oxygen in the world run out? (Paragraph 4.)
      (7) Look at paragraph four again. It tells us when plants give off oxygen and when carbon dioxide. How are conditions different when plants give off oxygen from when they give off carbon dioxide? (A process is involved here.)
      (8) Look at paragraph six. What happens if heart muscles do not get enough oxygen?
      (9) Let us look at paragraph seven. Why are paramedics very useful people?
      (10) (Thought question): What kind of first aid equipment should people keep at home or at work? (You might get different responses because parents' occupations differ.)

3. Teaching Skills.
   a. Vocabulary.
      (1) Antonyms exercise.
          Directions: Write an antonym (opposite) for each word listed. (These words can be placed on a chalkboard, and students can be called to the board to write the antonyms.)

          breathe freely _____   perish _____
          inhale _____   visible _____
          damaged _____   mountains _____
          (heart)
      (2) Contextual application.
          Charades (dramatic context).
          Directions: "I will give several of you a word on a card. Read the word. When I call on you, will you please act out your word."

sunlight	rescue	spark
climb	inhale/exhale	heart attack

      (3) Sentence context.
          Directions: "Please fill in each blank with a word from our lesson that makes the most sense. Several are tricky; you will have to think carefully."
          (a) When it gets hot and muggy, I feel as though I am going to _____.
          (b) Climbing _____ is a slow process.
          (c) If you tried to go to the top of Mt. McKinley, you would need a(n) _____ tank or two.
          (d) If you blow up a balloon with air from your lungs, the balloon will be full of _____ _____. (CO_2)
          (e) If even a _____ comes into contact with pure oxygen, an explosion may occur.
          (f) Plants are the opposite of people when it comes to breathing: plants "breathe" _____ _____ when it is daylight; people exhale it.
   b. Phonic Elements.
      Example: ch → /k/
      Ask how two known words look alike and how they sound alike. Develop the rule for pronouncing ch as it appears in the following words: chorus, stomach
      (1) Highlight the common element; develop the generalization, that is, the rule.
              chorus
          stomach
          The rule: In some words, ch is pronounced /k/.
      (2) Word building: (Going from known words to new words containing the phonic element just learned.)
          Directions: "Pronounce the first word. Now look at the partial word

below the first word. Write in the blank the phonic element we just studied." (Pause). "Now pronounce the word." (/krōm/) Continue in like manner with the remaining words.

(3) Other words containing ch → /k/. (Ask students for some words.) Some possibilities:

mechanics   chlorine   echo

schematic   cholera   chemistry

(4) Contextual application. (You may ask students for sentences or you may use the following for the underlined words:)

(a) Katie played beautiful chords on her guitar.

(b) Sam polished the chrome on Dad's car until it sparkled.

(c) Chlorine is used in purifying water.

(d) Jerry studied the schematic drawings so he could build his hi-fi set.

(e) Jill's 4-H club project was on hog cholera.

(f) Chyme is a substance found in stomachs.

(g) When the mechanic dropped his wrench in the huge airplane hangar, you could hear the echo.

c. Comprehension.

(1) Finding MRMs.

Research shows that teaching people to identify MRMs increases their reading comprehension. An MRM unit is comprised of three words. M stands for matter and R stands for relation. An MRM is really a meaning unit.

When teaching MRMs, don't get into a big discussion about grammar; just do them. Although a sentence may have more than one MRM (unit), do only one per sentence at the outset.

Do these exercises with the students; they should be actively involved. The sentences can be written on the chalkboard or placed on transparencies and projected onto a screen. Don't let the top students monopolize the exercise; call on various people.

(1) I'd like a glass of lemonade.   _____ of _____

(2) Jake was in the soup.   _____ in _____

(3) Cindy played the violin beautifully.   _____ played _____

(4) She gave the prize to John.   _____ to _____

(5) Leaves give off oxygen when   _____ when _____
    the sun is shining.[3]

(6) She was placed in the oxygen   _____ in _____
    tent until she recovered.

(7) Please run off copies of this   _____ run _____
    letter.[4]

(8) Our school has first aid equipment. _____ has _____

(9) Bring me the inhalator now.   _____ bring _____

(10) Until now he thought chloro-   _____ until _____
     phyll was purple.

---

[3] Oxygen when sun OR oxygen when shining. Other MRMs: leaves give oxygen; sun is shining.

[4] (You) understood: You run copies; copies of letters.

Oxygen

(1)   Oxygen is a life-giving gas. One could not live more than a few minutes without it. Food and water are also needed for life. But we can do without them longer than we can do without oxygen. Actually, we breathe in oxygen about 14 times every minute.

(2)   What is oxygen like? Oxygen is a bit heavier than air, but it has no odor, taste, or color. In fact, it is invisible. Yet, it is an element that is part of many things such as rocks, air, water, and food. Oxygen is also part of plants and all living things.

(3)   Oxygen has another important use. It is necessary if burning is to take place. If one blows out a flaming splinter of wood so that only a spark remains and then puts it into a test tube of oxygen, it will burst into flame. That also means that every time there is a forest fire much oxygen is used up.

(4)   If so many things use oxygen, why doesn't the supply of it run out? It isn't all used up because green plants come to the rescue. In direct sunlight, plants take in large amounts of carbon dioxide through their leaves. They use carbon dioxide to make their food and then give off oxygen as a "waste" product. So plants create oxygen for us to breathe. Some more "magic!" (Since plants cannot make food at night, they use a little oxygen and give off carbon dioxide.)

(5)   High above the earth the air gets "thin." That means there is less oxygen in the air. People who fly or climb very high mountains need extra oxygen. Therefore, they must take oxygen tanks with them.

(6)   A person whose heart starts to function very badly is having a heart attack. During such an attack the heart muscles may not get enough oxygen and the brain may become damaged. The person needs more oxygen right away or he/she may die.

(7)   At the first sign of a heart attack, one should call the emergency number 911. Paramedics will come and give the victim oxygen from a tank called an inhalator. Then they will take him/her to the hospital for more treatment. In the hospital he/she may be placed in an oxygen tent.

(8)   Paramedics are also called to help during fires. People who are caught in fires inhale smoke and may suffer lung damage. They need oxygen treatment right away. If they are not rescued in time, they may die from suffocation.

Sample Format for Individual or Group Reading Instruction

"Freckle, The Runt Pig"
From Sea to Sea
Silver Burdett 3^1, pp. 54–61.

I. READINESS.
   A. Background.
      1. Show pictures of a pig or pigs in a farm setting.
      2. Discuss how pigs are raised, how they are entered and judged at country fairs, and so forth.
   B. New Concept: runt
   C. New Words:

freckles	grow	hot	brought
runt	raise	friendly	butcher

1. Pairing new words with known words*:

   hunt   blow   rain   lot   fought

   runt   grow   raise   hot   brought

2. Reading new words in sentence context.
   a. Do you have freckles? Do you know somebody (else) who has freckles? (Tell us about it.)
   b. Why would a person not like to be called a little runt?
   c. Where do flowers grow?
   d. Do you know somebody who raises flowers?
   e. Do you like hot soup? What kind?
   f. Are little dogs friendly?
   g. Who brought you to school today?
   h. What is a butcher?
3. A checkup exercise.

   Directions: A word is missing from each sentence. Write in the correct word. The missing words are the new words that are in the questions you just answered.
   a. Grandma Smith _____ corn and peas in her garden.
   b. The red-headed boy had _____ .
   c. The _____ cut us a nice piece of meat.
   d. _____ people are nice.
   e. He _____ the book back today.
4. Play a word game for motivation and/or learning if needed.

II. READING THE STORY.

Options:
1. Do A, then B. (In this case, question 6 in B will not be needed.)
2. Do B, then A. (In this case, the guided reading question for A will not be needed.)

A. Silent Reading to Enjoy the Whole Story.
1. Setting the purpose: We know what happens to pigs when they get big. Let's find out in this story what happens to the pig named "Freckle."
2. Answer the guiding question after the story is read.

B. Teaching Comprehension Skills Through Guided Analytical Reading.*
1. Where did Freckle's home used to be?
2. Why did Mr. March think he would give Freckle away?
3. Do you think Freckle was expensive to feed? Explain.
4. What made the children feel proud?
5. I wonder how long they will stay proud. Let's read to find out.

III. TEACHING WORD IDENTIFICATION SKILLS.

A. Phonic Element (graphone): ir.
1. Highlighting the common element:

   bird

   girl

* Ask the pupil(s) how each pair is alike visually, and ask how they sound alike. Ask how they are different. Useful techniques such as the following may be used to identify the words and to put them into long-term memory: word-picture cards, knowing what a word is and isn't, and practice with a card reader.

* When a pupil has difficulty answering, the teacher will help him/her see the parts of the text that give cues to the answer. See further the section of the comprehension chapter in which a pupil was helped to logically analyze paragraphs in a *Weekly Reader Test* in order to obtain the correct answers.

(Use known words. Have pupil(s) pronounce the words. Have them indicate in what way the words sound alike. Ask how the words look alike. Have the like element underlined by one of the pupils. Ask what sound is said when we see the underlined part. Ask for a rule about pronouncing the ir.

2. Word building: The top word in each pair is a nucleus word. Have the newly learned element written in the blanks. Pupils pronounce the known word of each pair and then the word containing the element that has been written in.

shut   stem   see   batch
sh_t   st__   s_   b_ch

3. Contextual application:
   a. Do you wear a shirt?
   b. When you make a cake, you have to stir stuff.
   c. A birch tree has white bark.
   d. Yes, sir! I know this word.

4. Playing a game. (Select a game that will review this element and recently learned elements.)

B. Structural Element.
   1. Review the concept of closed syllables.
   2. Have the pupil(s) circle the closed syllables.

   little   hot   kitchen   summer
   children   open   biggest

   3. Note that the vowel in the closed syllable might be a "short sound" vowel.
   4. Have the closed syllable in each word pronounced.
   5. Have the entire word pronounced. If the "short sound" is not correct because the syllable is not accented, have the pupil try the alphabet sound or the schwa sound.

IV. FURTHER WORK IN COMPREHENSION AS NEEDED.
   A. Possibilities.
      1. Use Manzo's Re-Quest Procedure.
         a. Select appropriate paragraph (or two) of narrative or expository material.
         b. Teacher and pupil(s) read and quiz one another according to the Re-Quest procedure. (See comprehension chapter.)
      2. Select a different procedure from comprehension chapter.

V. TOUGHIES: thought   position   bother
   A. Types of Activities for Handling "Toughies."
      1. Compare each word with a known, similar word.
      2. Trace over the word with finger while saying the word. (Trace three times.)
      3. Utilize card reader such as the Language Master.
      4. Practice spelling and writing the word.
      5. Use the word in a note to a friend.
   B. Criterion for Mastery.
      If the pupil can correctly identify the word five days in succession, he/she knows it. You have to mix the given word card in with other word cards—known and unknown words—to be sure that the identification is valid.

Freckle, the Runt Pig

Freckle was a small brown pig. Before she came to live at Grass Lake School, her home was in Mr. March's barnyard.

Mr. March was the farmer who lived in the big white house near the school.

Freckle was a runt pig.

A runt pig is always smaller than the rest of the pigs in the barnyard. It has a hard time. It never gets enough to eat, because the other pigs push it away.

Freckle did not seem to grow at all. That was why Mr. March thought he would give her to the school.

The children and their teachers were glad to have a pig to raise. They made fine plans for her.

"We will feed her well, so that she will grow big and fat," they said. "Then, in the fall, we will have meat with our lunches."

There was a kitchen in the Grass Lake School. Every day, two or three of the big girls cooked something hot for lunch, and all the children ate together.

"Freckle will eat the bits left over from the hot lunch," said the cooking teacher.

Mr. Hall, the head of the school, looked pleased. "There are many schools where the children cook hot lunches," he said. "But not many schools raise their own meat."

The children smiled proudly. They were glad to think they were doing more than other school children did. They thought, too, of the lunches they would have.

So it was an exciting day when Mr. March drove up to the school with the little pig.

The children were disappointed when they looked at Freckle. She was so weak and thin!

"She is hardly as large as a puppy," they said. "And a hungry puppy, at that."

They put her in the pen that the boys had built for her. It was a small pen, but it seemed large when Freckle was in it.

The first day the pig was there, the girls in the kitchen made vegetable soup. They gave the outside leaves of the vegetables to Freckle.

"That is not enough for a hungry little pig," said one of the big girls.

So she took a big helping of soup to the pig. Most of the children gave Freckle bits from their own lunch boxes.

There were so many children that there was a big lunch for the pig after all.

"Such a little pig will never eat all that," they said. "And she seems almost afraid to eat. The other pigs have frightened her."

But when they went out to the pen after school, every bit of the lunch was gone. Freckle was asleep and seemed happy.

The little runt grew very fast. Everyone was surprised to see how much she could eat. Everyone was even more surprised to see how soon she stopped being thin.

Freckle soon learned to know when the school bus was coming in the morning. She would run to the side of the pen and make friendly sounds.

One time she got out of her pen. The children heard a funny noise at the front door. A teacher went to the door to see who was knocking. There stood Freckle, looking friendly and hungry.

After that, the boys made a higher pen for Freckle.

Once in a while Mr. March came to see the pig. Each time he came he was more surprised than the time before.

"Well, I never!" he would say. "She is not a runt pig any more."

Vacation time was coming. Mr. March said he would be glad to let Freckle stay in his barnyard with the other pigs.

"Freckle is strong enough to stand up for herself now," said Mr. March.

But the children did not want to let Freckle go back. They had a better plan. Some of the children who lived near would take turns feeding the pig.

So all that summer the children near by brought food to the pig. It was easy to get ears of corn or other vegetables from their homes.

When the children all came back to school in the fall, they ran to Freckle's pen. It was a big, strong pig that waddled up to the side of the pen.

The children were very proud.

By and by the time of year came when the farmers take their pigs to the butcher.

One morning Mr. March came to the school and said, "I shall be taking my pigs to the butcher soon. I'll be glad to take Freckle, too."

Mr. Hall looked around the big room where all the children were sitting. "Just think," he said, "of the delicious lunches we are going to have."

But no one looked happy. Some of the little girls had tears in their eyes.

That day in the kitchen the girls talked about the best ways to cook meat. Not one of the ways sounded good.

The next day, when the children were in the room with Mr. Hall, one of the big boys raised his hand.

"We children don't want to let Freckle go to the butcher," he said. "We know a man who will give us thirty dollars for her. And he will keep her always."

"We can take the thirty dollars and get a new icebox for the school," said a girl. "We have talked it all over. We don't want the butcher to have Freckle."

Mr. Hall seemed glad. "Well," he said, "Freckle is the school pig. You may do what you like with her."

The next morning Freckle was not in her pen. The children had carrot soup for lunch. There was no meat, but they were happy. They knew Freckle would like her new home with Mr. Brown.

PART FOUR: A SPECIAL WORD IDENTIFICATION TECHNIQUE

The Fernald Technique*

Stage 1: Students learn by tracing word.

a. Students trace word, with finger touching paper, saying each part of word as they trace it.
b. They repeat the process as often as necessary to write the word without looking at the copy.

* Based on the work of Grace M. Fernald. *Remedial Techniques in Basic School Subjects.* New York: McGraw-Hill Book Company, 1943.

c. They write it on scrap paper and then in the story they are developing.

d. After students write the story, it is typed for them and they read it in print.
e. Each new word learned is placed in alphabetical file.

The following points of technique are stressed:
1. finger contact is important.

2. "test": the students should never copy the word but always write it from memory.
3. always write word as a unit.

4. always put the word into a context.

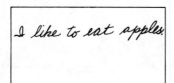

5. students say each word to selves or out loud as they write it.

6. type what they write and have it read before too long an interval passes.

I like to eat apples.

Stage 2: Same as stage 1, except tracing is no longer necessary after awhile.
  a. Look; say over to self while looking at the word.
  b. <u>Write</u> word without looking at copy.

| *tree* |

  c. Put words on index cards and file alphabetically.
  d. Students continue to <u>write</u> <u>freely</u> and to read the printed copy of what they have written.

| "The Apple Tree" | "The Apple Tree" |
| In our orchard we have a nice apple tree. We *~~ ~~ ~~* *~~ ~~ ~~* | In our orchard we have a nice apple tree. We r-m rl-i ic ɔ r -ii^ (ᴒ ʟ-'ᴒ ||=ʟ ᴄ+ |

  e. Students' stories are now longer.
  f. They write about everything that interests them as well as about their school subjects.

PART FIVE: PRACTICUM REPORT

My Field Experience
Maria Alvarez

For three weeks I had the opportunity to work with Alvin Kasten, Miss Beverly Murphy's student, at Caroline Brevard Elementary School in Tallahassee, Florida.

The classroom atmosphere is a pleasant one. The bulletin boards reinforce reading skills in an interesting way. The children's art work was always on display; this livens up the room and makes each child feel good. The room is always neat and has big windows to let the sunshine in. The times I was in the classroom the students were reading or doing independent work in a quiet manner. The students listened with respect to what Miss Murphy had to say.

Miss Murphy was very helpful and concerned about my work. Working with an understanding classroom teacher made the visits more pleasant. She showed concern for the students as people.

The reading materials Miss Murphy used for instruction included the following:

A Place for Me. Holt, Rinehart and Winston, Inc.

Special Happenings. Holt, Rinehart and Winston, Inc.

Joys and Journeys. American Book Company.

Cross Roads. Harper & Row, Publishers (used with the top group).

I also observed the shelves full of different books. A lot of books were collected by Miss Murphy. I was really impressed by the variety of books available. Resource books, story books, and a lot of interesting books to motivate were in her collection.

I noticed that the children also read different paperback books that they had ordered. Miss Murphy mentioned to me how they get a free book for every five the children order. She puts the free books on the shelves, adding to the children's class library. These books are being used. Miss Murphy has a certain time for reading books the children are interested in; I really admire her for doing that. It is important for them to want to read more.

Diagnostic Results

I tested two fourth-graders, Annie Lee and Alvin Kasten. After I analyzed the results of testing, I realized how similar the students' results were. Both students showed positive results on the majority of the tests. They both fell at the fourth-grade level in most of the categories.

Annie Lee is a nice girl who has a lot to give when she really applies herself. A lot of times I would catch her daydreaming, but when I had her attention and interest she showed surprising and good responses. She showed positive results throughout the diagnostic testing except in the phonics test. I feel Annie needs special help with consonant digraphs, vowel clusters, and "other combinations." Annie's perceptual abilities—visual discrimination, letter names, auditory discrimination, auditory blending—are very good and met the criterion of 70 per cent on all tests. On auditory blending she was only about half a year behind. Annie showed higher results (grade 5) on the Hafner Quick Reading Test, a word recognition test, than on the Woods-Moe Reading Test (grade 4.5).

In reading Woods-Moe passages, Annie's mistakes were mostly in repeating words and inserting extra words throughout the paragraphs. Annie's reading comprehen-

Name _Alvin Kasten_   Birthdate _10/13/68_
Grade Placement _4.7_   C.A. _9-6_
School _Caroline Brevard_   Examiner _Maria Alvarez_

READINESS Score		Percentage Correct	Criterion	CAPACITY Score
_10_	Visual Discrimination	100	70% /+/	_/_ Learning Rate Test
_8_	Letter Names	100	70% /+/	Hafner Verbal Comprehension Test
_8_	Auditory Discrimination	100	70% /+/	Verbal Age (V.A.) _10-3 (10.25)_
_7_	Auditory Blending	70	70% /+/	Verbal Grade Pl. _5.0_
				Verbal Comprehension Quotient _108_

		Gr. Pl.		
____	Auditory Memory	____	/-/	

READING

Word Recognition (Oral Reading)

Score		Gr. Pl.	Intelligence	
_41_	Hafner Quick Reading Test	_5.1_	Mental Age (M.A.) ____	
____	Hafner-Brown Quick Rdg. T.	____	Mental Grade Pl. ____	
____	Moe-Woods Reading Test	_4.5_	Intelligence Quotient ____	

Paragraph Comprehension

Score		Gr. Pl.	Listening Comprehension	
____	Moe-Woods Reading Test	_4.5_	Listening Age ____	
____	Hafner Multi-level Rdg. T.	____	Listening Grade Placement _5th_	
			Listening Quotient ____	

Phonics (Phoneme-Grapheme Associations)

% Correct		Known	Unknown
_100_	Consonant Blends	tr, sm, fr, gl, br, cl, pl, st, cr, pr	
_60_	Consonant Digraphs	wh, sh, th, ph, ch/ch/, ch/sh/	kn, th (unvoiced), gn, ch/k/
	Vowel Clusters		
_50_	group 1	ea, ea, ow ō, oa, oo/ů/	ou, ou, ow, ai, oo
_60_	group 2	oy, ue, oe, ie, ie, oi	ue, aw, au, au
_0_	group 3		ough, ough, ough, ough
			eigh, eigh, ei, ew, ew, ay
_80_	Other Combinations	wr, ing, ir, or, ur, alt, tion, er	tion, ar

sion skills fall at the fourth-grade instructional level; the fifth-grade level was too difficult for her. On the Hafner-Smith Verbal Comprehension Test, a capacity test, Annie rated at high fourth-grade level. What surprised me was how Annie's listening comprehension level was the same as her reading comprehension; once again, fifth-grade material was too difficult.*

Alvin Kasten was enjoyable to work with. The more questions you ask him and

---

* Because of space considerations, Annie's phonics test and verbal comprehension test answer sheets are not included. Her Record Form is included.

the more you talk to him, the more you realized he has a unique personality and the potential to achieve. Alvin showed positive results in most testing areas except auditory blending and phonics. In the phonics test, he showed deficits in consonant digraphs, vowel clusters, and other combinations. Alvin's basic perceptual ability is good, except in auditory blending and auditory memory. Alvin had a hard time remembering and repeating numbers backwards on the auditory memory test.

In word identification, Alvin scored higher on the Hafner Quick Reading Test (fifth-grade level) than on the Woods-Moe Reading Test (fourth-grade level). In oral reading of continuous context, Alvin made most of his mistakes in substituting words. The first time I tested Alvin on paragraph comprehension, he reached the instructional level at grade 3, but I noticed he wasn't himself. So I tested him again on Form A and Form B on the next visit just to be sure. As I thought, Alvin showed positive results on the fourth-grade level of the test.

On the Hafner-Smith Verbal Comprehension Test, Alvin reached the same verbal grade placement as Annie, 4.8. On the listening comprehension test, Alvin scored on the fifth-grade level.

Hafner Quick Phonics Test

Name *Alvin Kasten*

Grade *4th*

Directions: Have the subject read across the rows. Encode his response (according to the Merriam-Webster key) directly to the right of the stimulus. In test CD and VC he may give the phonemic options in any order. Encourage, but don't push. Count as correct any acceptable phonemic options which he may give. After the test is complete, circle incorrect responses, count number correct, and compute the percentages.

SCORE

LN: Letter Name. Directions: "Please tell me the names of these letters."

100 %   g   s   v   n   b   x   t   j   d   q   *10*/10

CB: Consonant Blend. (or Digraph: Consonant Diphone)

100 %   tr   sm   fr   gl   br   cl   pl   st   cr   pr *10*/10

(alternate)   troo   smoo   froo   gloo   broo

                   cloo   ploo   stoo   croo   proo

CD: Consonant Digraph. (or Digraph: Consonant Uniphone)

(Phonemic Options)

60 % kn   wh   sh   th/th/   ph/f/   gn (gun)   ch/ch   *6*/10

      /n/   /sh/   th   ch/sh/

                                                             ch

VC: Vowel Clusters. (or Vowel Phoneme Options)

Group one   ea/ē/   ou   ow/ō/   ai (air)   oa/ō/   oo/u̇/ *5*/10

50 %   ea   ou   ow   oo/ō/

Group two   oy/òi/   ue   aw   oe/ü/   au   ie/ī/   oi/òi/ *6* /10
60 %   ue   au   ie/ē/

Group three   ough   ough   eigh   ei   ew   ay *0*/10
— %   ough   ough   eigh   ew

OC: Other Combinations.

80 % wr/r/___ing/iŋ/   or òr   ur/ər/   ar/ər/   tion (tion)   er/ər/ *8*/10
         ir/ər/   alt/òlt/   cil (ce)

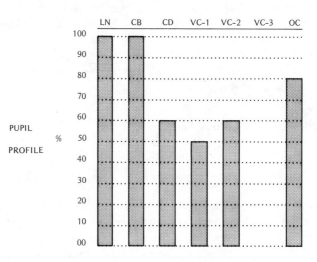

PUPIL
% PROFILE

Verbal Comprehension Test
Lawrence E. Hafner and Edwin H. Smith

School *Caroline Brevard* Name *Kasten*   *Alvin*
                                   Last   First

Teacher *Miss Murphy*   Birthdate *October 13, 1968*

Examiner *Maria Alvarez*   C. A. *9-6* Grade *4.8*

Date *April 15, 1978*   V. C. Age *10-3* V. C. Q. *108*

Record of Responses

3-0 _____ (3) _____
3-3 _____ (3) _____
3-6 _____ (3) _____
3-9 _____ (3) _____
4-0 _____ (3) _____
4-3 _____ (3) _____
4-6 _____ (3) _____
4-9 _____ (3) _____
5-0 _____ (3) _____
5-3 _____ (3) _____

5-6 _____	(3)	_____
5-9 _____	(3)	_____
6-0 _____	(3)	_____
6-3 _____	(3)	_____
6-6 _____	(3)	_____
6-9 _____	(3)	_____
7-0 _____	(3)	_____

7-3 _____	(3)	_____
7-6 _3_	(3)	*something you can spend*
7-9 _3_	(3)	*Columbus*
8-0 _3_	(3)	*eight left*
8-3 _3_	(3)	*something you can dig with*
8-6 _3_	(3)	*like a knife, sharp on end, skinny*
8-9 _3_	(3)	*15 cents*
9-0 _2_	(3)	*winter, summer, spring*
9-3 _2_	(3)	*make music*
9-6 _3_	(3)	*13 cents*
9-9 _3_	(3)	*6*
10-0 _0_	(3)	*—*
10-3 _0_	(3)	*may*
10-6 _0_	(3)	*O.K.*
10-9 _1_	(3)	*"Kinda" beats*
11-0 _3_	(3)	*9*
11-3 _0_	(3)	*India*
11-6 _3_	(3)	*all animals*
11-9 _0_	(3)	*silly, crazy*
12-0 _1_	(3)	*something you drink*
12-3 _0_	(3)	*—*
12-6 _0_	(3)	*8*
12-9 _0_	(3)	*—*
13-0 _0_	(3)	*—*

Basal age (bracket spanning 8-6 and 8-9)

Lesson Plan 1

(A brief description of an existing lesson plan)

"Tom and the Pirates," pages 150–154.
More Than Words/ Felder, Schafer.
Macmillan Publishing Co., Inc.

PREPARATION
Building Background—Discuss what a legend is. Display a map of North Carolina. Point out the island of Ocracoke. Use the map to guide the pupils in discovering why pirates might want to seek shelter in the inlet of Ocracoke.

(Lesson continues at the bottom of page 304.)

Name _Annie Lee_   Birthdate _Sept. 9, 1968_

Grade Placement _4.7_   C.A. _9-7_

School _Caroline Brevard_   Examiner _Alvarez_

READINESS Score	Percentage Correct	Criterion	CAPACITY Score
_10_ Visual Discrimination	100	70% /+/	_1_ Learning Rate Test
_26_ Letter Names	100	70% /+/	Hafner Verbal Comprehension Test
_8_ Auditory Discrimination	100	70% /+/	Verbal Age (V.A.) _10-9 (10.75)_
_10_ Auditory Blending	100	70% /+/	Verbal Grade Pl. _5.5_
			Verbal Comprehension Quotient _112_

	Gr. Pl.		
_9_ Auditory Memory	_4.0_	/+/	

READING

Word Recognition (Oral Reading)

Score		Gr. Pl.	Intelligence
_46_ Hafner Quick Reading Test		_5.6_	Mental Age (M.A.) _____
____ Hafner-Brown Quick Rdg. T.		____	Mental Grade Pl. _____
____ Woods-Moe Reading Test		_4.5_	Intelligence Q. _____

Paragraph Comprehension Score	Gr. Pl.	Listening Comprehension
____ Woods-Moe Reading Test	_4.5_	Listening Age _____
____ Hafner Multi-level Rdg. T.	____	Listening Grade Placement _4.5_
		Listening Quotient _____

Phonics (Phoneme-Grapheme Associations)

% Correct		Known	Unknown
_100_	Consonant Blends	tr, sm, fr, gl, br, cl, pl, st, cr, pr	
_60_	Consonant Digraphs	th, wh, ph, gh, sh, ch	kn, sh, th, /k/
	Vowel Clusters		
_60_	group 1	ea, ou, ow, oa, oo, oo	ea, ou, ow, ai
_50_	group 2	oy, aw, oe, ie, ie	ue, ue, au, au, oi
_50_	group 3	ough /ō/, ei, eigh /ā/, ay	ough, ough, eigh, ew, ough
_70_	Other Combinations	wr, ing, ir, or, ur, alt, er	tion, ar, cil

Lesson Plan 1 (cont.)
Developing Reading Vocabulary

pirates	pretended	chief	Ocracoke
cask	toting	Amos	Gale

Have students complete the 11 sentences by putting the correct word in the blank.

Independent Preparatory Work—Preparatory pages 78–79 in the Discovery Book.

INDEPENDENT SILENT READING

Use the table of contents by having the students locate the title of the story.
Purpose—Have students read pages 150–154 to find out what young Tom's ambition was.

Guided Oral Reading

a. Ask students questions that help them discover the feeling of the characters.

b. Have the students skim to note descriptive details.

c. Ask questions for understanding the behavior of story characters.

FOLLOW-UP

Independent Activities

a. Practice Exercise—Have each student underline the best answer to each question.
   Example: What did Tom do when he saw a ship coming?
   pretended   frowned   hoed

b. Exercise—Read each question and write the correct answer on the line.
   Example: Does ie in believe sound the same as ie in die or ie in Marie? _____

Teacher-Directed Activities

a. Reviewing the prefix re.

b. Recognizing cause-effect relationships.

c. Noting phonemic values for the digraph ie.

Provision for Individual Differences

a. Review words ending in teen and ty.

b. Note special terminology defining specialized vocabulary.

c. Use consonant substitution to review phonograms. -ask, -age, -ack, and -ame.
   Make minimal variations (substituting) with initial consonants.

d. Review consonant clusters sch, scr, spl, spr, squ, str, and thr. Have the student
   insert consonant blends to complete the underlined words in the paragraph.

Lesson Plans 2 and 3

Because of space considerations, lessons two and three are omitted; however, the logs on the lessons are included.

Lesson Plan 4

(Story from text "How I Became an Athlete," my own lesson plan, pages 48–52.)

KALEIDOSCOPE/ Durr, Windley, McCourt
Houghton Mifflin Company, Boston.

READINESS

A. Background
   1. Ask the student if he ever watched the Olympics on TV?
      What events did he like best?
      Does he know who Jesse Owens is?
   2. Ask Alvin if does he try his very best in everything?
      Is it important to always try your best?

3. Discuss where the Olympics took place last, and where it is going to take place next.

4. Ask Alvin, when a person writes a story about himself, what is this called? (Autobiography)

B. New Concepts: remedy   fate   doomed   massage

C. New Words: afford   posture   massage   fate
                 remedy   doomed   cripple   crutches
                 Olympic   absolute   impossible

1. Reading new words in sentence context.
   a. It takes hard training to join the Olympics.
   b. My baby brother is impossible to take care of.
   c. I can only afford to get one more candy bar.
   d. When I hurt my foot, I had to use crutches for a week.
   e. My mother's remedy always makes me feel better.
   f. Can I massage your back?
   g. My sister has a good posture from sitting up straight.
   h. Fate brought the brother and sister together again.
   i. When he fell down the stairs, he became a cripple.
   j. He was an absolute mess when he came back from playing football.

2. Playing a Word Game: afford   massage   fate
                            posture   doomed   impossible
                            remedy   absolute   cripple

   1. I cannot _____ that expensive dress.
   2. Sitting up straight helps me to have a good _____.
   3. The use of honey and lemon is my mother's _____ to help a sore throat.
   4. After a long hard day, I like someone to give me a good back _____.
   5. Mary felt that she was _____ to be a failure in math.
   6. Alice tried her _____ best to get an A on the test.
   7. After Tom's car wreck, he became a _____ for life.
   8. Tina believed that only her _____ will know if she is going to get married.
   9. It seems _____ for me to get all my homework done tonight.

D. Purpose: Read silently pages 48-52 and find out how Jesse's life was when he was younger and how Jesse became an athlete.

GUIDED READING
(p. 48)
1. What was one of the most wonderful moments of Jesse's life?
2. How many medals did Jesse win?
3. What was wrong with Jesse when he was a boy?
4. When did he start having trouble with his leg?
5. Was it all of a sudden that Jesse couldn't walk? Why?
(p. 49)
1. Was Jesse from a poor or rich family? Why do you think so?

2. What was Jesse's mother's remedy to help cure his leg?
3. What makes Jesse's mother so special?
4. Why did Jesse take up running?
5. What type of training did Jesse have to be a good runner?
6. Did Jesse have a chance to join a team? Why?

(p. 50)
1. Why was Jesse facing hard times?
2. Who are the two people in Jesse's life who helped him be a good runner?
3. How did Mr. Riley help him?
4. What moment in Jesse's life was even better than winning the gold medals in the Olympics?
5. Every night before bed, what did Jesse do?

(p. 51)
1. What is Jesse's method of running correctly?
2. What was it that Jesse thought that made him the best?
3. Was Jesse using all the ability he was gifted with?
4. What did Mr. Riley want Jesse to overcome?
5. What goal did Mr. Riley want Jesse to reach?

(p. 52)
1. Why was Jesse surprised when Mr. Riley asked him to work for a world record?
2. What event was Jesse most excited about in the Olympics?
3. What did Mr. Riley think was the most important thing in life?

TEACHING WORD-IDENTIFICATION SKILLS

A. Phonic Elements
    1. Consonant digraph ch, differentiating the three main sounds that represent ch.

church	chef	chord
chicken	chiffon	chorus

        a. Alvin read the words.
        b. He stated how the beginning of each word looked alike.
        c. He stated the three sounds that represent ch.
    2. A game identifying the different sounds.
       Alvin placed the correct card in the right section on the chart.

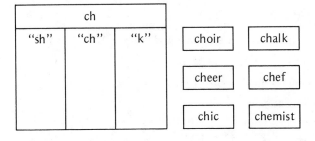

A. Phonic Element
    2. Vowel Cluster—Differentiating several sounds that are represented by ough.

Reinforcement Exercise

Today when I was walking
_ _ _ ough the store, I b _ _ _ _ t
myself some c _ _ _ _ medicine and
_ ough to make cookies.

ough
through
though
thought
cough

B. Structural Element
   1. Review the concept of prefix (auto).
      I always drive my <u>automobile</u> to work.
      Will you give me your <u>autograph</u>?
      I like to read <u>autobiographies</u> about famous people.

I discuss with Alvin each sentence.
   1. Automobile is a moving vehicle that runs by <u>itself</u>.
   2. Autograph is the signature of one <u>self</u>.
   3. Autobiography is a story that a person writes about him<u>self</u>.

Ask common prefix in each word.
Ask common meaning in each word.
Discuss as necessary.

TOUGHIES: WHAT DO YOU THINK?
   1. Ask Alvin what he thinks each sentence means.
      a. But slowly the coach's words <u>sank</u> in.
      b. Jesse your mother must have put <u>iron</u> in those legs when she was getting
         you well.
      c. But <u>fate</u> seemed to have other plans again.
      d. And when I was 9 years old, it went away <u>completely</u>.

Lesson Plan 5

(Story from text, "When Gerta Smiled," my own lesson plan)

<u>VALUES TO LEARN</u>/ Arnspiger, Brill, Rucker
Steck. Vaughn Company, Austin Texas, 1967

Preparation for Reading
1. Develop background. Have Alvin locate Sweden and Virginia on the globe so he
   will realize Gerta left a far country to come live in the United States.
   Discuss what type of transportation can get you from Sweden to the United
   States.

Ask Alvin if he has ever been new at a place, felt like a stranger, didn't know anyone? Ask him if he liked that feeling?

2. Present Vocabulary

Discuss what the new words mean.

New words: Sweden   Virginia
              delicious
              language
              snicker
              trembling

Complete sentences with the correct word.
a. My home state is _____.
b. An ice-cream sundae with butterscotch and fudge topping is _____.
c. My hands were _____ when I took my driving test.
d. I heard someone _____ when I tripped over the book.
e. I wish I could speak more than one _____.

3. Further preparatory work: Have Alvin connect a line to correct word.

Sweden   Spanish
Virginia   chuckle
delicious   country
language   taste good
snicker   state

4. Dictionary practice: Alvin looked up the words snicker and language in the dictionary

Reading the story

1. Silent reading—Alvin, please read and find out why Gerta decides to smile.
2. Guided Reading
   (p. 41)
   1. Has Gerta been in the United States a long time?
   2. Why did the students laugh at her?
   3. Why did Gerta feel her clothes in Sweden were good?
   4. Was Gerta comparing herself to others?
      Is it good to compare yourself to others?

Guided oral reading
   (p. 42)
   1. What type of expression did Gerta always have on her face?
   2. Why did Gerta's mother feel that Gerta had no friends?
   3. What advice did Mrs. Swenson give Gerta?
   4. What's so special about a smile?
   5. Why wasn't Gerta happy in the United States?
   (p. 43)
   1. Why did Gerta still have to wear the old clothes?
   2. What was Gerta's father's good news?
   3. Was it a good job?

4. Did Gerta get new clothes?

(pp. 44–45)

1. What activity did Miss Duke have the children do?
2. How did Gerta feel when it was her time to speak?
3. What makes you think Gerta doesn't speak clear English yet?

(p. 46)

1. How come Gerta thought the smiles were friendly smiles this time?
2. Can smiles always mean true happiness?
3. What was it that helped Gerta understand why they laughed?
4. How did Gerta arrive in the United States?
5. Did the classmates like what Gerta had to say?
6. What makes you think Gerta enjoys school now?
7. What did Gerta learn?
8. Would you have acted like the students? Why? or Why not?

Teaching Skills

1. Independent activities:

Practice Exercise—Underline the best answer.

1. How did Gerta feel about her first two weeks of school?
   sad   happy   bored
2. How did Gerta feel about her clothes?
   pleased   confused   unhappy
3. What did the class do when Gerta spoke?
   cry   clap   laugh
4. When Gerta came home, how did she feel?
   troubled   satisfied   bored
5. How did Mrs. Swenson and Gerta feel when Mr. Swenson told them the good news?
   interested   satisfied   excited
6. How did Gerta feel when she wore her new clothes?
   afraid   happy   proud
7. When it was Gerta's turn to speak, how did she feel?
   nervous   calm   excited

Independent activities.

Exercise on the sounds represented by ou and ow.

ou	ow
cloud	cow
rough	slow

a. Does the ou sound in cloud sound the same in foul or touch? _____
b. Does the ou sound in rough sound the same in out or tough? _____
c. Does the ow sound in low sound the same in grow or plow? _____
d. Does the ow sound in owl sound the same in snow or town? _____

Teacher-directed activities.

1. Sequence Game—Have Alvin put the correct sentence strip in the right order according to what happened from the beginning of the story to the end.
   Gerta went in the front of the class to talk about her family.

Gerta's father brought good news home about his new job.
Gerta is very unhappy at school.
Gerta makes friends and is happy at school.
Gerta's mother gives Gerta advice to smile and not to be so sad.

2. Teaching the two phonemic options for the grapheme oo.
Discuss the two different phonemes.

soon	crook
tool	stood
boot	wood
zoo	foot

Snap Game—Have Alvin snap once if the word he hears has the alphabet [long] vowel sound [phoneme] and have him snap twice if the word he hears has the silly [short] vowel sound [phoneme] and not to snap if he doesn't hear either sound.
The words I say are boo, took, blood, cool, boon, door. shook, room, floor, stood, tooth, broom, hook and flood.

3. Taking care of individual differences.

	prefix	root	suffix
unsuccessful	un	success	ful
prepare			
biography			
dislodgement			
selfish			
starless	star	star	less

Sentence Building—I had different strips of paper with nouns, determiners, adjectives, verbs, and phrases on them, so Alvin could build his own sentences.
Sentence Building Game—Alvin made the following sentences with the strips.
The silly boy swallowed a goldfish.
Each clown chased a spooky teacher.
Everyone waved to the class.
All the animals sang silly.

4. Related Activity—Alvin and I made a list of the things that make us smile (3-minute time limit). Alvin thought of 13 things and won.
The 13 things were Miss Murphy, his friends, his grandmother, eating ice-cream, watching car racing, a clown, funny car, a funny game, his baby cousin Frieda, a funny mirror, banana splits, the 3 Stooges, and the Little Rascals.

Log for Lesson 1

Alvin enjoyed the lesson about Tom and the Pirates. When we were building background, Alvin was able to locate the island Ocracoke on the map. Alvin told me what an island and an inlet are. Alvin had no problems with the new words; he completed the sentence exercise with no difficulty. He was interested in the words tote and cask. Since the story was about adventure, he enjoyed reading it. He had no problems answering literal questions such as, "What did they bring the cask for?"

and inferential questions such as, "What makes you think that Amos isn't being an understanding brother to Tom?" In the exercise on different feelings, Alvin showed he understood how each character felt in the different situations throughout the story. Alvin had to be reminded what a prefix was; but, after I explained, he understood what the re prefix stood for. He worked with different words that had the two sounds that ⟨ie⟩ represents. Alvin had no problem with this lesson, and I believe he found the exercises to be suitable. He was interested in pirates and expressed himself well in discussing the story.

Log for Lesson 2

The Stonecutter is an old tale with deep meaning. Since Alvin loves art, when we were developing background for the story Alvin enjoyed talking about sculptures and the tools stonecutters use. When I asked, "Have you ever wished you were someone else?" he mentioned wanting to be Tarzan or a rich, strong man. He had no problems with the new words although sunshade and carriage were new to him. As Alvin read the story silently and took notes of the different events, it took him time to express some events, but he took very good notes and knew when an event occurred in the story. The questions for the guided reading were mostly literal and he had no problems with them. Since this story has a deep moral meaning, which is that man should be content in what he does for a living and be happy for what he is, I asked more questions: (1) What was the author's message? and (2) Why is it important to be happy in what you do? and (3) Does what someone does always pay enough money to pay for living expenses? Alvin really thought about these questions, and he wasn't happy to realize some people don't make enough money to support themselves, because they have no other choice. He wasn't familiar with open and closed syllables, but after my explanation he did well. On the exercise about who had power over whom, he was able to look back at his useful notes and complete the exercise.

Log for Lesson 3

"Tiger on the Loose" did not interest Alvin as much as the others. He again enjoyed the discussion pertaining to the background of the story. We talked about tigers. He had no problem answering the questions; he read with good comprehension. The exercise with different types of vowels such as alphabet o, ⟨o⟩ → /ō/; "silly" e, ⟨e⟩ → /ē/; and ⟨a⟩ → /ä/ were quite a challenge for him, particularly the last association. Alvin liked breaking words into syllables. Finding the main ideas in a paragraph was not easy for Alvin. He was mostly guessing. Further instruction and related activities must be done in this area.

Log for Lesson 4 (The first lesson plan I wrote)

To my surprise Alvin really liked my lessons. They were more challenging for him, and the exercises reinforced some phonics skills and study skills. Alvin really liked "How I Became an Athlete." He liked talking about the Olympics; he remembered different events he had watched on TV. The only words Alvin needed help in understanding were fate, doomed, remedy, and massage. After the first exercise Alvin was able to complete the Word Game. He answered all the guided questions correctly.

Alvin had a hard time remembering that /k/ is a phonemic option for ⟨ch⟩. He enjoyed doing the ch chart game. Alvin was surprised that ⟨ough⟩ represented several different sounds. He completed the sentence exercise fine. The prefix auto was new to Alvin and took more sample sentences for him to grasp the meaning. On the "demon" sentences he had no problem translating the meaning into different words, that is, in paraphrasing.

Log for Lesson 5 (The second lesson plan I wrote.)

When Alvin read "When Gerta Smiled," he related his feelings. He didn't know Sweden was a country; so we went to a globe and I had him locate Sweden and also the state of Virginia. He was interested in the type of transportation you can take to get from Sweden to the United States. He again answered all the guided reading questions correctly, probably because of the careful preparation and the fact that he was reading on his instructional level. He also did correctly the exercise with the characters' different feelings.

Since Alvin had difficulty in knowing the two phonemes each represented by ou and ow, the exercise comparing known words having those graphemes helped him. His sequence skills are good; he ordered the sentences correctly. Alvin loved doing the game with the different ⟨oo⟩ graphemes, but needed to think more before "snapping." He had difficulty with knowing the difference between root and suffix. He had fun building his own "silly sentences."

Indications of Progress

From these lessons Alvin should be more comfortable with vowel clusters, developing study skills, answering inferential questions, and using structural analysis skills. I feel I expanded Alvin's skills with my individual discussions and questions.

Recommendations. Alvin needs more help with vowel clusters, developing the main ideas of paragraphs, and differentiating between roots and suffixes of words. I believe Alvin had a lot of potential, and expectations higher than third-grade level should be made.

Evaluation of Experience. I learned a lot during these past three weeks working with Alvin. I realized that to be a good teacher you should always be prepared and center activities around children's needs. It is a lot of work, but it's only fair to the students. Writing out my own lesson plans will give me more background for further teaching.

Miss Murphy and Alvin were enjoyable to work with. Alvin is a happy boy and loves art. He has an understanding personality. He has mentioned that he reads sometimes at home and enjoys school.

LEARNING ACTIVITIES

1. Using a variety of students (or the same students for all tests), administer, for practice, the following sets of tests to students. Follow procedures given in the Test Manual in this chapter. Score tests, make conversions of scores, where appropriate, to age-level and grade-level scores, enter data on Record Form(s), and write appropriate interpretations of your findings. Ask your instructor to help you as needed.

   a. Readiness tests.
   b. Capacity tests.

    c. Word-recognition (identification) tests.

    d. Reading comprehension tests.

    e. Phonic elements tests.

2. Under supervision of your instructor, make demonstration video tapes of your testing procedures to be critiqued for helpful suggestions and possibly, after refinement, for use as a demonstration tape in future classes.

3. With the help of your instructor, do a complete diagnosis of one or more students from an elementary or middle school classroom. Your instructor will help you set up this practicum experience by working with the appropriate college and school officials, including the all-important classroom teacher.

After scoring, converting scores to age-level and grade-level scores, where appropriate, entering data on Record Forms, and interpreting the results, write a complete diagnostic report.

4. Prepare teaching plans for improving the reading achievement of one or more of the students whom you tested. If you are working in the classroom with fellow students from your college class, you may be able to exchange diagnosed students in order to give each of you a small group of students who have similar levels of reading achievement and similar skills that need developing.

5. Teach the students five to eight developmental (corrective) reading lessons, or the number recommended by your instructor.

6. Under the guidance of your instructor, write a complete report,* including both the diagnostic and developmental phases of your work. It is suggested that you give one copy to the school, one to your instructor, and that you keep one for yourself. These reports should be considered confidential.

STUDY QUESTIONS

1. What steps are taken in studying the diagnostic data?

2. Relate the *Structural Guide for Report Writing: Reading* to the example of a report found in this chapter.

3. Write the key things you learned from studying the guide and the report.

RECOMMENDED READING

ABESON, ALAN and JEFFREY ZETTEL. "The End of the Quiet Revolution: The Education for All Handicapped Children Act of 1975." *Exceptional Children,* 44 (October 1977), 114–128.

CHARLES, C. M. *Individualizing Instruction.* St. Louis: The C. V. Mosby Company, 1976.

FARR, ROGER and NANCY ROSER. *Teaching a Child to Read.* New York: Harcourt Brace Jovanovich, Inc., 1979. Chapter 6.

FEELEY, JOAN T. "A Workshop Tried and True: Language Experience for Bilinguals." *Reading Teacher,* 33 (1) (October 1979), 25–27.

---

* Once the first set of reports has been handed in, the instructor will have a backlog of reports for students to study as an aid in their work.

KIBBY, MICHAEL W. "Passage Readability Affects the Oral Reading Strategies of Disabled Readers." *Reading Teacher,* 32 (4) (January 1979), 390–396.

KIRK, SAMUEL A., SISTER JOANNE MARIE KLIEBHAN, and JANET W. LERNER. *Teaching Reading to Slow and Disabled Learners.* Boston: Houghton Mifflin Company, 1978.

KLEIN, PNINA and ALLEN A. SCHWARTZ. *A Manual for the Training of Sequential Memory and Attention.* Seattle: Academic Therapy Publications, 1977.

MANGRUM, CHARLES T. and HARRY W. FORGAN. *Developing Competencies in Teaching Reading.* Columbus, Ohio: Charles E. Merrill Publishing Company, 1979.

PROPST, IVAN K., JR. and RICHARD B. BALDAUF. "Using Matching Cloze Tests for Elementary ESL Students." *Reading Teacher,* 32 (6) (March 1979), 683–690.

STANLEY, JULIAN C., WILLIAM C. GEORGE, and CECELIA H. SOLANO. *The Gifted and the Creative: A Fifty Year Perspective.* Baltimore: Johns Hopkins University Press, 1977.

STAUFFER, RUSSELL G. "The Language Experience Approach to Reading Instruction for Deaf and Hearing Impaired Children." *Reading Teacher,* 33 (1) (October 1979), 21–24.

VALETT, ROBERT E. *Valett Developmental Survey of Basic Learning Abilities.* Palo Alto, Calif.: Consulting Psychologist Press, 1966.

ZINTZ, MILES V. *The Reading Process: The Teacher and the Learner.* 3rd ed. Dubuque, Iowa: William C. Brown Company, 1980, Chap. 21.

REFERENCES

BLOOMER, RICHARD H. *Skill Games to Teach Reading.* Danville, N.Y.: Instructor Publications, 1973.

HERR, SELMA E. *Learning Activities for Teaching Reading.* 3rd ed. Dubuque, Iowa: William C. Brown Company, 1975.

KIRK, SAMUEL A. and JAMES J. McCARTHY. *Illinois Test of Psycholinguistic Abilities.* Champaign: University of Illinois Press, 1968.

MILLER, HARRY B. *Teacher's Programmed Educational Techniques in Reading.* Memphis, Tenn.: Al Graci Educational Service, 1974.

ROSNER, J. *Test of Auditory Analysis.* New York: Walker and Company, 1973.

SPACHE, EVELYN B. *Reading Activities for Child Involvement.* 2nd ed. Boston: Allyn & Bacon, Inc., 1976.

WAGNER, GUY and MAX HOSIER. *Reading Games: Strengthening Reading Skills with Instructional Games.* New York: Teachers Publishing Corporation, 1972.

SECTION V

Organizing for Better Reading Instruction

CHAPTER 9
Developing Interests, Tastes, and Motivation

OBJECTIVES:

As a result of studying this chapter the reader should be able to do the following:

1. *Explain how the extent of voluntary reading in a school might reflect the success of the total school reading program.*
2. *List three contributions wide reading experience makes to a child's learning, maturation, and socialization.*
3. *Describe three obstacles to voluntary reading by pupils.*
4. *List the general areas of reading preference of elementary pupils.*
5. *Describe two techniques for discovering the reading interests of a specific group of pupils.*
6. *List several sources for selecting good children's books.*
7. *List four guidelines for a school program to follow in expanding voluntary reading.*
8. *List five specific activities or techniques for generating interest in books.*
9. *Explain why poetry is generally low on the list of reading preferences of older pupils.*

A major goal of school reading programs is to develop in pupils a desire to read, an eagerness to turn voluntarily to books for pleasure and knowledge. Many authorities in reading believe that the true measure of the effectiveness of our instructional programs in reading is reflected in the extent to which our pupils read voluntarily. Schools have been accused of focusing their efforts on teaching pupils *how* to read and then promptly squelching their enthusiasm for reading by overemphasizing skill and fact learning. One parent recently told us, "My son's in the eighth grade and he certainly seems to be able to read all right. But he only reads what the teachers force him to. Can't they do something to make him like to read?"

319

About the only answers a teacher can give to the critics who complain that the schools are failing in their responsibility to make readers of children are (1) an expression of our awareness and concern and (2) an assurance of our efforts to learn more and improve. We are, despite the critics, doing a better job than ever before.

Perhaps we should also tell our public that teachers alone will not accept either the blame or the praise for making children want to read. To make readers of children, teachers, administrators, parents, and community leaders must share responsibility and concern. Where school officials are more interested in building a new gymnasium or swimming pool than in providing good school and classroom libraries; where communities spend more money decorating their streets for Christmas than on the maintenance of a good public library; and where parents provide a house with TV and automatic dishwasher but few books and little stimulating conversation, reading and books cannot seem very important to children. These obstacles are awesome to teachers, for they seem to be so completely beyond our control. But no good teacher throws up his red pencil in defeat because there are problems in teaching. He knows that there are successes even where all logic would predict failure. There are children from the most culturally destitute backgrounds who become book lovers because of teachers and school. The teacher knows too that, for far too many children, he alone is the example of what a reader is. He knows that if he can lead them to the discovery of the rewards and excitement of books, he will have done more for them than he could have by instilling all the other knowledge and skill that he possesses. The facts may be forgotten and the skills seemingly go unused, but the love of reading, once generated, will not easily disappear.

THE IMPORTANCE OF VOLUNTARY READING

Why read? The simple truth is that most of us read because it gives the pleasures of knowing, feeling, acting, learning, or of escaping from our own limited worlds. In the act of reading, as in witnessing a drama, we are able to go beyond ourselves, to be other people, in other places, doing other things. Through the projection of ourselves into the lives of characters in books we learn about ourselves and our relationships with our fellows, something of the general truth of being a human being. It is this knowledge that is the most important reward books have to offer; through it come compassion, insight, sensitivity, taste, and judgment.

Books are also functional, practical. Children should discover this while quite young. A book can tell the pupil what to feed his new guinea pig, how to make a box kite, or what the valves in an internal combustion engine do. Many an adult has learned to garden, repair his car, sew, plumb, or carpenter from a book or magazine. Very few such skills are beyond the scope of the person who can read.

Voluntary reading is also a vital adjunct to the school's program to improve reading skills. The pupil reading for pleasure is much like the skier who has left the demonstrations and lectures to try the slope. Here he applies what he learns. Skills awkwardly applied with concentrated effort at first gradually become habits, effortless and pleasant. To improve their reading, pupils must read.

But no matter how glib we teachers and parents may be about how valuable or rewarding reading is, we have difficulty convincing some children. One of the basic problems in engendering an interest in reading in children is that the rewards or effects of reading cannot be readily measured or demonstrated. The reward of reading is not tangible or immediately practical, and it is the nature of the immature learner to wish some concrete evidence of his learning, to visualize some possible results of his efforts. This the teacher will find difficult to provide. He can discuss the values we have mentioned, talk of the pleasure, as book-lovers have done for centuries, but he cannot "teach" it. The force that generates and maintains an interest in reading must come from the reading experience itself. Neither grades, praise, money, nor any other extrinsic reward will long sustain it.

IMPEDIMENTS TO VOLUNTARY READING

In addition to the general cultural conditions that make it more difficult for the teacher to develop an interest in reading, there are several ubiquitous competitors for children's time that complicate the task. Today's children have a multitude of out-of-school activities vying for their time and energy. We want our children to read for pleasure, but we also want them to study, take music lessons, dancing lessons, and riding lessons, go to parties, and take part in clubs, scouting, church activities, and so on. Equally important, they need adequate time to rest, work at a hobby, or simply play as they choose with friends and family. After a busy day at school, participating in even a few of these activities leaves little time for adequate rest, much less for reading. Parents must be aware of the debilitating effects of too many activities, and make certain that their children's time is reasonably spent. Every year pediatricians, reading specialists, and psychologists see children whose learning problems are a result of or are complicated by fatigue. No one, child or adult, reads or studies effectively when exhausted.

Television

In addition to all the activities mentioned here that demand pupils' time, television is thought by some authorities to be reading's major competitor. Some studies indicate that children spend more time watching television than in playing, studying, and reading combined. Whether or not this heavy dose of TV is harmful is a question that research has not answered. Some authorities suggest that carefully guided viewing offers many possibilities for enlarging children's interests and stimulating their imaginations. Some pediatricians and psychologists seem concerned that excessive TV viewing produces anxieties or other unfavorable personality quirks in children. Regardless of the outcome of future research into these problems, it is clear that the child who stays up too late watching the late movie is not able to function well in the classroom the next day. It is also safe to conclude that much of the time spent watching TV could be much more profitably spent in reading, studying, or working at a hobby.

Comic Books

Many elementary school children enjoy comic books. Some studies have concluded that nearly 90 per cent of children between eight and thirteen years old read comic books regularly. Many people, including teachers and psychologists, have been disturbed by this fact—simply because comics are poor reading material, others for fear that reading comics might lead to undesirable behavior, even delinquency. But there is little evidence to support this last notion, and many reading authorities discount it entirely.

It is easy to judge comics as poor, but that conclusion is not likely to have much effect on the children who enjoy them. If there is any valid reason for objecting to comic books, it is that they consume money and time that might be spent on material of better quality.

The School Reading Program

It may seem strange but the nature of a school's reading program can be an obstacle to voluntary reading. If the instructional program in reading emphasizes the teaching of isolated skills to the exclusion of actual reading, pupils may have little incentive to read. A danger inherent in some currently popular "behavioral approaches" to teaching reading can be that overemphasis on test-teach-test strategies along with detailed record keeping may leave little time for reading.

George Spache (1976) warns that a "skill-deficit" approach to teaching reading places an overemphasis upon decoding and other isolated skills: "Yet no one has been able to discover the proper sequence of training in specific areas, or even the best sequence within each skill area. Even the existence of the separate skills stressed, as in the area of comprehension, is doubtful."

Our purpose here is not to enter the controversy between those authorities arguing for a decoding, skill-centered approach (Groff, 1979; Walcutt, 1974) and those urging a "whole-language" approach (Smith, 1975; Hoskisson, 1979). We are suggesting that reading instruction should provide a balance between skill instruction and actual reading. The reading act itself—not workbook activities or exercises—must be seen by our pupils as the most important facet of our instructional program. Otherwise, they may conclude that teachers place little value on reading for pleasure.

CHILDREN'S READING PREFERENCES

Many teachers and researchers have conducted thorough investigations into both the general areas of children's reading interest and their specific book choices. A survey of research by Norvell (1966), Ashley (1970), Pieronek (1980), Meisel and Glass (1970), and Moray (1978) was the source of the following generalizations about children's reading interests:

1. A very high percentage of boys in grades 4–8 read comic books.
2. Children do more voluntary reading than many teachers suppose. Bright students read more than slow students.
3. The number-one choices of boys and girls in the elementary grades are stories of action, mystery, and adventure.
4. Both sexes dislike stories containing blatant moralizing and extensive description.
5. Sex is a more important determinant of reading interests than age or intelligence:
   a. Boys like animal stories, fantasy, science fiction, humor, biographies of famous men, and sports stories. They generally avoid stories of romantic love. In the intermediate grades boys read more non-fiction than girls.
   b. Girls generally have a wider range of interests than boys. They prefer adventure stories featuring female characters, stories of romance, sentiment, mystery, and biographies.
   c. Favorite magazines of intermediate boys are *Boys' Life, National Geographic, Popular Science* and *Popular Mechanics.*
   d. Intermediate girls included only *National Geographic* among their favorites and seemed to prefer magazines designed specifically for young people, such as *Child Life* and *Children's Digest.*
6. High-achieving intermediate grade pupils have more varied reading interests and read more than low-achievers. Low-achievers indicate a preference for books with a comic-book format.

Looking over this list one is struck immediately by the fact that children and adults are very much alike in their reading preferences. The largest-selling paperbacks in this country always include titles of suspense, mystery, and adventure. A large-scale research report in 1978, done for the Book Industry Study Group, surveyed the reading habits of adults in the United States (Monteith, 1980). This study reported that the most popular fiction categories were action and adventure stories, followed by historical fiction and historical romance. (Sadly, 39 per cent of the respondents in this survey indicated that they never read a book, although they do read newspapers and magazines.) The stories featured in the most popular women's magazines are similar to the types listed in young girls' reading preferences. It appears that the essential differences in adults' and young peoples' choices are not in the type of material but in the complexity of plots, maturity of characters, sophistication of language and style, and the like.

The research findings on children's reading interests have value as indicators of general patterns of their preferences, but teachers must be cautious in using them to select books for any particular child or perhaps even for an entire class. Children's interests change, partly as a result of shifting trends in television and movies, or perhaps as a result of new developments in science and technology widely reported in the news. The changing cycles of types of television programs may be fairly reliable guides to the changing interests of pupils.

Discovering What Pupils Like

In order to be effective in encouraging outside reading, it is advisable for teachers to find out all about the interests of their pupils. To do so they should take advantage of information from research and talk with librarians. More important, they should conduct informal investigations of their own, and these should produce more reliable information about their present pupils than any other source. One of the most direct ways to do this is through an interview in which the teacher asks the pupil about her hobbies, her club and sports activities, her favorite pastimes, comic books, and television programs, her pets, books, and the like. Specific questions such as "If you could write a book, what would it be about?" or "What kind of story do you most like to hear read aloud by your parents or teacher?" might be prepared beforehand to guide the interview.

In addition to the interview, observation of a child's daily activities and conversations in the classroom may provide clues to his interests. Another simple device is the interest inventory, which the teacher can prepare easily and administer to his entire class at the beginning of the year. The following teacher-made inventory may be reproduced for this purpose:

1. What do you do each day from the time school is out until dinner time? (play, chores, TV, lessons, sports?)
2. What kind of chores do you do at home?
3. What school subjects are your favorites? Why?
4. What TV programs do you watch regularly?
5. List your three favorite TV programs.
6. What movie have you seen recently that you enjoyed?
7. What are your favorite sports? Do you play any organized sports?
8. What school subjects do you enjoy least? Why?
9. What kind of places do you (or would you) like to visit?
10. What comic books do you read?
11. How much time do you spend reading at home?

12. Do you ever go to the public library? How often?
13. What magazines or newspapers do you read?
14. What kind of books do you dislike?
15. What kind of work do you like to do best?
16. Do you have any special hobbies? Any pets?
17. Underline three of the following subjects that you most enjoy reading about: (a) spies, (b) cowboys, (c) soldiers, (d) detectives, (e) sports heroes, (f) doctors and nurses, (g) boys and girls, (h) knights, (i) myths, (j) discovery and exploration, (k) fairy stories, (l) famous people, (m) war, (n) love, (o) school, (p) airplanes, (q) hunting and fishing, (r) animals, (s) science fiction, (t) true science, (u) "how-to" books, (v) others (name them).

In addition to specific questions about interests and activities, questions about family background, parents' occupations, travels, and so on, might also provide useful information. Such an inventory will provide clues to areas in which potential interests lie and in which present interests can be capitalized upon.

Selecting Books

Knowing what kinds of books pupils prefer is the first step in the battle to bring child and book together. Selecting specific books for the classroom library, books to which you can guide individual pupils, is the second problem. The following guidelines may be helpful:

1. Do not select a book because of attractive illustrations or cover.
2. Do not select a book simply because it is new.
3. Take your questions about books to an experienced children's librarian.
4. Read the book—don't give it to a child if you don't like it.
5. Consult a good source for specific recommendations and criticisms.

Sources. More than ever before, teachers have a wealth of good references to guide their choices of books. The following contain book lists, reviews, annotated bibliographies, or short annotations on the books they list. Many indicate the grade and interest levels of the books they list.

1. *Good Books for Poor Readers*, Spache (Garrard).
2. *A Teacher's Guide to Children's Books*, Larrick (Merrill).
3. *Best Books for Children*, Solomon (Bowker).
4. *Good Books for Children*, Eakin (University of Chicago).
5. *Children's Books Too Good to Miss*, Arbuthnot (Western Reserve University).
6. *A Basic Book Collection for Elementary Grades*, American Library Association.
7. *Growing Up with Paperbacks*, Kailin (Bowker).
8. *Children's Classics*, Jordan (Horn Book).
9. *Adventuring with Books: A Book List for Elementary Schools*, Guilfoile (Signet).

10. *Children's Books to Enrich the Social Studies,* Huus (National Council for the Social Studies).

The following periodicals carry regular features on children's books: *The Horn Book; Saturday Review; School Library Journal; Language Arts,* and *Reading Teacher.*

The following list of books, primarily fiction and poetry, was compiled from the authors' own preferences, from the recommendations of specialists in children's literature, and from the choices of many children. The list is merely a sampling of some books at each grade level that we believe teachers should know.

Kindergarten and Grade 1

Anderson, C. W., *Billy and Blaze* (Macmillan).
Angland, Joan W., *A Friend Is Someone Who Likes You* (Harcourt).
Association for Childhood Education, *Sung Under the Silver Umbrella* (Macmillan).
Banchek, Linda, *Snake In, Snake Out* (Crowell).
Bemelmans, Ludwig, *Madeline* (Viking).
Beskow, Elas, *Pelle's New Suit* (Harper).
Burton, Virginia, *Mike Mulligan and His Steam Shovel* (Houghton).
Crews, Donald, *Freight Train* (Greenwillow).
Dayrell, Elphinstone, *Why the Sun and the Moon Live in the Sky* (Houghton).
Fatio, Louise, *The Happy Lion* (McGraw).
Freschet, Bernice, *The Old Bullfrog* (Scribners).
Gag, Wanda, *ABC Bunny** (Coward-McCann).
Gag, Wanda, *Millions of Cats* (Coward-McCann).
Graham, Margaret, *Be Nice to Spiders* (Harper).
Hoban, Lillian, *Arthur's Prize Reader* (Harper).
Hoban, Russell, *A Birthday for Frances* (Harper).
Hoban, Russell, *The Stone Doll of Sister Brute* (Macmillan).
Hoffman, Hilde, *The Green Grass Grows All Around* (Macmillan).
Hutchins, Pat, *Rosie's Walk* (Macmillan).
Keats, Ezra Jack, *Peter's Chair* (Harper).
La Fontaine, *The Lion and the Rat* (Watts).
La Fontaine, *The Rich Man and the Shoemaker* (Watts).
Leaf, Munro,* *The Story of Ferdinand* (Viking).
Lobell, Arnold, *Grasshopper on the Road* (Harper).
Lobell, Arnold, *Mouse Soup* (Scholastic).
Mendoza, George, *The Gillygoofang* (Dial).
Miller, Jane, *Birth of a Foal* (Scholastic).
Minarik, Else, *Little Bear* (Harper).
Most, Bernard, *If the Dinosaurs Come Back* (Harcourt).
Mother Goose, *The Real Mother Goose* (Rand-McNally).
McCloskey, Robert, *Make Way for Ducklings* (Viking).
McGinley, Phyllis, *All Around the Town* (Lippincott).
Petersham, Maud and Miska, *Box with Red Wheels* (Macmillan).
Potter, Beatrice, *The Tale of Peter Rabbit* (Warne).
Rey, Margaret, *Curious George Goes to the Hospital* (Houghton).
Sharmat, Marjorie W., *Nate the Great and the Phony Clue* (Coward).

* Indicates Newbery Award winner.

Smith, William Jay, *Laughing Time** (Little).
Udry, Janice, *Moon Jumpers* (Harper).
Wyndham, Robert, *Chinese Mother Goose Rhymes* (World).
Zweifel, Frances, *Bony* (Harper).

Grades 2 and 3

Allard, Harry and J. Marshall, *The Stupids Have a Ball* (Houghton).
Anderson, C. W., *Pony for Three* (Macmillan).
Barclay, Gail, *The Little Brown Gazelle* (Dial).
Bendick, Jean, *Space and Time* (Watts).
Bishop, Claire, *The Five Chinese Brothers* (Coward).
Bond, Michael, *A Bear Called Paddington* (Houghton).
Brown, Margaret, *Wheel on the Chimney* (Lippincott).
Clymer, Eleanor, *The Big Pile of Dirt* (Holt).
Coatsworth, Elizabeth, *First Adventure* (Macmillan).
Dalgliesh, Alice, *Ride on the Wind* (Scribner).
d'Aulaire, Edgar and Ingri, *Benjamin Franklin* (Doubleday).
Elkin, Benjamin, *Gillespie and the Guards* (Viking).
Farley, Walter, *Big Black Horse* (Random).
Flack, Marjorie, *The Story About Ping* (Viking).
Flory, Jane, *The Unexpected Grandchildren* (Houghton).
Gannett, Ruth, *My Father's Dragon* (Random).
Haas, Merle, *The Story of Barbar* (Random).
Hann, Jacquie, *Where's Mark?* (Four Winds).
Haywood, Carolyn, *"B" is for Betsy* (Morrow).
Hurlimann, Bettina, *Barry: The Story of a Brave St. Bernard* (Harcourt).
Krahn, Fernando, *The Mystery of the Giant Footprints* (Dutton).
Lamorisse, Albert, *The Red Balloon* (Doubleday).
Lawson, Robert, *Ben and Me* (Little).
Leaf, Munro, *Wee Gillis* (Viking).
Long, Claudia, *Albert's Story* (Delacorte).
Matsutani, Miyoko, *The Crane Maiden* (Parent's Magazine).
Mayer, Mercer, *Appleard and Liverwurst* (Four Winds).
McClosky, Robert, *Burt Dow, Deep Water Man* (Viking).
Milne, A. A., *The House at Pooh Corner* (Dutton).
Niland, Deborah, *ABC of Monsters* (McGraw).
Raskin, Ellen, *Spectacles* (Atheneum).
Renich, Marion, *The Tail of the Terrible Tiger* (Scribner).
Rice, Eve, *Sam Who Never Forgets* (Greenwillow).
Sharmat, Marjorie W., *A Big Fat Enormous Lie* (Dutton).
Skorpen, Liesel, *Outside My Window* (Harper).
The Brothers Grimm, *The Four Clever Bears* (Harcourt).
Wiesner, William, *The Tower of Babel* (Viking).
Yashima, Taro, *Crow Boy* (Viking).

Grades 4, 5, and 6

Atwater, Richard and Florence, *Mr. Pepper's Penguins* (Little).
Baker, Russell, *The Upside-Down Man* (McGraw).

* Indicates Newbery Award winner.

Bontemps, Arna, *The Fast Sooner Hound* (Houghton).
Boston, Peter, *A Stranger at Green Knowe* (Harcourt).
Branscum, Robie, *The Saving of P. S.* (Doubleday).
Brink, Carol, *Caddy Woodlawn** (Macmillan).
Brooks, Walter, *Freddy Goes to Florida* (Knopf).
Bulla, Clyde, *The Sword in the Tree* (Crowell).
Burnett, Frances, *The Secret Garden* (Lippincott).
Butterworth, Oliver, *The Enormous Egg* (Little).
Canfield, Dorothy, *Understood Betsy* (Holt).
Carlson, Natalie, *The Family Under the Bridge* (Harper).
Carlson, Natalie, *The Happy Orpheline* (Harper).
Carroll, Lewis, *Alice's Adventures in Wonderland* (Macmillan).
Cleary, Beverly, *Ellen Tebbits* (Morrow).
Cleary, Beverly, *Henry Huggins* (Morrow).
Cleary, Beverly, *Ramona and Her Father* (Morrow).
Cleary, Beverly, *Ramona the Pest* (Morrow).
Coatsworth, Elizabeth, *The Cat Who Went to Heaven** (Macmillan).
Cresswell, Helen, *Absolute Zero* (Macmillan).
Cresswell, Helen, *Bagthorpes Unlimited* (Macmillan).
Daringer, Helen F., *Adopted Jane* (Harcourt).
DeAngelie, Marguerite, *The Door in the Wall** (Doubleday).
Defoe, Daniel, *Robinson Crusoe* (Macmillan).
DuBois, William P., *The Great Geppy* (Viking).
Edmonds, Walter, *The Matchlock Gun** (Dodd).
Estes, Eleanor, *Ginger Pye** (Harcourt).
Farley, Walter, *The Black Stallion* (Random).
Field, Rachel, *Hitty: Her First Hundred Years** (Macmillan).
Flora, James, *Grandpa's Ghost Stories* (Atheneum).
Gates, Doris, *Blue Willow* (Viking).
George, Jean, *My Side of the Mountain* (Dutton).
Gobble, Paul, *The Girl Who Loved Wild Horses* (Bradbury).
Hale, Lucretia, *The Complete Peterkin Papers* (Houghton).
Hurliman, Bettina, *William Tell and His Son* (Harcourt).
Jacobs, Joseph, *Fables of Aesop* (Macmillan).
Jarrell, Randall, *The Bat Poet* (Macmillan).
L'Engle, Madeleine, *A Swiftly Tilting Planet* (Farrar).
L'Engle, Madeleine, *A Wrinkle in Time* (Farrar).
Lofting, Hugh, *The Voyages of Doctor Doolittle** (Lippincott).
Lowry, Lois, *A Summer to Die* (Houghton).
MacGregor, Ellen, *Miss Pickerell Goes to Mars* (McGraw).
Mazer, Norma, *The Solid Gold Kid* (Dell).
Meigs, Cornelia, *The Covered Bridge* (Macmillan).
Nye, Robert, *Beowulf*
O'Hanlon, Jacklyn, *The Door* (Dial).
Paola, Tomie de, *The Quicksand Book* (Holiday).
Rich, Louise, *Star Island* (Watts).
Sachs, Marilyn, *Veronica Ganz* (Doubleday).
Saver, Julia, *Fog Magic* (Viking).
Seredy, Kate, *Magical Melons* (Macmillan).
Seredy, Kate, *The White Stag** (Viking).
Sewell, Anna, *Black Beauty* (World).

* Indicates Newbery Award winner.

Spellman, John, *The Beautiful Blue Jay and Other Tales of India* (Little).
Sperry, Armstrong, *Call It Courage* (Macmillan).
Stuart, Jesse, *The Beatinest Boy* (McGraw).
Todd, Ruthuen, *Space Cat* (Scribner).
Ventura, Piero and Marisa, *The Painter's Trick* (Random).
Withers, Carl, *Nonsense Tales from Many Lands* (Holt).
Wiggins, Kate, and Nona Smith, *The Fairy Ring* (Doubleday).
White, E. B., *Charlotte's Web* (Harper).

Grades 7 and 8

Anderson, Dave, and Milton Lancelot, *Upset* (Doubleday).
Bishop, Curtis, *Fast Break* (Lippincott).
Bosworth, Allan J., *All the Dark Places* (Doubleday).
Burnford, Sheila, *The Incredible Journey* (Little).
Butterworth, W. E., *Fast Green Car* (Norton).
Colum, Padraic, *The Children of Odin* (Macmillan).
Cunningham, Julia, *Drop Dead* (Pantheon).
Daugherty, James, *Danial Boone** (Viking).
Derleth, August, *The Moon Tenders* (Westminster).
Dubois, William P., *The Twenty One Balloons** (Viking).
Felsen, Henry, *Hot Rod* (Dutton).
Fon Eisen, Anthony, *Bond of the Fire* (World).
Forbes, Esther, *Johnny Tremain** (Houghton).
Frost, Robert, *You Come Too* (Holt).
Garnerk, Alan, *The Owl Service* (Walck).
George, John and Jean, *Vulpes, the Red Fox* (Dutton).
Graves, Robert, *Greek Gods and Heroes* (Doubleday).
Gray, Elizabeth, *Adam of the Road* (Viking).
Green, Roger, *Tales of Ancient Egypt* (Walck).
Harris, Mary K., *The Bus Girls* (Norton).
James, Will, *Smokey, The Cowhorse** (Scribner).
Keith, Harold, *Rifles for Watie** (Crowell).
Kelley, Eric, *The Trumpeter of Krakow** (Macmillan).
Kipling, Rudyard, *Captains Courageous* (Doubleday).
Krumgold, Joseph, *. . .And Now Miguel** (Crowell).
Krumgold, Joseph, *Henry III* (Atheneum).
L'Engle, Madeleine, *The Young Unicorns* (Farrar).
Lawson, John, *The Spring Rider* (Crowell).
O'Dell, Scott, *Island of the Blue Dolphins** (Houghton).
Poling, James, *The Man Who Saved Robinson Crusoe* (Norton).
Rankin, Louise, *Daughter of the Mountain* (Viking).
Rounds, Glenn, *The Blind Colt* (Holiday).
Spears, Elizabeth, *The Witch of Blackbird Pond** (Houghton).
Sperry, Armstrong, *Thunder Country* (Macmillan).
Twain, Mark, *Adventures of Tom Sawyer* (Macmillan).
Wersba, Barbara, *The Dream Watcher* (Atheneum).
Wier, Esther, *The Loner* (McKay).
Wilder, Laura, *By the Shores of Silver Lake* (Harper).
Wojciechowska, Maia, *Shadow of a Bull** (Atheneum).

* Indicates Newbery Award winner.

Note: Reprints of the annual annotated bibliography "Classroom Choices for 198_: Books Chosen by Children" can be obtained by sending a stamped, self-addressed envelope to The Children's Book Council, Inc., 67 Irving Place, New York, N.Y. 10003.

GUIDELINES FOR DEVELOPING READING INTERESTS

A program to develop lifetime reading habits requires more than occasional library visits, book reports, or assigned numbers of books for pupils to read. Such a program requires as careful deliberation as the plans to teach vocabulary or word-identification skills sequentially. Principles of learning, good psychology, compassion, and a rich knowledge of children's books and the pupils for whom they are intended are all necessary ingredients of an effective program stressing voluntary reading. The following guidelines may be helpful, for they attempt to take many of the factors mentioned here into consideration:

1. Develop needed reading skills in a sequential program that includes continual diagnosis of pupil needs. To be pleasurable, reading, particularly for the immature or reluctant reader, must be almost free from the necessity of struggling with word-identification or meaning problems.

2. Provide good books of appropriate difficulty levels on a wide variety of subjects; specifically choose most books for the classroom library with individual pupils in mind.

3. Display books colorfully; use the technique of the newsstand in having front covers in view.

4. Give pupils ample time for browsing and for voluntary reading as a part of the regularly scheduled school program. Do not relegate personal reading to moments pupils have free after completing another task or waiting for another activity.

5. Provide guidance to all children who need help in finding the right book. Although considerable freedom of choice is desirable, and many children will need little or no teacher direction, others need it. It is here that the teacher's knowledge of the pupils' abilities and interests proves invaluable.

6. Be a teacher who reads. Be enthusiastic about reading. Convey your pleasure in it. Talk about it freely and informally. Take your books to school and be "caught" reading by your pupils.

7. Be cautious about censuring pupils for reading any particular book. A better approach might be to discuss the material with them pleasantly, expressing your curiosity over its appeal. Try to lead them to something better that has similar characteristics.

Techniques for Developing Interests and Appreciation

The most pervasive characteristic of classroom practices that are successful in creating interest is that they somehow connect a pupil's needs, curiosity, awareness—some hunger for knowing or feeling—with reading. To make this connection a teacher must realize that books and children can be brought together easily, but unless there is a meaningful communication, the relationship is short-lived. The following activities and techniques are based on the premise that pleasure and satisfaction in reading should be "arranged" to whatever extent possible by the teacher. Many of them depend upon inducing children to read by setting up circumstances through which teacher and pupils share their pleasurable experiences.

1. Read often to children at all elementary levels. Even when time is limited, share a short poem or anecdote.

2. Encourage every child to talk about or even read aloud a portion of a book or story that he has enjoyed. Make the situation informal, pleasant, and without teacher criticism of either the material, the child's language, or delivery.

3. Maintain a reading center in the classroom with alternating committees of three or four pupils who are responsible for displaying their favorite books, magazines, or newspapers.

4. Form book-commercial committees, bringing together small groups of pupils who will be given freedom to "sell" their classmates on their favorites. Individuals might do this as well, but some teachers report that where committees are chosen so weaker students are together with better readers, the better students may be helpful to the poorer ones. Many of the poorer readers can make valuable contributions to the committee through the cleverness of their ideas to use in advertising. One key to the success of this technique is in allowing the pupils to choose any device to sell the book, from setting up a TV commercial to floating a gas-filled balloon in the room carrying the message.

5. Use paperbacks widely in the classroom. They are exciting to children because they are obviously not schoolbooks and they appear smaller and more colorful than most hardbacks. Encourage pupils to bring in their favorites to display, swap, or lend.

6. Try to make it possible for children to own books, even if you must contrive a way for them to earn them.

7. Be aware of television programming, school or civic theater plays, or films available to you related to some book you wish pupils to read. If possible, provide them with copies before the production appears. This may produce some exciting discussions about the differences in the media's versions.

8. Provide experiences from which voluntary reading may grow. Such experiences as are appropriate for use in content area studies or in language-experience activities may stimulate children, particularly disadvantaged ones, to want to know more. Be sure to provide guidance both before and after such an experience through discussion and questions. Find out what the students would like to know before the experience is shared. The following list of field trips may be helpful; some sample questions from students in a third-grade class are included with several of the locations:

    1. Visit to the zoo. Questions from pupils:
       a. Which animal makes the funniest noise?
       b. What is the biggest animal? the smallest?

     c. What do they do with a sick animal?

     d. How do they get an elephant to the zoo?

  2. Visit to a house under construction. Questions from pupils:

     a. How do they get a house level?

     b. Who shows the men where to put the boards?

     c. Where do the wires and pipes go in?

     d. How do they keep the bricks in a straight line?

  3. Visit to a farm. Questions from the teacher:

     a. How does the farmer decide what he will raise?

     b. What are the biggest problems with his crops?

     c. What must the farmer know about science and mechanics?

     d. What does the farmer do when the winter weather keeps him from growing things?

  4. Visit to a bottling works. Questions from the teacher:

     a. How many bottles are prepared in a minute?

     b. How do they make the drink bubble?

     c. How do they get the drink into the bottle and the carton?

     d. What are some of the ingredients that go into the drink?

Other fruitful visits might include those to a dairy, an airport, a publishing or printing firm, a lumber mill, a museum, a botanical garden (or a local greenhouse), a manufacturing plant, a radio or television station, a local newspaper, or a local site of historical importance. Books should be available that are related to most of these kinds of places, and pupils should be encouraged to browse in them both before and after a trip.

9. Provide a classroom atmosphere conducive to voluntary reading. Both the emotional and physical environment should be inviting. Provide for informal group work; keep book and book jacket displays, colorful bulletin boards, and a reading corner with comfortable chairs or floor pillows.

10. Give special incentives or rewards to children who need some initial thrust to get them started reading. Extrinsic rewards may not sustain interest; they may serve as a device to initiate the youngster into a self-satisfying reading experience. Many teachers report favorable results from using charts recording pupils' reading. The awarding of some special classroom job that the pupils desire or the awarding of a book of his own might motivate the reluctant reader. Often a few warm words of praise or extra attention may be incentive enough.

11. Use enrichment and follow-up activities judiciously. Enrichment activities that do not grow out of children's interests and ideas, out of their desire for self-expression, probably do more harm than good, particularly when the teacher follows up the basic-reader story with directions to "draw a picture of your favorite character," or "Write a paragraph telling me what you liked about the story."

12. Avoid formal, written book reports on voluntary reading. Talk about books informally; invite pupils' comments; challenge pupils to interest their classmates in a book. But don't punish pupils for reading or drive them to cheat themselves.

13. Have children keep informal records of their independent reading, perhaps on cards or in their notebooks. As their voluntary reading grows, they will be rewarded by the expanding records. Such a record will help them evaluate their own reading, and serve as a guide to the teacher in helping the weaker pupils.

14. In evaluating reading, use only those procedures that will help the child realistically assess his present reading accomplishments or provide new insights into his strengths and weaknesses for the teacher.

The following specific suggestions for classroom activities to encourage voluntary reading came from a list prepared by several hundred teachers at a recent workshop.

1. Have interested children write letters to the librarian requesting particular books which they have heard about.

2. Pupils might write a letter to a friend or classmate to recommend a book.

3. Create a colorful class mural depicting the various interests of the pupils. This will cut across all ability levels.

4. A puppet or marionette show to illustrate a story is sure to interest all primary children.

5. If a travel book has been read, the pupil might give an illustrated lecture using postcards, photos, slides, or magazine pictures.

6. Creating a series of original illustrations for a story requires good judgment in the selection of incidents.

7. The teacher's dramatic telling of only part of the plot of a good story is certain to send many pupils to the book.

8. A child's original book jacket may attract other children to the book.

9. A visit and talk by a local author or illustrator may send pupils to the library.

10. Children enjoy adding endings of their own and making other changes in a story.

11. Advertise books by having daily book-news announcements, brief skits; television shows; or bulletin board displays.

12. Have a book club in the room through which books are discussed, swapped, and purchased.

13. Keep a display of good magazines of various kinds, not overlooking those considered adult: *National Geographic, Life, Mankind, Scientific American, American Heritage, Science Digest, Reader's Digest.*

14. Organize a school- or system-wide book fair, calling on publishers, book stores, and community libraries to assist.

A NOTE ON POETRY

Poetry is language in its most delightful and exciting form. Why then are so many pupils and adults alienated from it? Why is it such a rarity at the high school level to find a boy who admits that he likes poetry?

There are no simple answers to these questions. It is clear, however, that the presentation of poetry in school is quite largely to blame: (1) Much of the verse presented is poor, unsuited to the interests and experiences of the pupils; (2) poetry is often presented as something to be "learned" rather than experienced and enjoyed; (3) poetry is often a vehicle for teaching oral interpretation, the poem being secondary to the mechanics of presentation; and, most important, (4) too few teachers appear to like poetry and present it with the enthusiasm it deserves.

To promote an interest in poetry, then, teachers must discover for themselves what poetry has to offer. If the teacher's knowledge of children's poetry is limited and his/her ability to present it in the classroom is weak, he/she should take a good course in children's literature or make a study of poetry and a good book on the subject of children's literature, such as Charlotte Huck and Doris Kuhn's *Children's Literature in the Elementary School* (Holt, Rinehart and Winston, 1979).

The teacher must seek ways to make poetry a regular and integral part of the entire language arts program. And there are many opportunities to bring in poems related to the content areas. There is hardly a subject about which there is not a poem children would enjoy.

Time for sharing favorite poetry should be a part of the language program. Pupils should be encouraged to write and read their own poetry. The teacher's presentation of short poetic forms such as the Haiku or ballad should be followed by pupils' attempts at writing, to demonstrate their proficiency as writers and to enhance their appreciation of the poet's work.

Marilyn R. Mazer tells of her experience in teaching pupils in the American School, U.S. Air Force Base, Tachikawa, Japan, how to write Haiku poetry.

> Writing Haiku poetry seems to like a suction force to young people. Haiku provides enough structure to guide the children, yet wide latitude for freedom of expression. Possessing an acute awareness for detail, children are natural "lookers." Haiku seems to exploit this special ability.
>
> In teaching Haiku, I impose only the restriction of pattern—17 syllables, three lines of 5–7–5 syllables, respectively. Usually it is attempted about three or four months after the beginning of school. During that time the children are involved in many language experiences that may prepare them for fashioning Haiku. They work on some figurative language-similes, metaphors, and alliteration. Using expressive verbs, writing vivid descriptive words and phrases to create clear mental pictures are a few of the activities the children engage in before writing the actual poems.
>
> I try to provide at least one creative writing experience a week. Frequently the children are asked to do impromptu writing, as the occasion arises. A sudden deluge of rain may inspire a descriptive sentence; snowfall may provoke a special mood; sounds of an insect invader may stimulate a need for expression. I merely capitalize on the freshness of seeing and feeling things the children, not totally manacled by conformity, seem to have.
>
> The day arrives to actually compose Haiku. Interest may be initiated in several ways. Teaching in Japan, I can relate a personal experience to trigger a discussion.

We may talk about art forms—Kabuki, Bunraku. Eventually we focus on the poem form peculiar to Japan; a brief history of Haiku ensues.

A film of Japanese life, pictures of Japan, Japanese prints, even scenes of nature clipped from magazines may all be employed as approaches to evoke interest.

I read many samples of Haiku—total immersion. Samples of children's work kept from previous years are shared. Reading Haiku translated from Japanese also contributes to the apprehension of this art form.

We discuss the subject range of Haiku. It usually deals with the seasons, or any aspect of nature. Along with the subject, the aim of Haiku is discovered. I might ask the children how they would capture an occurrence in nature, a fleeting scene to keep for posterity. The usual response: 'Take a picture.' I might then ask what we would do if we had no camera, or could not draw a picture. We could, of course, write it down. Haiku emerges as a word picture.

I never reject anything they write. I may, infrequently, suggest they think of a more expressive word should they become too trite. Rhyme is not necessary; in fact, it is detracting.

Often we illustrate the Haiku. I make a broadside of each using magic marker pens, and post them around the room with the young poets' names for all to enjoy.

Following are examples of Haiku written by Mrs. Mazer's pupils:

The chattering leaves
Twist and turn in the loud wind.
Autumn is here now. (Joey Felipe)

Rushing with the wind,
Whispering in the dark sky,
The leaves fall shyly. (Vickie Mitchell)

Lying on the ground,
I can see the clouds flying
Swiftly and lonely. (Roy Youngman)

The stars shone brightly
As the river rippled on
Its way through the night. (Terry Ann Mason)

The snow is clear white
The sun blazes pale orange
To bring new morning. (Susan L. Mercer)

SUMMARY

There are four key factors in developing enthusiastic readers: (1) an abundance of reading materials in the classroom—books, magazines, newspapers, reference sources, and so on; (2) adequate time for voluntary reading during each school day; (3) a teacher who loves to read and conveys this to the pupils;

and (4) a willingness on the part of the teacher to do the hard work of studying the pupil's abilities and interests and providing the necessary guidance to bring pupils to a book that might be right for them.

Classroom activities fostering interests focus on saturating the room with attractive and curiosity-provoking books and advertisements for books. It is indeed a rare child who, when books of appropriate difficulty levels are available, can resist a daily barrage of sights and sounds centered on the notion that reading is delightful.

LEARNING ACTIVITIES

1. Briefly explain how the nature of a school reading program might discourage recreational reading.

2. Suggest several specific books for children based upon currently popular television shows or movies.

3. Suggest several ways a teacher might build a classroom library over a period of several years at low cost.

4. Locate several poems that you think would appeal to the average sixth-grade boy. Explain why you think he might like them and how you would present them to him.

5. Imagine that you are a reading consultant in an elementary school where children's voluntary reading is at a low ebb. Make ten recommendations to improve the situation, involving the principal, teachers, parents, and pupils in both planning and specific activities.

6. Administer a reading interest inventory to a small group of pupils. Using the results, make a list of books you think they would enjoy reading.

7. Read the opposing arguments of Groff and Hoskisson in *The Reading Teacher* (Mar. 1979), pp. 647–659. Which approach (or combination of the two) might do most to engender wider recreational reading?

8. Observe the instructional reading program in a school and compare the amount of time spent on actual reading with that spent on skill building and workbook activities. To what extent, if any, are the two activities out of balance?

STUDY QUESTIONS

1. Explain how the extent of voluntary reading in a school might reflect the success of the total school reading program.

2. List three contributions wide reading experience makes to a child's learning, maturation, and socialization.

3. Describe three obstacles to voluntary reading by pupils.

4. List the general areas of reading preference of elementary students.

5. Describe two techniques for discovering the reading interests of a specific group of pupils.

6. List several sources for selecting good children's books.
7. List four guidelines for a school program to follow in expanding voluntary reading.
8. List five specific activities or techniques for generating interest in books.
9. Explain why poetry is generally low on the list of reading preferences of older students.

RECOMMENDED READING

ALEXANDER, J. E., (Ed.). *Teaching Reading.* Boston: Little, Brown and Company, 1979.

DEBOER, JOHN J. and MARTHA DALLMANN. *The Teaching of Reading.* New York: Holt, Rinehart and Winston, 1976, Chap. 11.

DIETRICH, DOROTHY M. and V. H. MATHEWS (Eds.). *Development of Lifetime Reading Habits.* Newark, Del.: International Reading Association, 1968.

GANS, ROMA. *Common Sense in Teaching Reading.* Indianapolis: The Bobbs-Merrill Co., Inc., 1963, Chap. 13.

HARRIS, ALBERT J. and EDWARD R. SIPAY. *How to Increase Reading Ability.* 7th ed. New York: David McKay Co., Inc., 1981.

HUCK, CHARLOTTE and D. KUHN. *Children's Literature in the Elementary School.* New York: Holt, Rinehart and Winston, 1979.

LAPP, DIANE and J. FLOOD. *Teaching Reading to Every Child.* New York: Macmillan Publishing Co., Inc., 1978, Chap. 5.

QUANDT, IVAN J. *Teaching Reading: A Human Process.* Skokie, Ill.: Rand McNally & Company, 1977, Chap. 10.

VEATCH, JEANETTE. *Reading in the Elementary School.* New York: The Ronald Press Company, 1966, Chaps. 13 and 14.

REFERENCES

ASHLEY, L. F. "Children's Reading Interests and Individualized Reading." *Elementary English,* 47 (1970), 1088–1096.

BYRES, L. "Pupils' Interests and the Content of Primary Reading Texts." *The Reading Teacher,* 17 (1964), 227–233.

CRISCUOLO, N. P. "Effective Approaches for Motivating Children to Read." *The Reading Teacher,* 32 (1979), 543–546.

CRISCUOLO, N. P. "More Miracle Motivators for Reluctant Readers." *Instructor,* 89 (8) (March 1980), 72–74.

FRASHER, R. S. "Boys, Girls and Pippi Longstocking." *The Reading Teacher,* 30 (1977), 860–863.

GROFF, P. "A Critique of Teaching Reading As a Whole Task Venture," *The Reading Teacher,* 32 (1979) 647–652.

HOSKISSON, K. "A Response to 'A Critique of Teaching Reading As a Whole Task Venture'," *The Reading Teacher,* 32 (1979), 653–659.

MEISEL, S. and G. G. GLASS. "Voluntary Reading Interests and the Interest Content of Basal Readers." *The Reading Teacher,* 23 (1970), 655–659.

MONTEITH, M. K. "How Well Does the Average American Read?" *Journal of Reading,* 23 (1980), 460–463.

MORAY, G. "What Does Research Say About the Reading Interests of Children in the Intermediate Grades," *The Reading Teacher,* 31 (1978), 763–768.

NORVELL, G. W. "The Challenge of Periodicals in Education." *Elementary English,* 43 (1966), 402–408.

PELTOLA, B. J. "A Study of Children's Book Choices." *Elementary English,* 40 (1963), 690–696.

PIERONEK, F. T. "Do Basal Readers Reflect the Interests of Intermediate Students?" *The Reading Teacher,* 33 (1980), 408–411.

ROGERS, E. and H. A. ROBINSON. "Reading Interests of First-Graders." *Elementary English,* 40 (1963), 707–711.

ROSS, P. "Getting Books into Those Empty Hands." *The Reading Teacher,* 31 (1978), 397–399.

SKELTON, D. "Pupils' Interest in Reading." *Elementary English,* 38 (1961), 246–249.

SLOVER, V. "Comic Book Versus Story Books." *Elementary English,* 36 (1959), 319–322.

SMITH, F. *Comprehension and Learning.* New York: Holt, Rinehart and Winston, 1975.

SMITH, M. and I. ENO. "What Do They Really Want to Read?" *Elementary English,* 38 (1961), 343–345.

STANCHFIELD, J. N. "Boys' Reading Interests As Revealed Through Personal Conferences." *The Reading Teacher,* 16 (1962), 41–44.

WALCUTT, C. C., J. LAMPORT, and G. McCRACKEN (with chapters by R. DYKSTRA). *Teaching Reading.* New York: Macmillan Publishing Co., Inc., 1974.

WITTY, P. A., A. M. FREELAND, and E. GROTBERG. *The Teaching of Reading, A Developmental Process.* Lexington, Mass.: D. C. Heath, 1966, Chap. 3.

WOLFSON, B. J. "What Do Children Say Their Reading Interests Are?" *The Reading Teacher,* 14 (1960), 81–82.

WRIGHT, G. "The Comic Book—A Forgotten Medium in the Classroom," *The Reading Teacher,* 33 (1979), 158–161.

YATVIN, J. "Recreational Reading for the Whole School," *The Reading Teacher,* 31 (1977), 185–188.

CHAPTER 10

Using Supporting Materials and Systems

OBJECTIVES

As a result of thoroughly processing the material in this chapter the reader should be able to state/explain the following:

1. *The meaning of reading disability and its incidence.*
2. *The result of not challenging gifted pupils.*
3. *Problems associated with some organizational patterns.*
4. *The meaning of proper instruction.*
5. *The characteristics of methods and materials that make self-instruction possible.*
6. *The meaning of supporting instructional materials.*
7. *The operation of programmed learning.*
8. *The key ideas and strengths of a number of reading instruction systems.*
9. *Six important considerations involved in the general logistics of reading instruction.*
10. *Operation of the* High Intensity Learning System(s).

Many students are not reading up to their potential. By definition, they have a reading disability. After reviewing a number of studies, Harris and Sipay (1976) estimated the incidence of reading disability to be about 12 per cent. This means that one student in eight or nine was not reading up to his/her potential.

These disability cases include students of all levels of ability. By plotting expected achievement based on capacity measures against actual achievement, one can show that for gifted students there is a greater discrepancy between reading achievement and expected achievement than for average students. Experience, too, shows that the result of not challenging the gifted can lead to ineffective, inefficient study habits and attitudes that result in lessened achievement as the rigors of academic life increase in later elementary and secondary school years.

Over the years many organizational plans and curriculum-adjustment procedures have been tried by schools to provide for individual differences in student ability. Most of these plans have been thoroughly described and evaluated by other texts in reading or curriculum development and for this reason will be touched on only briefly here.

Basically, most of the organizational patterns have concentrated on grouping pupils according to their reading ability, either within a grade level, as in most homogeneous grouping plans, or without regard for the student's actual grade placement, as in the interclass grouping plans. These plans have received similar criticisms from the experts: they unrealistically separate reading from the language areas and from the content areas; they do not ensure sequential mastery of skills; they do not ensure homogeneity of ability; they complicate the problems of grading and record keeping. In short, they do not accomplish the purpose of providing for the student's needs. It is a telling comment that none of the many plans tried over the years has proved so successful as to be recommended generally by a large number of objective experts in the field.

In view of the lack of success of such plans, most reading authorities seem to favor, as the most desirable means of providing for individual differences, the heterogeneous, self-contained classroom, provided that (1) the student load is reasonable (not more than 25), (2) the facilities and equipment are adequate, and (3) the teacher has good insight into the nature and potentials of the materials and a clear grasp of sound teaching principles.

Dahllof (1971) found that lower-ability students learn equally well in heterogeneously and homogeneously grouped classes, but medium- and high-ability students learn more in homogeneously grouped classes. One must question whether or not that finding would hold true in the various kinds of situations that exist in the schools. Zeichner (1978) in a study of 621 fifth- and sixth-grade students discovered that a person's sense of acceptance by the peer group is positively related to reading achievement.

PROPER INSTRUCTION

What does proper instruction mean? To us it means several things:

Direct Instruction and Self-Instruction. Not only must teachers interact with students and do a lot of explaining, cueing, and telling in order that students may learn how ideas on the printed page are related but teachers must help students get started with (and continue to monitor) related, independent self-instruction.

Teaching Students at Their Level. The classroom teacher would do well to look at teachers who are successful in teaching individuals because they introduce tasks always in terms of present achievement. One never sees a track coach, for example, who sets the high jump bar at five feet ten inches for a girl when the best she has ever done was five feet. Neither does a good piano teacher put into a level 5 book a student who has just completed a level 3 book. Whether in high jumping, piano playing, or reading, being placed at an incorrect level produces frustration, anxiety, and a poor self-concept—all of which interfere with ability to perform. In reading, such anxiety interferes with the ability to concentrate, to perceive well, and to think abstractly. The student will not be able to achieve at that too difficult level.

Too many students are placed in materials one or two (and more) levels too difficult for them. Students appreciate and respond well to instruction that is meaningful to them, that is, instruction at their level.

Pacing Instruction. Instruction should be paced so that a student can master material at each level before going on to new levels and more difficult material. People are hesitant about engaging in any (academic) activity in which they do not feel confident. Since mastery breeds confidence, the teacher must consider, too, the horizontal aspects of instruction. More practice should be given so that real competence and confidence result. Good reading teachers, like their colleagues in music and physical education, arrange for this. As an example of the success of mastery instruction, note the study by Katims and others (1977) who reported that learners receiving mastery learning-based instruction made greater gains in reading comprehension than did control groups not receiving such instruction. Briggs' (1972) study utilizing the *Sound Reading Program*—essentially a mastery approach—also vindicated mastery-learning instruction. A valuable discussion of mastery learning can be found in an article by Rupley and Longman (1978).

Eliciting Responses. Material should be introduced in such a way that every pupil will make many responses during a day and that he/she will make a large proportion of correct responses. Pupils need to make more responses during a day so that their time will not be wasted and they will learn more. To this end, they must be in some learning situations where they can read (at their level), can respond to questions, and then be immediately reinforced for their correct responses, and to a large extent, independent of the teacher—for it is obvious that a teacher cannot directly instruct at one time pupils who vary so greatly in achievement.

Encouraging Self-Instruction. So that independent, individual (self) instruction is possible, materials and methods should be made available that have some or all of the following characteristics:

1. Are sequentially and logically organized.
2. Are presented in optimal size steps.
3. Afford many opportunities to respond.
4. Are geared so that approximately 90 per cent of the pupil's responses will be correct.
5. Are geared so that pupil receives immediate feedback as to the correctness of responses.
6. Will teach all the basic reading skills plus concept development in content areas.

7. Could be used without disturbing other pupils in the classroom.

8. Could be used individually and in small groups.

9. Would actually instruct.

10. Would be supportive to the direct instruction of the teacher.

11. Would keep pupils profitably occupied in real instructional activities when not receiving direct instruction from the teacher or not engaging in project and other types of independent or small group activities.

This is not to say that direct reading instruction is not necessary, but a certain amount of self-instruction is useful, too.

SUPPORTING MATERIALS IN READING INSTRUCTION

The advances that make proper, individualized reading instruction possible are available. By supporting materials we mean programmed materials, audiovisual devices and programs, boxed kits, and computer-assisted instruction. Such materials permit a large degree of self-instruction that is sequential and permits numbers of children in the same classrooms who are at different achievement levels to be instructed at these different levels at the same time— at their own levels. At the present time there is interest in such proper, individualized instruction utilizing instructional supporting materials.

PROGRAMMED INSTRUCTION

Sullivan Associates Programs

The Prereading Program. The Sullivan Associates prereading program is written by M. W. Sullivan and Cynthia D. Buchanan. It acquaints pupils with printed symbols and the relationships of these symbols to speech sounds. The pupil completing the prereading course will know (1) the names of letters, (2) how to print letters, (3) that letters represent sounds, (4) which sounds *a, f, m, n, t, th,* and *i* represent, (5) that reading is done from left to right across the page, (6) that words are formed from groups of letters, and (7) how to read *yes* and *no* and the following sentences containing words made up of the letters listed in point 4:

I am an ant.	I am a pan.
I am a man.	I am tan.
I am a mat.	I am thin.
I am a pin.	I am fat.

As in other programmed materials, small amounts of information are given, a problem is posed, a response is elicited, and the response is then corrected or reinforced at once. In this way, the pupil can progress from simple letter discrimination toward more complex reading behavior or to reading words, sentences, and stories.

The Programmed Reading Program. The programmed reading program is comprised of 21 levels, with one book per level. Although pupils progress step by step through each book—and it is expected that they will be ready for the next book when they complete a given book—they are expected to pass an end-of-book test before proceeding to the next book. There are seven books in each of the three sequences in the program, and after each sequence a pupil must pass a special test before advancing to the next sequence.

Pages reproduced from Books 1, 5, and 11 in the Sullivan Associates Programmed Reading Series illustrate the program (see Figure 10-1). The left-hand column containing the answers is covered by the pupil. After each response he/she slides the marker down and checks to see if his/her response is correct.

To determine at which point a pupil (who is not a beginner) would enter a program, a placement examination is administered. In addition to the programmed readers and response books that are used in all three series, the first series has available word cards, filmstrips, supplementary story books, and ditto masters. Series 2 has available ditto masters and story books.

Strengths of the Sullivan Associates Programs. (1) Good record-keeping allows absentees or transfer pupils to pick up where they left off. (2) Pupils

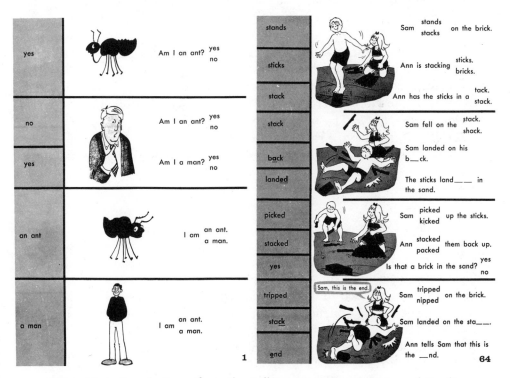

Figure 10-1. Sample Pages from the Sullivan Associates Programmed Reading Series. (Reprinted by permission from Programmed Reading: Books 1 and 5 *by Sullivan Associates. Published by Webster Division, McGraw-Hill Book Company.)*

progress step by step at their levels. (3) Active responses are required, and the program permits a pupil to make many correct responses. Correct responses are made at least 95 per cent of the time when a pupil is correctly placed in the program. (4) There is an immediate reward for correct responses and a correction for incorrect ones.

The Norelco Company Programs

The Norelco reading programs for upper elementary grades utilize a teaching machine (the Norelco EL–9001) and programmed materials. The programs are C5, *How to Improve Your Reading*; C10, *Figures of Speech*; and C12, *Words: Their Origin and Meaning*. The programmed material is contained on 3- by 5-inch microfiche cards, each of which has 198 individual instructional frames. Programs are available not only in reading but in a number of content areas. A teacher can also create his own materials, using Norelco's microfiche service to reproduce them on the cards.

The design of the selection system permits easy access to any microfiche card in the program and to any frame on a microfiche card. The response system has eight answer buttons and a reverse button for responding to instructional problems on each frame. The machine is designed to use linear programs and branching programs. An optional unit, the EL9002, allows for written responses.

Norelco "offers a programmed instruction course designed especially for teachers in training, teachers in service . . . who want to know more about programmed instruction and how to create their own programs."

Strengths of the Norelco Programs. The Norelco reading programs offer the following strengths: (1) The material is compact. (2) There is immediate feedback as to the correctness of the response. (3) Responses can be multiple-choice or written. (4) The system can be adapted to use teacher-written materials.

California Test Bureau

Lessons for Self-instruction in Basic Skills: Reading is a programmed course that teaches the following reading skills: (1) following directions, (2) reference skills, (3) reading interpretation I, and (4) reading interpretation II. Levels 4 through 6 were developed for pupils in grade 3 through high school.

The lessons can be used under the guidance of a teacher and in independent work. Each booklet is designed so that an individual can progress at his/her own level and rate.

Some of the lessons have multiple-choice features, and some allow a pupil to construct his own responses. If he chooses an incorrect answer, the text shows in what way he is wrong. When he makes a correct choice, the explanation of the answer reinforces his knowledge of principles.

Figure 10-2 is a segment of a lesson from Following Directions, Series C–D:

25

10th Street

The four rectangles above stand for city blocks. The dotted lines show the intersection of Monroe Avenue and 10th Street. A, B, C, and D are corner houses.

Each of the four houses is "at the corner of Monroe and 10th." But at which corner?

This little drawing will help:

Imagine that the second drawing is laid on the intersection. The four arrows would point to the four corner houses.

Now you see that House A is at the northwest (NW) corner of Monroe Avenue and 10th Street. You can also tell the location of the three other houses on the intersection.

Here is something for you to think about:

A person was told to go to the house on the south-east (SE) corner of Monroe and 10th.

Which house is at the SE corner?

It is House B. (No. 31)

It is House C. (No. 36)

It is House D. (No. 41)

31

It is House B.

 No, it is not. You were asked to find the house that is on the SE (southeast) corner. House B is not on that corner.

Imagine that the smaller drawing in No. 25 is laid on the intersection. To which house would the letters SE point?

Go back to No. 25.

36

It is House C.

 No, House C is not on the southeast corner of Monroe and 10th.

Return to No. 25. Read again the paragraph below the smaller drawing there. It will help you answer the question correctly.

41

It is House D.

 No doubt about it! The drawing at the right proves it.

Go to No. 24.

Figure 10-2. From "Following Directions," Series C-D of the Lessons for Self-instruction in Basic Skills: Reading by Miles Midloch (Consultants: Edward B. Fry and Lawrence W. Carrillo). Used by permission of the publisher, CTB/McGraw-Hill, Monterey, CA.) A revised edition, 1979, titled "Reading 400, Following Directions" is on the market. It seems to be suitable for students in the upper middle grades and above.

Strengths of the LSI Reading Program. The LSI Reading Program has certain strengths: (1) Several important reading skills are taught. (2) The lessons can be used independently or under the guidance of a teacher. (3) Some lessons allow constructed responses to be made. (4) Feedback shows *why* an answer is correct or incorrect. (5) The materials are easy to handle.

AUDIOVISUAL INSTRUCTION

Hoffman Information Systems (HIS)

The Hoffman Primary Language Arts and Phonics Program is designed for reading-readiness instruction. The sixty study units, divided into six sets with ten units in each set, are written by Phyllis Dole, Dorothy Andrews, and Joan Clary. The study programs, which are presented on the Mark IV Projector (as are all of the HIS programs), teach auditory discrimination, auditory memory, recognition of the visual symbols that stand for sounds, and the ability to print or draw letters. The letter symbols that represent the sounds are taught in both capital and lowercase forms. In each of the sixty units there is concept and language-usage development in the areas of science and natural phenomena, social studies, make-believe, family life, and mental health.

The entire Hoffman program may be used to advantage before formal instruction in reading print. Or it may be used in conjunction with developmental basal text instruction to support and reinforce phonics skills and the decoding process, as well as to enrich language aspects. Second- and third-grade pupils who need help in specific sounds may be assigned to certain study units to meet their individual needs.

HIS Reading Achievement Program Level 1 was written by Phyllis Dole, Dorothy Andrews, and Joan Clary. It is designed to provide individual and small group instruction in auditory and visual discrimination, basic sight vocabulary, phonetic analysis and structural analysis skills, concept development, and reading comprehension skills.

This program consists of sixty lessons of reading instruction, six sets of lesson albums with ten lessons in each set. Each audiovisual lesson is presented by means of two filmstrip sets and one record. Responses are made on *Do and Discover* worksheets. Associated with level 1 is a series of books called *Read to Learn* books. In these, pupils work to improve their understanding of the vocabulary that was introduced in the audiovisual presentation. There are twelve pages per book and there are sixty books, one for each lesson. Extensive use of the rebus concept is made in order to provide a larger context. At the back of each *Read to Learn* book are (1) a picture dictionary, (2) a set of flash cards that have the printed word on one side and a corresponding picture on the other (these cards can be cut out of the pages), and (3) a cumulative list of words.

HIS Reading Achievement Program Levels 2–6 is an audiovisual instruction system designed to provide individual and small-group instruction in auditory and visual discrimination, basic nucleus vocabulary, review of basic primary phonetic analysis and structural analysis skills, concept development, reading comprehension, and study skills. Level 2 is written by Phyllis Dole, Dorothy Andrews, and Joan Clary; level 3 is written by Phyllis Dole, and levels 4–6 are written by Louis Stoyanoff.

Each lesson album includes an audiovisual presentation of an original, factual, interesting story. Most of the color frames illustrate the story, but some of the frames are displays of visual text paralleling the audio signal. There are also sound effects for mood, setting, and realism.

The second presentation in the lesson, "Flashback on Facts," is designed to help develop comprehension and study skills. There is also reinforcement of new, technical, or scientific vocabulary.

The third segment, "Mirror on Meanings," is designed to develop vocabulary, which is presented audiovisually. The vocabulary meaning is presented in context and multiple meanings of words are dramatically presented.

In the last presentation, "Spotlight on Sounds," word-analysis skills are developed.

During these presentations visual and audio displays of information are made, questions are asked, and answers are given. After a person makes a response in his workbook, he pushes a button on the projector and the answer frame appears on the screen. He receives immediate reinforcement or correction.

When a pupil finishes a reading lesson, he is given a printed copy of the story in an attractive illustrated brochure called the *Encore Reader*. Following the story is a list of key words.

Each study album or lesson presents a dramatic story of high interest. The story content has been selected to have appeal to persons of a wide range of ages. The lessons, therefore, can be used to instruct young children as well as adults.

The Hoffman Reading Program can be used for individual or small group instruction through the use of earphones. Group instruction is facilitated by use of a jackbox that connects several sets of earphones.

The light, durable Mark IV Projector may be placed on a table or in a study carrel. Its operation does not disturb pupils engaged in other activities.

Strengths of the Hoffman Language Arts, Phonics, and Reading Programs. The following strengths are found in the Hoffman Langue Arts, Phonics, and Reading Programs: (1) All the language arts—reading, spelling, listening, and writing—are emphasized. (2) Concepts are developed in several content areas. (3) Individualized self-instruction is made possible by the unique methods of audio and visual display of stories and lessons. (4) The equipment is easy to handle and is easily moved about in the room. (5) The stories are interesting to children and adults. (6) *Encore* reading materials make it possible to take home a copy of the story to read to parents and to keep. (7) The system can be used as a supportive, supplementary program, as the main program, or as a remedial program.

Educational Progress Corporation

Audio Reading Kits (ARK) provide a reading development program consisting of four levels: *Alligator, Bear, Cougar,* and *Dolphin*. They were designed to help weak or below-level readers in grades 1 through 6 learn the basic decoding and comprehension skills they failed to learn in earlier instruction.

Lessons in the ARK program have been developed within ten interest areas:

Animals and Pets	Sports, Games, and Hobbies
Myth, Folklore, and Fantasy	The Lives of People
Mystery and Adventure	The Paths of History
Human Relations	The World of Science
Humor	The World of Work

The components of ARK lessons are (1) lesson cards and instructional tapes, providing quality instruction and motivation through the use of dramatization, sound effects, and a teacher; (2) activity sheets, with audio accompaniment, that provide reinforcement of each lesson subskill: the additional story content and artwork printed on the activity sheets further explicate the characterization, themes, and plot lines developed in the lesson story; (3) marking pencils and plastic sleeves, which are easily cleaned for further use; and (4) teacher's guide explaining the rationale and organization of the program and detailed information to help the teacher implement the program.

Overview of the ARK Program:

Level	Skill	Readability	Grade level
Alligator	Simple and Advanced Phonetic Word Analysis	1.0 - 2.0	1 - 3
Bear	Simple and Advanced Phonetic Word Analysis	1.0 - 2.0	2 - 4
Cougar	Phonetic Word Analysis Structural Word Analysis	1.0 - 2.5	4 - 6
Dolphin	Advanced Phonetic Word Analysis; Structural Word Analysis	1.5 - 2.5	5 - 6

Audio Reading Progress Laboratory (ARPL) Revised is an eight-level, audio-tutorial reading instruction program designed to supplement the content of basal reading series and to develop basic word analysis and comprehension skills of students of varying reading abilities in grades 1 to 8.

Audio instruction leads the student through each lesson, moving at a natural pace to facilitate blending of sound to support meaning. Significant emphasis to content is given by the speech patterns of tone and pause. Through imitation and inference the student applies language strategies to learning to read.

Because of the close coordination of the audio instruction and the student lesson page the learner can acquire new skills as well as practice old ones.

Each lesson is based on learning objectives. The reading skills taught fall into five basic categories: phonetic word analysis, structural word analysis, comprehension, vocabulary, and study skills. Comprehension is emphasized in each lesson. Teacher's guides are provided for each level of the program.

The ARPL: Level A Program is the preparatory level of the previously discussed program. It is designed to assist young children to develop the skills that undergird reading. The components of the level A program are audio tapes, reading progress books, teacher's resource books, circular game board, alphabet letter boards, wooden game cubes, deck of game cards, and a game spinner.

Independent Reading Skills Laboratory (IRSL) is a series of three laboratories that enrich and extend the comprehension skills of the average or above-average readers in grades 1 through 6. The IRSL is designed so that a number of students can use it at the same time. The program offers readers positive enjoyable reading experiences and uses these experiences to develop recall, comprehension, thinking, and vocabulary skills.

The components of the IRSL are (1) *student booklets* containing modern and classical readings from a wide variety of interest areas; (2) *dramatapes* of the literary selections, all related by theme to selections in the *student booklets*; (3) study cards, geared to the booklets, that provide three types of exercises: direct recall questions, comprehension skill exercises, vocabulary exercises, and a teacher's guide.

Educational Developmental Laboratories

EDL publishes a number of programs designed to improve reading and study skills of pupils at various levels.

EDL Listen and Read. *The EDL Listen and Read* program, by Stanford E. Taylor and colleagues is designed to develop both listening and reading abilities; it consists of a series of 30 audio tapes and a workbook that contains an exercise for each tape. Through careful listening and workbook exercises, which entail reading, students get practice in various phases of the skill or concept involved.

Set D-F, developed for students reading at levels 4–6, has lessons on skills such as identifying main ideas, using details, comparing, recognizing cause and effect, making inferences, predicting outcomes, using maps and graphs, using PQR (Preview, Question, Read), outlining, summarizing, interpreting figurative language, and interpreting poetry.

Set G–L, developed for students reading at levels 7–12, would be appropriate for good readers in the upper grades of elementary school. The first two lessons show the interrelationships of listening, language, and reading. The next set deals with increasing understanding of words, sentences, and paragraphs, and their use in expressing ideas. The third group of lessons teaches study skills, and the last 11 lessons encourage critical reading and listening as well as the enjoyment of a variety of literary forms. Each lesson lasts about 30 minutes.

EDL Aud X. *The EDL Mark 4 Aud-X* is an audiovisual teaching device utilizing cartridge-loaded filmstrips with matching cassettes. The filmstrips contain photographs, illustrations, words, or other graphic material. The audio mode presents teaching content, lesson directions, and appropriate sound effects or music. When a pupil is finished responding to a question, he/she presses a button and advances to the next frame for correction or reinforcement.

In the readiness stage the pupil learns (1) the relationships between letters and sounds. (2) the name of each letter, and (3) how to discriminate each letter from other letters.

In beginning-reading instruction, the Aud-X can display a word on the screen at the same time the record gives the spoken form, so that a connection can be established between the printed word and its speech sound. The construction of a word can be shown by dropping and adding letters through rapid frame changes.

EDL Controlled-Reading Program. *The EDL Controlled-Reading Program* is divided into two parts, the readiness phase and the reading phase. The filmstrips that contain the reading material are used in a machine called the EDL Controlled Reader.

The readiness phase is designed to develop in pupils such abilities as concentration, observation, retention, discrimination, and logical reasoning. The six picture nouns filmstrips show pictures of 120 nouns that are commonly referred to in beginning reading in order to ensure recognition of familiar objects and to speed word-picture-experience association. The categories filmstrips present everyday objects in such categories as tools, tableware, vegetables, and household articles. Training builds on and expands experience and develops the ability to classify and to see relationships among common objects. Visual discrimination filmstrips were developed to improve the ability to note gross and minute differences existing among objects. The reasoning filmstrips were developed to strengthen the ability of pupils to see relationships between objects by identifying things that are used together or often found together and to tell why the things are related. The auditory discrimination filmstrips help a pupil hear similarities in the way words begin or end.

The reading phase is designed to develop word recognition, vocabulary, and comprehension skills. During Controlled Reader training, reading material is uncovered and covered as a slot travels across the screen from left to right. The slot can be stopped and started for vocabulary, pictures, or oral reading. For silent reading the automatic speeds ranging from 60 to 1,000 words per minute can be used.

EDL Word Study Skills Program. This reading skills support system teaches phonics, structural analysis, and usage skills with 85 sound-filmstrip lessons and 26 teacher-taught lessons. Instruction, reinforcement, evaluation, and reteaching are given for each lesson with reading levels from 1–4 and interest levels 1–6. Criterion-referenced tests are available for each performance objective.

The Controlled-Reading Program covers a wide range (preprimer to level 14). At the primary levels the materials are written to correlate with such basal programs as those published by Allyn & Bacon; American Book; Ginn; D. C. Heath; Houghton Mifflin: Macmillan; Row, Peterson; Scott, Foresman; and Silver Burdett.

The stories can be used for silent and oral reading. They are designed to help develop sight vocabulary, reading fluency, and comprehension.

From reading level 4 through level 14 each student has a *Controlled-Reading Study Guide.* The complete text of each selection may be surveyed before it is read in the Controlled Reader. After reading a selection on films, a student takes the comprehension quizzes on the film story. The student answers detail, inference, and main idea questions in addition to a "think about" question to start group discussion, creative thinking, and work on individual essays. Also included is a Progress Chart.

Other EDL Programs. *EDL Comprehension Power Paragraphs and Sentences* by Dorothy Dietrich and others is a controlled reading program similar in nature to the program just described. Designated labels are from grade 3 to grade 8. The Comprehension Power filmstrips were developed to combine perceptual training with the development of a number of important comprehension skills.

EDL Listen, Look, and Learn is a beginning reading instructional program that uses a number of techniques and media that enlist the several sensory learning modalities of a pupil. Special features of the program include building of auditory and visual perception skills, a multilevel high interest library, films, filmstrips, and recordings. Also available are programs in listening, word attack, and comprehension. The total system provides instruction from kindergarten through grade 6.

Individual progress is furthered by a combination of self-instruction, team learning, and group learning. The program provides the instructional materials and teachers guides needed for 205 days of beginning reading instruction.

In the *EDL Study Skills Library,* second edition, by H. Robinson and others, each lesson is designed as a self-directed reading activity. Using these materials, each student can work at his/her own level and rate. In order to ensure a student's being able to read and comprehend the selections and instructions, he/she is started in the material one year below his/her reading instruction level.

The Study Skills program develops both comprehension and study skills. The chief study skills are interpretation, evaluation, organization, and reference. Each lesson deals with a particular study skill and is carefully developed in these steps: (1) skill explanation, (2) example, (3) application to content just read, and (4) checking work against the answer key.

At each level, from third reading level through ninth reading level, there are three kits available—in science, in social studies, and in reference skills. To keep track of their progress, students keep their own records and maintain a lesson-to-lesson progress chart. Figure 10–3 shows segments of a lesson designed to teach comprehension and study skills.

EDL Listen and Think is a program designed to develop listening comprehension and its concomitant listening skills. The skills are organized around four key areas: analysis, interpretation, appreciation, and criticism. After a skill

STUDY THESE KEY WORDS:

skull (skul)
 The bones of the head. *The skull protects the brain.*

gland (gland)
 A part of the body that produces substances which help the body to work properly. *Glands make the liquid which moistens the mouth.*

lens (lenz)
 A part of the eye that directs light rays upon the layer of cells that receives images. *Glasses help the lenses in our eyes to make better images.*

mag ni fy ing lens (mag′ na fī′ ing lenz)
 A specially made piece of glass which makes an object appear larger than it really is. *A microscope contains a special kind of magnifying glass.*

nerve (nèrv)
 A stringlike bundle of tiny living threads in our bodies along which messages can travel to and from the brain and spinal cord. *Nerves that end in the tongue help you to taste things.*

Have you ever wondered how our eyes are able to do so many tasks? This science selection describes the parts of the eyes and how they work.

SURVEY the selection by quickly reading the headings and looking at the pictures and their captions.

hat, āge, cāre, fär; let, ēqual, term; it, īce; hot, ōpen, ôrder; oil, out; cup, pút, rüle, üse; ch, child; ng, long; th, thin; ŦĦ, then, sh, measure; ə represents a in about, e in taken, i in pencil, o in lemon, u in circus.
From the Thorndike-Barnhart School Dictionaries, courtesy Scott, Foresman and Company.

OUR EYES

READ the selection carefully to find out:
 How do your eyes work?
 What are some ways in which your eyes are protected?
 What does the lens in the eye do?

Look closely at some of the parts of an eye. The colored part is called the *iris*. The black part in the center of the iris is called the *pupil*.

The pupil is an opening in the iris. The pupil looks black because the inside of the eye is dark. Light reflected from things around us goes into the eye through the pupil.

There is a clear covering over the front of the eye. You can see this clear covering by looking at someone's eye from the side.

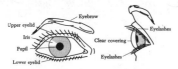

How Pupils Act

Pupils can change in size. They are small when the light is bright. They are large when the light is dim. When you go into a bright place, your pupils close and keep out some of the light. When you go into a dark place, your pupils open and let in as much light as possible. When you go into a dark theater on a sunny afternoon, at first you cannot see your way to a seat. After a few minutes you can see your way. Your pupils have opened and let in more light.

Do your eyes hurt when you turn on a bright light after being in a dark room? Your pupils are large in the dark room. They let in so much bright light that your eyes hurt. After a few minutes, however, you can see better and your eyes are comfortable.

DID YOU UNDERSTAND WHAT YOU READ?

Choose the Best Answer

1. The colored part of the eye is called the
 a. pupil.
 b. lens.
 c. iris.

2. Light reflected from things around us enters the eye through the
 a. pupil.
 b. lens.
 c. iris.

3. When you go from a dark room into a bright room, the pupils of your eyes
 a. become smaller.
 b. become larger.
 c. remain the same size.

7. The writer of this selection is most interested in showing us
 a. how well our eyes are protected.
 b. what happens in order for us to see.
 c. how much our eyes are like cameras.

True or False

8. Tears are present in your eyes all the time.

9. The eye is shaped much like a camera.

10. The lens can become thicker or thinner.

Figure 10–3. Lesson F-6, "Our Eyes"; and "Study Skill Lesson," "Classifying (the Heart), from EDL Study Skills Laboratory, *by H. Alan Robinson, Stanford E. Taylor, and Helen Frackenpohl; contributing authors, Maxine Hall, Alvin Kravitz, Charlotte Reynolds, and Ruth Wells (Educational Development Laboratories, Inc., Huntington, N.Y. Reprinted by permission.)*

CLASSIFYING

An important skill for the science student is classifying. This means arranging statements or things in groups that go together.

The paragraph below gives information about the heart. In classifying the information, the parts of the heart could be listed under one heading, and the functions (what the heart does) could be listed under a second heading. Read the paragraph and then look at the headings A and B to see how the information in the paragraph is classified.

> The heart is divided into two parts, a left chamber and a right chamber. Each chamber is also divided into two parts. The upper part of each chamber is called an auricle. The auricles receive blood from the body. The lower part of each chamber is called a ventricle. Blood enters the ventricles from the auricles and is pumped into the body again. The right ventricle sends blood to the lungs. The left ventricle sends blood to other parts of the body. There are valves between the auricle and ventricle in each chamber. Valves control the direction of the flow of blood.

A. Parts of the Heart

1. The heart has a left and a right chamber.
2. Each chamber has an auricle and a ventricle.
3. There are valves between the auricle and ventricle in each chamber.

B. Functions of the Heart

1. Auricles receive blood from the body.
2. Blood enters the ventricles from the auricles.
3. The right ventricle sends blood to the lungs.
4. The left ventricle sends blood to the rest of the body.
5. Valves control the direction of the flow of blood.

Now go to your worksheet for practice in classifying.

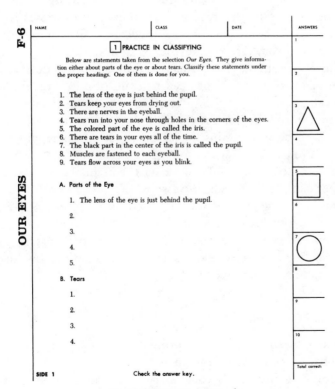

OUR EYES

F-6

NAME		CLASS	DATE	ANSWERS

☐1 PRACTICE IN CLASSIFYING

Below are statements taken from the selection *Our Eyes*. They give information either about parts of the eye or about tears. Classify these statements under the proper headings. One of them is done for you.

1. The lens of the eye is just behind the pupil.
2. Tears keep your eyes from drying out.
3. There are nerves in the eyeball.
4. Tears run into your nose through holes in the corners of the eyes.
5. The colored part of the eye is called the iris.
6. There are tears in your eyes all of the time.
7. The black part in the center of the iris is called the pupil.
8. Muscles are fastened to each eyeball.
9. Tears flow across your eyes as you blink.

A. Parts of the Eye

1. The lens of the eye is just behind the pupil.

2.

3.

4.

5.

B. Tears

1.

2.

3.

4.

SIDE 1   Check the answer key.

Figure 10-3 (Continued).

is introduced through taped material, problems are posed and the student responds to these problems in a lesson book.

Programs A and B are listening-thinking skills that provide a foundation for beginning reading. Programs E and F (grades 3–6) deal with reading skills, organization skills, literary interpretation skills, and critical thinking skills.

Strengths of the EDL Programs. The EDL programs (1) teach a wide variety of reading, study, and listening skills; (2) cut across many reading levels; (3) are, to a large extent, designed for self-instruction; (4) are interesting; (5) provide rapid feedback to the learner; (6) provide instruction in several sensory modes; and (7) utilize appropriate technology.

Craig Reading Skills I Program. The *Craig Reading Skills I Program* was developed by John E. Gordon and Eugene C. Gibnery. It is a sixteen-lesson program designed to improve the reading skills of upper elementary or junior high school pupils who are reading at the fourth-grade level. The subject matter is aimed at the interest level of students 13 to 15 years of age.

The *format* of the lessons presented on the Craig Reader and in the lesson books is much like that of other Craig programs. The content is different from that of other programs. Each skills slide teaches a specific English or reading skill; some of the skills taught are context clues, roots, use of dictionary, sentence types, skimming, and outlining. Each vocabulary slide contains ten new words per lesson. The words are defined and used in meaningful context. Pupils use these words in the reading selections and exercises following each vocabulary slide. Each reading selection draws on a different curriculum area— science, literature, history, art, social studies, sports.

Craig Reading Program B. *Craig Reading Program B* was developed by Selma Herr. It is designed to improve the reading skills of pupils reading at the upper elementary levels.

There are two books in this program. Book One starts at the seventh-grade reading level. Each book contains 24 lessons; these lessons, which are done in twenty-four 45-minute training periods, can be completed in 9 to 18 weeks. Although the core program is self-directive, the manual gives many suggestions that the teacher can use to enrich the lessons.

The program is designed to develop such skills as recognizing the main idea, finding facts, syllabication, skimming, interpreting cartoons, and editorial reading. Lesson titles include the following: comprehension, organization, word power, reading in different ways, purposeful reading, dividing words into syllables, and reading the newspaper.

Bell and Howell Corporation

The Bell and Howell Corporation produces the *Language Master Program,* designed to provide self-instruction in word recognition. It teaches (1) sight words, (2) phonic elements, (3) vocabulary, (4) structural elements, (5) word-building techniques, and (6) word-analysis techniques.

The material consists of a Language Master device and boxes of cards; each card contains a printed message and a corresponding spoken message. The spoken message is prerecorded on a strip of audio tape running the length of the bottom of the card.

To operate the device a card is placed into it. As the card is drawn through the device, the pupil hears the spoken message and sees the printed message at the same time. In this manner, he/she learns to associate the visual message with the audio message, that is, the printed word with the spoken word. Further pupil involvement is possible because the audio tape on the cards is a two-track tape. The word printed on the card is recorded on one track or band; the other track is blank so the pupil can record his/her rendition of the word. On the playback, he/she can listen and compare the two recordings. The pupil continues recording and playing back until satisfied with the performance compared to the prerecorded models on the other track.

Also available are boxes of blank cards. The teacher can use these cards to develop additional words and phrases to supplement teaching plans.

Set I, Sound Blending and Beginning Phonetic Skills:

Card	Visual and Audio Display	Card	Visual and Audio Display
2	a s as	79	rot rod rock
3	a t at	138	lit let lot
4	a n an	171	win wine
5	a n d and	172	hid hide
6	a n t ant	191	aid ail aim

Set III, Word-Building and Word-Analysis Techniques:

Card	Visual and Audio Display	Card	Visual and Audio Display
30	age wage ↑ [1 second interval on voice display]	88	paint painted painting painter
		157	ed u ca tion ↓↑↗ education [fraction of a second pauses on voice display]
55	think thin thing	199	The sun is bright. Jack is his son.

Strengths of the Language Master Program. Two strengths characterize the Language Master Program: (1) Direct individualized and small-group instruction is made possible in the following skills and abilities: phonic readiness, recognition of sight words, recognition of phonic elements, vocabulary growth, and recognition of phrases. (2) The Language Master can be adapted for use with other reading programs and methods.

BOXED KIT LABORATORIES

Science Research Associates (SRA)

The development of compact reading laboratories in boxed-kit form was pioneered by Don H. Parker for Science Research Associates (SRA). Each of the SRA reading laboratories contains a large number of lessons designed to teach power of reading, rate of reading, and listening skills. Each reading lesson has an illustrated story followed by comprehension, word meaning, and phonic-analysis exercises. The lessons are printed on slick, durable cardboard folders. A placement test is given to each pupil (individually or in a group situation) in order to determine at which level he/she should begin work in the program. When correctly placed at his/her level, a pupil should score between 85 and 100 per cent in the reading exercises.

SRA Reading for Understanding (Junior Edition) Program. The *SRA Reading for Understanding (Junior Edition) Program* by Thelma G. Thurstone is a set of 400 reading-comprehension exercises, utilizing 4,000 reading paragraphs. The first exercises in the laboratory are at the 3.0 grade level; the last ones are at 14.0⁺ grade level. Minimum ability for beginning the program are those reading skills taught in the primary grades. The exercises emphasize reasoning, inference, and interpretation skills.

Basic steps in the program are (1) setting goals, (2) giving the placement test, (3) scoring the test, (4) assigning practice levels, (5) selecting pupil leaders, (6) checking pupil progress, (7) advancing the pupils, and (8) evaluating progress.

The design of the exercises is simple. A typical exercise at the 2.8 level looks like this one[1] [card 1, first paragraph]:

> 1. Billy and Jane went to visit a farm. When it was time to go home, Billy said, "I don't want to leave. I like the farm. When I grow up, I want to be
>
>   A — happy."   B — a farmer."   C — rich."   D — strong."

The following is one of a number of exercises at the 8.1 level [card 50, fourth paragraph]:

> 4. The scallop is a vagabond. It does not cling to rocks or settle in beds on the bottom of the ocean, but is constantly
>
>   A — eating.   B — idle.   C — traveling.   D — learning

Strengths of the SRA Programs. The SRA Programs show the following strengths: (1) Reading improvement lessons are provided in a multilevel program ranging from grade one through college. (2) Basic, important reading skills are taught. (3) The reading selections are informative and interesting. (4) Ex-

---

[1] This exercise and the exercise that follows are from *Reading for Understanding*, Junior Edition, by Thelma G. Thurstone. © 1963, Science Research Associates, Inc. Reprinted by permission of the publisher.

cellent placement tests place a pupil at his/her level. (5) Feedback is positive and reinforcing because the pupil works at his/her level and rate. (6) Correct placement and continual positive feedback (reinforcement) are motivating to the pupil. (7) Color coding differentiates levels and makes it easy for the pupil to find correct materials and to know his/her relative standing in the program. (8) SYNCROTEACH,™ in the Reading Laboratories by Parker, gives the pupils all the necessary directions for using the program so that the teacher is freed for other teaching tasks. (9) The teacher's manuals are comprehensive.

COMPUTER-ASSISTED INSTRUCTION (CAI)

Computer-assisted instruction (CAI) in reading was pioneered by Richard Atkinson at Stanford University in cooperation with the Brentwood School in East Palo Alto, California. In CAI, according to Carson (1969), a pupil is guided by a computer through an instructional course geared to his/her abilities. Through CAI the curriculum author can use a computer to present educational material to pupils. The pupil sits at one of several instructional terminals and works with a teletypewriter device (and/or a cathode ray tube) through which (1) the computer presents information and questions, accepts and analyzes responses, and keeps performance records that are used in making reports and (2) the pupil reads and makes responses.

Instructional material developed for CAI systems can be likened to a series of textbooks that have been broken down into small pieces of information. The pupil progresses through the material on an *individual path*—at his own pace and level—and in terms of his previous performance. (Carson, 1969).

CAI makes immediate reinforcement of correct responses possible. When an error is made, the pupil may be given hints, another try, or remedial instruction. Correct answers are immediately rewarded; errors are spotted before misconceptions become fixed in the pupil's mind.

CAI is used for instruction in various content and skill areas in addition to reading. The critical reader will ask about some of the reported research conclusions on CAI. Bundy (1967) reports that (1) students learn at least as well by CAI as by conventional methods, (2) they learn in less time, (3) students can work on different programs at the same time, (4) the computer can adapt and modify its teaching logic in response to student performance and background, (5) the computer can provide great flexibility in terms of data collection and information presentation, (6) it offers great promise as a simulation device (University of Illinois' PLATO System), (7) CAI can help mentally retarded children to read, and (8) students generally react favorably to CAI.

Boettcher (1981) demonstrated the value of microcomputers as an aid in improving reading comprehension in the elementary schools.

There is a great need for improving reading competence. Instructional technology provides indispensable tools for teaching all pupils to read up to their capacity through making possible self-instruction based on pacing and mastery principles. Determining the point in a program at which the pupil begins is crucial to proper instruction. Educational Development Laboratories, Science Research Associates, Sullivan Associates, and the Hoffman Information Systems have their own easy-to-administer-and-score inventories for all or some of their programs. In some of the program manuals one can find names of reading tests that are useful in placing pupils correctly in programs. Chapter 7 of the present book provides information on reading measurement and evaluation.

LOGISTICS OF READING INSTRUCTION

Logistics is the art of getting materials and people to the right place at the right time in order to get a job done efficiently and effectively. Teachers need to develop the logistics of reading instruction in order to help pupils read up to capacity and to help themselves to work at maximum efficiency and effectiveness.

The logistics of reading instruction involves six important considerations:

Availability of Adequate Programs and Devices

Teachers must have adequate programs and devices available. They will need to choose those that best meet the children's needs. Further practical considerations in the selection of programs involve the size and plan of the room and the money that can be provided to purchase the programs.

Familiarity with the Programs

The teacher must be familiar with the purposes of these programs and know. how best to use them. Some of the programs are designed to be supportive of direct instruction; other programs can bear the brunt of the instruction program in reading. Observation of the materials in use and experimentation by the teacher will help him/her to decide the combination of programs that will best serve the pupils.

Selection and Arrangement of Classroom Equipment and Materials

Carefully designed and appointed classroom experience centers contain the equipment and materials needed for excellent instruction (see Figure 10-5). Types of equipment and furnishings needed for instruction paced to the learner include the following: chairs, tables, easel chalkboards, movable book racks, rugs and/or carpeting, chalkboards, bulletin boards, shelves, overhead projector, filmstrip projector, cartridge tape players, carrels, storage bins, storage cabinets, partitions, science laboratory, globes, maps, charts, models, and other audiovisual devices for presentation of lessons.

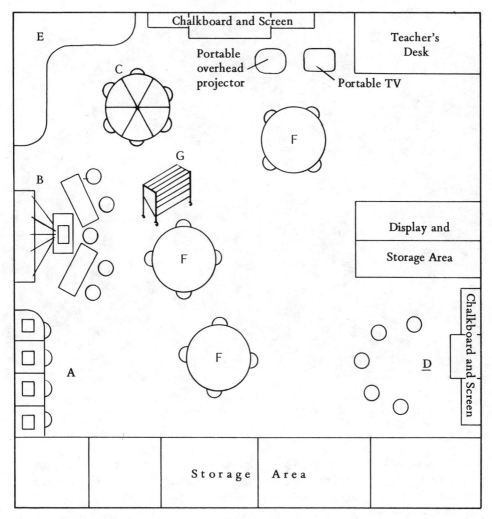

Figure 10–4. Design for a Classroom Experience Center in Which Instruction Can Be Individualized.

(A) Individual carrels. For automated self-instruction utilizing such devices and programs as *Hoffman Reader; EDL Controlled Reader,* and microcomputers.

(B) Small group projection area. For automated self-instruction utilizing such devices as *EDL Controlled Reader, Jr.*

(C) Individual and/or small group area. Self-instruction using such programs and devices as *B-H Language Master;* group self-instruction using *Hoffman Readers.*

(D) Small group direct instruction area. Basal reader instruction; linguistic reader instruction.

(E) Science Corner.

(F) General purpose work areas.

(G) Movable book racks.

Figure 10–5. Children in an Experience Center Learning How to Operate Devices That They Will Use for Independent Self-instruction. (Courtesy E & S Associates, Inc.)

The children in the photograph (Figure 10–5) are at work on learning programs that aid in (1) improving reading skills and (2) developing concepts in content areas. The carrel and equipment depicted are part of a learning or experience center concept developed by E & S Associates, Inc., one that may be part of a classroom or may be housed in a special room.[2]

These centers can be equipped and used for advanced, average, and slow learners, for the culturally advantaged as well as the culturally deprived child. They are predicated upon the well-established and substantiated principle that each child learns best through his own experiences of things, including a wide variety of instructional materials.

The Experience Center concept suggests that all instructional materials be assembled in one place and coordinated by a person who is able to deal with all media and is informed about their utilization and their influence on learning. The Experience Center should be the place where teachers can locate or create the best possible materials for children.

[2] The carrel pictured in Figure 10-5 is obtainable from E. & S. Associates, Inc., 2204 Mt. Meigs Road, Montgomery, Alabama 36107.

Self-instructional materials can be selected from among the following programs, already described in this chapter:

1. *Bell and Howell Language Master Programs.*
2. *California Test Bureau Lessons for Self-Instruction in Reading.*
3. *Educational Development Laboratories (EDL) Listen and Read Program.*
4. *EDL Controlled-Reading Program.*
5. *EDL Comprehension Power Paragraphs and Sentences.*
6. *EDL Study Skills Library.*
7. *EDL Listen, Look, and Learn Program.*
8. *EDL Word Study Skills Program.*
9. *Educational Progress Corporation Audio Reading Kits, Audio Reading Progress Laboratory Revised, and Independent Reading Skills Laboratory.*
10. *Hoffman Information Systems Language Arts, Phonics, and Reading Program.*
11. *Norelco Reading Program.*
12. *Science Research Associates (SRA) Reading Laboratories.*
13. *SRA Reading for Understanding Programs.*
14. *McGraw-Hill Sullivan Reading Program.*

Assigning Pupils to Appropriate Specific Materials and Levels Within Materials

Pupils achieving at the same level or pupils with like needs may be taught by appropriate materials on a small-group basis. For example, up to six children at a time may work in the same lesson (without disturbing the rest of the class) at the Hoffman Reader, because the earphones of the children can be plugged into a convenient jack box. Other small groups of children or individuals can be working on the Hoffman Readers at the same time. Similar small groups and individuals can work in various EDL materials. Group leaders can be appointed or elected.

Furthermore, pupils can work individually at all of the self-instruction programs described in this chapter. They can work on these materials at any time during the day, freeing the teacher for direct instruction in reading, in other skill areas, and in other subject areas. Pupils with individual needs can be taught with self-instruction materials on an individual basis, skipping those segments of lessons or those lessons whose skills they may have already mastered.

Showing Pupils How to Use Self-Instruction Materials

Although the pupils can do most of the self-instruction on their own, once they get started, they will initially profit from instruction in how to use the laboratories, kits, programmed materials, and audiovisual instructional programs and devices. Much of this preliminary instruction can be done on a small-group basis and is well worth the relatively small amount of time involved. Most reading supervisors will be glad to help the teachers who feel they need help, although teacher's manuals accompanying the programs are usually sufficient for most teachers.

The programmed materials such as the Sullivan program and the LSI proram, and audiovisual reading programs such as the Hoffman Reading Program have immediate, automatic feedback built into the programs, and therefore correction and record-keeping are no problem. Most of the programs provide means for keeping records of pupil work and for charting pupil progress, but they are usually not very difficult to teach to the children.

Scheduling Pupils for Self-Instruction and Direct Instruction in Reading

Theoretically, children would not need to be scheduled once they got started with their work. For practical reasons a teacher might want to schedule most of the reading instruction, allowing some latitude for eager beavers and/or special problem cases who might want to or need to get more self-instruction. Any schedule for the use of technological devices should be posted where pupils can see it.

Modern school architects are producing a variety of classroom structures which are well adapted to individual and small group self-instruction. One of these developments is the pod arrangement. The pod is a very large room that contains several classes. Within each of these class clusters there is room for desks, tables, cabinets, work areas, and so forth. In the center of the pod is a large area where various kinds of self-instructional reading materials (software) and story books are placed in movable and stationary racks, carts, and tables. Pupils from the classes in the pod have equal access to these materials. Because of the spaciousness of these areas and because the floors of the better pods are carpeted, traffic and acoustic problems are minimal.

The pod arrangement is ideally suited for the use of individually prescribed instruction in reading. At the beginning of the week the teacher prescribes the self-instruction work for each pupil. These prescriptions are placed on prescription forms (See illustration). At various times during the day or at a set time pupils check their prescription sheets, obtain the appropriate instructional material, and work their assignments. At times, several pupils may be working with the same material. They may elect, or the teacher may plan for them, to work together and to discuss why they answered a question in a particular way.

Of course, classroom instruction will utilize various approaches to teaching in order to attain educational goals. The teacher is still at the heart of the teaching-learning milieu. However, since he/she has the welfare of pupils uppermost in mind, he/she will, in teaching children also utilize teacher-pupil dialogue; independent study (projects, unit activities); study of realia, models, and so on; observation; classification; experimentation; and some of the newer methods of self-instruction made explicit by educational technology.

Reading Prescription Sheet

Name ___John Brown___

Date ___April 5-9___

Materials	Monday	Tuesday	Wednesday	Thursday	Friday
Enchanted Gates	pp. 61, 62	63, 64	65, 66	67, 68	
Microcomputer (Program A)	Unit 1		*		*
Phonics We Use C	70		71		72
SRA Aqua Lab Ib		16		17	18

*dependent on previous progress

High-Intensity Learning Systems

Moore (1979) describes the High-Intensity Learning Systems (HILS)[3] as a commercially prepared systems approach to individualized reading instruction that "allows one teacher to operate numerous reading curricula per day, using materials from numerous publishers." More than 400 instructional objectives, each with its own criterion assessment instruments, are incorporated into the program. There are, of course, instructional prescriptions available for each objective.

Characteristics of the system are that it is:

1. *Diagnostic/prescriptive.*

2. *Individualized.* A variety of materials is used to help the teacher in fitting the content, rate, and level to each student.

3. *Motivating.* Students get immediate feedback to their responses.

4. *Definitive.* Both teacher and learner know what is to be learned, what materials will be used, and what must be done to show mastery.

5. *Intensified.* Students not only are taught to use the system but are also trained to use their time to the fullest. "Except during training, teacher talk and overt direction are kept to a minimum."

6. *An open system.* It is continuously being revised and improved by the publisher, the individual teacher, and the school system.

Moore suggests that establishing a HILS lab involves one (large) bare room and 100 boxes filled with materials. In the Harford County, Maryland public schools, hardworking teachers and aides with the assistance of a consultant from the publisher put the lab together in several weeks. Anyone who wants to set up such a lab would need to use one of the HILS consultants or a teacher who has successfully organized and operated one of the labs.

In the Harford operation a teacher-manager and an aide "managed com-

---

[3] High-Intensity Learning Systems (HILS 2), revised edition. New York: Random House, 1978.

fortably with approximately 110 students spending 40 minutes in the lab each day." There were six classes daily, leaving about two hours for planning, paperwork, and modification of materials.

Initial student placement is based on a brief reading test called the Basic Test of Reading Comprehension. The results of this test, that is, knowing the child's "subsystem," allow the teacher to select several check-in tests at the appropriate level. There will be some tests from each of the four areas: word study, vocabulary, comprehension, and study skills. These results are directly related to instructional objectives (IOs). Appropriate prescriptions for IOs not achieved are circled in the back of the Student Record Book.

Next, the student learns by doing, by working on the instructional prescriptions at his/her own pace and level in individualized materials. Upon completion of the assignment the student takes a check-out test. If the prescriptions were well chosen, the student usually demonstrates mastery of the IO at this point. A plastic envelope lapboard allows materials to be used nonconsumably.

All materials except check-in and check-out tests are self-checking. Each learner records his/her progress on a progress plotter. This plotter and recorded data are brought to the teacher or aide when the student wants a check-out test. A record of the student's success is noted both in the Student Record Book and on the wall chart where each student's name is posted. These are quite satisfying procedures for most students.

The "six areas of the room are designated with color-coded, illustrated signs hanging from the ceiling. One of the codes—p for poetry, w for workbooks, c for cassette or audiovisual, k for kits, r for reading, or g for games—appears in each prescription, directing the student to the correct areas of the room." Arriving there, students locate the material that is coded to match their prescription.

How to use the lab is taught and practiced in training. The training is a period of daily "old-fashioned" teaching lasting one to two weeks. Students are also taught during this time to:

1. "Do a book" (follow the steps that result in a book conference).
2. Fill out a progress plotter and use a conversion chart to convert scores into percentages.
3. Use equipment and materials in the lab.
4. Know what kinds of behavior patterns are expected of them.

The free reading of trade books is another basic factor in the design of the HILS program. Reading is done for pleasure; no reports are required.

When students enter the lab they pick up their packets. Each packet consists of the Student Record Booklet, a lapboard, special marking crayon, pencil, progress plotters, and kit markers (to be placed in the spot where a card or lesson is removed so it can be returned to the proper place). Packets are returned to storage when students are finished.

The labs are used in Harford County by upper elementary, below-average students. However, HILS labs can be used by a wide range of students from primary through high school levels. It must be emphasized that lab work *supplements* regular reading instruction in the classroom.

Prior to the use of the labs, students averaged five months of reading growth for each grade attended; that is about 0.5 for each month in school. Post-tests of third-graders using the HILS system showed 1.47 month of reading growth for each month attended; fourth-graders, 1.36; and fifth-graders, 1.42.

SUMMARY

Large numbers of students are not reading up to their potential because they do not receive proper instruction, which would require, among other things, teaching all students at their reading instruction levels through an ongoing, self-perpetuating program that fosters optimally effective, individual instruction of all students.

Organizational plans that have separated reading from both language and content areas and that in other ways have failed to meet student needs have fallen short of that goal.

Proper instruction means teaching students at their reading instruction level, pacing instruction so that they can master material at each level before going on to new levels and more difficult material, and making available to teachers and students materials and methods that make independent, individual self-instruction possible.

Because a teacher is neither omniscient nor omnipresent, he/she needs the help that is now available from supporting materials and systems. By that we mean programmed materials, boxed laboratories, audiovisual devices and programs, computer-assisted instruction, and organizational systems.

These developments make possible individualized self-instruction that is impossible without them. And they keep students profitably occupied in real instructional activities when not receiving direct instruction from the teacher or not engaging in projects and other types of independent or small-group activities that produce educational growth. Supporting materials are designed to supplement the teacher's instruction; they are not designed to replace it.

The logistics of reading instruction relates to the organization of the classroom or systems in reading centers. It means getting the right kinds of programs to the students at the right time so they can be helped to profit from both supporting materials and from direct teaching by the teacher. Only then will all students be able to read up to capacity and be able to help themselves to work at maximum efficiency and effectiveness.

LEARNING ACTIVITIES

1. Interview a music teacher, an elementary teacher, and a track coach to get their ideas on the methods they use to pace instruction. Also inquire about the value of such pacing.

2. Talk with some fellow students who are studying a foreign language or math. Ask them if instruction is being paced to their abilities and needs. Find out what could be done to help the instructor pace the instruction properly.

3. Go to a curriculum center that has reading instruction materials. Compare two or more types of reading instruction materials that use a programmed learning format.

4. If possible, observe elementary students using programmed materials. What do the students seem to like about the material? Dislike? Which kinds of students seem to be helped the most?

5. Arrange to observe the use of material such as the Hoffman Information System programs or something similar. If possible, try out the material. What are your reactions?

6. Arrange to observe and/or use material such as the *Audio Reading Kits* developed by the Educational Progress Corporation. Would you use such material? Explain why or why not.

7. Compare several reading kits that are designed to accomplish the same things.

8. Write to several companies that produce supporting reading materials and ask them to send copies of research reports on their materials. Discuss any reports you receive with your instructor. If there is no research on a given set of materials, ask the company the reason for the lack and ask your instructor to comment on the lack of research.

9. Ask your instructor if anyone at your school or in your area is using the PLATO computer system for reading instruction. Arrange to go to the PLATO computer center for a demonstration. Also arrange for a demonstration on the use of microcomputers for reading instruction.

10. If there is a reading instruction system (such as HILS) in your area, arrange, preferably with the help of your instructor, to observe the system in operation. What are your reactions to the system?

STUDY QUESTIONS

1. Discuss the meaning of reading disability and its incidence.
2. What may happen if gifted pupils are not challenged?
3. Discuss problems connected with some organizational plans.
4. What, in your estimation, is the import of the research by Dahllof and that by Zeichner?
5. Explain what proper instruction means. Do you favor such instruction? Explain.
6. What are the characteristics of methods and materials that make self-instruction possible?
7. What is meant by supporting instructional materials?
8. How does programmed learning work?
9. Select three reading instruction programs and state their key ideas and strengths.
10. Do the six important considerations involved in the general logistics of reading instruction seem logical to you? Explain.
11. Outline or write a brief summary of how the *High-Intensity Learning System* works.

RECOMMENDED READING

ALEXANDER, J. ESTILL (Ed.). *Teaching Reading.* Boston: Little, Brown and Company, 1979.

BRICK, MICHAEL. "Fountain Valley Reading Support System for Teachers." *Reading Improvement,* 13 (Summer 1976), 66–70.

CARNINE, DOUGLAS and JERRY SILBERT. *Direct Instruction Reading.* Columbus, Ohio: Charles E. Merrill Publishing Company, 1979.

COOPER, J. DAVID, EDNA W. WARNCKE, PEGGY A. RAMSTAD, and DOROTHY A. SHIPMAN. *The What and How of Reading Instruction.* Columbus, Ohio: Charles E. Merrill Publishing Company, 1979, 335–381.

DOLLY, JOHN P. and VANA H. MEREDITH. "The Use of Mastery Learning As a Classroom Management Model." *Educational Technology,* 17 (April 1977), 26–29.

FARR, ROGER and NANCY ROSER. *Teaching a Child To Read.* New York: Harcourt Brace Jovanovich, Inc., 1979, Chap. 9.

HOLLANDER, SHEILA K. "Reading: Process and Product." *The Reading Teacher,* 28 (March 1975), 550–553.

INDRISANO, ROSELMINA. "Managing the Classroom Reading Program." *Instructor,* 87 (January 1978), 117–120.

KOENKE, KARL. "Toward Effective Use of Teacher Aides." *Reading Teacher,* 32 (8) (May 1979), 996–999.

MANGRUM CHARLES T. and HARRY W. FORGAN. *Developing Competencies in Teaching Reading.* Columbus, Ohio: Charles E. Merrill Publishing Company, 1979, Modules 10 and 11.

MATTLEMAN, MARCIENE and MICHAEL H. KEAN. "Project Management to Improve Reading Instruction." *Educational Technology,* 13 (September 1973), 13–14.

RUDE, ROBERT T. "Objective-based Reading Systems: An Evaluation," *Reading Teacher,* 28 (November 1974), 169–175.

SILVERBLANK, FRANCINE. "The New Technologies Can Work." *Reading Improvement,* 11 (Winter 1974), 17–19.

SPUCK, DENNIS W. and STEPHEN P. OWEN. "Individualized Instruction: Its Structure and Management with Computer Assistance." *Educational Technology,* 16 (September 1976), 35–40.

SULLIVAN, MAUREEN. "What Is the Instructional Systems Approach to Reading?" *Educational Technology,* 13 (September 1973), 15–18.

REFERENCES

BOETTCHER, JUDITH V. "Developing Comprehension Skills via Computer in an Elementary classroom." Presentation at the 26th annual Convention of the International Reading Association in New Orleans, April 1981.

BRIGGS, BARBARA C. "An Investigation of the Effectiveness of a Programmed Graphemic-Option Approach to Teaching Reading to Disadvantaged Students." *Journal of Reading Behavior,* 5 (Winter 1972–73), 35–46.

BUNDY, R. F. "Computer-assisted Instruction: Now and for the Future." *Audiovisual Instruction,* 12 (1967), 344–348.

DAHLLOF, U. *Ability Grouping, Content Validity and Curriculum Process Analysis.* New York: Teachers' College Press, 1971.

HARRIS, ALBERT J. and EDWARD SIPAY. *How to Increase Reading Ability.* 6th ed. New York: David McKay Co., Inc., 1976.

KATIMS, MICHAEL and others. "The Chicago Mastery Learning Reading Program: An Interim Evaluation." Paper presented at the annual meeting of the American Educational Research Association, New York, N.Y., 1977. (ED 137 737).

MOORE, JULIA T. "A Systems Approach to Individualized Reading." *Reading Teacher,* 32 (8) (May 1979), 951–955.

PALMER, BARBARA C. and LAWRENCE E. HAFNER. "Black Students Get an Edge in Reading." *Reading Horizons,* 19 (4) (Summer 1979), 324–328.

RUPLEY, WILLIAM H. and BONNIE L. LONGNION. "Mastery Learning: A Viable Alternative?" *Reading Teacher,* 32 (3) (December 1978), 380–383.

SIBAYAN, BONIFACIO P., LORNA Z. SEGOVIA, and EDILBERTO P. DAGOT. "Who Profits From Self-Learning Kits (SLKS)?" Philippine Normal College Research Series No. 2. Manila, the Philippines: Philippine Normal College, 1976.

SMITH, EDWIN H., C. GLENNON ROWELL, and LAWRENCE E. HAFNER. *The Sound Reading Program.* Waco, Texas: Educational Achievement Corporation, 1972.

ZEICHNER, KENNETH. "Group Membership in Elementary School Classrooms." *Journal of Educational Psychology,* 70 (4) (August 1978), 554–564.

APPENDIX A

Readiness, Reading, and Capacity Tests

Outline

READINESS TESTS
    A. Individual Readiness Tests
        1. Visual Discrimination Test
        2. Auditory Discrimination Tests
            a. Rhyming Test
            b. Middle Sound Test
            c. Beginning Sound Test
        3. Auditory Blending Test
        4. Letter Knowledge Test
WORD-RECOGNITION TEST (Individual Test)
    A. Hafner Quick Reading Test
VOCABULARY TEST (Group/Individual)
READING COMPREHENSION TEST (Group/Individual)
INDEPENDENT WORD-IDENTIFICATION SKILLS TESTS
    A. Individual Independent Word-Identification Skills Tests
        1. Hafner Quick Phonics Test (A Phonemic Options Test)
        2. Phonic Elements Tests
            a. Consonant Sounds Test
            b. Consonant Blends Test
            c. Consonant Digraphs Test
            d. Vowel Digraphs Test
            e. Diphthongs Test
            f. Special Combinations Test
            g. Final "e" Rule Test
        3. Structural Elements and Principles Tests
            a. Dividing Words into Syllables Test
            b. Closed Syllable Rule Test
            c. Open Syllable Rule Test
            d. Prefixes Test
            e. Suffixes Test

INDIVIDUAL READING APTITUDE TESTS
  A. Hafner-Smith Verbal Comprehension
  B. Testing Learning Rate in Reading
  C. Individual Mental Abilities Point Scales
     1. General Information
     2. Auditory Memory Span
     3. Proverbs
     4. Vocabulary
STUDY-REFERENCE SKILLS INVENTORIES
SAMPLE INFORMAL READING INVENTORIES

INFORMAL CAPACITY AND READING TESTS

Student Information:

Name _____ Date _____

Grade _____ School _____

Examiner _____ City _____ State _____

READINESS

Individual Readiness Tests

Visual Discrimination Test

Directions: There are three words in each part of the test. One word is different from the other two. Draw a line under the different one. [Do the first three with the pupil(s). Make sure the pupil(s) understand how to do the test before proceeding with the remaining items.]

A. cat   cat   bee
B. shop   milk   shop
C. fat   flake   flake
1. best   am   best
2. buy   tree   tree
3. pouch   teach   teach
4. reading   reading   ridden
5. purpose   porpoise   purpose
6. scare   scare   share
7. capacity   capacity   capacitor
8. considerable   consideration   consideration
9. interpretive   interpretative   interpretative
10. beep   deep   deep   Criterion: 70%

Auditory Discrimination Tests

Rhyming Test

Directions: I will say three words. Two of them rhyme. One does not. Tell me the word that does not rhyme. [Do the first three items as examples].

A. day   say   do
B. bring   trick   sing
C. pry   try   tree
1. look   cook   sock
2. prize   cries   most
3. seed   fight   feed
4. hot   corn   horn
5. like   bike   wait
6. play   by   say
7. delight   bright   joke
8. pine   train   pain   Criterion: 75%

Middle-Sound Test

Directions: I will say two words. You tell me if they have the same middle sound.

A. bat   cab
B. pin   tap
C. tell   tent
1. dug   club
2. hot   mud
3. bad   mat
4. pick   fill
5. rain   like
6. bought   cause
7. set   dim
8. cute   suit   Criterion: 75%

Beginning-Sound Test

Directions: I will say three words. Two words will begin with the same sound; one will start with a different sound. Listen: "can, carry, sing." Which word started differently? [sing] Let's try another: "tell, boy, tank." Which word started differently? [boy] Now let's do some more.

1. man   too   mix
2. wool   wind   fun
3. go   boy   green
4. nice   seat   so
5. dig   door   pen
6. jump   jam   tack
7. bake   pick   barn

8. noise   new   mean
9. walk   chalk   chair
10. fun   land   fan   Criterion: 70%

Auditory-Blending Test

Directions: [Read the sounds to the child at a rate of one sound per second.]
I will say the sounds of a word slowly. You say them fast so you can figure out
the word. Tell me the word.

A. i - t
B. o - f
C. u - p
1. a - m
2. s - o
3. i - s
4. t - a - p
5. or - an - ge
6. pl - ea - se
7. ta - bl - e - t
8. r - ea- d - ing
9. bir - th - day - s
10. ca - rr - o - t - s   Criterion: 70%

Letter-Knowledge Test

Directions: Here are some letters. Read the letters to me.

b   d   v   z   o

h   s   x   f   q

l   a   c   w   u

p   j   e   g   y

t   n   i   k   m

r

Hafner Quick Reading Test (Expanded Version)

School Grade _____   Name _____

School _____   Number Correct _____

Date _____   Reading Grade Placement _____ *

Directions: Have student read down first column until an item is missed. Then drop
back two rows and read across. If the row is then read correctly, proceed. If not,
drop back until a row is read correctly. Stop when 5 consecutive items are missed.

* Reading Grade Placement = (Number Correct/10) + 1. Example for student who scores thirteen:
RGP = (13/10) + 1 = 1.3 + 1 = 2.3.

1. bed	ride	funny	old	ground
catch	name	in	she	could
2. floor	together	river	minute	question
thank	enough	anyone	happen	lady
3. empty	which	stupid	glance	island
rather	weight	easily	alive	certain
4. saucer	command	future	majesty	encourage
orchard	quiver	improve	range	trumpet
5. flexible	emperor	operator	enclose	niece
warmth	mosquito	ravine	neglect	ceiling
6. mortal	physician	essential	geranium	document
possess	scroll	monstrous	forfeit	orphanage
7. complexion	conceit	reluctant	siege	monotonous
geology	chivalry	plague	unique	asylum
8. nourish	exquisite	camouflage	intrigue	hereditary
occupant	mythology	calamity	juror	reinforce
9. accomplice	regime	grimace	ecstacy	belligerent
idolize	encore	judicial	stealthy	physique
10. cynical	annihilate	uncouth	marital	deteriorate
reimburse	linear	anonymous	suave	feign
11. awry	guise	slovenly	emaciated	typify
indict	boudoir	glower	cuisine	meander
12. gauche	prosaic	visage	bourgeois	inveigle
quiescent	liaison	pedagogy	iridescent	myriad
13. inchoate	chimerical	miscegenation	sinecure	schism
satiate	avarice	matrix	cynosure	hyperbole

Reading Vocabulary Test (Group or Individual)

Date _____ Name _____

Grade _____ Number Correct _____

School _____ Reading Grade _____

Placement _____

Directions: (The examiner should read the following directions and explain how to do the sample exercises, A and B.): "Read the sentence part and then find which word best completes the sentence. Note the capital letter by the answer and write it in the blank to the left of the sentence."

_____ A. An oak is a kind of _____.
　　　A. book　　B. tree　　C. cloud　　D. bird　　E. song
_____ B. A person who is nice is _____.
　　　A. smart　　B. dumb　　C. tall　　D. funny　　E. good
_____ 1. An apple is a kind of _____.
　　　A. fruit　　B. bread　　C. color　　D. bush　　E. vegetable
_____ 2. A person who can do something is _____.
　　　A. clumsy　　B. big　　C. proud　　D. nice　　E. able

_____ 3. The top of a road is its _____.
A. frame   B. divider   C. curve   D. speed   E. surface

_____ 4. If a person is not smart, he is _____.
A. stupid   B. bright   C. silly   D. wild   E. stooped

_____ 5. A big snow storm is a _____.
A. blizzard   B. cyclone   C. snowflake   D. tornado
E. blanket

_____ 6. Something that breathes is _____.
A. food   B. alive   C. happy   D. wide   E. dead

_____ 7. A fat person is not _____.
A. tall   B. lean   C. nice   D. big   E. bad

_____ 8. People who think well are _____.
A. dumb   B. naughty   C. fat   D. clever   E. loose

_____ 9. Tearing down means _____.
A. company   B. repairing   C. wrecking   D. crying
E. sadness

_____ 10. If you are sure, you are _____.
A. good   B. stiff   C. glittery   D. lonely   E. certain

_____ 11. A group of peach trees is called _____.
A. a forest   B. an orchard   C. groovy   D. a chore
E. an orchid

_____ 12. Arrows are kept in a _____.
A. quiver   B. statue   C. pasture   D. bucket   E. quilt

_____ 13. A person who is unafraid is _____.
A. brave   B. a nag   C. convenient   D. twinkly   E. skilled

_____ 14. If you get better, you _____.
A. sleep   B. reply   C. improve   D. worsen   E. try

_____ 15. An empty house is _____.
A. big   B. vacant   C. impossible   D. homey   E. pretty

_____ 16. North America is a _____.
A. state   B. harness   C. country   D. company
E. continent

_____ 17. Cowboys work out on the _____.
A. gulch   B. holster   C. hacienda   D. range   E. stall

_____ 18. Where something comes from is called its _____.
A. sauce   B. home   C. place   D. source   E. homeland

_____ 19. When you make up your mind, you make a _____.
A. decision   B. brain   C. incision   D. sculpture
E. declaration

_____ 20. One kind of musical instrument is the _____.
A. choir   B. scalpel   C. conductor   D. waltz   E. trumpet

_____ 21. Animals that eat in the pasture are _____.
A. loafing   B. whimpering   C. grazing   D. braying
E. gorging

_____ 22. A magician often uses his _____.
A. wand   B. ears   C. sash   D. won   E. watch

_____ 23. Celebrating the Fourth of July is a _____.
A. concert   B. custom   C. parade   D. skyrocket   E. band

_____ 24. A big ditch is a _____.
A. merchant   B. stream   C. ravine   D. compass   E. slope

_____ 25. A person who tries to solve crimes is a _____.
A. warden   B. mayor   C. detective   D. prisoner
E. fireman

_____ 26. Someone who does as he is told is _____.
A. a rebel   B. hen-pecked   C. silly   D. stubborn
E. obedient

_____ 27. A nice smell is _____.
A. ugly   B. fragrant   C. odd   D. fragile   E. weird

_____ 28. A column is a _____.
A. pillar   B. shirt   C. sickness   D. vegetable   E. medicine

_____ 29. A light is often suspended from the _____.
A. roof   B. sky   C. basement   D. ceiling   E. floor

_____ 30. A thing that can carry malaria is the _____.
A. fly   B. mosquito   C. June Bug   D. spider   E. muskox

_____ 31. Something that is great is _____.
A. happy   B. imaginary   C. tremendous   D. yearning
E. natural

_____ 32. A person who is not cared for is being _____.
A. hospitalized   B. loved   C. teased   D. helped
E. neglected

_____ 33. A special dream in which something is revealed by God or an angel is a
_____.
A. halo   B. round   C. nightmare   D. vision   E. festival

_____ 34. A person's name at the close of a letter is called his/her _____.
A. handwriting   B. salutation   C. signature   D. nickname
E. signboard

_____ 35. An untrue story that has a special lesson is known as a _____.
A. fable   B. novel   C. biography   D. lie   E. rhyme

_____ 36. To keep something in good condition is to _____ it.
A. preserve   B. neglect   C. refine   D. prepare   E. destroy

_____ 37. Four singers are usually called a _____.
A. trio   B. choir   C. quartet   D. chorus   E. quintet

_____ 38. People who are shy are _____.
A. stubborn   B. conceited   C. ashamed   D. dumb
E. timid

_____ 39. One who gives the enemy military secrets is a _____.
A. traitor   B. document   C. major   D. vault   E. baron

_____ 40. To live in a place is to _____ it.
A. belittle   B. occupy   C. rent   D. interpret   E. consider

_____ 41. Defying authority is being in _____.
A. support   B. variation   C. rebellion   D. consultation
E. cahoots

_____ 42. To breathe air out is to _____.
A. forfeit   B. elongate   C. inhale   D. exhume   E. exhale

_____ 43. Half of a ball can rightly be called a _____.
A. hemisphere   B. pie   C. dance   D. prism   E. ionosphere

44. The short story is a kind of —————.
    A. nonfiction   B. poem   C. biography   D. magazine
    E. fiction

45. A clever disguise or way of concealing something is a _____.
    A. siege   B. serenade   C. still   D. moat   E. camouflage

46. An unverified story circulated about someone is a _____.
    A. kernel   B. documentary   C. rumor   D. tangle
    E. history

47. One type of poisonous liquid is _____.
    A. penicillin   B. rum   C. venom   D. witch hazel
    E. battery acid

48. One kind of respiratory sickness is called _____.
    A. appendicitis   B. headache   C. restitution   D. influenza
    E. measles

49. To cry over the death of someone is to _____.
    A. brood   B. mourn   C. nourish   D. knell   E. grill

50. You can call a building and a tower _____.
    A. strands   B. thermostats   C. structures   D. basements
    E. spires

51. To sing a love song to someone is to _____.
    A. serenade   B. bellow   C. promenade   D. waltz
    E. harmonize

52. Starting a flame is _____ one.
    A. quenching   B. igniting   C. smoldering   D. enveloping
    E. repealing

53. A person who is fascinating is _____.
    A. repining   B. starry-eyed   C. beautiful   D. meditative
    E. intriguing

54. To exile someone is to _____ him.
    A. inform   B. create   C. import   D. elect   E. banish

55. A severe epidemic is sometimes called a _____.
    A. plague   B. quarantine   C. traction   D. revolution
    E. typhoon

56. An angry person could rightly be called _____.
    A. subtle   B. angulate   C. docile   D. petulant   E. enacted

57. Meat-eating animals are _____.
    A. omnivorous   B. captious   C. herbivorous   D. wan
    E. carnivorous

58. A supply that is gone is _____.
    A. replenished   B. revoked   C. depleted   D. ponderous
    E. vigilant

59. A _____ is a type of tool.
    A. ragout   B. valance   C. gimlet   D. vacuole   E. limoge

60. One kind of beetle is the _____.
    A. scarab   B. nosegay   C. tarantula   D. notornis   E. lemur

61. A dying business is _____.
    A. simulated   B. moribund   C. effusive   D. stalwart
    E. murky

_____ 62. A swamp is (a) _____.
    A. descant   B. fen   C. kaka   D. meadow   E. vale

_____ 63. To cut off is to _____.
    A. sensitize   B. secrete   C. restore   D. sever   E. abort

_____ 64. To steal is to _____.
    A. pilfer   B. emanate   C. humiliate   D. desecrate   E. jibe

_____ 65. A high point in someone's career can be called its _____.
    A. entourage   B. accessory   C. ebb   D. zenith   E. echo

_____ 66. A beggar is also known as a(n) _____.
    A. mendicant   B. dolt   C. alms giver   D. monad
    E. escheat

_____ 67. Someone who is a comfort is a(n) _____.
    A. blanket   B. hero   C. smidgeon   D. solace   E. amnesty

_____ 68. Stubborn people are also called _____.
    A. belfries   B. obdurate   C. bairns   D. viscous
    E. miniscule

_____ 69. A fearful person is _____.
    A. foolhardy   B. wizened   C. jocular   D. weak
    E. timorous

_____ 70. One who is thin and tired-looking is _____.
    A. weird   B. pensive   C. ardent   D. gaunt   E. corpulent

Answer Key to the Reading Vocabulary Test

1. A	25. C	49. B
2. E	26. E	50. C
3. E	27. B	51. A
4. A	28. A	52. B
5. A	29. D	53. E
6. B	30. B	54. E
7. B	31. C	55. A
8. D	32. E	56. D
9. C	33. D	57. E
10. E	34. C	58. C
11. B	35. A	59. C
12. A	36. A	60. A
13. A	37. C	61. B
14. C	38. E	62. B
15. B	39. A	63. D
16. E	40. B	64. A
17. C	41. C	65. D
18. D	42. E	66. A
19. A	43. A	67. D
20. E	44. E	68. B
21. C	45. E	69. E
22. A	46. C	70. D
23. B	47. C	
24. C	48. D	

Reading Grade Placement Equivalents of Raw Scores on the Hafner-Jolly Reading Vocabulary Test

RS	RGP	RS	RGP	RS	RGP
1	1.6	25	5.2	48	10.3
2	1.7	26	5.4	49	10.6
3	1.8	27	5.6	50	10.9
4	1.9	28	5.8	51	11.3
5	2.0	29	6.0	52	11.6
6	2.1	30	6.2	53	11.9
7	2.2	31	6.4	54	12.2
8	2.3	32	6.6	55	12.6
9	2.4	33	6.8	56	12.9
10	2.5	34	7.0	57	13.2
11	2.6	35	7.2	58	13.5
12	2.7	36	7.4	59	13.9
13	2.8	37	7.6	60	14.2
14	3.0	38	7.8	61	14.5
15	3.2	39	8.0	62	14.8
16	3.4	40	8.2	63	15.1
17	3.6	41	8.4	64	15.4
18	3.8	42	8.6	65	15.7
19	4.0	43	8.8	66	16.0
20	4.2	44	9.0	67	16.3
21	4.4	45	9.3	68	16.6
22	4.6	46	9.6	69	16.9
23	4.8	47	10.0	70	17.3
24	5.0				

Hafner Reading Comprehension Test (Group or Individual)

Name _____

Grade _____

Raw Score _____

Reading Grade Placement _____

Directions: (To beginning readers): "Find the star on the page. Do you see it? Next to the star is the sentence. The sentence is 'My name is Jim'. Do you see it? The next sentence is I am a _____. A word is missing. What word do you think should be in the blank? (Pause for responses). Move your pencil to the right and find the capital A. Do you see the four words? Find the word boy and draw a line under the word boy. (Check the responses.) Now read the next sentence. What word comes after blue. See the capital B under the blank? That means you go to the capital B on the right to find the correct answer. What word comes after blue? (Pause) Yes, it is house. Draw a line under it. The next blank has a 1 under it. Find the answer and mark it. (Pause) Now do as many as you can."

Level 1

* My name is Jim. I am a _____.
 ___A___

I live in a blue _____. My blue
 ___B___

house is _____ big. It is little. _____
 ___1___ ___2___

have a big brother _____ a cat. We
 ___3___

like _____ play in our yard. _____
 ___4___ ___5___

we run so hard _____ fall on the
 ___6___

ground.

Level 2

_____ day we got in _____.
 ___7___ ___8___

Mother cleaned the floor _____ we
 ___9___

walked on it _____ it got dry.
 ___10___

Level 3

Jack _____, "Wait a minute,
 ___11___

Mother. _____ you want to be
 ___12___

_____ that we don't walk _____
 ___13___ ___14___

your wet floor, you _____ put up
 ___15___

a sign. _____ we wouldn't make the
 ___16___

Level 4

_____ journey across the wet
 ___17___

_____." .
 ___18___

Mother's Side of the Story

"This was quite a _____ for a
 ___19___

mother to _____. After a bit of
 ___20___

Level 5

_____ I took command and
 ___21___

_____ as they had asked."
 ___22___

A.	girl	B.	house
	boy		sky
	wagon		frog
	hat		tree

1. so	2. We	3. and
very	I	for
not	Can	frog
red	Mother	now

4. our	5. Something	6. we
the	Sometimes	he
an	Besides	they
to	Look	head

7. The	8. time	9. because
Some	trouble	and
One	better	yet
Last	asleep	until

10. before	11. Sprat	12. After
after	Jones	As
until	said	If
lazily	jumped	Hey

13. sad	14. up	15. carefully
old	on	won't
grumpy	around	needn't
certain	behind	should

16. Often	17. bus	18. flour
Then	happy	wall
How	stilted	surface
There	stupid	lake

19. decision	20. have
sign	come
discovery	make
journey	do

21. preparation	22. did
relief	went
mystery	hoped
encouragement	came

Mr. Brown's Occupation

Mr. Brown, Jim's father, _____
                              23
to have a very _____ job. He is the
                 24
_____ of a police helicopter.
    25

23. is   24. low   25. mechanic
    and   suspicious   owner
    in   interesting   player
    appears   dumb   pilot

Level 6

_____ has an immense amount
   26
_____ work, in my hunble
   27
_____ . He helps other policemen
   28
_____ traffic on crowded roads,
   29

26. Police   27. of   28. home
    He   in   estimation
    Jim   hard   language
    It   from   situation

29. over
    guide
    supplant
    help

Level 7

_____ at times he pursues _____
   30   31
bank robbers and other _____ of
                         32
criminals.

    Although he _____ to do many
                  33
routine _____ in his job of
          34

30. then   31. past   32. kinds
    if   fleeing   old
    when   funny   parts
    and   with   mean

33. how   34. habits   35. stifling
    will   tasks   helping
    has   vital   avoiding
    comes   happenings   abetting

Level 8

_____ crime and enforcing laws,
   35
_____ has always served with
   36
_____ . Part of his success
   37
_____ due to the intensive _____
   38   39
which he received, and _____
                         40

36. it   37. treachery 38. happens
    he   hesitation   is
    man   distinction   were
    then   camouflage   by

39. training   40. all
    rewards   what
    heat   that
    courtesy   some

Level 9

is due to his _____ mind and his
                41
cool _____ .
       42

Grandma Brown

41. stealthy   42. dedication
    melancholy   badge
    lamentable   expansion
    ingenious   jurisdiction

    Grandma Brown is a _____ reading
                         43
teacher. Suffice it _____ say, she
                      44
enjoys teaching _____ people how to
                  45

43. remedial   44. for   45. feudal
    dejected   can   delinquent
    festive   we   illiterate
    grouchy   to   brazen

Level 10

read. _____ factors account for her
     46

_____ success in teaching. One
  47

_____ real mutual trust existing
  48

_____ her and her students.
  49

Level 11

_____ second is the excellent
  50

_____ she received at the _____ .
  51   52

Another factor is her _____
                      53

intuition. Then the final _____
                          54

in her great success _____ a
                     55

Level 12

mentor are the _____ skill with
               56

which she _____ the sometimes
          57

nebulous problems _____ the
                  58

prodigious and also _____ manner
                    59

in which she _____ these problems.
             60

Level 13

How the _____ of life
        61

seemed to _____ exemplified in these
          62

brief _____ ! Please do not take
      63

_____ at our manner of _____
  64   65

aspects of our characters' lives.

46. Numberless
    Five
    Confounding
    Which

47. poor
    gratifying
    mediocre
    piteous

48. are
    has
    sees
    is

49. by
    for
    between
    happily

50. One
    That
    My
    The

51. oratory
    symposium
    quandary
    curriculum

52. university
    high school
    book store
    library

53. fastidious
    unerring
    statistical
    impending

54. things
    factors
    scores
    deficits

55. as
    with
    story
    in

56. obsequious
    gauche
    chimerical
    consummate

57. creates
    identifies
    redresses
    vindicates

58. freeing
    and
    or
    in

59. sagacious
    voracious
    vicarious
    ostentatious

60. adjures
    sublimates
    inveigles
    rectifies

61. vicissitudes
    sycophants
    panegyrics
    judicatures

62. have
    me
    be
    come

63. cupidities
    vignettes
    satraps
    irascibilities

64. datura
    fruition
    panache
    umbrage

65. vindicating
    desiccating
    exacerbating
    delineating

Answer Key for the Reading Comprehension Section of the Hafner Comprehensive Group Reading Inventory

1. not
2. I
3. and
4. to
5. sometimes
6. we

7. one	8. trouble	9. and
10. before	11. said	12. if
13. certain	14. on	15. should
16. then	17. stupid	18. surface
19. decision	20. make	21. encouragement
22. did	23. appears	24. interesting
25. pilot	26. he	27. of
28. estimation	29. guide	30. and
31. fleeing	32. kinds	33. has
34. tasks	35. stifling	36. he
37. distinction	38. is	39. training
40. some	41. ingenious	42. dedication
43. remedial	44. to	45. illiterate
46. five	47. gratifying	48. is
49. between	50. the	51. curriculum
52. university	53. unerring	54. factors
55. as	56. consummate	57. identifies
58. and	59. sagacious	60. rectifies
61. vicissitudes	62. be	63. vignettes
64. umbrage	65. delineating	

Conversion Table for the Hafner Reading Comprehension Test

Raw Score	Grade 16 % tile	Grade Placement	Raw Score	Grade Placement
65	93+	——	34	5.8
64	91	——	33	5.7
63	89	——	32	5.6
62	85	——	31	5.4
61	80	——	30	5.3
60	74	——	29	5.2
59	68	——	28	5.0
58	62	16.5	27	4.8
57	54	16.1	26	4.7
56	45	15.3	25	4.6
55	37	14.4	24	4.4
54	28	13.8	23	4.3
53	21	13.5	22	4.2
52	15	13.1	21	4.0
51	10	12.8	20	3.8
50	6	12.4	19	3.7
49	4	11.9	18	3.6
48	3	11.0	17	3.4
47	2	10.2	16	3.3
46	1	9.4	15	3.2
45	——	8.8	14	3.0
44	——	8.1	13	2.8
43	——	7.5	12	2.7

Raw Score	Grade Placement
42	7.0
41	6.6
40	6.5
39	6.4
38	6.3
37	6.2
36	6.1
35	6.0

Raw Score	Grade Placement
11	2.6
10	2.4
9	2.3
8	2.2
7	2.0
6	1.8
5	1.7
4	1.6
3	1.5
2	1.4
1	1.2

Individual Phonics Tests

The Hafner Quick Phonics Test

Name _____

Grade _____

Directions: Have the subject read across the rows. Encode his response (according to the Merriam-Webster key) directly to the right of the stimulus. In test CD and VC he may give the phonemic options in any order. Encourage, but don't push. Count as correct any acceptable phonemic options which he may give. After the test is complete, circle incorrect responses, count number correct and compute the percentages.

SCORE

CLN: Consonant Letter Name. <u>Directions</u>: "Please tell me the names of these letters."

_____%   g   s   v   n   b   x   t   j   d   q   /10

VLN: Vowel Letter Name. <u>Directions</u>: "Please tell me the names of these letters."

_____%   i   o   a   u   e   /5

CB: Consonant Blend. (or Digraph: Consonant Diphone)

_____%   tr   sm   fr   gl   br   cl   pl   st   cr   pr   /10
(alternate)   troo   smoo   froo   gloo   broo
              cloo   ploo   stoo   croo   proo

CD: Consonant Digraph. (or Digraph: Consonant Uniphone)
               (Phonemic Options)

_____%   kn   wh   sh   th   ph   gn   ch   /10
                         th   ch
                                         ch

VC: Vowel Clusters. (or Vowel Phoneme Options)

Group one ea   ou   ow   ai   oa   oo   /10

_____%   ea   ou   ow   oo

Group two oy   ue   aw   oe   au   ie   oi   /10

_____%   ue   au   ie

Group three   ough   ough   eigh   ei   ew   ay   /10

_____%   ough   ough   eigh   ew

OC: Other Combinations.

_____%   wr ____ ing   or   ur   ar   ____tion   er   /10
                    ir   alt   cil

	CLN	VLN	CB	CD	VC–1	VC–2	VC–3	OC
100	. . . .
90	. . . .
80	. . . .
70	. . . .
PUPIL 60	. . . .
%	
PROFILE 50	. . . .
40	. . . .
30	. . . .
20	. . . .
10	. . . .
00	. . . .

Structural Elements and Principles Test

Dividing Words into Syllables Test

Directions: Here are some words and nonsense words that you may divide into syllables. Draw a line between the syllables that you find.

ago	batter	baby	captain	open	Atlantic
past	behind	cry	Pacific	imi	chammer

oprak   delo   nokrim   sattle   lėpstan   jying

rable   fy

Closed Syllable Rule Test

Directions: These nonsense words start with "f-f-f" and end with <u>too</u>. Please read them for me.

fettoo   fattoo   fittoo   fottoo   futtoo   fyttoo

Open Syllable Rule Test

Directions: These nonsense words start with "f-f-f" and end with <u>too</u>. Please read them for me.

fetoo   fatoo   fitoo   fotoo   futoo   fytoo

Prefixes Test

Directions: Here are some prefixes. Please read them for me.

ab   ad   be   com   de   dis   en   ex   in   pre

pro   re   sub   un

Suffixes Test

Directions: Here are some suffixes. Please read them for me.

ary   ive   ance   ity   ious   ence

ic   ent   sion   ly   ous   ment

ful   tion   ure   ness   ate   able

ant

Hafner-Smith Aptitude Test   (See Test Manual for directions.)

3-3 _____ (3) Tell me your name . . . last name, too.
                   (Two names, three months; one, one month.)

3-6 _____ (3) Please draw a circle like this one:
                   (Point to a circle on back of answer sheet.)

3-9 _____ (3) What do you do when you are hungry?
                   (Eat: three months; ask someone for food: one month.)

4-0 _____ (3) Sister is a girl; brother is a . . . .
                   (Boy)

4-3_____(3) What is a knee? (Point to your knee.)

4-6_____(3) I am going to say something. When I am finished, you say it:

        1) I am going to get a drink for Mama.
           (You cannot repeat the sentence for the subject. The first sentence is an example, but if he/she gets it correct, he/she gets the full three months' credit. If he/she misses it, do the second sentence. In effect, the subject gets two chances (sentences) to earn three months' credit. The sentence must be repeated exactly.)

        2) Look at the pretty flag on the flagpole.

4-9_____(3) Name two things that are green.
           (One does not find a testing room that necessarily has green in it. If it happens to have these things—fine. The basic idea is for the person to recall something green. No cues, please.)

5-0_____(3) What is a ball? . . . Tell me what a ball is.
           (At this age, either a use for the ball or a description merits three months' credit. The criteria will change at the 6–0 level.)

5-3_____(3) Please draw a square like this one.
           (Point to the square on the back of the answer sheet.)

5-6_____(3) A scissors and a piece of broken glass both _____.
           (The task is for the subject to supply the correct word so you must speak the sentence to show the expectancy. Words such as cut, slice, pierce, or puncture are considered correct.)

5-9_____(3) Please repeat this sentence when I am finished. OR I am going to say a sentence. You say it when I finish.

        Jim likes to play with his wagon and bicycle.

6-0_____(3) What is an apple?
           (Fruit: three months; gives some legitimate use such as "You eat it," two months; describes it (more than saying, "It's round,"): one month.)

6-3_____(3) What is a rabbit?
           (Animal: three points; use such as, "You eat it" or "It's a pet": two months; describes it: one month.)

6-6_____(3) Print your name here, please.
           (Two names: three months; one name: two months. Name should be printed in space on back of the answer sheet.)

6-9_____(3) How are a penny and a dime alike? What are they both?
(Money or coins: three months; use: two months; describes them, giving common features: one month.)

7-0_____(3) Please draw a diamond like this one:
(Point to diamond on back of answer sheet.)

7-3_____(3) Sally had four pencils and her father gave her three more. How many did she have then?
(Begin timing as soon as you have finished stating the problem. Timing must be precise to the second. Time limit is 30 seconds. If subject asks for a repetition of the problem, repeat it, but the timing keeps going. Only one repetition is allowed. The subject may not use pencil (or pen) and paper; neither may the numbers be displayed. This is in keeping with the procedures on other major ability tests. Answer is seven.)

7-6_____(3) What is a nickel? ———
(Money or coin: three months; use: two months; describes it: one month)

7-9_____ (3) Who is the president of the United States? . . . First and last name.
(Two names: three months; one name: two months.)

8-0_____ (3) A boy had 11 marbles and lost three. How many did he have then?
(Same rules as problem at 7-3. Time limit, 30 seconds. Answer: eight.)

8-3_____ (3) What is a shovel?
(Tool: three months; use: two months; describes it: one month.)

8-6_____ (3) What is a sword?
(Weapon: three months; use: two months; describes it: one month.)

8-9_____ (3) At five cents each, what will three pieces of candy cost?
(Fifteen cents. Thirty-second time limit with same rules applying as in previous arithmetic reasoning items.)

9-0_____ (3) What are the seasons of the year?
(Winter, summer, spring, fall: three months; three seasons: one month.)

9-3_____ (3) How are a piano and a guitar alike?
(Musical instruments: three months; use, such as "You play them" or "You make music with them": two months; describes likeness, such as, "They both have strings": one month.)

9–6 _____ (3) Two girls had 26 marbles. They divided them so that each girl got the same number of marbles. How many marbles did each girl have then?
(Thirteen.)

9–9 _____ (3) How many things make a half dozen? (Six.)

10–0 _____ (3) What does scorch mean?
(Burn something so that its color is changed: three months; Parch with great heat: three months; to intensely censure or criticize someone: three months; burn with an iron (or other hot instrument): two months (if explained to show change of color of material or quality of material, then, three months.)

10–3 _____ (3) What month sometimes has only 29 days?
(February.)

10–6 _____ (3) What is a thorn?
(1. pointy branch; sticker 2. something that wounds, annoys, or causes discomfort.)

10–9 _____ (3) What does the heart do?
(Pumps blood; circulates blood: three months; beats: one month.)

11–0 _____ (3) Four girls had 36 apples. They divided them so that each girl got the same number of apples. How many apples did each girl get? (30-second time limit; same procedures as in 7–3 level. Correct answer: Nine.)

11–3 _____ (3) What is the capital of France?
(Paris.)

11–6 _____ (3) How are a robin, a bear, and a spider alike?
(They are animals: three months; some like function(s): two months; like part of body: one month.)

11–9 _____ (3) What does ignorant mean?
(Not knowing; uninformed; lacking knowledge or training: three months for any one of these.)

12–0 _____ (3) How are champagne and brandy alike?
(Both are alcoholic or intoxicating beverages: three months; both make you drunk: two months; both liquids or something to drink: one month.)

12–3 _____ (3) Who wrote The Adventures of Huckleberry Finn?
(Samuel Langhorn Clemens or Mark Twain: three months; Clements or Twain: two months.)

12-6 _____   An artist earned $48. She was paid $12 for each painting. How many paintings did she sell?
(30-second time limit; same procedures as previously. Correct answer: Four.)

12-9 _____   In what war was the Battle of Yorktown fought?
(Revolutionary War.)

13-0 _____   What does disease mean?
(Sickness; ailment; infection; dysfunction of part of body caused by environment, infection, and the like: three months for any one of these.)

13-3 _____   How are paper and gas alike?
(Both are potential energy sources; both fuels: three months; both burn: one month.)

13-6 _____   What is the name of the national anthem of the United States?
(Star Spangled Banner.)

13-9 _____   Fifty-four is three fourths of what number?
(30-second time limit; Display the numerals. Correct answer: 72.)

14-0 _____   What does cluster mean?
(A bunch; things grouped together: three months.)

14-3 _____   If you buy four dozen eggs at 60 cents a dozen, how much change should you get back from three dollars?
(60-second time limit; Display the numerals. Correct answer: 60 cents.)

14-6 _____   How tall is the average American woman?
(Any answer between and including 5 feet, 1½ inches, and 5 feet, 4½ inches.)

14-9 _____   How are an ounce and a mile alike?
(Both are measures.)

15-0 _____   What does flaw mean?
(Imperfection; defect; not perfect; something wrong with something.)

15-3 _____   If three radishes cost seven cents, how much would 18 radishes cost?
(60-second time limit; Same procedures as at age level 7-3. Answer: 42 cents.)

15-6_____ Who invented the telephone?
            (Alexander Graham Bell: three months; Bell: two months.)

15-9_____ What is a sternum?
            (Answer: A breastbone; the bone in the chest area to which the
            ribs are attached or subject points to it.)

16-0_____ How are a piece of wire and an aluminum pan alike?
            (Both are metal.)

16-3_____ If you pay nineteen cents a glass for milk and buy five glasses of it,
            how much change would you get back from a dollar?
            (45-second time limit. Same procedures as at age level 7-3.
            Answer: 5 cents.)

16-6_____ Where is Bolivia?
            (South America.)

16-9_____ What does ramble mean?
            (1. to roam about, 2. to talk or write aimlessly, 3. to grow or
            spread out in all directions.)

17-0_____ What does belligerent mean?
            (1. at war, 2. of war; of fighting, 3. seeking war; warlike,
            4. showing a readiness to fight or quarrel.)

17-3_____ Fourteen is one third of what number?
            (30-second time limit. Same procedures as at age level 7-3.
            Answer: 42.)

17-6_____ In what part of an engine are air and gas mixed?
            (Carburetor.)

17-9_____ What profession did Ernest Hemingway, Mark Twain, and Edgar
            Allen Poe have in common?
            (1. Writing; or they were authors, 2. Journalism.)

18-0_____ What does envoy mean?
            (1. a messenger; agent; representative, 2. a diplomat.)

18-3_____ Seventeen is one quarter of what number?
            (30-second time limit. Same procedures as at age level 7-3.
            Answer: 68.)

18-6_____ For what theory is Albert Einstein famous?
            (Relativity or special relativity.)

18-9_____   Who commanded the American Expeditionary Forces in World
              War I?
                   (Pershing; General John J. Pershing.)

19-0_____   What does anticipate mean?
                   (To look forward to; foresee; expect.)

19-3_____   How much are 13 1/4 and 16 7/8.
                   (30-second time limit. Same procedures as at age level 7-3.
                   Answer: 30 1/8.)

19-6_____   Where are Christchurch and Auckland located?
                   (New Zealand.)

19-9_____   What important substance does the pancreas secrete?
                   (Insulin.)

              (The test items themselves should not be given to the school—
              only the results in terms of verbal comprehension age and verbal
              comprehension quotient.)

Testing Learning Rate in Reading

1.0   Thesis: The best way to see if a child is ready to learn to read is to teach
       the child some words and see if he can remember them.

2.0   Basic steps in the process.

2.1   Prepare picture-word cards of words to be taught.
2.2   Teach the words to a small group of children.
2.3   After one hour, test each child apart from the others to see how many words
       he/she remembers.

3.0   Preparing the learning-rate test.

3.1   Select three to eight words depending upon the ability of the group.
3.1.1 The meanings of the words must be known to the children.
3.1.2 The words should be reasonably colorful so that many illustrations may be
       given in the teaching—concrete words, action words, for example:

water	baby	truck	catch	eat	funny
clown	letter	radio	ride	play	pretty
glass	tree	fork	kick	laugh	happy
apple	house	table	run	cry	
flower	chair	guitar	sing	come	
pencil	drum	plate	drink	jump	
bus	girl	orange			

3.1.3 Remember that a combination of long and short words would be easier to learn than words of the same length. Try to use words of similar length when testing learning rate in reading. All words starting with the same letter (or in some other way quite similar) would be difficult to learn.

3.2 Print the words and illustrations on cards of equal size.

side 1: | ball ◖ | side 2: | ball |

4.0 Teaching the words to the children.

4.1 The method.

4.1.1 Present the picture-word side of cards to the children. (Let's say we will teach the words clown, funny, play, truck, sing, orange.)

4.1.2 Point to the word clown and say, "This word is clown. Look at it closely; say clown."

4.1.3 Have two children use the word clown in a sentence. (You might need to cue a child with a question such as
    1. What do clowns do?
    2. Where can you see a clown?)

4.1.4 Present the picture-word side of funny.

4.1.5 Point to the word funny and say, "This word is funny. Look at it closely; say funny."

4.1.6 Have two children use the word funny in a sentence.

4.1.7 Review the word clown. Hold up word side of the clown card. Ask what the word says. Point to the first two letters. Say, "Here are the first two letters of clown. Now look at the rest of the letters."

4.1.8 Next hold up word side of the funny card. Point to the first two letters. Say, "Here are the first two letters of funny. Now look at the rest of the letters."

4.1.9 Have children discriminate between clown and funny, using word side of cards.

4.10 Present the remaining words in like fashion; then review them and help children discriminate among them.

4.11 Play a game with the children: Scramble the order of the cards. Present each word card (word side). Ask children to look at word and say it. Let children check as you turn to the picture-word side. (Set aside the word or words they still seem to have trouble with and finally present these and have children note differences in structure of the word.)

4.12 Place word cards in combinations such as

| funny | | clown |

Have children read them.

4.13 Scramble all the word cards and run a final check. (This method of teaching a person to identify printed words can be used any time you need to teach such words.)

5.0   Test: After one hour test each child individually, away from other children. On a record sheet which contains the words you teach, record + for correct responses and o for incorrect responses.
(Note: Use thick enough cards so pictures don't show through.)

Individual Mental Abilities Point Scale

This is an informal test of mental abilities found useful in reading. It contains types of items found in readiness tests and types found in intelligence tests. All tests are to be administered orally. The numbers of the auditory memory span test are to be read at a rate of one per second.

Local norms can be built for this test. Comparison of students' mental ability scores on these tests with the mental ability scores (on this same test) of known good and poor readers at certain chronological age levels can lead to the development of reading achievement expectancy patterns.

The average student will probably not give correct responses on the Proverbs Test until age fourteen or fifteen. Very bright students may begin to give correct responses at age nine or ten, and bright students at age twelve.

Since the tests have very high ceilings, they can be used with older students for appropriate measurement and evaluation.

Individual Mental Abilities Point Scale

Name _____ Age _____

Birth date _____ Grade _____

School _____

City _____ State _____

Examiner _____ Reading instructional level _____

Test	Points	Standard Score*	Percentile Rank*
General Information	_____	_____	_____
Auditory Memory Span	_____	_____	_____
Proverbs	_____	_____	_____
Vocabulary	_____	_____	_____
Total	_____	_____	_____

General Information Test [Maximum points = 25]

Directions: I am going to ask you questions about many different things. Here is a sample question: Who is the President of the United States? [Scoring—one point for each correct response]

1. Name one of the colors in the United States flag.

* One may need to consult (a) a test and measurements text or a statistics text or (b) a friend for help in determining these statistics.

2. What is a canoe?
3. How many inches are in a foot?
4. What do you call the shape that has three sides?
5. On what date is Christmas Day?
6. What is the name of our national anthem?
7. What do you call the person who fixes water pipes in people's homes?
8. What is the chief officer or ruler of the state called?
9. How far is it from St. Louis to Chicago?
10. What is the name of the bank of earth or concrete that is built to hold back a river so it won't overflow its banks?
11. Where is Montreal?
12. How long is a football field from goal line to goal line?
13. How many feet are in a mile?
14. What mountains run from Maine to Alabama?
15. What is a cathedral?
16. What is Patrick Henry's most famous saying?
17. What is the capital of Australia?
18. Which country gave the Statue of Liberty to the United States?
19. What kind of energy does a motor use?
20. What metal is processed from hematite?
21. Where is "the cradle of civilization"?
22. What does tempus fugit mean?
23. What is the capital of West Germany?
24. What is the lingua franca of central east Africa?
25. Who was the "Angelic Doctor"?

Auditory Memory Span Test

Directions: I am going to say some numbers. When I finish a set, I want you to say them after me. For example: I say 4 - 2 and you say ___. [Wait for response. Mark + for correct and 0 for incorrect. If the subject gets the first set of an item correct, proceed to the next item. If he fails the first set of an item, give him the next set. When he reaches his ceiling on the forward section, proceed to the backward section. Score: highest number of digits correctly repeated forward plus highest number of digits repeated backward; for example, if a subject's highest level forward is E and his highest backward is C his score is 6 + 4. or 10.] [Maximum points = 18.]

Forward		Backward	
A.	4 - 2	A.	3 - 7
	2 - 9		6 - 9
B.	7 - 3 - 8	B.	5 - 4 - 8
	4 - 7 - 1		7 - 1 - 9
C.	9 - 3 - 2 - 6	C.	3 - 7 - 6 - 2
	3 - 7 - 1 - 5		5 - 8 - 2 - 3
D.	8 - 1 - 3 - 4 - 6	D.	8 - 6 - 1 - 3 - 9
	7 - 6 - 8 - 2 - 9		5 - 1 - 7 - 2 - 8

Forward	Backward
E. 4 - 2 - 7 - 1 - 6 - 3	E. 7 - 2 - 4 - 9 - 3 - 5
1 - 8 - 2 - 5 - 4 - 7	4 - 9 - 7 - 3 - 8 - 1
F. 9 - 3 - 8 - 7 - 4 - 2 - 1	F. 5 - 7 - 6 - 2 - 9 - 4 - 1
6 - 2 - 7 - 4 - 1 - 3 - 8	2 - 6 - 5 - 9 - 1 - 8 - 3
G. 9 - 5 - 6 - 2 - 8 - 3 - 6 - 4	G. 4 - 2 - 8 - 5 - 7 - 3 - 6 - 1
5 - 3 - 1 - 6 - 2 - 7 - 4 - 8	7 - 9 - 6 - 1 - 8 - 2 - 5 - 4
H. 8 - 2 - 3 - 7 - 6 - 2 - 9 - 1 - 5	H. 1 - 6 - 5 - 8 - 4 - 7 - 3 - 9 - 2
6 - 8 - 2 - 7 - 3 - 5 - 1 - 4 - 9	5 - 1 - 7 - 9 - 6 - 2 - 4 - 8 - 3

Proverbs Test

Directions: I will read some sayings to you. Please tell me what they mean. [Scoring: one or two points each, depending upon completeness of response. Credit is not given for literal responses such as, "When you spill something, you shouldn't cry about it." The response should be generalized.] [Maximum points = 22.]

1. Don't cry over spilt milk.
2. Big trees from little acorns grow.
3. Haste makes waste.
4. Don't put all your eggs in one basket.
5. Honey catches more flies than vinegar.
6. A fool and his money are soon parted.
7. God helps those who help themselves.
8. A stitch in time saves nine.
9. A word to the wise is sufficient.
10. Little strokes fell great oaks.
11. A soft answer turneth away wrath.

Vocabulary Test

Directions: Say each word to the student. Ask the student the meaning of the word. Write the response in the space after the word. If the student says he/she does not know it, write D. K. after the word. Allow one point for each minimally correct answer. Allow two points for responses that show good understanding. [Maximum points = 88.]

	Approximate Vocabulary Age Level
A. What is a <u>cat</u>?	
B. What is a <u>balloon</u>? or What do we mean by a <u>balloon</u>?	

	Approximate Vocabulary Age Level
1. apple _____	6- 0
2. lamp _____	6- 2
3. airplane _____	6- 4
4. bridge _____	6- 6
5. shelf _____	6- 8

	Approximate Vocabulary Age Level
6. drum	6-10
7. giant	7- 0
8. zoo	7- 2
9. river	7- 4
10. arrow	7-10
11. mechanic	8- 4
12. badge	8-10
13. discover	9- 2
14. detective	9- 6
15. tailor	10- 2
16. pyramid	10- 6
17. construct	10-10
18. merge	11- 2
19. plunge	11- 8
20. gentle	12- 2
21. scuff	12- 8
22. artery	13- 2
23. prompt	13- 8
24. enlist	14- 2
25. mummy	14-10
26. splendid	15- 6
27. remedy	16- 2
28. marsh	16- 8
29. inquire	17- 2
30. apparel	17- 8
31. cease	18- 2
32. frail	18- 8
33. unwieldy	19- 0
34. upbraid	20- 0
35. persevere	21- 0

	Approximate Vocabulary Age Level
36. resolute _____	22- 0
37. tangible _____	23- 0
38. bonny _____	24- 0
39. probity _____	25- 0
40. atavistic _____	26- 0
41. truculent _____	27- 0
42. arras _____	28- 0
43. pasquinade _____	29- 0
44. cunctatious _____	30- 0

Sample Study-Reference Skills Inventories*

Social Studies: Your Town and Mine, level 3 text (Ginn)

I. Location of Information
  A. Index. Use the index to answer the following questions:
    1. On what pages does the book tell about forests? [pages 100–103]
    2. On how many pages does it tell about clothing made from wool? [7]
    3. Name two other headings under which you could find information about meat. [Food, Animals]
  B. Table of Contents
    1. On what page does the unit about the homes in the town begin? [page 100]
    2. In what chapter would you find information about vegetables? ["A Trip to a Truck Farm" or "Mr. Hill's Grocery Store"]
    3. In what chapter would you find information about growing cotton? ["Cotton and Linen for Our Clothes"]
  C. Dictionary [Beginning Thorndike and Barnhart]
    1. Find the following words: (1) floss (2) tame
    2. Locate the words underlined below and tell what they mean as they are used in the sentence:
      a. I make the distance to be ten feet.
      b. The knight wore a coat of mail.
    3. Using the guide words at the bottom of the page, pronounce the following words:
      a. The Indians grew a corn called maize. [māz]
      b. The colors made the dress look gaudy. [gôd′ i]

---

* These are sample tests. The idea here is for teachers to construct tests to fit the materials they are using in their classrooms.

II. Selection and Evaluation.
   A. Topic of a Sentence
      1. What is the topic of the last sentence on page 40? [grain elevator]
      2. What is the topic of the first sentence on page 43? [filling flour bags]
   B. Topic Sentences
      1. What is the topic sentence of the third paragraph on page 52? [Too many cattle cannot be put into one pasture.]
      2. What is the topic sentence of the first paragraph on page 26? [first sentence]
   C. Topic of a Paragraph
      1. What is the topic of the first paragraph, second column, page 47? [greenhouse]
      2. What is the topic of the next-to-the-last paragraph on page 54? [animal fat]
   D. Main Ideas
      1. What is the main idea of the last paragraph, column one, page 107? [Making bricks is one of the oldest kinds of work.]
      2. What is the main idea of the first paragraph, column two, page 107? [Bricks are made to be used in different ways.]
      3. What is the main idea on page 119? [Water is needed for power, drinking, ships, and so on]
   E. Recognizing Important Details
      1. [Read page 83.] How is silk thread made?
      2. [Read page 81.] Where does linen come from?

III. Organization
   A. Outlining
      1. Outline the first paragraph on page 27. [Or one may ask the pupil to write the important ideas.]
      2. Outline page 53.
   B. Summarizing
      1. Summarize the first three paragraphs on page 122.
      2. Summarize page 35.
   C. Following Sequence of Events
      1. [Read the first three paragraphs on page 73.] Describe what is done with sheep's fleece after it reaches the mill.

IV. Special Skills
   A. Skimming
      1. Locate the paragraph that tells how cotton grows. [page 177]
      2. Read the sentence which tells what rayon is made from. [Last paragraph, page 85.]
   B. Reading/Interpreting Pictorial Aids
      1. Answer the question asked above the picture on page 221.
      2. Map, page 186.
         a. Which direction would you travel to reach Mexico from the United States? [south] from Africa? [west]
         b. What country is east of Poland? [U.S.S.R. or Russia]

Science: Discovering with Science, level 4 text

I. Location of Information
   A. Table of Contents
      1. On what page does the chapter start that is entitled, "The Air We Live In?" [page 86]
      2. In which chapter would you be able to read about oceans, lakes, and streams? ["The Waters of the Earth"]
   B. Index
      1. On which page can you read about the telegraph? [page 180]
      2. How many pages would give you information about tin? [two; 251 and 252]
      3. On how many pages could you read about insects? [six; 21, 31, 149–151, and 203]
   C. Skimming and Locating Information [Use Index.]
      1. Name two kinds of plants that you can grow by grafting. [apple trees and rose bushes; page 139]
      2. Locate the sentence that states that arctic terns are great travelers. [page 26, last paragraph]
      3. How long do eels live in fresh water? [six or seven years; page 208]
II. Selection and Evaluation
   A. Topic
      1. What is the topic of the first sentence on page 39? [leaves]
      2. What is the topic of the first paragraph on page 39? [evergreen trees]
   B. Main Idea
      1. Locate the paragraph that tells how a tidal wave is started. [page 83, last paragraph]
      2. What is the main idea of paragraphs 2, 3, and 4 on page 57? [Farmers in different areas have to grow crops that will mature during the growing season.]
III. Organization
   A. Outlining
      1. Outline page 45
   B. Summarization
      1. Summarize page 27.
IV. Specialized Skills
   A. Reading a Chart
      1. There is a weather record on page 63. The wind blew from what direction on December first? [N.E.]
   B. Reading a Time-zone Map
      1. Using the map on page 75, tell me how many time zones there are in the United States. [four]
      2. Using this same map, tell me whether the sun rises first in New York or Chicago. [New York]
V. Following Directions
   A. Locate the names of plants mentioned in this book that grow in the desert and plants that grow in the jungle. Make a list of each of these. When you

have finished, tell me whether you have the longer list for the desert or the jungle. [Desert plants: saguaro, barrel cactus, strawberry cactus, prickly pear, tree cacti. Jungle plants: rubber trees, orchids, ferns, tall trees.]

Sample Informal Reading Inventories

SAMPLE ONE

1. Story: "The Whoopee-Hide Adventure," by Alice Alison Lide. Segment from pages 183–185.
2. Book: *From Sea to Sea*, ed. by Nila B. Smith.
3. Publisher: Silver Burdett Company, 1946.
4. Level: 3^1.

> Directions: Try to develop interest in the story by telling the pupil the story is about Bobby and his sister Polly, who live in a little house high up on Pine Hill. Their mother is having a quilting party in order to finish sewing some quilts. Today Mother's friends came to help her and they brought their children with them. The children have work to do and Bobby Boy and the other small boys have just run off to get some firewood. Then say, "Please read the rest of the story silently to find out what happens and then I will ask you some questions about it."

The girls had to keep the fires going under the cooking pots. But they played all kinds of games, too. The best game of all was "Whoopee Hide."

Polly was IT because the party was at her house. As the others scampered off, Polly sang the Whoopee-Hide song.

A bushel of wheat, a bushel of rye.
All not ready, shout out "I."

Polly sang about the bushels of wheat and rye three times. By then there were no more shouts. So she called "Whoopee" to tell the others that she was coming.

Then she set out to hunt for them.

Polly had a long hunt before she found the children, who were hiding behind rocks and stumps.

Was everyone in? No, not all. Where was little Sally?

The other girls hunted, but never a sign of little Sally. Aunt Betsy and all the others left the quilting frame and the boys, too, started to hunt.

Where could the child be? They looked everywhere, running around the house and across the yard. At last they all ran down the path that led to the spring.

Near the spring Polly saw something under the big wash pot that was turned upside down. It was a bit of bright pink cloth.

Yellow Dog saw it, too, and barked and pawed at the pot excitedly.

Many hands took hold of the big pot and raised it a little way. There, under it was poor little Sally, curled up in a ball.

Out she rolled, so glad to be free that at first she could not say anything.

At last the words came.

"I saw this pot leaning upside down against a rock," said Sally, "I thought it a grand hiding place. I squeezed in under it. Then bang! Down it fell on top of me.

"If a stone had not held it up a little bit, I would not have had a breath of air."

"Let's be thankful for that stone," said Aunt Betsy Brown, as she took Sally in her arms.[1]

Comprehension Questions [15 points each]

1. What did the children shout if they weren't ready?

   _____

2. Where were the children hiding?

   _____

3. What was turned upside down?

   _____

4. Who held Sally after she was saved?

   _____

Score: _____

Interpretation Questions [10 points each]

5. Why were there no more shouts after Polly sang the song three times?

   _____

6. Why was it lucky that several people found Sally under the big, heavy pot?

   _____

7. How do you think Sally felt under the pot?

   _____

8. How did the stone save Sally's life?

   _____

Score: _____

Total: _____

	Criteria Met	
Silent Reading: _____ points or % comprehension	Yes	No
Oral Reading: _____ % accuracy	Yes	No

An Informal Reading Inventory
(Comprehension, Pronunciation, and Vocabulary)

SAMPLE TWO

Readability level = 7.7

[1] Reprinted by permission of Silver Burdett Company.

Plane Airways*

Skyways, or airways, are routes through the air followed by airplanes in flight. Most airways extend thousands of feet above the ground. Jet routes are above 25,000 feet altitude.

Each airway is ten miles wide. This results in each airplane being surrounded by a large block of airspace ten miles wide, twenty-five to fifty miles long, and two thousand feet high.

In the United States there are more than 65,000 miles of airways. These are operated by the Federal Aviation Agency. This agency's regulation is called air-route traffic control. The control centers receive flight plans and reports from pilots. The centers keep in contact with the pilots by means of radio.

Planes are separated in flight levels according to their destinations. They fly west and south at even-numbered thousands of feet altitude. Airplanes flying east or north must fly at odd-numbered thousands of feet altitude. When above towns or cities, at least 1,000 feet altitude must be maintained.

Today pilots are aided in their flights by radio, light beacons, and radar. In the early days of airplane flights, the airways were simply routes over which pilots flew as they looked for such landmarks as towns, lakes, mountains, and rivers.

\# of errors _____

% correct _____   (Divide # of errors by 2 and subtract from 100 to get % correct)

Do silent reading and answering of questions first. Then have the subject read orally. Mark pronunciation errors on duplicate copy of the selection. Finally, have the student define the vocabulary items in the last part of the tests.

Plane Airways

Literal Comprehension (15 points each)

_____ 1. What can you tell me about an airway? (Any detail.)

_____ 2. Who operates the more than 65,000 miles of airways in the United States? (Federal Aviation Agency)

_____ 3. Where do pilots send their flight plans and reports? (To air-route traffic control or traffic control or control center)

_____ 4. Give me an example of a landmark. (Any of the following: town, lake, mountain, river - or any correct example of a landmark)

Interpretation (10 points each)

_____ 5. What might happen in flying if there were no airways? (There would be many crashes)

_____ 6. How does a radio help a pilot in his work? (Any reasonable answer

* Used by permission of Harper and Row Publishers.

relating to communication useful in his job, for example, communicate with control centers)

_____ 7. Why would a plane flying west probably not crash into a plane flying north? (They fly at different altitudes.)

_____ 8. How did pilots use landmarks? (navigation guides, or they helped the pilots tell where they were going)

_____ TOTAL

		Criteria Met	
Silent Reading: _____ points or % comprehension		Yes	No
Oral Reading: _____ % accuracy		Yes	No

Vocabulary: (Read the items to the student and ask him or her to define them.)

1. skyways	4. regulation	7. agency	10. communicate
2. altitude	5. destination	8. landmark	
3. radar	6. navigation	9. ascent	

Kits and Audiovisual Aids, Games and Toys, Books, Workbooks

READINESS MATERIALS

Kits and Audiovisual Aids

ALPHA Time Kit. Focuses on basic readiness skills through creative activities with 26 inflatable dolls. Contains 3 LP records, duplicating masters, and 26 booklets emphasizing consonant sounds. *Arista Corp.*

BFA Comprehension Skill Kit A. Activity books and reading cards focusing on information skills, organization skills, evaluation, and generalization. A cassette story introduces each of the four skill areas. Provides a teachers' manual and self-check answer books. *BFA.*

Building Pre-reading Skills: Kit A and Kit B. Kit A contains 172 illustrations; designed to develop language, thinking, and perception skills undergirding success in learning how to read. Kit B contains picture, word, and letter cards plus teacher's manual. Designed to teach auditory discrimination skills, association of selected consonant letters with their sounds, use of context plus beginning sounds to determine a response orally, and the visual forms of selected consonants. *Ginn.*

Dandy Dog's Early Learning Program. Story picture books, story records, do and learn records, learning activities, learning charts, learning pads, animated slides, and handbook and planbook for the teacher. For headstart, nursery schools, kindergartens, slow learners, non-English-speaking children, and first grades. *American Book.*

Developing Cognitive Skills in Young Learners. Seven color filmstrips designed to deal with the following dimensions of cognitive development: grouping and categorizing, contrasts and opposites, relative space and size relationships, concept ordering and discrimination, sequence of ideas, making inferences and judging antecedents and predicting outcomes. Primary. *Educational Activities, Inc.*

EFI Special Language Program. Designed to help the verbally disadvantaged children, this program teaches such areas as parts of the body; directions; basic language patterns; classification, labeling; descriptive statements; and simple logic. Grades K–1. *Electronic Futures, Inc.*

English as a Second Language. Utilizes colored cartoon storybook, filmstrip, and choice of banded record, tape, or cassette. Guidebook. *Kenworthy.*

Gateway to Good Reading. Reading readiness program of auditory discrimination and visual perception. Forty tapes and thirty response booklets. *Imperial Productions, Inc.*

Goldman-Lynch Sounds & Symbols Development Kit. Two audio cassettes, teacher's manual, symbol cards, pocket chart, word cards, sentence strips, puppets, and picture cards. This kit is designed to develop and extend auditory discrimination ability, knowledge of phoneme-grapheme relationships, and extend good speech habits in kindergarten and grade one. *American Guidance Service.*

Hoffman Primary Language Arts Phonics Program. Designed to teach (1) perceptual and language skills and (2) concepts in several content areas. Auditory and visual stimuli are presented together. Through visualization of language in picture stories and word games, children learn sound-symbol relationships. The program is also designed to teach the structure of English and many concepts in the following content areas: science and natural phenomena; social studies; make-believe, fairy tales; family attitudes; and mental, physical and emotional health. Grades K–2. *Hoffman.*

Life in a Nutshell. Color filmstrips and long-play records are used to present vicariously important background and life experience for children. Grades K–1. *Educational Electronics, Inc.*

Peabody Language Development Kits. Designed to stimulate and develop facets of oral language: reception, conceptualization, and expression. Contain stimulus cards, manual of lessons, story posters, tapes, intercom set, and puppets. Preschool and early primary. *American Guidance.*

Readiness for Learning: A Program for Visual and Auditory Perceptual Motor Training. Visual and auditory perceptual-motor training, letter-knowledge and word-knowledge training. Grades K–1. *Lippincott.*

The Reading Bridge. Kit designed for children who need special help in beginning reading. Focuses on letter names, sight words, sentence recognition and word families. Provides a teacher's guide, ten books, and reward tokens. *BFA.*

Reading Readiness. Self-instructional program of 60 film lessons each 50 frames long to be used in a multiple-choice viewer. Designed to teach perceptual skills and 72 basic words. *Educational Projections Corp.*

Reading Readiness. Kit contains cassettes and a teacher resource guide to develop auditory perception and listening skills. *JAB.*

Reading Readiness Skill Starters Kit. Contains skill-development activities in both reading and mathematics. Includes activities with main ideas, left to right sequencing, interpreting illustrations, auditory and visual discrimination, context clues, and sequence of events. *Random House.*

St. Louis Program. An individualized approach to reading readiness and speech improvement that utilizes audio tapes, cassettes and printed materials. *Imperial Productions, Inc.*

Sounds for Young Readers Series. This listening series, which utilizes phonograph records, is designed to promote auditory acuity and discrimination. Volumes 1–3 for grades K–3. *Educational Activities, Inc.*

Speech-to-Print Phonics. Inductive approach to teaching of auditory discrimination and phonic element skills. Oral exercises plus practice with flash cards and pupil pads. Grades K–1. *Harcourt.*

Visual Perception Skills. Color filmstrips treating visual memory, visual-motor coordination, visual constancy, visual discrimination, visualization, figure-ground perception, and visual matching. *Educational Record Sales.*

Games and Toys

Animal Finger Puppets. Tiny, dressed-up animals sit on children's fingers as children invent situations and dialogues. Five puppets with wooden heads and cloth bodies. Ages 3–8. *Creative Playthings, Inc.*

Bigmouth Puppets. Simple rubber puppets for make-believe fun. Alligator, crow, bullfrog, whale. Ages 3–8. *Creative Playthings, Inc.*

Classification Game. Interiors of a food market, clothing store, toy store, and pet shop yield context clues for classifying forty-eight picture cards. *The Instructo Corp.*

Design Cubes. One-inch painted cubes. Can be combined in a large variety of patterns and structures. Ages 4–8. *Creative Playthings, Inc.*

First Experiences with Consonants and Vowels. Materials designed to involve the total child; they use visual, kinesthetic-tactile, and auditory learning styles; help develop ability to recognize relationships between letters and sounds. *The Instructo Corp.*

Foldaway Play Screen. Three-panel screen can be a grocery store, post office, railroad station, or theater. The panels are hinged to open at various angles. Ages 3–10. *Creative Playthings, Inc.*

Folk Marionettes. Make six international wooden puppets gesture, dance, and perform. Easy to operate. Ages 5–12. *Creative Playthings, Inc.*

Integrated Community Workers. Policeman, fireman, laborer, captain, mailman, and conductor. Each 6 inches high; bendable. *Creative Playthings, Inc.*

Junior Handyman. Real handsaw, hammer, 6-foot folding rule, carpenter's pencil, metal square, large-headed nails. Ages 4–8. *Creative Playthings, Inc.*

Magnetic Letters. Seventy plastic letters, upper and lower case. Each contains a small magnet. Ages 3–12. *Creative Playthings, Inc.*

Our Town. Experimental city planning can be done with this array of houses, skyscrapers, stores, government buildings and municipal landmarks, plus trees, shrubs and vehicles (made of hardwood). Ages 4–8. *Creative Playthings, Inc.*

People Finger Puppets. These puppets sit on children's fingertips as children "bring them to life." Wooden heads, cloth bodies. Ages 3–8. *Creative Playthings, Inc.*

Playtown Farm. Several animals, barn with stalls, tractor, and a farmer and his wife. Ages 2–9. *Creative Playthings, Inc.*

Playtown Garage. Tank truck for deliveries, tow truck, gas pump, and garage. (Also available Playtown Firehouse, Marina, and Airfield.) Ages 3–9. *Creative Playthings, Inc.*

Puppet Showplace. Setting for puppet performances. Ages 4–10. *Creative Playthings, Inc.*

Puppet Stage. Sturdy puppet stage. Draw curtains, vinyl backdrop. Colorful. Hinged for easy storage. Ages 5–12. *Creative Playthings, Inc.*

Picture Readiness. Game in which children match pictures in order to learn to pay attention and to perceive details, skills that are needed in beginning reading. *Garrard.*

Reading Lottos. Designed to aid language development. Child names each object as he matches pictures. Later he learns to associate each picture with its printed name. Up to six players. Ages 4–7. *Creative Playthings, Inc.*

Tote Desk. Child can carry this 4-pound portable desk. Paper roll under chalkboard surface unrolls to cover surface. Tear off at bottom. *Creative Playthings, Inc.*

Sequence Puzzles. The sequence of events is determined by the child and he arranges pictures in a logical sequence. Four puzzles. Ages 4–7. *Creative Playthings, Inc.*

Who Gets It? A series of cards, each of which contains nine labeled pictures. Concept learning and perhaps incidental learning of sight words. *Garrard.*

Workbooks

Readiness Through Phonics. Phonics readiness skills are taught through use of the readiness book. Other books in the series are for grades 1–4 and K–1. *Educational Activities, Inc.*

Readiness for Reading. A beginners' workbook that can be used with (1) beginning reading books and (2) the Picture Word Cards by the same publisher. Stories are read by the teacher. The work pages for the pupils are designed to teach pupils attention, perception, and good work habits. *Garrard.*

Readiness for Learning Workbook. Perceptual-motor training for kindergarteners or beginning first-graders. Level 1 deals with development of such skills as co-ordination, control, and understanding of easy instructions. Level 2 materials can be used to attempt establishment of lateral dominance. In level 3 the following skills of particular importance to reading are introduced: perceiving letter groupings, associating printed symbols and corresponding spoken words and speech sounds. *Lippincott.*

BEGINNING READING

Kits and Audiovisual Aids

ALPHA Phonics. This kit provides materials to teach phoneme-grapheme relationships to 25 students. Cassettes, duplication masters, cards, and books covering the phonic elements. *Arista.*

AVS-10. Utilizes self-contained viewing screen and loudspeaker. Forty cartridges provide the input of phonic-linguistic type lessons. *CBS Laboratories.*

Comprehension Skill Kit A & B. Boxed materials include teacher's guide, four cassette tapes, reading cards, and answer books. Focuses on information skills, organization skills, evaluation skills, and generalization skills. Designed for independent activities. *BFA.*

EDL Controlled Reading Program. At the beginning levels the materials are written to correlate with basal reading programs. The stories can be used for silent and oral reading and are designed to develop sight vocabulary, reading fluency, and comprehension. Audiovisually presented lessons. *EDL.*

EDL Listen, Look, and Learn. Beginning reading instruction program using techniques and media that enlist the several learning modalities of a pupil. *EDL.*

First Level Reading Program. Beginning reading program that utilizes 100 filmstrips divided into 12 topics. Filmstrips contain all manner of stories as well as many content area topics. Level 2 (grade 2) and level 3 (grade 3) programs available. *Educational Projections Corp.*

HIS Reading Achievement Program Level One is designed to provide individual and small-group instruction in beginning reading skills by means of audiovisually presented lessons. As part of the lesson, responses are made on *Do and Discover* worksheets. Associated with level 1 is a series of books called *Read to Learn* books. Pupils work in these books to improve their understanding of the vocabulary introduced in the audiovisual presentation. Illustrations in filmstrips and worksheets are appropriate and esthetically delightful. Other associated materials. *Hoffman.*

Learning With Laughter. Each kit contains a color filmstrip, cassette, poster and game. Emphasis on phonics and word-attack skills through humorous stories. *Prentice-Hall.*

Read Along with Me. Home instruction of beginning readers through having the child follow in a booklet as the words of the text are heard on the record. *PR.*

Read On. 30 cassettes, 73 ditto masters, scoring cards, diagnostic chart, and criterion tests. Skills taught include discrimination, phonics, word structure, and comprehension. *Random House.*

Reading for Beginners Series. Primary level reading skills taught in four films. Deals with such skills as sounds, word shapes, words, word parts, context clues. *Coronet.*

Reading Skill Center. A kit of materials for independent activities and games dealing with word analysis, spelling, reading, and plays for oral reading. Available at primary and intermediate levels. *Curriculum Associates.*

Rolling Readers (First, Second, Third). Six-sided plastic blocks with a word "printed" on each side. Can be arranged in many different combinations to form sentences. *Scott.*

Sound-Blending Cassette Program. Audio program with duplicating master activity book emphasizing the blending of phonic elements into whole words. *Ideal.*

Sounds and Symbols. An audio cassette program with duplicating masters designed to teach writing, recognizing the letters, and matching letters and sounds. *Educator's Publishing Service.*

System 80. Programmed learning system utilizing a machine for audiovisual presentation of lessons. Individualized instruction in important beginning reading skills. Grades K–3. *Borg-Warner.*

Books and Workbooks

The following reading series are designed to be used by the teacher to teach beginning reading skills.

Alice and Jerry Basic Reading Program. Harper.
Bank Street Readers. Macmillan.
Basic Reading Series. Lippincott.
Betts Basic Readers. American Book.
Bookmark Reading Program. Harcourt.
Chandler Language-Experience Readers. Chandler.
City Schools Reading Program. Follett.
Developmental Reading Series. Lyons.
Early-to-Read Program. i/t/a Publications.
Economy Reading Program. Economy.
Exploring Reading Series. Stone.
Gateway to Reading Treasure Series. Laidlaw Bros.
Ginn Reading 360. Ginn.
Harper and Row Basic Reading Program. Harper.
Invitation to Adventure Series. Benefic.
Learning to Read Series. Silver Burdett.
Macmillan Reading Program. Seventies Edition. Macmillan.
Merrill Linguistic Readers. Merrill.
Miami Linguistic Readers. Heath.
New Basic Readers: Seventies Edition. Scott F.
Open Highways Program. Scott F.
Open Court Basic Readers. Open Court.
Project Read. Behavioral.
Prose and Poetry Series. Singer.
Read System. American Book.
Reading Essentials Series. Steck.
Reading for Interest Series. Heath.
Reading for Meaning Series: Seventies Edition. Houghton.
Sequential Steps in Readings. Harcourt.
Sheldon's Basic Reading Series. Centennial Edition. Allyn.
Singer/Random House Literature Series. Random House/Singer.
Sounds of Language Series. Holt.
SRA Basic Reading Series. SRA.
Structural Reading. Random House/Singer.
Winston Basic Readers. Holt.
Young America Basic Reading Program. Lyons.

The following materials are designed largely for self-instruction by the pupils.

Sullivan Reading Program. With these programmed materials children are taught readiness skills and reading skills at their own rate. Self-teaching in format, the programmed texts emphasize active responses, immediate feedback of answers, and a high percentage of correct responses. Skills carefully sequenced. *Webster.* (Other self-instruction materials are listed in the kits and audiovisual section of this beginning reading division.)

Games

Games suitable for use in beginning reading instruction will be found in the section on basic sight vocabulary and word identification.)

BASIC SIGHT VOCABULARY AND WORD IDENTIFICATION

Kits and Audiovisual Aids.

Auditory and Visual Discrimination. Learn to differentiate words that look alike and sound different and those words that sound alike and look different. Two long-play records and twenty charts. *Richards.*

Basic Phonics Program. Alphabet, blends—117 basic sounds with key words for extra practice. Four long-play records. Twelve co-ordinated wall charts. Manual. Grades K–3. *Richards.*

Creative Rhymes Program. Features rhyming of words as an aid to building a phonetic vocabulary. Two long play records. Eight coordinated charts. Grades K–3. *Richards.*

Discovery Reading Program. A phonic program for beginning readers that uses a discovery format. The first thirty films are on the alphabet; the remainder treat decoding. Pupils respond orally or in booklets. Use in conjunction with a basic reading program or independently. *Psychotechnics.*

Elementary Phonics Program. This audiovisual instructional program is designed to teach consonant sounds and vowel sounds. A magnetic tape at bottom of each printed card provides the audio component when the card is inserted into the Language Master device. *Bell.*

Filmstrips for Practice in Phonetic Skills. Four filmstrips developed to provide practice on fundamental phonetic skills. Grades 1–2. *Scott.*

Linguistic Word Pattern Program. Utilizes printed cards with magnetic tapes. When the card is inserted into the Language Master device, the pupil sees the printed words and elements and also hears them pronounced. In this program are presented the three major vowel-consonant patterns that characterize English spelling. *Bell.*

Magnetic Chalkboard on Stand. Designed to be the means by which many word and reading games and lessons can be executed. Magnetic upper- and lower-case letters, numbers, and math symbols. *Creative Playthings, Inc.*

Picture-Word Association Program. Interesting associations of pictures and words for reading readiness and sight vocabulary. Two long-play records. Fourteen co-ordinated charts. Grades K–1. *Richards.*

Reading Series. A series of 41 color filmstrips for teaching phonetic and structural analysis; also learning the use of the dictionary, reading for understanding, and using books efficiently. *Pacific.*

Sound Way to Easy Reading. Consists of a teacher's guide, four long-play records, and fifteen phonics charts, which are available on transparencies or in the wall chart size. *Bremmer.*

SRA Reading Laboratories. Series of boxed kits or laboratories containing graded materials for development of basic reading skills of word identification, vocabulary, comprehension, and rate. Manual. Placement tests. Grades 1–13. *SRA.*

Tactics in Reading. I and II. Boxed kit of exercises providing instruction and practice in use of context, structural and phonic analysis, use of the dictionary, and meaning skills. For advanced pupils in upper elementary grades. *Scott.*

System 80. Programmed learning system utilizing a machine for presentation of lessons and feedback. Designed to aid teacher by giving pupils individualized instruction in recognizing letters of alphabet, initial sound-symbol relationships, and beginning reading vocabulary. Grades K–3. *Borg-Warner.*

Perceptamatic Reading Series Materials. Designed to reinforce reading skill teaching by the teacher, these kits at eight reading levels sharpen visual perception, develop word-attack skills, and help build vocabulary skills. Uses tachistoscopic projector. *Rheem Califone.*

Books and Workbooks

Attention Span Stories. Five low readability level books for developing concentration. One-page episodes with colorful illustrations and skill exercises. *Jamestown.*

Be a Better Reader Series. Designed to develop phonics, syllabication, prefixes and suffixes, and meaning skills in a context of content reading materials. Grades 4–12. *Prentice.*

Building Reading Skills. Complete series for teaching phonics skills; also available, Teacher's Phonics Skill Builders. Grades 1–6. *McCormick.*

Comprehension Skill Series. Each book deals with one skill: main ideas, sequencing, organization, vocabulary, etc. Available for grades 4 through 8. *Jamestown.*

Conquests in Reading. An aid in teaching such word-identification skills as phoneme-grapheme relationships, compound words, prefixes, suffixes, and syllabication. Dolch sight words also taught. *Webster.*

Cordts Phonetic Books. Three books designed to teach basic word identification skills: *I Can Read, Hear Me Read, Reading's Easy.* Grades 1–3. *Benefic.*

Encore Readers. A series of reading anthologies for the first three grades. Stories illustrated with photos and drawings. Contains poetry and nonfiction along with exciting children's stories, myths, fairy tales, and skill activities. *Scott, Foresman.*

Eye and Ear Fun. Extensive phonics program. Grades 1–6. *Webster.*

Happy Times with Sound Series. A comprehensive course in phonics. Four books. *Allyn.*

I Can Write a Book. For grades 2 and 3, builds new vocabulary with phonics instruction, spelling, and usage using a cloze technique. *Curriculum Associates.*

Kid's Stuff. Book of reproducible activities for centers of various types dealing with spelling, listening, speaking, and reading. *Teacher's Market Place.*

Lift-Off to Reading. Reading program for pupils who have perceptual, motor, or verbal handicaps. Grades 1–6. *SRA.*

Modern Reading Skilltext Series. Deals with word-recognition skills and a host of other important reading skills. Diagnostic tests in each book. Eighteen skill tapes for each book. Upper elementary. *Merrill.*

My Little Pictionary. Handy reference to aid development of sight-word vocabulary. *Scott.*

My Picture Dictionary. Aid for independent development of sight vocabulary. *Ginn.*

My Second Pictionary. Scott.

Newbery Award Reading Program. Twenty-five award-winning books ranging in reading difficulty level from grade 3 through 8. Activity cards are provided for each book along with a teacher's guide. *Sunburst.*

The New Phonics We Use. Systematic, established phonics program. Grades 1–8. *Random.*

Phonovisual Phonics Program. May be used with other reading instruction materials such as basal readers. Key pictures and letters on charts help develop association of phonic elements and their corresponding sounds. Also available are a readiness book, transition book, game book, consonant and vowel workbooks, record of sounds, magnetic boards and so on. *Phonovisual.*

Scrambler Reading Series. Ranging in readability from 2.5 to 4.0, with higher interest levels, this series is designed for poor readers in the intermediate grades. Comic book format presents stories, each followed by skill activities. *Xerox.*

Star Wars Attack on Reading. A comprehension skills reader-workbook, illustrated with drawings and photographs from the "Star Wars" film. Available for grades 4 through 6. *Random House.*

Syllable Concept. Sixty-four cards designed to develop skill in syllabicating words. Grade 3⁺ *Educators.*

Ways to Read Words, More Ways to Read Words, and Learning About Words. Basic word-identification skills. Grades 2–4. *Teachers.*

Word Attack Manual. Workbook with a variety of advanced exercises in phonics, word-structure, dictionary skills, and spelling. Separate answer booklet. Suitable for intermediate grades and up. *Educator's Publishing Service.*

Words I Like to Read and Write (A picture dictionary). *Harper.*

Games

Baffle. Anagram-type game for developing a pupil's ability to construct patterns and words. *Lyons.*

Basic Sight Vocabulary Cards. Dolch's 220 words that make up 50 to 75 per cent of all reading material. Directions for playing games with the cards. *Garrard.*

Cagey. Anagram-type game stimulates the pupil's vocabulary potential through the use of three-, four-, and five-letter patterns. *Lyons-Carnahan.*

Click-a-Word. Designed to aid spelling. Ages 8-adult. *Creative Playthings, Inc.*

Comprehension Soup. A group of six separate games with cards, game board, and directions. Each game focuses upon a different skill: opposites, concepts, synonyms, and sentence comprehension. *Scott Resources.*

Consonant Cards. Designed to teach a number of consonant elements. *Garrard.*

Consonant Lotto. Designed to give ear training by helping children hear how a word begins. Pictures are used. It also teaches which sounds go with which consonants or consonant combinations. Beginning consonant and consonant combinations of the words are printed on the picture cards. Grade 1. *Garrard.*

Consonant Race. A board game to reinforce recognition of beginning consonant sounds and 72 sight words. *Childcraft.*

Capture. Board game that gives pupil experience in discrimination of syllables in words. *Lyons.*

Cross Country. Board game that encourages pupil recognition of phoneme-grapheme relationships through diacritical marks and phonetic spellings. *Lyons.*

Cross-Over. Anagram-type game developed to challenge the pupil's vocabulary capacity through word-building. *Lyons.*

Ends 'n Blends. Combines consonant blends and blends with word patterns or families. Helps teach many new words. Grades 1–6. *Educational Games, Inc.*

Fun with Phonics Program. Interesting phonics games—Phonics Bingo and Sound Down. Games are called on records as children play along on individual cards. Two records, sixty cards, twenty charts. *Richards.*

Listen. Domino game that stimulates pupils to recognize and spell common beginning consonant digraphs and clusters. *Lyons.*

Lively Letters. Game for learning letters and sounds. Children see a cut-out letter, say the sound, and imitate an action associated with the letter. *Curriculum Associates.*

Lucky Duck. This card game is designed to improve a person's skill in discriminating short vowel sounds. *Lyons.*

Mice Twice. Domino game designed to encourage pupils to hear long vowel sounds and to associate these sounds with the correct spelling patterns. *Lyons.*

No Nonsense. Card game designed to give experience in building words through reinforcing morphemic principles. *Lyons.*

Picture Word Builder. Contains common words and pictures and die cut words that fit properly with the pictures when identified correctly. Classification exercises included. *Milton Bradley.*

Phonetic Quizmo. Designed to aid reading and spelling competence, this game is played like Lotto to teach sounds of letters and groups of letters. *Milton Bradley.*

Phonics Soup and *Consonant Soup.* Each of these games focuses upon some aspect of phonics through a series of game board activities. Cards, spinners, tokens, and directions are provided. *Scott Resources.*

Picture Word Cards. Teaches nouns commonly found in beginning readers by associating a picture with a printed word. *Garrard.*

Popper Words. So called because the sound should "pop" into mind instantly when the pupil sees the word. Set 1, easier half of the Dolch 220 Basic Sight Vocabulary; set 2, harder half. *Garrard.*

Reading Games. A series of games to develop word analysis skills and improve understanding of basic language concepts. Includes games with contractions, rhymes, synonyms, homonyms, and other aspects of vocabulary development. *Childcraft.*

Rolling Phonics. Set of blocks, containing phonic elements, which can be used as an aid in teaching phonics skills. *Scott.*

Scat Cat. Designed to enrich the pupils' experience with application of phoneme-grapheme relationships through word-building patterns. *Lyons.*

Sight Phrase Cards. Comprised of 144 cards. On each is printed a phrase such as "down the street" and "we were." *Garrard.*

Snail Trail. Board game emphasizing reinforcement of beginning consonant sounds that have consistent spellings. *Lyons.*

Sort-a-Card Game. Helps build basic vocabulary through interesting series of matching and memory games for two to eight players. *Milton Bradley.*

Sound Hound. Rummy-type game emphasizing reinforcement of final consonant sounds. *Lyons.*

Spill and Spell. A fine classroom game to brush up on spelling. *Parker Brothers, Inc.*

Ship-Shape. Bingo-type game emphasizing phoneme-grapheme relationships in beginning or ending consonant digraphs—*ch, ng, sh, th. Lyons.*

The Syllable Game. Designed to teach quick recognition of common syllables and sounding of long words by dividing into syllables. *Garrard.*

Toll Road. Board game for giving experience in building words through reinforcement of morphemic principles. *Lyons.*

Vowel Lotto. Designed to give ear training by helping pupils hear the vowel sounds in words. Pictures are used. It also teaches which sounds go with which vowels or vowel combinations. Words and vowel combinations of the words are printed on the picture cards. Grades 1–2. *Garrard.*

Webster Word Wheels. Over sixty word wheels. As a wheel is turned various combinations of phonic elements and word families combine to make words. *Webster.*

VOCABULARY AND CONCEPTS: GENERAL AND CONTENT AREAS

Kits and Audiovisual Aids

Audio-Reading Progress Laboratory. This is a developmental audio reading program in vocabulary, word analysis, comprehension, and study skills. Based on delineation of behavioral objectives. Provides immediate feedback and reinforcement. Individualized instruction. Grades 1–10. *EPC.*

Base and Place Kit. Helps develop understanding of bases other than the decimal system; readiness concepts for computers. Ages 6–12. *Creative Playthings, Inc.*

Clues to Reading Progress. Comic book format magazines and accompanying skill tapes range from levels 2.0 to 5.0. All reading and skill activities are directed by the tapes. Separate test booklets are provided. An advanced *Clues* kit focuses on comprehension skills through the same format. *Educational Development Corp.*

Contained Reading. A machine-centered program using mechanical pacers, tachistoscopes, and audio tapes, covering ranges from first through sixth grade. Each lesson story is presented by machine and some reading from workbook, followed by comprehension and vocabulary activities. *AV Concepts.*

Context-Phonetic Clues Kit. Designed for grades 2 through 4, this kit contains 300 activity cards focusing upon spelling patterns and phonograms. The child is presented three words in isolation, all containing one phonogram, and selects each of the words to fit an appropriate context. *Curriculum Assoc.*

Curriculum Developmental Reading Program. Level 4: 11 sets of filmstrips, averaging 14 filmstrips per set. Reading skills taught through content areas of social studies, science, mathematics, and art. Levels 5 and 6: similar programs. *Educational Projections Corp.*

Design for Reading Tutorial Program. Designed for paraprofessionals to help teachers give individual attention. Provides a step-by-step tutor's guide, workbook, and activity sheets, cards, and a guide for the supervisor. *Harper & Row.*

Discover Your World Program. Series DW–11, China; DW–12, Pakistan; DW–13, India. This is a transparency series designed to help teach concepts in the following areas about each country: geography, history, anthropology, sociology, economics, and political science. Teacher's guide. Elementary and high school. *AEVAC, Inc.*

Electric Invention Box. Wire, light bulbs, switches, push buttons, bell, buzzer, miniature motor, and six-volt battery. Carrying case. Ages 6–12. *Creative Playthings, Inc.*

Expanded Vocabulary Kit. Six giant symbol cards, 279 giant word cards, in 7 vocabulary categories. Child's reading book, teaching book, phonograph recording and other accessories. Ages 4–8. *Creative Playthings, Inc.*

How to Develop a Good Vocabulary (filmstrip). *Educational Projections Corp.*

Importance of Vocabulary, The (filmstrip). *Educational Projections Corp.*

Individualized Reading from Scholastic. Basic components are a collection of one hundred good paperback books (and paper bookcases) for children and a collection of teaching aids and devices. Wide range of topics including fantasy, history, animals, science. "Conference" cards are tools to help the pupil share with his teacher during a conference his interest in the books he reads. Notes of pupil's status, achievement, and needs entered in printed "Individual Conference Pages" kept in a loose-leaf notebook. "Activity" cards provide the pupil with suggestions for worthwhile followup activities. "Skill Activity" cards suggest games for learning word-identification and word-meaning skills. Reading diary available to each pupil. Workbook of master sheets for reading exercises. Grades 2–6. *Scholastic.*

Mathematics Kits by the Learning Center. Three-dimensional plastic and wood manipulative devices to help teach basic mathematical concepts to pupils. *Creative Playthings, Inc.*

MISSION: READ. A kit with 20 copies of 20 stories and 20 skill exercises, answer keys, and manual. Skills include word-recognition, vocabulary, listening, spelling, comprehension. Attention given to attitudes and values. *Random House.*

The RISE Program. A series of anthologies with skillbooks and teachers' guide, designed for superior students. *Open Court.*

Science Adventures. Forty full-color captioned filmstrips in ten sets: atoms and their energy; magnetism and electricity; weather; nature of light; four metallic elements; the cell: basic unit of life; astronomy; electronics; automation; important chemical elements. Grades 5–9. *Filmstrip.*

Solar Science Projects. Low-cost solar energy projects to construct and use; diagrams included. *Scholastic.*

Student Project Planetarium. Table-top planetarium designed to help pupils explore relationships of the sun and planets. Instructions. Ages 9–17. *Creative Playthings, Inc.*

Who Makes Words? (film). Explains how words originate. Grades 4–6. *Coronet Films, Inc.*

Whys of Elementary Science. Utilizes a filmstrip program to apply scientific principles to everyday life. The 48 filmstrips are divided into 12 sets of four each. The sets are headed: weather; simple machines; plants; animal life; our sky; electricity and magnets; light and eyes; the earth's surface; heat; our bodies; the astronaut and space travel; the sea. All filmstrips utilize a narrative approach in which two children learn and apply scientific principles in everyday life around them. Grades 1–4. *Filmstrip.*

Word Clues. In learning vocabulary by this program, the pupil is required to syllabicate words, pronounce them, read them in a sentence, and write definitions. Used with flash-x sets, filmstrips, discs, and tach-x sets and filmstrips. Tests available. Grades 7–13. *EDL.*

Words in Motion. Self-directing tape cassette program with worksheets and management chart. Designed to teach a variety of vocabulary and word analysis skills to pupils in grades 4–6. *Macmillan.*

Games and Toys

Conestoga. An historical game about the Oregon Trail. Up to eight children can play at once. *Saalfield.*

Classification Game. Context clues are provided by the interiors of several types of stores in order to aid classification of 48 picture cards. *Instructo.*

Glory Road, Black History Games. Learning games about such great black Americans as Crispus Attucks, Harriet Tubman, and Matt Henson. *Creative.*

Go Gin. This is a strategy game to build vocabulary and aid spelling. *Ideal Toy.*

Model Kits. With these kits youngsters can build cars, motorcycles, spacecraft, aircraft, and ships. *Revell.*

Play Family Farm Set. Designed for free play and developing vocabulary and speech, this set contains nineteen pieces made of wood and plastic materials. A barn and a silo act as a storage unit. *Fisher-Price.*

Remcraft Space Science Kits. Chemical compound forming, weather forecasting, jet propulsion, mechanical physics. Especially good for older boys who are interested in science. *REMCO.*

Undersea World of Jacques Cousteau. Good game for learning some oceanology concepts. *Parker Brothers.*

V-8 Engine. This toy is made to help develop mechanical skills. It actually works and should be appealing to boys. *Child Guidance.*

Wff 'n Proof. Game of logic that is a series of 21 progressively more difficult games. The games use symbols for words. Logical, orderly thinking is rewarded. Includes 36 logic cubes, timer, 224-page game manual. Ages 6–adult. *Creative Playthings, Inc.*

Books and Workbooks

Be a Better Reader Series. N. B. Smith. Designed to help pupils learn general and subject-matter vocabularies. Grades 4–12. *Prentice.*

Building Reading Power. Series of fifteen booklets in programmed learning format designed to improve vocabulary and comprehension. Grade 5[+]. *C. E. Merrill.*

Dictionary of Basic Words. This dictionary contains over 21,000 entries and features full-color illustrations on nearly every page. Age 9–adult. *Children's Press.*

Grow in Word Power. E. Moreda (ed.). Exercises from the high school edition of Reader's Digest. Grade 7⁺. *Reader's Digest.*

Lessons for Self-Instruction in Basic Skills: Vocabulary. E. B. Fry. Programmed booklets designed to teach vocabulary. Grades 3–9. *CTB.*

Macmillan Reading Spectrum. Consists of eighteen booklets providing systematic instruction in word identification, vocabulary development and reading interpretation. Grades 4⁺. *Macmillan.*

New Practice Readers. C. R. Stone and C. C. Grover. Each of seven books in the series contains brief reading selections and related exercises designed to improve vocabulary and comprehension. Books A–G; grades 2–8. *Webster.*

Unesco Science Book. Incorporates more than seven hundred easily done and clearly explained demonstrations and experiments that require everyday items found around the house. Prepared under the aegis of UNESCO. Ages 8–15. *Creative Playthings, Inc.*

Vocabulary Development. L. Deighton. Programmed workbooks that provide a variety of exercises. Grades 3–8. *Macmillan.*

Word Clues. Several vocabulary workbooks. Emphasize reasoning through use of reading context. Related recordings available. Pupil does the work and checks it himself. *EDL.*

Words Are Important. H. C. Hardwick. Series of books designed to teach more unusual words in the *Teacher's Word Book* by Thorndike and Lorge. Reviews to help "nail down" words. 7⁺. *C. S. Hammond & Co.*

COMPREHENSION AND STUDY-REFERENCE

Kits and Audiovisual Aids

Audio Reading Progress Laboratory. Developmental reading program that makes extensive use of an audio approach. The program supplements and is correlated with basic reading programs. Reading progress lessons are geared to attaining specific performance objectives. The four strands that run through the program are (1) phonetic and structural word analysis, (2) comprehension, (3) vocabulary, and (4) study skills in basic curriculum areas. Strands 1 and 2 are in all levels, grades 1–8, strand 3 is included in all levels except level 1; strand 4 begins at grade-5 level. Several grade spans at each level. Levels 1–8, readability levels grades 1.5–10. *EPC.*

Building an Outline (film). Step-by-step procedures for developing an outline. 7⁺ *Coronet Films, Inc.*

Doing an Assignment (filmstrip). Clues on what to do and what not to do when working on an assignment. Grade 7⁺ *EP.*

Doing Homework (filmstrip). Ways of getting to the task of doing homework profitably. Grade 7⁺ *EP.*

Finding Information (filmstrip). How to save time in finding the information needed. 7⁺ *EP.*

Hoffman Reading Achievement Program. Audiovisual presentation of stories and followup lessons for developing a variety of reading skills. Stories are interesting to young and old alike. Many content area concepts are taught. Self-instructional program. Grades 1–6. *Hoffman.*

How to Read Essays (film). Tips to help make essay reading more enjoyable and profitable. 7⁺ *Coronet Films, Inc.*

How to Read Novels (film). Helps unveil the mysteries of reading the novel. 7⁺ *Coronet Films, Inc.*

How to Read Plays (film). Helps the student learn to read plays with more finesse. 7⁺ *Coronet Films, Inc.*

How to Read Poetry (film). How to get more out of poetry and increase one's liking for it. Grade 7[+] *Coronet Films, Inc.*

How to Remember (film). Specific procedures for tackling study tasks. Grades 7–9. *Coronet Films, Inc.*

How to Study (filmstrip). Provides a number of useful tips that help improve the results from time spent in study. *EP.*

Importance of Making Notes (film). Explains why it is a good idea to make good notes. Grade 7–9. *Coronet Films, Inc.*

Library Skills. These skills are taught by Minisystem—a self-contained instructional package composed of a tape reel or cassette program, 30 pupil activity sheets correlated with the taped instruction sequence, and a teacher's guide. *Electronic Futures, Inc.*

Listen and Read Program. Thirty tapes and a workbook designed to help pupils develop listening, comprehension, study and critical reading skills. Grades 7–9. *EDL.*

Listen Well, Learn Well (film). Key ideas for increasing learning through improving listening skills. Grades 4–6. *Coronet Films, Inc.*

Listening Progress Laboratory: Series 789. Designed to develop concepts that will provide general background and also an information base for various reading endeavors. The following basic listening skills are developed: tracking, focusing, discriminating, recalling, attending, following directions, and following actions. Cognitive listening skills developed are topics, main ideas, details; note-taking and summarizing; fact and opinion; tone and mood; creative anticipation; cause and effect; inference; critical analysis. The laboratory contains content material in literature, music, science, social studies, speech, and culture. Grades 7–9. *EPC.*

Making an Outline (filmstrip). How to organize ideas for presentation 7[+] *EP.*

Making Sense with Outlines (film). Basic procedures for developing and using outlines in academic work. Grades 4–6. *Coronet Films, Inc.*

Maps Are Fun (film). Making and reading maps. Grades 4–6. *Coronet Films, Inc.*

Primary Reading. A self-contained supplemental program designed to teach various skills including study skills. Uses tapes, portable cassettes, printed material, and teacher's manual. Grades K–3. *Imperial Productions, Inc.*

Reading Improvement Skill File. Comprehension and vocabulary development are emphasized in this program. There are 180 graded, illustrated, color-keyed exercises in this multilevel program. Selections are on a wide variety of topics. Grades 6–13. *The Reading Laboratory, Inc.*

SRA Reading for Understanding, Jr. and Sr. Each boxed laboratory contains four hundred lesson cards containing four thousand brief exercises designed to teach comprehension, meaning, and interpretation skills. Grades 3–12. *SRA.*

SRA Reading Laboratories. Boxed laboratories designed to teach word identification, word meaning, comprehension, and rate skills. Labs are available at various levels. Grades 1–14. *SRA.*

Tachisto-o-Films. Designed to develop such skills as attention and concentration, vocabulary, phrase reading comprehension, and retention. Four levels: primary, intermediate, junior high, senior high. Also special word-identification filmstrips. *Learning Through Seeing, Inc.*

Thinking Box. A teaching tool developed specifically to improve critical thinking skills. Utilizes 240 skill development cards that present activities requiring thought processes such as classifying, hypothesizing, and criticizing. Student also works out answers to questions that help him determine how he came to solutions while engaged in the previous thought processes. Also self-help thinking-skill cards, student reference books, student activity record sheets, and teacher's guide. Six curriculum and interest-content sections. Twelve thinking operations. 6[+] *Benefic.*

Using a Library (filmstrip). How to take advantage of all the resources of a library. *EP.*

Using Maps and Globes. Uses Minisystem to teach important reference skills. *Electronic Futures, Inc.*

Using Reference Books (filmstrip). Finding and using the best reference materials for a particular task. *EP.*

We Discover the Dictionary (film). Shows the importance of the dictionary and how it can be used to the best advantage. Grades 4–6. *Coronet Films, Inc.*

Wheel Transparencies. Fifty-nine transparencies for use with an overhead projector. Teach vowel and consonant phonic elements. *Cambosco.*

Writing a Research Paper (filmstrip). How to gather, organize, and present information. 7+ *Jam Handy.*

Books and Workbooks

Be a Better Reader Series. Variety of word identification, vocabulary, comprehension, and reference skills taught in a setting of the content areas of social studies, new math, literature, and biological and physical sciences. Grades 4–12. *Prentice.*

Building Reading Skills. Many exercises designed to develop word recognition skills and word, phrase, and sentence meanings. Grades 1–6. *McCormick.*

Everyready Series. High-interest-low-difficulty-level readers with titles such as *Cases of Sherlock Holmes* and *The Gold Bug and Other Readers.* Reading level 4. *Webster.*

Gates-Peardon Reading Exercises. Help to develop the following abilities: noting details, understanding directions, getting the general significance, and predicting outcomes. Elementary grades. *Teachers.*

McCall-Crabbs Standard Test Lessons in Reading. Rate of reading and comprehension skills emphasized in these booklets. Each booklet contains 78 lessons. Book A, grades 2–4; B, 3–5; C, 4–6; D, 5–7; E, 7–12. *Teachers.*

McCall-Harby Test Lessons in Primary Reading. Thirty reading comprehension exercises for pupils in grades 1 and 2. *Teachers.*

Map Skills Project Books. Paperback books to help teach basic map skills. Many illustrations. "Try Your Skills" quizzes every few pages for pupil self-check. Book 1, grade 2; book 2, grade 4; book 3, grade 5. *Scholastic.*

New Practice Readers. Designed to teach pupils to note details, identify antecedents of words, identify words similar in meaning, detect opinions, and select true statements. Grades 2–8. *Webster.*

New Reading Skilltext Series. Develops several vocabulary and comprehension skills. Story context plus exercises. Grades 1–6. *Merrill.*

Progress in Reading. One book designed to develop interpretation, reference, and reading-speed skills. Grade 7. *Steck.*

Reader's Digest Reading Skillbuilders. Interesting stories plus exercises for developing word identification, vocabulary, and comprehension skills. Audio lessons available. Grades 2–8. *Reader's Digest.*

Reading Essentials Series. Ten worktexts designed to develop a variety of reading skills. Such titles as *Fun Time* and *Mastery in Reading.* Grades 1–8. *Steck.*

Reading for Meaning Series. Workbooks for levels 4 and 5 emphasize word meaning, detailed meanings, and central thought. Books 6–12 also include organizing and summarizing skills. Grades 4–12. *Lippincott.*

Reading Success Series. Six worktexts of high interest, low readability, designed for students 10 to 16 years old. Emphasis in the exercises is on inductive teaching of word-identification skills. *Xerox.*

Reading Spectrum, The. Multilevel program of vocabulary development lessons contained in skill booklets. The lessons are self-directing and easy for the pupil to correct. Also available, two sets of books from grade 2 reading level to grade 8 level. *Macmillan.*

Something New to Do. Designed to develop comprehension skills. Grades 1–2. *Schmitt.*

Sonic Readers. Illustrated stories plus recorded narration. Primary. *EP.*

Study Type of Reading Exercises: High School Level. Work-type reading materials for senior high school students or advanced pupils in the upper elementary grades. *Teachers.*

Directory of Publishers

Abelard. Abelard-Schuman, Ltd., 6 W. 57th St., New York, N.Y. 10019

Abingdon. Abingdon Press, 201 8th Ave. S., Nashville, Tenn. 37203

Academic Therapy Publications, 1543 Fifth Avenue, San Raphael, Calif. 94901

Addison. Addison-Wesley Publishing Co., Sand Hill Road, Menlo Park, Calif. 94025

AEVAC, Inc. 404 Sette Drive, Paramus, N.J. 07652.

Aladdin. Aladdin Books, see American Book Company.

Allyn. Allyn & Bacon Books, Inc., Rockleigh, N.J. 07647

American Book. Orders to Van Nostrand-Reinhold Books, 450 W. 33rd St., New York, N.Y., 10001

American Ed. American Education Publication, Inc., 55 High St., Middletown, Conn. 06457. A Xerox company.

American Guidance. American Guidance Service, Inc., Publishing Bldg., Circle Pines, Minn. 55014

American Interstate Corp., Mundelein, Ill. 60060

American Library. American Library Association. Order Dept., 50 E. Huron St., Chicago, Ill. 60611

American Opt. American Optical Co., Southbridge, Mass.

Americana, Inc. (a subsidiary of Grolier, Inc., 575 Lexington Ave., New York, N.Y. 10022).

Appleton. Appleton-Century-Crofts, Inc., see Meredith Corp.

Arista. Arista Corp., 2440 Estand Way, Concord, Calif. 94524

Association for Childhood Education International, 3615 Wisconsin Ave., N.W., Washington, D.C. 20016

Audio-Visual. Audio-Visual Research Co., 1509 8th St. S.E., Waseca, Minn. 56093

AV. AV Concepts Corp., 30 Montauk Blvd., Oakdale, N.Y. 11769

AVID Division, P. M. & E. Electronics, Inc., 10 Tripps Lane, East Providence, R.I. 02914

Baldridge. Baldridge Reading and Study Skills, Inc., 14 Griggs St., Greenwich, Conn. 06830

Barnell Loft, Ltd., 111 South Centre Ave., Rockville Centre, N.Y. 11570

Basic Books, Inc., Publishers, 404 Park Ave. S., New York, N.Y. 10016

Bausch. Bausch & Lomb Optical Co., Rochester, N.Y. 14602

Beckley-Cardy Co., 1900 N. Narragansett Ave., Chicago, Ill. 60639

Beginner. Beginner Books, see Random House.

Behavioral. Behavioral Research Laboratories, P.O. Box 577, Palo Alto, Calif. 94302

Bell. Bell and Howell Co., Audio Visual Products Division, 7100 McCormick Road, Chicago, Ill. 60645

Benefic. Benefic Press, 10300 W. Roosevelt Rd., Westchester, Ill. 60153.

Benson. H. Benson, 2121 Westbury Court, Brooklyn, N.Y. 11225

BFA. BFA, CBS Publications, 2211 Michigan Avenue, Santa Monica, Calif. 90406

Dick Blick Co., P.O. Box 1269, Galesburg, Ill. 61405

Bobbs. The Bobbs-Merrill Co., Inc., 4300 W. 62nd St., Indianapolis, Ind. 46268

Book Lab Inc., 1449 37th St., Brooklyn, N.Y. 11218

Borg-Warner. Borg-Warner Educational Systems, 7450 N. Natchez Ave., Niles, Ill. 60648

R. R. Bowker Company, 1180 Ave. of the Americas, New York, N.Y. 10036

Stanley Bowmar Co., Inc., 4 Broadway, Valhalla, N.Y. 10595

Milton Bradley Co., Springfield, Mass. 01101

Bremmer. Bremmer-Davis Phonics, Inc., 161 Green Bay Road, Wilmette, Ill. 60091

Burgess Publishing Company, 428 South 6th St., Minneapolis, Minn. 55415

Cadmus. Cadmus Books, see Hale.

Califone. See Rheem Califone.

California. California Test Bureau, a Division of McGraw-Hill Book Company, Inc., Del Monte Research Park, Monterey, Calif. 93940

Cambosco. Cambosco Scientific Co., Inc., 342 Western Ave., Boston, Mass.

Cenco Educational Aids, 2600 S. Kostner Ave., Chicago, Ill. 60623

Chandler. Chandler Publishing Company, 124 Spear St., San Francisco, Calif. 94105

Chicago. See University of Chicago Press.

Child Guidance. Child Guidance Toys, Inc., 1055 Bronx River Ave., Bronx, N.Y. 10472

Childcraft Equipment Co., Inc., 155 E. 23rd St., New York, N.Y. 10010

Childrens. Children's Press, Inc., 1224 W. Van Buren St., Chicago, Ill. 60607

Children's Book Centre, 140 Kensington Church St., London W 8, England

Clinical. Clinical Psychology Publishing Co., Brandon, Vt. 05733

College Skills Center, 101 W. 31st St., New York, N.Y. 10001

Combined Book Exhibit, Inc., Scarborough Park, Albany Post Road, Briarcliffe Manor, N.Y. 10510

Committee on Diagnostic Reading Tests, Mountain Home, N.C. 28758

Conrad Publishing Co., Box 90, Bismarck, N.D. 58501

Consulting. Consulting Psychologists Press, 577 College Ave., Palo Alto, Calif. 94306

Continental Press, Inc., Elizabethtown, Pa., 17022

Copp Clark Publishers LTD, 517 Wellington St. W., Toronto 2B, Ontario, Canada

Coronet Films, Inc., 65 E. South Water St., Chicago, Ill. 60601

Council for Exceptional Children, Orders to National Education Association of the United States, Publishing-Sales Section, 1201 16th St., N.W., Washington, D.C. 20036

Coward. Coward-McCann, Inc., 200 Madison Ave., New York, N.Y. 10016

Craig Corporation, 3410 S. La Cienega Boulevard, Los Angeles, Calif. 90016

Creative. Creative Environments, Inc., 565 Fifth Ave., New York, N.Y. 10017

Creative Playthings, Inc., Edinburg Rd., Cranbury, N.J. 08540

Creative Visuals, P.O. Box 310, Big Spring, Tex. 97920

Crowell. Crowell Collier and Macmillan, Inc., 866 Third Ave., New York, N.Y. 10022

Curriculum. Curriculum Associates, 5 Esquire Rd., North Billerica, Mass. 01862.

Curtis Audio Visual Materials, Curtis Publishing Co., 641 Lexington Ave., New York, N.Y., 10022.

Davis A. V. Service, 713 S. W. 12th St., Portland 5, Ore.

Day. The John Day Company, Inc., 62 W. 45th St., New York, N.Y. 10036

Delacorte Press. See Dell Publishing Company.

Dell. Dell Publishing Company, 750 Third Ave., New York, N.Y. 10017

Developmental Learning Materials, 3505 N. Ashland St., Chicago, Ill. 60657

Dexter & Westbrook, Ltd., 111 South Centre St., Rockville Centre, N.Y. 11570

Dial. The Dial Press, Inc., 750 Third Ave., New York, N.Y. 10017

Dodd. Dodd, Mead & Company, Inc., 79 Madison Ave., New York, N.Y. 10016

Doubleday. Doubleday & Company, Inc., 277 Park Ave., New York, N.Y. 10017

Dutton. E. P. Dutton & Co., Inc., 201 Park Ave., New York, N.Y. 10003

E & S Associates, Inc., 2204 Mt. Meigs Road, Montgomery, Alabama 36107.

EB Auditory Products, 4807 W. 118 Place, Hawthorne, Calif. 90250

Economy Co., 1901 N. Walnut, Oklahoma City, Okla. 73105

EDL. Educational Development Laboratories, Inc. (a Division of McGraw-Hill Company, Inc.,) 284 Pulaski Road, Huntington, N.Y. 11744

Edmund Scientific Co., 101 E. Gloucester Pike, Barrington, N.J. 08007

Educational. Educational and Industrial Testing Service, San Diego, Calif. 92107

Educational Activities, Inc., 1937 Grand Ave., Baldwin, N.Y. 11520

Educational Development Corp., 4235 South Memphis Drive, Tulsa, Okla. 74145

Educational Electronics, Inc., 3017 N. Stiles, Oklahoma City, Okla. 73110

Educational Games, Inc., P.O. Box 3653, Grand Central Station, New York, N.Y. 10017

EP. Educational Projections Corp., 527 S. Commerce St., Jackson, Miss. 39201

Educational Record Sales, 157 Chambers St., New York, N.Y. 10007

Educators. Educators Publishing Service, Inc., 75 Moulton St., Cambridge, Mass. 02138

Edukaid of Ridgewood, 1250 E. Ridgewood Ave., Ridgewood, N.J. 07450

Electronic Futures, Inc., 57 Dodge Ave., North Haven, Conn. 06473

Embossograf Corp. of America, 38 W. 21st St., New York, N.Y. 10010

Encyclopaedia Britannica Inc. per BIP., 425 N. Michigan Ave., Chicago, Ill. 60611

EPC. Educational Progress Corporation, 8538 E. 41st Street, Tulsa, Okla. 74145

Essay. Essay Press, Box 5, Planetarium Station, New York, N.Y. 10024

ETA Division. A. Daigger and Co., 150 W. Kinzie St., Chicago, Ill. 60610

ETB. Educational Test Bureau, Educational Publishers, Inc., 1525 N. State Parkway, Chicago, Ill., 60610

ETS. Educational Testing Service, 20 Nassau St., Princeton, N.J. 08540

Exemplary Center for Reading Instruction, 3690 South, 2860 East, Salt Lake City, Utah 84109

Eye Gate House, Inc., 146–01 Archer Ave., Jamaica, N.Y. 11435

Fearon Publishers, Inc., 2165 Park Blvd., Palo Alto, Calif. 94306

Field. Field Enterprises Educational Corporation, 510 Merchandise Mart Plaza, Chicago, Ill. 60654

Filmstrip. Filmstrip House, Inc., 432 Park Ave. South, New York, N.Y. 10016

Fisher-Price. Fisher-Price Toys, Inc., East Aurora, N.Y. 14052

Follett. Follett Educational Corp., 1010 W. Washington Blvd., Chicago, Ill. 60607

Four Winds Press, 53 W. 44th St., New York, N.Y. 10036

Funk. Funk & Wagnalls Company, Inc., a Division of Readers Digest Books, Inc., 380 Madison Ave., New York, N.Y. 10017

Garrard. Garrard Publishing Company, Champaign, Ill. 61820

General Learning Corp., 3 E. 54th St., New York, N.Y. 10022

Ginn. Ginn and Company, Waltham, Mass. 02154

Globe. Globe Book Company, Inc., 175 Fifth Ave., New York, N.Y. 10010

Golden. Golden Press, Inc., 850 3rd Ave., New York, N.Y. 10022

Golden Gate Junior Books, Box 398, San Carlos, Calif. 94070

Grolier. Grolier Educational Corp., 845 3rd Ave., New York, N.Y. 10022

Grossett. Grossett & Dunlap, Inc., 51 Madison Ave., New York, N.Y. 10010

Grune & Stratton, Inc., 757 Third Ave., South, New York, N.Y. 10017

Gryphon Press, 220 Montgomery St., Highland Park, N.J. 08904

Hale. E. M. Hale & Co., Inc., 1201 S. Hastings Way, Eau Claire, Wis. 54701

C. S. Hammond & Co., Inc., 515 Valley St., Maplewood, N.J. 07040

Harcourt. Harcourt Brace Jovanovich, Inc., 757 3rd Ave., New York, N.Y. 10017

Harper. Harper and Row, Publishers, Inc., 30 E. 33rd St., New York, N.Y. 10016

Harvey. Harvey House, Inc., 5 S. Buckout St., Irvington-on-Hudson, N.Y. 10533

Hastings. Hastings House, Publishers, Inc., 151 E. 50th St., New York, N.Y. 10022

Heath. D. C. Heath & Company, 285 Columbus Ave., Boston, Mass. 02116

The Highsmith Co., Inc., Fort Atkinson, Wis. 53538

Hoffman. Hoffman Information Systems, 5623 Peck Road, Arcadia, Calif. 91006

Holiday. Holiday House, Inc., 18 E. 56th St., New York, N.Y. 10022

Holt. Holt, Rinehart and Winston, Inc., 383 Madison Ave., New York, N.Y. 10017

Horn Book, Inc., 585 Boylston St., Boston, Mass. 02116

Houghton. Houghton Mifflin Company, 2 Park St., Boston, Mass. 02107

Ideal Toy. Ideal Toy Corporation, 200 Fifth Ave., New York, N.Y. 10010

Illinois. See University of Illinois Press.

Imperial Productions, Inc., 247 W. Court St., Kankakee, Ill. 60901

Initial Teaching Alphabet Publications, Inc., Orders to Pitman Publishing Corporation, 20 E. 46th St., New York, N.Y. 10017

The Instructo Corp., Paoli, Pa., 19301

International Reading Association, 6 Tyre Ave., Newark, Del. 19711

International Universities Press, Inc., 239 Park Ave. S., New York, N.Y. 10003

IPAT. Institute for Personality and Aptitude Testing, 1602–04 Coronado Drive, Champaign, Ill. 61820

Jam Handy. Jam Handy School Service, 2781 E. Grand Blvd., Detroit, Mich. 48211

Jamestown. Jamestown Publishers, P.O. Box 6743, Providence, R.I. 02940

The Judy Co., 310 N. 2nd St., Minneapolis, Minn. 55401.

Kenworthy. Kenworthy Educational Service, Inc., P.O. Box 3031, Buffalo, N.Y. 14205

Keystone. Keystone View Co., Meadville, Pa. 16335

Kingsbury. See Remedial Education Press.

Knopf. Alfred A. Knopf, Inc., 825 Third Avenue, New York, N.Y. 10017

Laidlaw Bros., a Division of Doubleday & Company, Inc., 36 Chatham Rd., Summit, N.J. 07901

Language. Language Research Associates, 950 E. 59th St., Chicago, Ill.

Lantern. Lantern Press, Inc., 257 Park Ave. S., New York, N.Y. 10010

Learning Through Seeing, Inc., 8138 Foothill Blvd., Sunland, Calif., 91040

Lerner. Lerner Publications Company, 241 First Ave. N., Minneapolis, Minn. 55401

Lippincott. J. B. Lippincott Company, E. Washington Square, Philadelphia, Pa. 19105

Little. Little, Brown and Company, 34 Beacon St., Boston, Mass. 02106

Lothrop. Lothrop, Lee & Shepard Company, Inc., 419 Park Ave., New York, N.Y. 10016

Lyons. Lyons & Carnahan, 407 E. 25th St., Chicago, Ill. 60616

McCormick. McCormick-Mathers Publishing Co., Inc., 450 W. 33rd St., New York, N.Y. 10001

McGraw-Hill. McGraw-Hill Book Company, Inc., 330 W. 42nd St., New York, N.Y. 10036

McKay. David McKay Company, Inc., 750 Third Ave., New York, N.Y. 10017

Macmillan. The Macmillan Company, 866 Third Ave., New York, N.Y. 10022

Macrae. Macrae Smith Co., 225 S. 15th St., Philadelphia, Pa. 19102

Maico Hearing Instrument, Inc., 7375 Bush Lake Rd., Minneapolis, Minn. 55435

Melmont. Melmont Publishers, 1224 W. Van Buren St., Chicago, Ill. 60612

Meredith Corporation, 440 Park Ave. S., New York, N.Y. 10016

Meredith Press, 250 Park Ave., New York, N.Y. 10017

Merrill. Charles E. Merrill Books, Inc., 1300 Alum Creek Drive, Columbus, O. 43216

Messner. Julian Messner, Inc., 1 W. 39th St., New York, N.Y. 10036

Milton Bradley Company. East Longmeadow, Mass. 01101.

Minnesota. See University of Minnesota Press.

Morrow. William Morrow & Company, Inc., 105 Madison Ave., New York, N.Y. 10016

National Computer Systems, 4401 W. 76th St., Minneapolis, Minn. 55435

National Council of Teachers of English, 1111 Kenyon Rd., Urbana, Ill. 61801

National Reading Conference, Inc., c/o Gordon Gray, Godfrey Hall, Clemson University, Clemson, S.C. 29631

Nelson. Thomas Nelson & Sons, 1626 Copewood St., Camden, N.J. 08103
Nevins. C. H. Nevins Printing Co., Pittsburgh, Pa.
New Century. See Meredith Corp.
New York Times Teaching Resources, 100 Boylston St., Boston, Mass. 02116
Noble. Noble & Noble, Publishers, Inc., 750 3rd Ave., New York, N.Y. 10017
Norelco. North American Phillips Corporation, Training and Education Systems, 100 E. 42nd St., New York, N.Y. 10017
Open Court. Open Court Publishing Company, Box 402, La Salle, Ill. 61301
F. A. Owen Publishing Co., 7 Bank St., Dansville, N.Y. 14437
Pacific. Pacific Productions, 2614 Etna St., Berkeley, Calif. 94704
Parents. Parents' Magazine Press, 52 Vanderbilt Ave., New York, N.Y. 10017
Parker Brothers, Inc., 190 Bridge St., Salem, Mass. 01970
Perceptual Development Laboratories, 6767 Southwest Ave., St. Louis, Mo. 63143
F. E. Peacock, Itasca, Ill.
Personnel. Personnel Press, Inc., 191 Spring St., Lexington, Mass. 02173
PEL. Psycho-Educational Laboratories, 1729 Irving Ave. S., Minneapolis, Minn.
PESA. Psychological-Educational Services Association, P.O. Box 87, Pebble Beach, Calif. 93953
Phonovisual. Phonovisual Products, Inc., 4708 Wisconsin Ave., Washington, D.C. 20016
Pioneer. Pioneer Printing Co., 306B Flora, Bellingham, Wash. 98225
Plays, Inc., Publishers, 8 Arlington St., Boston, Mass. 02116
Portal Press, Inc., a Division of John Wiley & Sons, Inc., 605 3rd Ave., New York, N.Y. 10016
PR. Programmed Records, Inc., 154 Nassau St., New York, N.Y.
Prentice. Prentice-Hall, Inc., Englewood Cliffs, N.J. 07632
Priority. Priority Innovations, Inc., P.O. Box 792, Skokie, Ill. 60076
Psychological. Psychological Corp., 304 E. 45th St., New York, N.Y. 10017
Psychological-Educational Services Association, Pebble Beach, Calif.
Psychological Test. Psychological Test Specialists, Box 1441, Missoula, Mont. 59801
Psychotechnics, Inc., 7433 N. Harlem Ave., Chicago, Ill. 60648
Putnam. G. P. Putnam's Sons, 200 Madison Avenue, New York, N.Y. 10016
Rand. Rand-McNally & Company, P.O. Box 7600, Chicago, Ill. 60680
Random. Random House, Inc., 201 E. 50th St., New York, N.Y. 10022
Reader's Digest Services, Inc., Educational Division, Pleasantville, N.Y. 10570
The Reading Institute of Boston, 116 Newbury St., Boston, Mass. 02116
The Reading Laboratory, Inc., 55 Day St., South Norwalk, Conn. 06854
REMCO. Remco Industries, Inc., 200 Fifth Ave., New York, N.Y. 10010
REVELL. Fleming H. Revell Company, 4223 Glencoe Ave., Venice, Calif. 90291
Rheem Califone, 5922 Bancroft St., Los Angeles, Calif. 90016
Richards. Richards Research Associates, Inc., 353 Shangrila Circle, Plainwell, Mich. 49080
Frank E. Richards, Publisher, 215 Church St., Phoenix, N.Y. 13135
The Reilly & Lee Co., 114 W. Illinois St., Chicago, Ill. 60610
Remedial Education Press, Kingsbury Center, 2138 Bancroft Place, N.W., Washington, D.C. 20008
Remedial Reading Service, School of Education, The City College of the City University of New York, Convent Ave. and 135th St., New York, N.Y., 10031.
RIME Associates, P.O. Box 252, Paramus, N.J. 07652
Ronald. The Ronald Press Company, 79 Madison Ave., New York, N.Y. 10016
Saalfield. Saalfield Publishing Company, Saalfield Square, Akron, O. 44301
Schmitt. Schmitt, Hall & McCreary Co., 527 Park Ave., Minneapolis, Minn.
Scholastic. Book Services, Scholastic Magazines, 50 W. 44th St., New York, N.Y. 10036
Scholastic Testing. Scholastic Testing Service, Bensenville, Ill.
School house. School house Industries, Inc., 170 Central Ave., Farmingdale, N.Y. 11735

Science for Visual Education, Inc., 1345 Diversey Parkway, Chicago, Ill. 60614
Scott. Scott Resources, Inc., P.O. Box 2121, Fort Collins, Colo. 80522
Scott. William R. Scott, 333 6th Ave., New York, N.Y. 10014
Scott F. Scott, Foresman and Company, Glenview, Ill. 60025
Charles Scribner's Sons, 597 Fifth Avenue, New York, N.Y., 10017
Seabury. The Seabury Press, 815 2nd Ave., New York, N.Y. 10017
Selchow and Righter Co., Bay Shore, N.Y. 11706
Selected Academic Readings, Associated Educational Services Corp. 630 Fifth Ave., New
    York, N.Y. 10003
Silver Burdett. Silver, Burdett Company, a Division of General Learning Corp., Box 2000,
    Morristown, N.J. 07960
Simon. Simon & Schuster, Inc., 1 W. 39th St., New York, N.Y. 10018
Singer. L. W. Singer, Inc., a Division of Random House, 501 Madison Ave., New York,
    N.Y. 10022
Society for Visual Education, Inc., 1345 Diversey Parkway, Chicago, Ill. 60614
Special Child Publications, Inc., 4535 Union Bay Pl., N.E., Seattle, Wash. 98105
Special Education Materials Development Center, 2020 R St., Washington, D.C. 20009
Speech and Language Materials, Inc., P.O. Box 721, Tulsa, Okla. 74101
Spoken Arts, Inc., 59 Locust Ave., New Rochelle, N.Y. 10801
SRA. Science Research Associates, Inc., 259 E. Erie St., Chicago, Ill. 60611
Steck. Steck-Vaughn Co., P.O. Box 2028, Austin, Tex. 78767
Study-Scope Company, P.O Box 689, Tyler, Tex. 75701
Sunburst. Sunburst Publications, 41 Washington Avenue, Pleasantville, N.Y. 10570
Systems for Education, Inc., 612 N. Michigan Ave., Chicago, Ill. 60611
Teachers. Teachers College Press, Columbia University, 525 W. 120th St., New York, N.Y.
    10027
Teachers. Teacher's Market Place, 16220 Orange Avenue, Paramount, Calif. 90723
Teaching Resources, Inc., 100 Boylston St., Boston, Mass. 02116
Teaching Technology Corp., 5520 Cleon Ave., North Hollywood, Calif. 91601
Tecnifax Corp., 195 Appleton St., Holyoke, Mass. 01040
Tempo Books. See Grosset.
3M Visual Products, 2501 Hudson Rd., St. Paul, Minn. 55119
Titmus Optical Vision Testers, 1312 W. 7th Street, Piscataway, N.J. 08854
Tweedy Transparencies, 207 Hollywood Ave., East Orange, N.J. 07018
University of Chicago Press, 5750 Ellis Avenue, Chicago, Ill. 60637
University of Illinois Press, Urbana, Ill. 61801
University of Minnesota Press, 2037 University Ave. S.E., Minneapolis, Minn. 55455
Vanguard. Vanguard Press, Inc., 424 Madison Ave., New York, N.Y. 10017
Viking. The Viking Press, Inc., 625 Madison Ave., New York, N.Y. 10022
Wagner. Harr Wagner, see Field Enterprises Educational Corp.
Walck. Henry Z. Walck, Inc., 2 Park Ave., New York, N.Y. 10016
Warne. Frederick Warne & Co., Inc., 101 Fifth Ave., New York, N.Y. 10003
Washington Square Press, Inc., a Division of Simon & Schuster, Inc., 630 Fifth Ave., New
    York, N.Y. 10020
Watts. Franklin Watts, Inc., 575 Lexington Ave., New York, N.Y. 10022
Webster. Webster Division of McGraw-Hill Book Company, Inc., Manchester Rd., Man-
    chester, Mo. 63011; 330 W. 42nd St., New York, N.Y. 10036
Wenkart. Wenkart Phonic Readers, 4 Shady Hill Square, Cambridge, Mass. 02138
Western. Western Publishing Co., School and Library Department, 1220 Mound Ave.,
    Racine, Wis. 53404
Western Psychological Services, 12035 Wilshire Blvd., Los Angeles, Calif. 90025
Westminster. The Westminster Press, 925 Chestnut St., Philadelphia, Pa. 19107
Wff 'n Proof, P.O. Box 71, New Haven, Conn. 06501

Whitman. Albert Whitman and Co., 560 W. Lake St., Chicago, Ill. 60606
Wilson. H. W. Wilson Company, 950 University Avenue, Bronx, N.Y. 10452
Winston. See Holt, Rinehart & Winston, Inc.
Winter Haven Lions Research Foundation, Inc., Box 112, Winter Haven, Fla. 33880
Word Making Productions, P.O. Box 305, Salt Lake City, Utah, 84110
World. World Publishing Company, 110 E. 59th St., New York, N.Y. 10022
Xerox Corp., Curriculum Programs, 245 Long Hill Rd., Middleton, Conn. 06457

Index